JOURNAL OF A SOMER

Journal of a Somerset Rector

1803–1834

JOHN SKINNER

EDITED BY
HOWARD AND PETER COOMBS

Oxford   New York

OXFORD UNIVERSITY PRESS

1984

Oxford University Press, Walton Street, Oxford OX2 6DP

London Glasgow New York Toronto
Delhi Bombay Calcutta Madras Karachi
Kuala Lumpur Singapore Hong Kong Tokyo
Nairobi Dar es Salaam Cape Town
Melbourne Auckland

and associated companies in
Beirut Berlin Ibadan Mexico City Nicosia

Oxford is a trade mark of Oxford University Press

The 1822–32 portion of the Journal was first published by John Murray in 1930
This edition first published by Kingsmead Press 1971
First issued as an Oxford University Press paperback 1984

British Library Cataloguing in Publication Data
Skinner, John
Journal of a Somerset rector, 1803–1834.
1. Camerton (Somerset)—Social life and customs
I. Title   II. Coombs, Howard
III. Coombs, Peter
914.23'8   BX5199.S6
ISBN 0–19–281416–8

Printed in Great Britain by
Richard Clay (The Chaucer Press) Ltd.
Bungay, Suffolk

Preface

THE *Journal of a Somerset Rector* edited by Howard Coombs and Rev. Arthur N. Bax was published by John Murray in 1930, and dealt with the years 1822–32.

At the time, the subject seemed to be exhausted, but during the year 1933 we were informed that the British Museum had purchased from a London bookseller a further twenty-five volumes of the Rev. Skinner's MSS. Twenty-one of these are autograph Journals, and the other four are volumes of miscellanea, two of which are labelled "Camertonia". One of these proved to be of unusual interest: it was entitled "The Liber Niger of Camerton" and presents a unique, if unedifying picture of English village life in the early part of the last century.

In this volume, the record has been amplified by the *Black Book of Camerton* as well as passages from the story of Skinner's earlier years which could not find a place in the first volume, and also by important additions from the years 1832–4.

Skinner wrote steadily under the inspiration of a favourite motto:

> Nulla dies sine Linea
> Since life so soon must close, would we retain
> The hope of living to our friends again?
> Let each succeeding day which speeds so fast
> Afford some leisure to record the past—
> To note with pencil, or describe with pen,
> The works of Nature or the ways of men,
> So that, when summoned from this changeful scene,
> These records may declare we once have been,
> Nor purblind loitered on the arduous road
> Which leads through Nature's works, to Nature's God.

His handwriting was almost illegible, but the Journal was transcribed by his brother Russell, who devoted much labour to the task. He transcribed at the rate of 25 pages a day, or upwards of 5,000 words, but not always without incurring his brother's criticism. It was an ill day for the Journal when he died in December 1832; indeed it continued only for another two years, and the last five years of his life are shrouded in silence, during which time he seems to have summarised certain periods of his life at Camerton as if to present the

PREFACE

volumes for posterity in the most favourable light, and to ensure, as Virginia Woolf has noticed, that posterity should be in no doubt as to the evils with which he had to contend, and that he was not to blame for them.

The volumes of the Journal are largely filled with sketches and records of tours, mostly of little general interest, for if he visited the British Museum he would begin to catalogue its contents, and his notes on the places through which he passed are mainly of the guide-book description. Hundreds of pages are filled with archaeological detail and theory, mostly dead stuff, but the Parochial Journal, where it exists, throws much light on the life of a Somerset village at the beginning of the nineteenth century. Among his papers were found the following instructions, written in August 1839 just two months before his death:

"I Bequeath all the books to the British Museum for my country-men's benefit. May they know how to value such a territory as this as it ought to be valued, and unite in maintaining its ancient institutions inviolate till the last. England, I love thee still!

JOHN SKINNER"

Since the publication of the original volume, we are fortunate in having the essay on John Skinner by Virginia Woolf which was published in the *Common Reader of 1932* under the heading "Two Parsons".

It is a brilliantly penetrating, yet sympathetic study of Skinner, and forms a fitting introduction to the new work. We are grateful to Mr. Quentin Bell, Angelica Garnett and The Hogarth Press for permission to use it. The lecture by Dr. Hunter to the Bath Field Club in 1872, which is given in Appendix III, is of interest for its reference to contemporary opinion of Skinner by one who knew him well.

Contents

Note

The extract on pages 4–9 is from *The Common Reader* by Virginia Woolf, copyright 1925 by Harcourt Brace Jovanovich, Inc.; renewed 1953 by Leonard Woolf. It is printed here by permission of Harcourt Brace Jovanovich, Inc., the author's literary estate, and the Hogarth Press.

Particulars of Camerton Living

Written by MR. JAMES STEPHENS,

Squire of Camerton, *circa* 1800

CAMERTON RECTORY, seven miles from Bath on the Wells Road, consists of a very good Rectorial House, offices and stables, gardens, etc., and forty acres of Glebe, annual value £63.

The Glebe is all meadow and pasture, lying compact and for the most part near the Parsonage House.

Annual composition for the great and small tithes of the Parish of Camerton at 3s. in the £, which is low, £180.

Thirty acres in the Parish of Wellow and pay to Camerton, now taken in kind, £3.

A district of land in Woodburrow, also adjoining to Camerton, compounded for by the present Rector at £5 10s. per annum, but is worth £10.

The tithes of the Hamlet of Cridlingcot in the said Parish of Camerton, compounded for by the present Rector at £36 6s. 2d., but worth £54.

Easter Offerings and Surplice Fees, acknowledged by the present Rector to be communibus annis £10 10s., which makes the value of the Living amount to £320 10s., Deduct for taxes and Curates stipend £50, and the nett income which remains will be £270 10s.

The duty is very easy, viz, only once a Sunday, and occasional burials, etc., etc.

The present incumbent[1] is 72 years of age.

The Rectorial House, nearby in the centre of the Parish, is in very good repair and within a small distance of the Church. The house consists of a hall, two parlours, and kitchen, etc. The bedrooms are sashed.

The Parish of Camerton abounds in coal of the very first quality, where considerable works are now carrying on, and when taken from under the Glebe, which it will be in the process of working, the Rector will be entitled to his free share (they have purposely avoided the Glebe and Churchyard).

[1] Rev. John Prowse, 1759–1800.

Extract from Camerton Register

MEMORANDUM.—On May 27, 1811, it was required by Government that the Overseers of every Parish should go on that day from house to house in order to ascertain the number of dwellings and the inhabitants they contained, a proper return of which they were to make to the Justices of the district.

The Clergy were at the same time required to send a list to the Bishop of the aggregate number of Births, Burials and Marriages for the preceding ten years, specifying the number and sex of persons baptized and buried each particular year, so that a proper estimate might be formed of the population of Great Britain as to its increase or diminution.

	Males	Females	Total
Number of Baptisms during 10 years	129	122	251
Number of Burials during 10 years	73	62	135
Number of Marriages during 10 years			44
Houses in Camerton Parish, A.D. 1811	151		
Number of Inhabitants	786		

Introduction

JOHN SKINNER was born in 1772, at the OLD HALL, Claverton, Bath, the son of Russell Skinner of Newtown House, Lymington, Hampshire, a descendant of Robert Skinner (1591–1670), successively Bishop of Bristol, Oxford, and Worcester. His mother was Mary Page, who was born at Tottenham High Cross, Middlesex. He was educated at Cheam School and Trinity College, Oxford, which he entered on November 16, 1790, graduating B.A. in 1794, and M.A. in 1797. He has stated that his childhood was darkened by a duel near his mother's house in 1778 between Count du Barry and Count Rice in which the former was shot through the heart.

In 1794 he went to Lincoln's Inn, but sometime afterwards he decided to take Holy Orders.

The Rev. Richard Graves who gave him his title, was a man of some note, and was from 1750–1804 the Rector of the beautiful village of Claverton, in the valley of the Avon about three miles from Bath. Claverton had been the home of Ralph Allen, the original of Fielding's "Squire Allworthy". Old as he was, when Skinner came under his influence, Graves must have done much to form the views and tastes of the younger man. Skinner attributes to him the early bias his mind received for the study of antiquities, and perhaps his want of sympathy with Methodism was also due to Graves, who had satirised it in "A Spiritual Quixote."

John Skinner was ordained Deacon in 1797 and Priest in 1799 by Dr. Charles Moss, Bishop of Bath and Wells, and has left us a brief notice of his ordination, which was the prelude to an excursion through Somerset, Devon, and Cornwall.

On the evening of September 20, 1797, he left his mother's house at Claverton, accompanied by Le Marquis de Kermel a French emigrant, intending to reach Wells to sleep, but they were detained the night at Old Down Inn, six miles short of their intended stage, by rain. Early the next morning, they crossed the bleak Mendip Hills and breakfasted with his brother William at Wells.

Skinner was afterwards examined for Priests' Orders by the Subdean, Mr. Moss (the son of the Bishop), who desired him to preach the Ordination Sermon the following Sunday. He spent the rest of Thursday in walking the quiet town with his companion

1

until dinner-time, and the evening in a visit to Wookey Hole. The next three days were spent in composing and preaching the Ordination Sermon, and on September 25, having taken leave of his companion, who returned to Bath, he left Wells at twelve, having been detained this long to receive his paper of ordination from the Bishop.

In the Autumn of 1799 John Skinner resigned his curacy at Claverton to take up one at South Brent (now Brent Knoll). He approached his new parish in a way which should ensure at least some measure of respect in a country village. Brent Knoll, at one time an island, is a conspicuous hill rising from the moors near the mouth of the Parrett, in Somerset. "Having learned," he tells us, "that I might ascend the Knoll on horseback, and get to Mr. Phelp's house on the opposite side by only leaping one hedge, I took that direction".

John Skinner did not stay long at Brent Knoll. In 1800 his uncle, the Rev. John Haggard, Rector of Bennington, Herts, assured him "a comfortable independence by purchasing" for him the living of Camerton, and thither he removed in the Spring of that year.

His predecessor, the Rev. John Prowse, had held the living for fifty-one years, and during his long incumbency things had perhaps gone a little awry. John Skinner has put on record on some blank pages of the Parish Register some of the problems he had to face. Unhappily he carried with him to Camerton too much of the lawyer's instinct developed by his early training, for either his complete happiness or success as a country parson. He found the parsonage in a very dilapidated state. The old Manor House was too close to the Church and Rectory. In after years the Jarrett family, who derived much of their wealth from the West Indies, pulled down the old house, and built at a distance from the Church the stately Camerton Court.

To the Squire of the day, a Mr. Stephens, from whom the Jarretts inherited the property, it seemed a simpler solution to offer a new site for the Rectory and £300 towards building a new house, on condition that the site of the existing one was made over to him. After mature reflection Skinner declined the proposal; but as, on his own reckoning, it cost him upwards of £1,000 to repair, or rather, almost to rebuild his house, it seems to have been a want of statesmanship on his part to refuse an offer which might well have been of advantage to the Rector, and might have removed a source of friction between them.

As life went on Skinner came to regard his home as Naboth's vineyard and his Squire as Ahab, and in time this feeling grew almost to an obsession. Nor was this all. A little investigation in the Parish Register brought to light an encroachment on the churchyard which had been connived at, and must be looked into. Here we have the key to many of the troubles of John Skinner's life. In those days squires had power, and sometimes used it without scruple to further their own interests. The John Prowses purchased peace by calling Overseers and Churchwardens to witness that things were as authority wished them to be, and left to their successors diminished rights for Church and Rectory. John Skinner resisted and led a troubled life. He never lacked courage, and he was truly conscientious in his decisions. "I have held the living now upwards of thirty years," he wrote towards the end of his life, "and I have never, either through fear or favour, given up one of the rights which belonged to the Rectory."

In 1805 he married Anna, daughter of Mr. Holmes of Edmonton. In rapid succession five children were born: Laura in 1806; Fitz Owen in 1808; Anna in 1809; Joseph Henry in 1810; and lastly Eliza Tertia in 1811, who died as an infant. Of these only two survived him—Fitz Owen, who entered at Lincoln's Inn and became a barrister, and Anna, who married William Robert Augustus Boyle of Lincoln's Inn.

For five years John Skinner found happiness, and then the shadows began to close in and never passed again.

In 1809 his elder brother, Fitz Owen, who was in the Navy and in command of a sloop, showed the grave symptom of spitting blood and was carried off by his brother to their Mother's house in Hertfordshire, where he was tenderly nursed by John Skinner and his sisters, Eliza and Emma. Fitz Owen died in his brother's arms on May 23, 1810, but not before he had passed on the infection to his sisters, who died soon after.

John Skinner hurried home to find his wife who had also paid a long visit to Hertfordshire "very poorly and bad". Early in 1811 she gave birth to a daughter who died of consumption at the age of three months, and then followed the great tragedy of his life—the death of his wife in 1812. These two tragedies, the deaths of his brother and his wife are the subject of separate chapters in the Journal.

In 1813 he wrote, "The mortality in my family has been great

3

indeed, as I have lost my wife and child, two sisters and a brother, two great-uncles and my father-in-law". On June 27 of that year he gives evidence of his own narrow escape; probably his love of the road and of the open-air saved him, and his readiness to ride or walk or to go by water in order to see people and places, rather than to study speed and ease. The Editors are of the opinion that the Camerton scene as Skinner found it, cannot better be described than in the essay by Virginia Woolf, and this is given in its entirety.

PETER COOMBS

The Rev. John Skinner

A whole world separates Woodforde, who was born in 1740 and died in 1803, from Skinner, who was born in 1772 and died in 1839.

For the few years that separated the two parsons are those momentous years that separate the eighteenth century from the nineteenth. Camerton, it is true, lying in the heart of Somersetshire, was a village of the greatest antiquity; nevertheless, before five pages of the diary are turned we read of coal-works, and how there was a great shouting at the coal-works because a fresh vein of coal had been discovered, and the proprietors had given money to the workmen to celebrate an event which promised such prosperity to the village. Then, though the country gentlemen seemed set as firmly in their seats as ever, it happened that the manor house at Camerton, with all the rights and duties pertaining to it, was in the hands of the Jarretts, whose fortune was derived from the Jamaica trade. This novelty, this incursion of an element quite unknown to Woodforde in his day, had its disturbing influence no doubt upon the character of Skinner himself. Irritable, nervous, apprehensive, he seems to embody, even before the age itself had come into existence, all the strife and unrest of our distracted times. He stands, dressed in the prosaic and unbecoming stocks and pantaloons of the early nineteenth century, at the parting of the ways. Behind him lay order and discipline and all the virtues of the heroic past, but directly he left his study he was faced with drunkenness and immorality; with indiscipline and irreligion; with Methodism and Roman Catholicism; with the Reform Bill and the Catholic Emancipation Act, with a mob clamouring for freedom, with the overthrow of all that was decent and established and right. Tormented and querulous, at the same time conscientious and able, he stands at the parting of the

4

ways, unwilling to yield an inch, unable to concede a point, harsh, peremptory, apprehensive, and without hope.

Private sorrow had increased the natural acerbity of his temper. His wife had died young, leaving him with four small children, and of these the best-loved, Laura, a child who shared his tastes and would have sweetened his life, for she already kept a diary and had arranged a cabinet of shells with the utmost neatness, died too. But these losses, though they served nominally to make him love God the better, in practice led him to hate men more. He was fixed in his opinion that the mass of men are unjust and malicious, and that the people of Camerton are more corrupt even than the mass of men. But by that date he was also fixed in his profession. Fate had taken him from the lawyer's office, where he would have been in his element, dealing out justice, filling up forms, keeping strictly to the letter of the law, and had planted him at Camerton among church-wardens and farmers, the Gullicks and the Padfields, the old woman who had dropsy, the idiot boy, and the dwarf. Nevertheless, however sordid his tasks and disgusting his parishioners, he had his duty to them; and with them he would remain. Whatever insults he suffered, he would live up to his principles, uphold the right, protect the poor, and punish the wrongdoer.

Perhaps the village of Camerton in the year 1822, with its coal-miners and the disturbance they brought, was no fair sample of English village life. Certainly it is difficult, as one follows the Rector on his daily rounds, to indulge in pleasant dreams about the quaint-ness and amenity of old English rural life. Here, for instance, he was called to see Mrs. Gooch—a woman of weak mind, who had been locked up alone in her cottage and fallen into the fire and was in agony. "Why do you not help me, I say? Why do you not help me?" she cried. And the Rector, as he heard her screams knew that she had come to this through no fault of her own. Her efforts to keep a home together had led to drink, and so she had lost her reason, and what with the squabbles between the Poor Law officials and the family as to who should support her, what with her husband's extravagance and drunkenness, she had been left alone, had fallen into the fire, and so died. Who was to blame? Mr. Purnell, the miserly magistrate, who was all for cutting down the allowance paid to the poor, or Hicks the Overseer, who was notoriously harsh, or the ale-houses, or the Methodists, or what? At any rate the Rector had done his duty. However he might be hated for it, he always stood up for the rights of the down-trodden; he always told people of their faults, and convicted them of evil. Then there was Mrs. Somer, who kept a house of ill fame and was bringing up her daughters to the same profession. Then there was Farmer Lippeatt, who, turned out of the Red Post at midnight, dead drunk, missed his way, fell into a quarry, and died of a broken breastbone. Wherever one turned there was suffering, wherever one looked one found cruelty behind that suffering. Mr. and Mrs. Hicks, for example, the Overseers, let an infirm pauper lie for ten days in the Poor House without care, "so that maggots had bred in his flesh and eaten great holes in his body." His only attendant was an old woman, who was so failing that she was unable to lift him. Happily the pauper died. Happily poor Garratt, the miner, died too. For to add to the evils of drink and poverty and the cholera there was constant peril from the mine itself. Accidents were common and the means of treating them elementary. A fall of coal had broken Garratt's back, but he lingered on, though exposed to the crude methods of country surgeons, from January to November, when at last death released him. Both the stern Rector and the flippant Lady of the Manor, to do them justice, were ready with their half-crowns, with their soups and their medicines, and visited sick-beds without fail. But even allowing for the natural asperity of Mr. Skinner's temper, it would need a very rosy pen and a very kindly eye to make a smiling picture of life in the village of Camerton a century ago. Half-crowns and soup went a very little way to remedy matters; sermons and denunciations made them perhaps even worse.

The Rector found refuge from Camerton neither in dissipation like some of his neighbours, nor in sport like others. Occasionally he drove over to dine with a brother cleric, but he noted acrimoniously that the entertainment was "better suited to Grosvenor Square than a clergyman's home—French dishes and French wines in profusion," and records with a note of exclamation that it was eleven o'clock before he drove home. When his children were young he sometimes walked with them in the fields, or amused himself by making them a boat, or rubbed up his Latin in an epitaph for the tomb of some pet dog or tame pigeon. And sometimes he leant back peacefully and listened to Mrs. Fenwick as she sang the songs of Moore to her husband's accompaniment on the flute. But even such harmless pleasures were poisoned with suspicion. A farmer stared insolently as he passed; some one threw a stone from a window; Mrs. Jarrett clearly concealed some evil purpose behind her cordiality. No, the only refuge from Camerton lay in Camulodunum. The more he thought of it the more certain he became that he had the singular good fortune to live on the identical spot where lived the father of Caractacus, where Ostorius established his colony, where Arthur had fought the traitor Modred, where Alfred very nearly came in his misfortunes. Camerton was undoubtedly the Camulodunum of Tacitus. Shut up in his study alone with his documents, copying, comparing, proving indefatigably, he was safe, at rest, even happy. He was also, he became convinced, on the track of an important etymological discovery, by which it could be proved that there was a secret significance "in every letter that entered into the composition of Celtic names." No archbishop was as content in his palace as Skinner the antiquary was content in his cell. To these pursuits he owed, too, those rare and delightful visits to Stourhead, the seat of Sir Richard Hoare, when at last he mixed with men of his own calibre, and met the gentlemen who were engaged in examining the antiquities of Wiltshire. However hard it froze, however high the snow lay heaped on the roads, Skinner rode over to Stourhead; and sat in the library, with a violent cold, but in perfect content, making extracts from Seneca, and extracts from Diodorus Siculus, and extracts from Ptolemy's *Geography*, or scornfully disposed of some rash and ill-informed fellow-antiquary who had the temerity to assert that Camulodunum was really situated at Colchester. On he went with his extracts, with his theories, with his proofs, in spite of the malicious present of a rusty nail wrapped in paper from his parishioners, in spite of the laughing warning of his host: "Oh, Skinner, you will bring everything at last to Camulodunum; be content with what you have already discovered, if you fancy too much you will weaken the authority of real facts." Skinner replied with a sixth letter thirty-four pages long; for Sir Richard did not know how necessary Camulodunum had become to an embittered man who had daily to encounter Hicks the Overseer and Purnell the magistrate, the brothels, the ale-houses, the Methodists, the dropsies and bad legs of Camerton. Even the floods were mitigated if one could reflect that thus Camulodunum must have looked in the time of the Britons.

So he filled three iron chests with ninety-eight volumes of manuscript. But by degrees the manuscripts ceased to be entirely concerned with Camulodunum; they began to be largely concerned with John Skinner. It was true that it was important to establish the truth about Camulodunum, but it was also important to establish the truth about John Skinner. In fifty years after his death, when the diaries were published, people would know not only that John Skinner was a great antiquary, but that he was a much wronged, much suffering man. His diary became his confidante, as it was to become his champion. For example, was he not the most affectionate of fathers, he asked the diary? He had spent endless time and trouble on his sons; he had sent them to Winchester and Cambridge, and yet now when the farmers were so insolent about paying him his tithes, and gave him a broken-backed lamb for his share, or fobbed him off with less than his due of cocks, his son Joseph refused to help him. His son said that the people of Camerton laughed at him; that he treated his children like servants; that he suspected evil where none was meant. And then he opened a letter by chance and found a bill for a broken gig; and then his sons lounged about smoking cigars when they might have helped him to mount his drawings. In short, he could not stand their presence in his house. He dismissed them in a fury to Bath. When they had gone he could not help admitting that perhaps he had been at fault. It was his querulous temper again—but then he had so much to make him querulous. Mrs. Jarrett's peacock screamed under his window all night. They jangled the church bells on purpose to annoy him. Still, he would try; he would let them come back. So Joseph and Owen came back. And then the old irritation overcame him again. He "could not help saying" something about being idle, or drinking too much cider, upon which there was a terrible scene and Joseph broke one of the parlour chairs. Owen took Joseph's part. So did Anna. None of his children cared for him. Owen went further. Owen said "I was a madman and ought to have a commission of lunacy to investigate my conduct." And, further, Owen cut him to the quick by pouring scorn on his verses, on his diaries and archaeological theories. He said: "No one would read the nonsense I had written. When I mentioned having gained a prize at Trinity College . . . his reply was that none but the most stupid fellows ever thought of writing for the college prize." Again there was a terrible scene; again they were dismissed to Bath, followed by their father's curses. And then Joseph fell ill with the family consumption. At once his father was all tenderness and remorse. He sent for doctors, he offered to take him for a sea trip to Ireland, he took him indeed to Weston and went sailing with him on the sea. Once more the family came together. And once more the querulous, exacting father could not help, for all his concern, exasperating the children whom, in his own crabbed way, he yet genuinely loved. The question of religion cropped up. Owen said his father was no better than a Deist or a Socinian. And Joseph, lying ill upstairs, said he was too tired for argument; he did not want his father to bring drawings to show him; he did not want his father to read prayers to him, "he would rather have some other person to converse with than me." So in the crisis of their lives, when a father should have been closest to them, even his children turned away from him. There was nothing left to live for. Yet what had he done to make every one hate him? Why did the farmers call him mad? Why did Joseph say that no one would read what he wrote? Why did the villagers tie tin cans to the tail of his dog? Why did the peacocks shriek and the bells ring? Why was there no mercy shown to him and no respect and no love? With agonising repetition the diary asks these questions; but there was no answer. At last, one morning in October 1839, the Rector took his gun, walked into the beech wood near his home, and shot himself dead.

VIRGINIA WOOLF

1803

The Threatened Invasion

I RECEIVED a letter from Mr. Briant, Clerk of the General Meetings, dated, Ilminster, July 9, 1803, requesting me to summon my parishioners and lay before them plans adopted for the internal defence of the country in case of invasion. Schedules were also delivered which were to be filled up with the names of those willing to serve, either as volunteers in arms, or as overseers for the driving of cattle in case of necessity, or as overseers of waggons, or guides on horseback to conduct the army, or as pioneers; the live and dead stock of the parish was also required to be returned by the farmers, with the number of their waggons and teams, and the names of the servants who might conduct them.

Accordingly I gave notice for the assembling of the inhabitants, and as Mr. Stephens was at home, with the office of Deputy Lieutenant for this division (Bath Forum) I thought that gentleman would be the proper person to take the lead in the business. We met at his house, and the schedules were filled up according to the directions we had received. I therein entered my name as Volunteer in the ranks, supposing I could render my country more effective service in this manner than in any other. Mr. Stephens and about a dozen besides, having also enrolled their names as willing to bear arms, but there was no return made of Pioneers.

Some days afterwards I received a letter from the Bishop, wherein he advised the Clergy to remain quiet at their Livings and take upon them the measures to be adopted in their several parishes. This mode of procedure, furthered by the advice of General Simes, his Lordship recommended as the best the Clergy of the Diocese could follow. I therefore withdrew my name from the list of volunteers, and resolved to render myself as serviceable as possible in the more pacific office which might be allotted me; nevertheless resolving privately to learn the Broad Sword exercise, to be prepared in case of emergency.

Sunday, July 17

I called a General Meeting of the inhabitants of Camerton (by a notice which I read in Church) for the following day at 10 o'clock, but, as there happened to be a field day for the Volunteers at the same time, only three of the parishioners attended. Not being able to enter upon business with so small a number I adjourned the meeting till the following day at the same hour. In the interim I rode around the parish, calling at the farmer's houses to request they would attend the meeting, otherwise it would be impossible for me to make the requisite returns.

In the evening I called on Mr. Stephens to speak concerning a body of Pioneers, as the colliers did not put themselves forward as they had done at Radstock and elsewhere. Mr. Stephens argued that he had power to appoint a Company of Pioneers from his own Volunteers, and that he thought would be sufficient, I did not agree with him, first, because his own complement (which according to the proposals he made to Government was to be full 600 men) would thereby be diminished; secondly, if the Volunteers were to be ordered from home, the Pioneers amongst them could afford no local service, supposing the approach of an enemy. I therefore resolved at the meeting to endeavour to persuade a Corps of Pioneers to enrol themselves from amongst the colliers to be prepared to act on the spot in case of emergency.

July

A collier called Robert Paine received in his house a stranger named Holford, who, having experienced many hardships at sea, in order to avoid being pressed again took refuge among the Collieries and worked with Paine at the pits, lodging and boarding with him and his family.

After labouring for some weeks beyond his strength he was seized with a pain in his side, cough and spitting of blood, which ended in a consumption.

When Walters, the carpenter, who lived near him at Wick Lane informed me of his situation I immediately visited him, but found the poor fellow so far gone in a decline that no medical aid could be of any service.

He made no complaint whatever and seemed perfectly resigned to his fate, uniting fervently in the prayers I delivered at my different visits, and declared his wish to be relieved from the painful life he had experienced; indeed his horror of the sea service was beyond anything I ever met with, for having been pressed as a landsman I fancy he was very severely treated on board, no excuses being made for his ignorance and incapacity.

11

I was much interested with him and with his host Paine, who told me he had taken him in from charity, clothed him from head to foot at his own cost and paid all the expenses of his illness, but could get nothing from the Overseers of the parish, to whom he had applied for a little assistance, having a large family of his own to maintain and nothing but what he got from his labour.

I gave what I thought might relieve the present necessities, and promised I would speak to the Overseer myself. I did so. He replied he could not give the parish money to strangers; that the man did not belong to Camerton, therefore he had no business to relieve him, if anyone did, it ought to be the Coalowners, since he had caught his illness in their service. I replied it was our business to relieve actual distress in a pauper who was too ill to be removed to his own parish; but I could effect nothing either by threats or by persuasions. In the meantime the man died, and Paine applied for assistance to bury him, which was also refused him.

I was so disgusted at this behaviour I called a Vestry in order to mention it to the farmers, but no one attended it, except G. Coombs who keeps the Camerton Inn [now "The Jolly Collier"].

I then went to Paine and gave him what I thought might reimburse him, determining to have the conduct of the Overseer brought before the Magistrates at Bath, but Goold, the Bailiff of the Coal Works called on me to say, although the Overseer ought to have paid somewhat towards funeral expenses, yet I had been much deceived by Paine in his statements: that he, as payer to the workmen, could prove that the deceased had a right to all that had been laid out upon him by Paine, since it was purchased with his own money, for every halfpenny he gained by his work, which was pretty considerable (as he worked two tons a day) he gave into Paine's hands who was to find him in necessaries for his labour, and that it was for interested motives alone that Paine had received him into his house and had continued to provide for him.

On extending my enquiries among the neighbours I found that William Goold had not deceived me in this representation, and I verily believe the honest sailor lost his life by over exertion to gain money for his selfish designing host, whom he considered as his benefactor in the first instance because he had received him into his home.

Another stranger from Ireland a little before this, named Culling Macnab, who also worked in the coal pits, being much intoxicated on

Saturday night was drowned by falling into the Canal, and afterwards a collier of the name of Cook killed by some loose earth at the bottom of the pit falling upon him, his two sons who were working close by providentially escaped, and endeavoured to dig away the earth from their father, but could not do it in time to save his life, but were near enough to hear him exclaim, "My poor lads, it will soon be over with me."

Aaron Horler, another collier, was killed in a very extraordinary manner. He had been drinking at the public house, whence, after behaving in a violent manner by dancing on the tables and stools, etc., and insulting some of his associates there assembled, he walked to the Lower Pit and, it is supposed, endeavoured to slide down the rope (by which the coal is hauled) to the bottom; but going too quick, not being able to retain his hold, he fell down many fathoms and was dashed to pieces, his hands being much burnt by the velocity with which the rope passed through them before he let go his hold. A person going down the pit about ten o'clock to feed the asses kept under-ground was presented with this horrid spectacle on his descent, and was so much frightened as not to recover himself for some time.

But how horrid soever these accidents may be, they are trifling compared to what was attempted by some diabolical wretch, who it is supposed had a spite against one of his comrades, and wilfully cut the rope, all but one twist, hoping that when it was his turn to descend by it he might be destroyed, and not only the object of his malevolence but all who happened to be let down at the same time, which is sometime six in number, men and boys. By the greatest providence the injured rope was noticed by one of the men preparing to descend, and thus they were saved from destruction.

On the colliers shewing me the rope I offered two guineas to any person who might give me the clue to lead to the perpetrator of this diabolical transaction.

Suspicion fell upon a man of revengeful disposition, but it never could be brought home to him. One really shudders at the bare thought of such wickedness.

A woman called Rebecca, who was recommended to me by my Mother as cook on my return from my tour, formed an acquaintance with West the Collier (the same person who defrauded the ringers of half-a-guinea) on coming from Bath to my house, and used to entertain him whenever she could without fear of detection; indeed one night when I heard a man's voice I followed him into the orchard, but he escaped at the further end by getting over the hedge. He afterwards married her, and I believe there was no collier within ten miles who could swear so fluently as she did.

I afterwards engaged a middle-aged man to be in the house, but I soon found he was as bad as the rest—receiving his friends in my house when I was absent, and never going to Bath without taking something to his children who resided there. I came to the knowledge of the particulars owing to a quarrel between my two female servants, one of whom was quite a girl, yet it seems he did not think her too young to trifle with as well as the other. So at last the rival queens, not being able to accord together, the younger came with a formal complaint, saying that she could not continue any longer with me as Richard and Harriet lived together improperly. As I had myself seen and reproved him for kissing the girl, I was not at a loss to account for her feelings on the subject. I therefore paid her her wages, and, sending for the man and woman, mentioned what I had heard, and not perceiving anything in their reply to invalidate the girl's testimony I paid them also both, and dismissed them immediately. A village girl whom I then took on the recommendation of a labourer working in my garden of the name of William Heal, whose niece she was, left me as suddenly because my sister refused her permission to go to Timsbury Revel.

Not knowing where to hear of a servant I engaged old widow King, who lived at Claverton, to come over for a time till I could suit myself.

1804

An Expedition to Weymouth and The Royal Yacht

THIS morning I left Camerton with the design of spending a few days with my brother Fitz Owen, stationed at Weymouth, on board the "Royal Sovereign" yacht. I was on horseback by seven, and passing by Shepton Mallet and Ansford Inn without stopping, arrived about eleven at Sherbourne—a thirty-mile stage; here, whilst my horse was baiting, I called upon young Phelps at the Grammar School, and asked permission for him to accompany me to Lord Digby's about a mile from the town.

Remounting my horse about two, I proceeded to Alton (Pancras) to take up my quarters at a gentleman's house for the night; after a very hospitable reception and entertainment I went to bed about twelve.

I was persuaded by my obliging host to continue here over the day, in order to enjoy the amusement of shooting over the Manor, which abounds in game. We contrived to bring home three brace and a half of birds, a leash of which fell to my share; after an early dinner we tried our success again in the evening, but without killing a bird.

Two other gentlemen came over this morning to breakfast, and I was induced to accompany them with my gun, but the weather proving insufferably hot and the birds shy, I parted company, and taking leave of the hospitable family at Alton pursued my way to Weymouth, where I arrived about 5 o'clock.

Wishing to see my brother as soon as possible, I hired a boat to go on board the "Royal Sovereign" (sailing in the Bay) immediately. The Royal Family had left her, but as the yacht had taken a longer cruise than usual, the evening closed in before they came to their moorings; the boatmen persuaded me to row back to Weymouth and return with the "Sovereign's" barge to the yacht, after the Royal

Family had landed. Accordingly we waited till we saw the grandees disembark at the pier head, when making myself known to the coxswain, whose face I remembered when on board the "St. Fierenze," he took me into the barge, where I sat in state to be rowed by 14 fine fellows dressed in blue uniform; but my pride was of short duration for some malicious demon, envious of my grandeur, conjured up a thick mist that so completely enveloped us that instead of reaching the yacht we rowed at random for two or three hours in the Bay till the boat's crew were on the point of shipping their oars, and probably we should have continued on the water all night, had we not fortunately procured a compass of a cutter lying at anchor, whose cable we ran athwart before we percevied her.

We were enabled to return to Weymouth about 11 p.m.

September 13

Having passed a miserable night at my brother's lodgings, tormented with all manner of vermin, I rose at 6 o'clock my right eye completely closed by the bite of a bug. About an hour was passed in walking round the town and esplanade, and bathing. I afterwards hired a boat and got on board the "Royal Sovereign" yacht, where I found my brother well, and happy to see me after the adventure of last night.

Breakfast being concluded, he conducted me over this beautiful Vessel. She is, in burthen, about 300 tons, and fitted up with every convenience that can be imagined, having below deck three superb rooms, two of them adorned with crimson damask, and panels of the finest mahogany, the windows plate glass, with large mirrors to each door of the apartments; the third chamber is painted white and gold, the flooring adorned, like the rest, with beautiful carpeting.

It is here that the officers at present mess, but when the King[1] is on board this room is occupied by the Lords in Waiting and attendants. In fine weather the Royal Family sit on Couches upon deck under a canvas awning, which stretches to the mainmast, the Queen's Band always attending, arranged under the canopy at the stern of the ship. His Majesty's suite when the ship's under sail continue on the forecastle with the Captain and Officers, without they are particularly sent for by the Royal party.

All orders respecting the management of the ship are given in a low voice, so as not to be heard by those astern; indeed, the running

[1] George III.

rigging is so well contrived that there is never the least noise in hauling up or lowering the sails; in short, a polite drawing-room cannot be better regulated than is this elegant floating palace.

The King and the Princesses have hitherto sailed every day since their arrival, Sundays excepted. His Majesty usually dines at one with some of the Princesses. When the Queen is on board, she takes a later repast.

Two other yachts, the "Augusta" and the "Charlotte," and two frigates, the "Aeolus" and "Crescent," besides two cutters, always sail in Company with the "Royal Sovereign," which is the Commodore bearing the standard of England at the mast head.

Having viewed everything as well as the time would permit, my brother informed me the barge was waiting, which was to go on shore for the Royal Family, he had given directions to them to receive me on board; I accordingly resumed my proud station at the stern of the most beautiful boat that was ever built, and flew through the water to the pier head; indeed the rowers exerted every nerve, as they saw the carriages conveying the Royal Family driving to the spot with all speed, and I am sure my anxiety was still greater when I observed them stopping, and the King, Queen, and Princesses alighting, before we arrived at the steps. To disembark thus in the face of Royalty was what not even a courtier could have wished, and would for the moment have exchanged my situation with the humblest person in the crowd. I scrambled up the steps as quick as I could, and was fortunately recognised by Sir Harry Neale,[1] who was waiting at the landing place to attend the King, and he kindly relieved me from any embarrassment, and I passed on without further observation. When the barge had got half way to the yacht the royal salute was fired by all the ships, which produced a grand effect.

The weather being fine I hired a boat, and sailed about the Bay till half-past six o'clock when I returned to dine on board the "Sovereign."

In the evening I accompanied my brother to the play, and slept on a mattress on the floor of the King's Head Hotel. The expense of this day's boating alone was 17/6, as the watermen demand 3/- an hour. This seems an exorbitant price, and will, I fear, curtail my water excursions.

[1] Admiral Sir Harry Burrard-Neale (1765–1840) of Walhampton, Hants, Member of Parliament and second Baronet. (*See also* Burrard.)

I rode this morning to the Isle of Portland and visited the camp in the neighbourhood of Weymouth, where the two regiments of the Somerset and Staffordshire Militias are quartered. The day was insufferably hot, and the road dusty. The want of foliage on this coast certainly detracts much from its beauty and convenience as a place of public resort.

This day being appointed for a review of the Hanoverian Cavalry near Maiden Castle, on the road to Dorchester, I accompanied my brother and another gentleman, on horseback, to the ground where we arrived about eleven, and fortunately procured a good situation to see the troops march in succession before His Majesty: they are a very fine body of men, and appeared to go through their evolutions with the utmost precision; their charge is indeed tremendous and rendered still more so by the terrific shouts and clashing of swords with which it is accompanied.

The King and the whole company seeemed highly to applaud this warlike rehearsal. When it was concluded, we directed our course to Dorchester, two miles distant where we procured a comfortable dinner at the "Fountain" Inn; returned in the evening in time to get to the play, and I retired to my mattress before twelve.

I bathed before breakfast, and afterwards went to Church, but it was with the greatest difficulty I procured a sitting there, every part being astonishingly crowded but at length Mrs. Hemming accommodated me with a seat in the gallery, which gave me an opportunity of seeing the Royal Family to advantage. Besides the King and Queen, there were in the same pew the Princesses Elizabeth, Mary, Sophia and Amelia, with the Dukes of Kent, Sussex and Cambridge. Indeed they are an exceedingly fine family, and appeared very attentive to the discourse preached by Mr. Daubigny, of Bath.

After Church I walked on the esplanade, and went on board the "Sovereign" with a party of ladies; but in the evening attended the dress promenade at the Rooms. The Royal Family appeared a little after eight, and spoke in the most affable manner to those introduced to them; whilst they walked up to the saloon to the tea room, the Staffordshire Band playing airs and marches the whole time.

Having procured a table for the party I attended, we drank tea, and returned by moon-light on board the Royal yacht to sleep, where I was accommodated with a much more comfortable bed than I have had for three nights.

After breakfast my brother lent me the jolly boat to take me to the "Augusta" yacht, about 200 yards off the "Sovereign" he having introduced me to Captain Foot[1] in order to give me an opportunity of sailing at the same time they did, as it is not permitted for anyone to be in the King's ship, except the Royal suite, when the family are on board.

The "Augusta" is one of the oldest vessels in the service, having been employed by George I in his frequent excursions to Hanover. The cabin is comfortably fitted up in the old fashioned way with gilt leather, opening to a little bedroom in which that Monarch often reposed. She is not above 180 tons in burthen, but has three masts and mounts eight four-pound brass guns. When the salute was fired I thought they would have deafened me, as the ringing of the brass conveys a more piercing sound than the heavy report of an iron gun.

We had a very pleasant sail, running down as far as Lulworth, and tacking backwards and forwards in the Bay. Whenever we passed under the stern of the "Sovereign" our shrouds were manned, and the sailors gave three cheers in compliment to the Royal party. The same was observed by the other ships. I found we sailed the worst of the fleet. At 2 p.m. we lay by to dinner, and I enjoyed a very comfortable repast and excellent wine. When the King sails everything is provided on board the yachts and cooks are sent to dress the provisions.

Captain Foot appeared a sensible gentlemanly man, and I had every reason to be gratified by his politeness.

As soon as the yachts came to their moorings, boats put off with the Captains of the attendant ships to wait on His Majesty, and see him safe into the barge. A salute was fired as the barge was going to the shore, and this concluded the business of the day. Returning on board the "Sovereign" to my brother I found the mess just sitting down to dinner; indeed, it was supper time with me, for I went to bed at nine.

[1] Captain E. J. Foote, 1767–1833 (later Vice-Admiral Sir E. J. Foote).

This morning after bathing, I went on board the "Charlotte" yacht, commanded by Captain Lowry and had a delightful sail in the Bay. It blew a fresh gale, which gave animation to the scene; indeed it was a beautiful sight to see the frigates, cutters and yachts, cruising on different tacks, and cheering the "Royal Sovereign" as they passed under her stern. The "Charlotte" is larger than the "Augusta," and is fitted up in a superior style. She was built for the purpose of bringing over the Queen from Germany, and was considered at that time a very beautiful vessel, but compared with the "Royal Sovereign" she falls vastly into the background.

I found the Officers pleasant and obliging men, and Mrs. Lowry who was on board, seemed a most charming woman but there was a degree of hauteur about the Captain, that to a landsman is not very agreeable.

We dined at 2 and in the evening I returned on board the "Royal Sovereign."

The complement of Officers to each of these yachts is nearly similar, there being a Captain, Lieutenant, Doctor, Purser, and Master. The "Sovereign" as Commodore has two Midshipmen in addition. The pay of the Captain is about £600 p.a. as they have equal rank with the Commanders of second Rates. The Doctor's and Purser's pay is in proportion, but the Lieutenant's is not augmented.

The great advantage of being in the Royal Yacht was the prospect of promotion. My brother, who sailed with Sir Harry Neale from the time he was eleven years old, and was in the "San Fierenze" frigate many years, received a promise not long since from the King of being made Master and Commander as soon as the Yacht returned to Deptford.

The manner of His Majesty's giving this promise was in the highest degree gratifying to a young man. The very first day he came on board he said he was glad to find a "San Fierenze" man as his Lieutenant, for he should always have the greatest regard for any Officers from that Vessel (alluding to the gallant manner in which they behaved during the mutiny at the Nore), and putting his hand on his left shoulder he told him he should have an Epaulette there whenever the yacht left Weymouth. Indeed, his Captain, Sir Harry Neale, has been a most steady friend and has taken every opportunity of advancing his interests in a way that merits our warmest thanks and esteem.

I bathed and breakfasted, after which I rode a circuit of six or seven miles round Weymouth. The country is very bare and barren, affording few interesting rides or walks; therefore I am less surprised to see, the Company prefer the Esplanade, to the village of Wick, or the shingly beach at Portland. There are no retired Vallies or shady coverts, to shield one from the scorching Sun, which at present is intolerable; but wherever you turn yourself, it is all one wide expanse; on one side the level Ocean, on the other, the plain unbroken surface of the Downs. In the evening, however, at the Rooms, there was a pleasing variety of animated beauties which amply repaid for all disappointments as to other prospects.

I had the felicity of dancing with Miss Daubigny, and spent a very agreeable evening.

Today, having packed up my little portmanteau, and settled my bills, I took a final leave of Weymouth.

On mouting my horse I was concerned to see a great alteration in his appearance, during the short time he was here, although I had to pay at the rate of a guinea a week for his keep, at the Livery Stables. The poor animal seems literally starved, his ribs starting through his skin, we were therefore obliged to move slowly to Alton, where I had promised to dine, and take up my quarters for the night.

At Ansford Inn near Castle Cary, I baited my horse for a couple of hours, and got a mutton chop; afterwards continuing my route, leaving Shepton Mallet a little to my right, I passed through Farmborough and Paulton and arrived at Camerton a little before nine, having experienced a most pleasant tour, but as a little drawback to my satisfaction, found one of my female servants much indisposed in consequence of a brutal assault made on her by Mr. Stephens's gardener during my absence, whom I shall be under the necessity of bringing to justice, if his master does not himself punish him, which I do not think at all likely, knowing his own sentiments on this head.

My housekeeper, Mrs. King, came into the room and told me there had been a sad business during my absence; that Lizzy Cottle had been so ill with fits that she was obliged to send her to Chilcompton to be under Mr. Flower's care; that the occasion of these fits was a violent assault made upon her by Lowe, Mr. Stephens's gardener, some time before, when she was going one evening through the plantation for my letters to the Red Post; that Lowe had taken her up in his arms and carried her into the thickest part of the coppice wood with the intent to ravish her, and if Joseph Heal had not fortunately come by he would certainly have accomplished his purpose.

On hearing this I spoke to the girl myself, who confirmed what had been told me by Mrs. King.

Next morning, Sunday, I sent for Joseph Heal, and wrote down what he deposed on the subject. I then called on Mr. Stephens and mentioned the heinous conduct of his servant. Mr. Stephens said that he was sorry to hear of it, that he could scarcely believe the account I had been told as he had an excellent opinion of Lowe, who was a married man, and seemed to be going on very steadily in his business.

I mentioned as a confirmation Joseph Heal's deposition, and read it to him.

Mr. Stephens said it would be better to hear what the man Lowe had to say for himself. I readily assented. He was sent for into Mr. Stephens's study. Mr. Stephens said that Mr. Skinner had brought a very serious charge against him, and asked what he had to say for himself. He replied that he was very sorry for what he had done, but declared solemnly he had only meant to kiss the girl, and should not have done that but that he had taken a little too much drink, a friend having called upon him in the morning; that he had not taken her from the road, and had not the most distant idea of offering her any violence.

When the man was gone Mr. Stephens told me he did not know what to make of the business; but on my urging him to give a summons as a Magistrate, that the man might appear before the Justices at the following meeting, he declined, saying it was a delicate situation for him to act in, it being his own servant, etc.

On speaking with the girl's father he told me Lowe had been with him previous to my coming home, and said he would give him anything if he would not inform Mr. Skinner of it, as it certainly would be the means of his losing his place; but Cottle, the father, would not hearken to him, and had determined mentioning everything to me, even if Mrs. King had not done it.

On Monday I sent Cottle to Mr. Day, the Justice at Hinton, to lay his complaint before him on the violence offered to his daughter. In the upshot Lowe appeared before the Magistrates, and there the matter was settled out of Court. They took the view that, "as the father seemed disposed to a reconciliation, and as the girl herself did not seem to be very rancorous against the man, it was better they should make up the matter, and as Lowe offered to pay five guineas and make an apology they thought it might end there."

I had not undertaken to bring the matter forward through any enmity or dislike of the man, for previous to this business I had entertained a good opinion of him, but through a conviction that I should not be doing my duty otherwise.

1805

I must mention an occurrence which took place when the workmen were engaged in the Parsonage, which would be called second sight in Scotland, and in this country amongst the Methodists *a manifest and miraculous indication of the Spirit:* but as I can account for the circumstances by natural causes, I will briefly state it in this place and my unvarnished interpretation of the vision:

As I expected Mr. Holmes and his daughter to pay their first visit at Camerton after my marriage, I was anxious to get the Parsonage somewhat in order for their reception. Workmen had been employed in painting the premises, and some masons set to work in altering the dining parlour, the ceilings of which they rose nearly two feet, carrying that of the bedchamber nearly three feet into the roof; the old casements were taken away and some gothic windows (made after my drawings) put in their stead. The largest of these windows, which is in three compartments, in the dining-room, I was very anxious to have in its place before the arrival of my friends, and assisted the masons as long as we could see on the Saturday night in getting in the stone jambs and arches, holding up myself the different pieces in their places till they walled them in; yet, notwithstanding all our exertions, there was an opening in the wall left just above the window on the outside, which the masons promised to come early on Monday morning to fill up before Mr. Holmes arrived.

On going to bed, my mind fully impressed with the operations of the day, I slept for awhile, then awoke much alarmed at a dream which represented the stone window frame at which we had been working thrown down with a terrible crash, and all the wall of the house quite to the roof lying in fragments about it. I was so struck with the apparent disaster that I awoke my wife, exclaiming "See, there the window is all broken to pieces," and it was nearly a minute before I could be convinced that it was all a dream.

On the Monday morning, not finding the mason and his lad at the Parsonage, as they promised, I went down to the Camerton Inn, where I found they had been drinking all the Sunday, and saw the old man, Masters, who promised to come up without his lad, who

24

he said was gone home. I thought he looked very queer and stupid, but had no idea at that time of the morning of his being in liquor. His business was merely to get some mortar and to wall up the aperture, about a foot square, which he might have done in an hour at the farthest; but he seemed to set about it very awkwardly and unwillingly, and while my back was turnèd to give directions to the servants I heard a dreadful noise of something falling, and running into the garden saw my dream in every respect verified . . . the window gone and a large chasm down from the roof to the ground, the mason meanwhile stamping and roaring like a madman, saying it was a great mercy he had not been destroyed, as he was just pulling away a loose stone when all came down at once, and if he had not been fortunately on one side he must have been crushed to pieces.

The impression I received certainly accounted for my dream, but the chances were more than a thousand to one that it became realized. How many dreams we have which make equally strong impressions which never are realized and we think no more of them! This happened to come to pass and it appears wonderful though it was no good fortune to me, as I was obliged to have a new window frame made by Sumpsion, and had the mortification of having the side of my house open when my company arrived.

September 18

A little boy of the name of Cottle, son of the Schoolmistress, was killed in the coal pit by some loose ground falling upon him. He was only eight years old, and had worked a year.

Surely the parents and the proprietors of the works are to blame for permitting such little boys to work, who cannot possibly take care of themselves and must be ignorant of the dangers they are exposed to; but what is not sacrificed to the shrine of covetousness?

> Quid non mortalia pectora cogis,
> Auri sacra fames?

Memorandum. The father of this boy is a striking example of one making everything which is sacred subservient to his own interest. As long as his wife had the direction of my School, and used moreover to be paid according to the number she brought to Church a penny for each, both he and she professed to be attached to the Establishment; but when I dismissed her from the office, having discovered she was improper to fill it . . . being very artful and inattentive to the children, from that moment she left off coming to Church, whilst her husband, who worked as a collier and sometimes as a gardener, under Goold became a strong Methodist and a constant attentant on Chapel. But after Reynolds came in Goold's place as bailiff, who happened to be a Baptist, Cottle, in order to pay court to him, and retain his employment, became of that sect, and leaving Red Hill Meeting he transferred his attendance to the Baptist Meeting at Paulton.

Having been informed of these changes, on meeting him one day on the canal towing path where I was walking with my Newfoundland dog, I threw a piece of stick into the water, which he brought out just as Cottle was passing by, I then said, "Mr. Cottle, I understand that you have been taking a plunge too." He asked me what I meant, for he did not exactly comprehend me. I said, "Why in the Baptist Meeting-house;" if he had not already done it I supposed he soon would: that I hoped after all his changes he would be right at last. He was first Churchman, then Methodist, now Baptist; perhaps he would now try the Catholic persuasion, especially if a Catholic were made bailiff of the Works. He said he thought there was no harm in endeavouring to improve himself and collect instruction: that he wished to resemble the bee which went from flower to flower collecting sweets, not making any distinction between the flowers he got it from. I replied there was another insect called a spider which also went from flower to flower, but instead of collecting sweets converted all she got into poison. My opinion was it were better to remain steady and to listen to those who could most contribute to his good by delivering wholesome doctrines; that a rolling stone collected no moss, nor was it possible for him among a variety of opinions to decide which were founded on reason or in error.

He did not feel my reproof in a manner indicative of its being likely to do any good, so he went *his* way and I *mine*.

N.B. This man I have heard since is now become indifferent to all religion, that he sings and drinks with the younger Reynolds, who is quite a freethinker, in low life, beats his wife and is careless of his children.

Cottle drowned himself in the canal one night after a quarrel with his wife. They have turned out very indifferently; indeed the one who lived with me, and afterwards went into service in Bath, was got with child by an apprentice she kept company with, admitting him into the house where she lived, and had the impudence to deny the situation she was in, declaring the pangs she felt in labour was a violent stomach ache, till a little witness soon made an appearance who cleared it all up. I always knew her to be an artful girl, and perhaps in Lowe's business she had given him encouragement before he proceeded to such lengths. Another of Cottle's daughters was on the town I find at Bristol, but is now married to a silly young man who took a fancy to her.

Such are the consequences of instability, in religion it cuts at the root of all order and morality amongst the people.

Besides the versatility of this Vicar of Bray in low life there was another occurrence took place in the parish about this time, equally indicative of the omnipotent power of gold in changing the outward appearance of man and making him assume a character very different from his own. The instance I allude to was exemplified by William West, the collier, who married a servant who had lived with me.

This fellow was everything but what he ought to be, namely, an honest man. On my coming to Camerton he cheated the ringers of half of what I gave them. He afterwards, when his wife was taken ill and died, ran away, leaving a large family on the parish, and continued away, no one knew where, for many months. He then returned well dressed and in good plight, with a watch and plenty of money in his pocket, and afterwards married my servant, who by all accounts was able to play her part as well as himself, as will be seen in the sequel. She had been married before to a man living at Sodbury in Gloucestershire, and was left a widow with two boys, who worked in the coal pits with West after his marriage.

It seems there was a charitable donation in the parish (to which these children belonged in right of their father) for putting out the poor as apprentices, the fee for each being £5. West, having an eye to this money, dressed himself in his Sunday's clothes, and assuming a deal of consequence went to Sodbury, pretending he was a farmer living at Camerton and had seen the boys, and would, if approved of, take them both as apprentices. The Overseers had the prudence to write to me before they concluded the agreement or had the articles drawn out, asking if there were a Farmer West of the description he gave of himself at Camerton. I soon found out the mystery, and wrote them a faithful account of the person who was intreating with them for the apprentices, saying he was a tricking fellow who already derived considerable advantage from the boys working with him in the pits, and with regard to the apprentice fee it would be all thrown away as he had no business to instruct them in beyond their present engagement.

West after a while, with his wife, left the parish and went to Town, and what afterwards became of them no one knows.

(The woman, West, when a widow died in poverty at Cridlingcot, and I attended her at the last.)

1806

A MAN of the name of William Bowler was drowned in the brook. The accident was occasioned so far as I could learn from intoxication. At his funeral I took the opportunity to address the people assembled in Church before we went to the grave, and as they seemed very attentive I hope my admonitions were not thrown away.

William Britain, another collier, was killed in the coal pits by a shocking accident. He was riding in a small coal cart underground drawn by an ass, which vehicle is usually employed to convey the coal from different parts where it is dug to the large store below the mouth of the pit, but was then empty. As the ass was going along at a brisk pace he did not observe he was come to a spot where the roof of the passage was much lower than it was before, and, neglecting to stoop his head, his back was bent double by the sudden violence of the shock and his spine snapped. The poor fellow was drawn up and lived some hours, but his extremities were quite paralysed. He was son to poor old Britain who occasionally works for me. The brother who is left will be of little comfort to him, as he is a sad fellow, indeed quite a savage.

March 22

James Edwards, whose business it was to see the coal brought to land at The Old Pit, in reaching over too far in order to stay the basket which was coming up, fell to the bottom and was dashed to pieces. Horrid to say, his last word was an oath when he found himself going. He left a widow and four children at Cridlingcot.

July 12

On returning from Combe Hay, about half-past 9 or 10 o'clock (for I had dined with Mr. Gardiner[1] after having performed Evening Service at Wellow.) I heard a violent disturbance in the lane opposite the Red Post Inn. On going thither I found two young men fighting, one stripped to the waist, the other with his coat and waistcoat off; two others seemed to be engaged in the affray, Abrahams, the black-smith, was endeavouring to part them, as did also another young man

---

[1] Reverend Edmund Gardiner M.A., 1741–1827, vicar of Wellow and later of Tintern Parva.

who I am acquainted with; there was also standing by Swift (and his wife, I believe,) who works in Mr. Purnell's garden, Carter's wife (late Gullick) was I think also there and some other females. On asking what was the occasion of this disturbance I found they had been drinking at the Red Post, and were quarrelling about one of the females. I begged them to disperse, which they did, I heard afterwards from Abrahams, almost directly.

July 19

On my way to Wellow to do duty there I spoke to Gay the Landlord of the Red Post Inn, and told him I certainly should represent his house as a disorderly one. He seemed inclined to be impudent, but I did not hear what he said as I rode on directly.

Two or three times previous to this I had represented to Mr. Purnell (of Woodborough) the bad goings on at the Red Post, as I conceived it behoved him in his double capacity of Magistrate and owner of the house to restrain such outrages against the peace, but he took no trouble to attend to my representations. On the contrary I understand that Gay considers himself rather countenanced than otherwise by Squire Purnell, who consults him on all occasions. I had also threatened Coombs to have his licence taken away, if he permitted such drunkenness and riot. Indeed I consider these two public houses are the principal causes of all the licentiousness and insubordination, poverty and consequent misery of the lower orders; but as there is no Magistrate who is on the spot to restrain them, for Mr. Purnell will do nothing, they go on just as they choose. (Gay got into poverty and was put into prison, and died badly, although the Methodists, I suppose, gave good assurance) Tis here they learn:

> The road that leads from competence and peace
> To indigence and rapine, till at last
> Society, grown weary of the load,
> Shakes her incumbered lap and casts them out.

Respecting Joseph Lippiatt. This man I had taken to work in my garden after I had parted from William Heal, and during the time he lived with me lost my favourite Newfoundland dog, Mungo. At first I was going to offer a reward, but was dissuaded by Mr. Ensor from so doing, who thought it might be the means of my losing him again! I did not therefore do as I proposed in the first instance, but told Lippiatt I would give him half-a-crown if he could procure any intelligence of him. In the course of three weeks he came open mouthed to me just after breakfast and asked whether I had not promised to give half-a-crown if he would give me any intelligence of the dog? I replied I certainly did, and should do so if he knew anything about him. "Yes, Sir," says he, "I caught him as he was running away up the hill, and put him into the stable." When I went to look at the poor fellow he was overjoyed to see me, but I was concerned to see such an alteration, as he was nothing but skin and bone.

After a little I began to consider the history that Lippiatt had told me, and after a little cross-questioning found he had fabricated this story under the idea of getting the half-crown. The truth of the matter was the poor animal had made his escape from the place where he had been detained and found his way home again, with very little inclination to wander away as the knave pretended. I, instead therefore of giving him half-a-crown gave him a good rating for his deception.

Not long after, when the dog was following my horse over the Old Bridge at Bath, a woman stopped me and asked if he belonged to me. On my answering in the affirmative she said he had been kept by her upwards of three weeks, and that in that time she had had him cried, but could hear of no owner; that the manner he came into her possession was as follows: she, living close by the river side, one night heard a dreadful howling and barking; on getting up early she found the dog with a large stone tied to his neck, which had not been sufficiently heavy to drown him, but, sticking in the mud at the bottom of the river, prevented his getting away, and gave him liberty to crawl upon the bank and no further. Having cut the cord she took him home and provided for him in the best manner she was able. Having satisfied the woman I was left quite in the dark as to the person who could have taken the trouble to injure my dog.

Sometime in October, 1806, Lowe came to me saying that he had appointed Thursday for the christening of his child, and hoped that I would make it convenient to attend. I replied I should be ready to christen it on the Sunday following, either during Morning or Evening Service, but I should not think of attending on a weekday, and he might be well acquainted with my reasons for declining it, as he never attended Church himself therefore he had no right to expect I should put myself out of the way to please him. I accordingly baptized the child on the Sunday I appointed (October 26).

I mention this circumstance as connected in my opinion with an event which took place shortly after.

Mr. Holmes and his daughter came from Town on a visit to me. We were sitting after dinner when we were startled by the report of a gun close at hand. I immediately expressed my surprise at the firing at that hour (about 7 p.m.) and so close to the premises, but could make but little comment on the business as another report, equally loud, made me run hastily into the garden.

I saw the cook and housemaid standing by the back kitchen door, apparently much alarmed. They said they were sure someone had fired at my dog, Mungo: that they saw clearly the flash of the gun both times. On asking which way they supposed the person had gone who had done it, they said, towards the Church they believed. I went out of the door going to the Village. Although the moon was not bright there was sufficient light for me to see fifty or sixty yards before me, and there was no person in that direction. On my way back to my own house I met Farmer Burfitt's shepherd's boy, who said that Mr. Lowe and his wife were come up to his house. It immediately struck me that Lowe was the person who had fired into my premises, and it was very easy for him to have got away from me by turning into the door to Mr. Stephens's garden close to my field; indeed no doubt remained in my mind but that he was the aggressor. Under this impression I walked up the hill to Burfitt's; Lowe and his wife and child and Mrs. Burfitt were in the kitchen.

I immediately taxed him with having fired into my premises. He strongly denied it, and proceeded in the most abusive terms to insult me, saying amongst other things that he had it in his power to punish me pretty severely, and did not know indeed whether he could not have deprived me of my Living. I asked him in what way? Because, he said, I married him without having a certificate of his Banns being published in his wife's parish. I told him he was a great scoundrel for speaking on this business, since if there were any fault it was on his side, as he informed me the Banns were published at St. James's, and there was a person who attended his marriage at Camerton who said he could take his oath he had heard them published three Sundays. He also (Lowe) promised to get me a certificate from the Clergyman who had published them. I demanded where that man was, for I would bring him forward to account whether he spoke true or not. Lowe replied he knew where the man was, but would not tell me.

After a great deal of violent, gross behaviour, during which his wife and Mrs. Burfitt did all they could to restrain him, I left the house, but told him previously I should certainly call upon Mr. Stephens and mention the particulars of his conduct, and if he did not take notice of it I must have recourse to other means of punishing him. He said he cared no more for Mr. Stephens than for me; he was no longer his servant; he had given him notice, and meant to quit him; that he was quite independent, and would count guinea for guinea with me any day; and a great deal of similar abuse. I left him and returned to my house.

The following day I called upon Mr. Stephens, mentioned the insult I had sustained through the firing into my premises; told him I had offered a reward for the discovery of the offender: that it behoved him as much as myself to endeavour to bring him to punishment, for if these things were suffered with impunity, his turn would be next.

Two stories I have heard within these few weeks of this man Lowe's conduct with respect to women and drinking which are astonishing. So that in order to supply a fund for carrying on his profligate life he had recourse to a variety of frauds, and took up money on various pretences from the people in the neighbourhood. All the people whom he was connected with more or less had reason to remember the plausibility with which he got them to lend him money. Jonas Weeks informed me that he ordered at Bath, at a house of ill fame, a little before he left the place a guinea's worth of punch for the woman, etc. He also heard a history of his having endeavoured to set his apartments on fire, yet notwithstanding all these outrages I heard his friends at Camerton and Bath essayed to get him a place as gardener at Lady Waldegrave's, but he went there in such a state of intoxication to offer himself that he was of course refused. He afterwards went into Devonshire, and I had a letter from his wife saying she was in distressed circumstances, and wishing to have a certificate of her marriage at Camerton, which she considered as her parish.

Besides this business of Lowe's I had occasion to notice to Mr. Stephens the conduct of his footman, Binden, who got Heal, the washerwoman's daughter, with child. The father (Amos Heal) having mentioned the circumstance to me in such a manner it appeared the man was highly culpable.

Mr. Stephens, instead of enquiring into the affair, merely said if he was obliged to attend the private conduct of his servants he should have enough to do, and never took any further notice of it; indeed he could not well reprove his servants for a conduct which his example had probably taught them to pursue.

1807

I HAD had occasion to notice the behaviour of a woman of the name of Sarah Summers, who kept company with Coward, a servant of Burfitt's.

In the beginning of November, 1806, she came to me saying she wished to have the Banns asked between Coward and herself. I told her that it had been mentioned to me that her husband was alive, and therefore it would be very wrong in her to think of being asked without she was certain he was dead. She said it was all false what folks said about his being alive; that he went to the East Indies as a soldier upwards of seven years ago, and had never been heard of since.

I accordingly asked the Banns in Church. Just as the parties were preparing to be married the husband made his appearance at Camerton, and on enquiring for his wife found out her residence and surprised her by his coming so unexpectedly upon her; whilst he on his part was no less astonished at finding four children, instead of the one he had left when he went abroad. However, as reproofs and complaints were useless, like a second Socrates he forgave the frail one and took her again to his bosom, and for near a month they lived together, I understand, in perfect conjugal felicity; but, unfortunately, the husband returning from his work in the coal pits sooner than was expected, found his rival with his wife. He beat her as long as he could without absolutely killing her, and immediately left the strumpet, going to take up his abode at Timsbury. The man afterwards married a Timsbury woman by licence at Bristol, his wife meanwhile continued to keep company with Coward. I often admonished and threatened her, and when she had another child sometime afterwards spoke to the Overseer to represent it to the Justices, which he did not do because Coward offered to maintain it.

35

1808

THE officer has just called upon me previous to his delivering the Citation to Joseph Goold.

On perusing it I find there are three following Sundays specified wherein the singers are described as interrupting the Catechism: this was in fact the case. The complaint I bring against Goold is for brawling and insolent behaviour to me in *Church last Sunday*, and the interruption then given to the catechising the children.

From my first residence in Camerton till the present time I have contributed towards supporting a School in order to instruct the poor in reading and working, the Schoolmistress having charge, above all, to learn them their Catechism in the week-days, and to see them attend Church on Sundays where they were to be examined in the progress they had made in this important duty after the Morning Service.

With regard to the conduct of my Churchwarden, it appears to me in every respect my duty to represent it as I have done, otherwise all ecclesiastical regulation must be at an end, as all civil has long since been, in my parish: that a person whose office it is to preserve decency in the Church should be the first to violate it: that he should openly disown all authority and subordination to his Rector, and appear as the champion of disobedience; all this is so directly contrary to his oath and office that I should be myself very culpable if I did not appeal to the authority of the laws to support me in the discharge of my duty.

Joseph Goold, having received the Citation from the officer, called on me and requested I would not prosecute the business further; in future he promised to pay every proper attention to me and his duty: that the expense he already would incur would amount to £3 10s. 6d. The same day Mrs. Goold, the mother, happened to be of the most essential service in putting my wife to bed of a healthy boy. As my obligation was of such a kind I could not better repay it, I imagined, than by forgetfulness and forgiveness of her son's behaviour. The proceedings were stopped, and so the affair ended.

Joseph Goold's wife being very near her time, and very apprehensive her delivery would prove fatal to her, I have called on her, not only as I think it my duty so to do, but also to show I do not retain any remembrance of the past.

He seems sensible I have done him a kindness and appears more civil than usual, but he is *a bad fellow*.

1809

WILLIAM BRITAIN, of Cridlingcot, died of a consumption, brought on in a great measure by excessive drinking. I attended him several times before his death, and he declared solemnly to me that the Red Post public house had been his ruin; that frequently on a Sunday he had left his home with the intention of going to Camerton Church, but as he crossed Whitebrooks Lane in his way thither something used to draw him away as it were, contrary to his better resolutions, and take him up the hill, where there were always a number of people assembled drinking all the Sunday morning: he was heartily sorry in being thus led away in opposition to his better judgment; he knew how wrong he had acted, but it was now too late to think of that; but he imagined it to be a duty he owed to mention to me how things were going on at that place, that others might not fall into the same errors he had done.

The Methodists had been about him, and told him that if he had only a proper faith he should save his soul; but he knew he must repent sincerely, and he only regretted he had not left off his sins before they left him.

He seemed to die very penitent.

Another man at Cridlingcot, T. Sperring, who had worked some time as a Collier in Wales, died also of consumption. I was with him about a week before his decease, at a house in the same row where Benjamin Rossiter lives, and after speaking to him for a while on general topics, respecting a future state, etc., he said he wanted nothing further, being assured of his salvation, that his pardon was sealed by Christ who was all in all, and notwithstanding his weak state he tried to raise himself up in his bed and catch at something above him. I asked what he did that for? He was catching, he said, at the foot of the Lamb. This reminded me of the horrid profanations I witnessed in the Meeting of the Jumpers at Caernarvon; but surely this man (Sperring) did not leave the temple (of the world) so well justified as the other more humble publican who said, "Lord, have mercy upon me a sinner."

On going for letters I met Farmer Bush at the bottom of Radstock Hill, and said to him I wished to have some conversation respecting

38

the tithe of the ground he bought of Charles Dando, as he had not settled the price. I told him on an average the people of Cridlingcot paid me 4s. 9d. an acre; that I supposed he would have no objection to pay that sum. He answered, indeed he never would; that what he had was not worth 3s. nor would he give me more. I felt hurt at his violent manner, and said the best way then of settling the business was by taking it up. He replied I might do as I chose, he knew me, and had heard a good deal of me; that the people around knew me well enough. He said he would give me 2s. in the £. I told him, after his unprovoked insolence I would not waste any time by speaking to him: that respecting his tithe he should hear further on a future occasion. On leaving him he called out, *he* was not afraid of parsons.

Monday, July 11

Bush called this morning before 8 o'clock, said he was very sorry for what passed on Saturday, and was ready to pay my demand for the tithe. I told him I could fix no sum till I had seen the ground; as he expressed his sorrow for the offence he had given I would not let that weigh with me in putting my price on the ground; that I would appoint some future day for meeting him on the spot. I said what appeared most insolent on his part was the conclusion of his conversation, "that he was not afraid of parsons." He said he was very sorry for having thus spoken in heat: that he was well aware that all proper respect ought to be paid to superiors, etc.

Memorandum. Bush afterwards agreed to my terms.

August 6

This day died of an inflammation of his bowels a collier of the name of Lockyear. I more particularly notice his demise as many circumstances previously occurred which to my mind appeared certain indications of the warnings of that Almighty Power who willeth not the death of a sinner, but had rather that he should turn from his sins and be saved; yet he refused to hear, and was cut off in his sins and died most impenitent. He lost his first wife in 1806, and not long after united himself to a second, a niece of Goolds. I married them. About three weeks after, before I was up in the morning, the servant knocked at the door and informed me that Lockyear's wife had drowned herself in the Canal.

The first time I had an opportunity I spoke seriously to Lockyear; told him how much it behoved him to be careful of his religious conduct, since God had in a more especial manner called him to serious thoughts, for not long before he was lying without any hope of recovering in the hospital at Bath. Still he continued in his old course, drinking and everything that was bad. Last week he caught a cold, and on Saturday, hearing that the doctor had pronounced him in danger, I went to him and found him lying in great pain. I entreated him most earnestly to think of his state; that he was on the brink of Eternity. But his mind was not to be worked on, the pain of his body absorbed all considerations; the sight to me was most distressing. On getting up early this morning I was going to repeat my exhortations. Before I got to his house I heard he was dead. The impression is most awful! May we all profit by it. I find that William Hill, a Methodist collier, had been to him in his last moments and extorted from him a declaration that he had faith in Christ, which is considered as a sufficient satisfaction for an ill-spent life and as a sure passport to Heaven. What delusive, what diabolical doctrines both for those who die and those who live! His sister told me she had no doubt he was gone to a blessed state, for these were the last words he spoke before he died.

August 8

About ten o'clock in the morning, when going down to the house where Lockyear died to enquire the time of the funeral, I heard a most violent quarrelling in a field near Red Bridge belonging to William Goold, and soon saw him beating a lad called Moses Heal as hard as he could with a stick, swearing in the most outrageous manner all the time. The lad tried to escape, and got to the gate of the field. Having broken one stick Goold took another, kicking at him at the same time with the greatest fury imaginable. When I called to him he at length left off. I went up to him and asked the meaning of this savage behaviour. He told me the lad was injuring his property, and that he had a right to thrash him for so doing. I told him he had no business to take the law in his own hands in the manner he did, that, besides, he had made use of the most shocking oaths, and which I certainly should inform a Magistrate of and have him fined for his behaviour. He said he cared not what I did; that he would not stop his mouth for me when I was passing by, and words to this effect. By this time he had walked to his own house, the next door to the one in which Lockyear died; his wife and another woman came out and, hearing his insolence to me, begged him to be quiet and remember the state of him who lay dead. He would not listen to their advice, but redoubled his insults by saying he should go back to his field and thrash the other lads who were there, and I might come and witness his so doing if I chose. I told him his conduct should certainly be taken notice of. I turned into the field to see if he did beat the other two lads, but only heard him abusing them.

I then walked with Moses Heal to Mr. Purnell at Woodborough, and laid a complaint against William Goold upon oath, stating only one of the expressions he made use of, namely, "God damn you." Although he repeated this kind of imprecation over and over again.

Purnell granted a summons, which he said he would send to Burfitt, the constable, to deliver; Goold was to appear before him the following day at eleven.

August 9

On going this day to Mr. Purnell's rather before eleven I found that Burfitt and Goold had been there before me. Mr. Purnell told me that he had made much ado about paying the fine, saying he had not sworn at all, etc; however, he did at last pay two shillings. Mr. Purnell, for some reason best known to himself, forgave him the shilling which he might have charged for the summons, and they went away, Burfitt and Goold, to Lansdown Fair.

August 18

Moses Heal having procured a warrant for William Goold, he went before the Justices this day; they decreed that he should pay the sum of six shillings and the expenses of the summons, etc. Old Mother Heal, mother to the lad, I found went with them. Moses Goold saw them in Bath, and said if her son proceeded in the business against his brother he would kill him, or words to that effect. What a charming brood we have in the place in these Goolds.

August 20

Whilst walking in the village, as I generally do between Morning and Evening Services in order to see things are tolerably quiet, I saw a boat laden with coal going down the Canal. On enquiring whose it was I found that it was under the direction of William Goold, junr, who carried coal for his brother, Joseph Goold. I told the boys who were with it how improper it was to be boating coal on a Sunday,

and begged they would tell their master I should notice the impropriety of this behaviour. The name of the barge was "Vulcan No. 7."
On Monday I went to Goold's, found he was with the boat, and was not expected home for a day or two. I desired they would send him to my house when he came home. Friday he came up after breakfast, said he was very sorry for what he had done, but was fearful he should not get his coal up into the country if he had not done as he did, as there was likely to be a stoppage on the canal; that he knew I might have him fined, but if I would not proceed against him he never would be guilty of the like in future.

What a hopeful set are these Goolds! proper shoots from the old stock, one and all alike!

I performed Evening Service at Timsbury. Whilst reading the Prayers I experienced an open insult from some of the congregation in the gallery, as the people made such a constant hawking, in the manner the audience at a theatre expresses disapproval of an actor on the stage, I was obliged to tell them to leave off, otherwise I could not proceed with the Service. Then they stopped.

After Service, the Clerk told me there was to be a funeral at six. I desired him in future, if there was to be a funeral on a Sunday, to have it ready just after Service. I returned home to dinner, and went again to Timsbury a little after six.

A man told me the corpse had been waiting twenty minutes.

When the funeral service was concluded I returned to the Church. Finding the Clerk there alone I asked the meaning of that hawking when I was in the reading desk, saying if the people wished to insult me I wished to know their reason for so doing; that I had long known there were underhand dealings against me, I only wished to bring my adversaries above ground; that if the Methodists interrupted me in the discharge of my duty they might find they had the worst of it; he was at liberty to tell them so.

At the time of the (Timsbury) Revel I thought the behaviour of the people reprehensible, there being a wedding in the morning, and it was conducted with such indecorum I was obliged to tell the young man who was to be married, if he laughed in such a manner again I would stop the Service.

Going with Mr. Crang where the Club assembled before their march a drunken collier, half naked, came and laid himself down near the spot, talking all manner of nonsense, and another came out from the shed offering one beer.

Thinking it better not be a party concerned in this merriment before Church, I told Mr. Crang I should go into the Church, and wait till the people came, which I did.

I certainly shall not be much inclined to take charge of Mr. Barter's[1] flock again, without he keeps them in better order.

October

Whilst walking between Churches into the Village I met George Coombs, alehouse keeper, accompanied by his two pointers. On his saying it was a fine day I replied it was so, and had hoped it might have tempted him to have extended his walk to the top of the hill. He said he had been there. I asked him whether he had seen a building called a Church in his walk? I had been spending an hour there, and it would have given me pleasure to have seen him of the company. "Why, Sir," he replied, "my wife was there," I said she was so, and was constant in her attendance, and it gave me much satisfaction when I saw her in her place, and only wished she could persuade him to follow her example: that the reason I took that opportunity of speaking to him was for his own good, and to give him advice he would one day thank me for; that I had been at Camerton nine years, and was sure I could speak to a certainty I had never seen him nine times within the Church walls during that period: that the reason I had refused preaching to the Camerton Club on Whitsuntide was solely on that account because he was the Steward and many, I might say most, of the members never thought of setting their foot within the walls of the Church on the Sabbath, and I considered it a mere mockery to do it by way of parade at another time; therefore I declined preaching to them, but if they would shew themselves more regular in their attendance on me in future they might depend on my attendance on them, and giving them a sermon every year and doing all in my power to promote their Association. He thanked me and, finding him inclinable to be civil, I thought it a good opportunity of urging the necessity of reformation in his general conduct, as I had heard some things very much to his disadvantage. I said, as we were alone I should urge upon him the consideration of the uncertainty of human life, and assure him that if any man was cut off in his sins he would be exposed to a certainty of punishment in another world; that repentance should not be referred to a deathbed, it was requisite to set about it

[1] Reverend W. B. Barter, 1783–1825, Rector of Timsbury.

immediately; that in short, if he did not perform the duties of his station and reform those he so continually transgressed, he would if taken hence *go to Hell*. He, having been nettled before at what I had advanced, said, "*I don't believe there is such a place*." I was most sorry, I replied, to hear such a sentiment from his mouth, as there was an end of all reformation if he had brought his mind to this belief. I advised him, therefore, never to adopt this pernicious doctrine on trust, but turn his thoughts towards serious subjects, which would not only make him happier and better in this life, but, what was of more consequence, extend his claim to an eternal felicity hereafter.

He then went his way, and I mine.

1810

EDITOR'S NOTE. *In 1809, five years after the Weymouth trip, his brother Fitz-Owen is introduced to us again. The King's word had held good; promotion had come. He had lately been appointed to the command of the sloop "Trinculo", which was fitting out at Portsmouth. He had been ill, but John Skinner found him better than he had been but thought him very thin. Now occurred the first of the series of tragedies which permanently saddened Skinner's life. These extracts are taken from entries written afterwards.*

MY brother had shown so grave a symptom as spitting blood, but he would not hear of quitting his ship. He could not bear the thought of his ship going to sea, perhaps making a good prize whilst he was absent: that she was just the kind of thing he had set his heart on so long, and when appointed to her could not bear the thought of relinquishing the object of his first wishes. The symptoms returned, and it was evident even to the sufferer that he could not go to sea. Leave was obtained, and I carried my brother off for change of air and rest to Hertfordshire to my Mother's house.

In February, 1810, I was summoned again to Hertfordshire as my brother was growing rapidly worse. I found him almost a skeleton and more than usually weak and nervous. He ascribed his condition to the too great use of digitalis, or foxglove, of which he took for upwards of ten weeks, eight grains per diem, till at length his sight became affected and he became subject to violent spasms. Baron Dimsdale[1] was consulted and put him on a different diet. He was ordered to drink three quarts of whey per diem, to take opium in small quantities to relieve his cough and occasionally to eat fish and light meats, though he did so with very little appetite.

On being pressed by my brother as to what had passed between us, I made known to him that his days were numbered.

"Why did you not tell me, dear John?" he said. "I have much to do and to think of. It was cruel to leave me in ignorance of my situation." I begged him to be composed. He said he was perfectly so, though at first it was a little sudden to know that he would not recover; all along he thought he was weak, but expected the Spring

---

[1] Baron Dimsdale, son of the celebrated Thomas Dimsdale (1712–1800), created Baron by the Empress Catherine of Russia.

would bring him about again; however, if it was God's will he should
not, he was perfectly satisfied. He then exacted a solemn promise
from me not to leave him again till the last. I asked him if he should
feel more comfortable if I slept in his room; he said undoubtedly
he should. I then ordered a bed on the floor. I got but little sleep,
but found myself less agitated than I had reason to expect. How
provident it is that when great exertions are requisite I have ever
found a proportionate degree of strength for the occasion, never
have I been left destitute of help from above. *Deus sit laus*.

After breakfast on March 15, my brother set in order his affairs.

"You will find in my writing desk an account of the debts I owe,
and which my Mother has agreed some months ago to settle." The
list, I found, contained the sums for which he was indebted to his
agents for sums advanced, amounting to about £380, two tailor's
bills about £70 and Mr. Goodwin £100; there were two or three
smaller articles, amounting in the whole to £6 or £7. He begged I
would take care the tailors were paid soon, as their bills had been
due some time. He said, that indeed, all things considered, he had
much rather be called home now; he had suffered much confinement
and pain, which he should by no means like to go over again.
Besides, supposing he recovered, his prospects were by no means
promising, though Lord Mulgrave[1] had given his word to him for a
ship, yet he might be out of office before he was in a state to go to
sea again; and he dreaded the fitting out of a new ship; unavoidably
he must run in debt with his Agents for the outfit, and should he not
take prize money, must live considerably beyond his pay. He begged
that I would one day or other explain to my Uncle Haggard that he
was obliged to draw upon his Agents for the money he owed, having
had to change his ship twice in less than two years; that when he
commanded the "Hindustan" it was very expensive going backwards
and forwards carrying passengers for whom he had to keep a table
like a packet; that the service the "Goldfinch" was employed in was
somewhat similar, and that the expense could not be supported unless
prize money fell in the way, which was a great chance, and he had not
been so fortunate as to make any, though he had endeavoured to
do his duty.

He expressed a wish to receive the Sacrament.

The following day, dear Fitz told me he wished to be buried in the
parish Church, his best hat and sword to be put in the coffin with

[1] Henry Phipps, 1st Earl of Mulgrave, 1755–1831; 1st Lord of the Admiralty, 1807.

him. "I charge you, John," he added, "Not to let my body suffer any dishonour from the nurses or the people who are employed." "There are many in the Navy," he said with a sigh, "who now think little of my death, and will be sorry when they hear of it; there were many pleasant fellows I knew, and I know they liked me, and will think of me when I am no more."

I then read to him, and turned his mind to the ceremony of the Sacrament he was to join in next day. "You know, John, I received it once at Camerton; that was the only time, I wish I had done it oftener; it was not through disregard, but for want of proper opportunities. When at sea I always said my prayers, and often read the Service to the sailors. As I said before, I never wilfully or premeditatedly set about doing evil. What evil I have done was through the impulse of the moment; when I came to myself I repented of it, and made resolutions, as far as I was able, of avoiding the like in future."

Editor's Note. About this time, the promised visit to Uncle Haggard[1] was carried out, and the following extract vividly describes the old gentleman. . . .

"I found him just going out coursing with his servants, three greyhounds and three spaniels; he wished to turn back but I preferred accompanying him. We beat the common fields two hours. I happened to find a hare setting, which the dogs killed after a long course, which the old gentleman seemed highly interested in. How surprising it is to see a man between 80 and 90 years of age (really 86) enjoying the strength and spirits to enter into amusements of this kind; he has had the living of Bennington 54 years, and probably in the whole of that time has not missed a season either coursing or shooting. I see no manner of alteration in him, and he is exactly the same as when I used to visit him before I went to Oxford, which is nearly twenty years ago. He wears the same-formed blue greatcoat, the hood covering his wig, a three-cornered hat above, square-toed boots rising above his knee, short spurs scarcely visible, a long stick, and mounted on a little pony. He entered as clearly into conversation as he was accustomed to do, asked me many particulars about poor Fitz, then about my living and the Methodists, saying that they were gaining ground in his country, that Dr. Heath, at Walkern, was so annoyed with them that he threatened to leave the place. The old gentleman remarked that he made no doubt, ere twenty years were

---

[1] The Rev. John Haggard (1723–1813), Rector of Bennington, Herts. (1759–1813).

over our heads, they would expel us (the regular clergy) from our seats; however, we ought to thank ourselves for it through our inattention and supineness."

March 20

I received a letter from my dear Anne, who begged so hard to be permitted to come over here for a few days I could not refuse her, and wrote that she might, on the condition she refrains from the sick-room, as in her situation any uneasiness or exertion may be attended with the most serious consequences. She arrived on March 24 about one. She went into his room and stayed till dinner time. He was much pleased at talking over past occurrences with her.

April 3

FitzOwen said that he could do without my sleeping in his room, and begged I would occupy the room above with Anne. I told him I would consider the business, and it was finally so arranged.

April 8

Mr. Goodwin has promised to drive Anne on Thursday to Edmonton. Poor thing, she is very low at the idea of leaving me; with the prospect of a long journey and a confinement, whilst I am absent from her, no wonder her spirits are depressed.

In view of FitzOwen's emaciated frame I am certain his dissolution cannot be far off, and how could I answer it to myself to leave him and be absent during his last moments, especially after the solemn promise I gave him when he knew himself to be in danger? Alas! it is a trying situation, when one must perforce neglect one duty in the performance of another.

April 12

FitzOwen slept tolerably, and I found on getting up that he had dressed himself and was sitting in his chair, but on his complaining of fatigue I persuaded him to go to bed again, as I perceive his yesterday's exertion was too much for him. Poor Anne was very low and said she could not take leave of FitzOwen, therefore she did not go into his room. Baron Dimsdale called about eleven; at one the chaise arrived that was to convey Anne and myself to Hoddesdon. She was more nervous than I ever remember to have seen her; poor creature, it is indeed a trial to her, but I trust she will be supported under it.

We had an early dinner with the Goodwins, at four he and Mrs. Goodwin took charge of Anne in their carriage to Edmonton, I walked back to Hertford.

April 15

FitzOwen had a bad night, his cough troublesome. An old ship-mate, Mr. Goodwin, called soon after breakfast, and about one o'clock another friend of FitzOwen's, Mr. Allen; they were with him the greater part of the day.

I accompanied Baron Dimsdale in his carriage to the East India College two miles from Hertford, as he was kind enough to say he would shew me over the building and introduce me to the professors.

FitzOwen has exhausted himself by talking. Although one cannot but feel gratified by these attentions of his friends, still in his weak state their visits are prejudicial.

I wrote to Anne.

April 18

I put my intention into execution of going to see Anne at her father's. I left Hertford in the seven o'clock coach for Edmonton, where I arrived at half past ten, and had the happiness of finding her and little Laura quite well. After breakfast I walked with Anne across the fields to Warren's[1]. He himself appears much as usual, if anything thinner. The whole duty of so extensive a parish must be very prejudicial to his weak lungs, I wish he could be persuaded to take a curate, but he says he has been so much plagued by the negligence and inattention of the last he had much rather perform the whole duty himself.

April 22

I was called up before six this morning. On going in to FitzOwen I found his cough almost incessant, and this continued till eight o'clock. I could not tell what to do to relieve him, but gave him more laudanum than he had been accustomed to take. This medicine, which used almost immediately to quieten him, seems to have lost its effect, the poor fellow looks more languid and spent than I have yet seen him; he found himself too weak to receive the Sacrament as he had

[1] Rev. Dr. Dawson Warren, Vicar of Edmonton.

intended, but I read the Psalms and Lessons of the day (Sunday). I stayed in his room the whole of the day excepting at dinner time.

I read this evening to him, in addition to the usual prayers, the Office of the Visitation of the Sick, with which he seemed most gratified, and begged I would continue to read it to him daily. Baron Dimsdale told me he thought him worse than when I left him.

April 24

FitzOwen was asleep, and seemed so composed I made a sketch of him as he lay in his bed; dear fellow, these slight memorials will, I know, be valuable to me hereafter.

April 27

I learnt from Mr. Bradley the apothecary, whom I met in my walk, his surprise that FitzOwen had lingered on so long, as he says he had no hope from the beginning of his recovery. Be this as it may, his treatment of him by giving him the digitalis so long and in such large quantities cannot be defended, as his so doing can only be attributed to ignorance or, what is equally bad, to obstinacy.

April 29

FitzOwen, poor fellow, seems hastening rapidly to the termination of his career! May his transition be easy. As it may take place suddenly I have ordered my bed to be made again in his room, that I may be with him during the night. After his evening's dose of laudanum he got up and seemed quite alive again, wishing me to write a memorial to Lord Mulgrave before he goes out of office, stating his situation and services, and begging his interest for promotion. Alas! how do we cling to life to the very last gasp! The other day he had some of his clothes altered by the tailor; but it is a real comfort to know he is prepared for the stroke whenever it arrives.

May God bless him and my dear Anne and children is my fervent wish, may they be spared to me as pledges to insure my exertions, and render this wretched life somewhat interesting. If it were not for this consideration how vapid would everything appear, how much should I wish my cable unloosed in order to sail in company with my friend and brother; but my probation is not yet accomplished nor my warfare completed! Oh, Almighty God! let me ever entertain the same thoughts on the subject of death I now do; let me never be attached to the world, that I may regret leaving it when summoned hence, but on the other hand let me never think too lightly of the awful change. Thy will be done at all times and in all circumstances. Ten o'clock, April 29.

April 30

I was rather alarmed this evening by finding I spit blood, but as I have had a sore throat the whole day, suppose it proceeds from that cause. I hope I shall not add to the list of invalids. I trust I may hear comfortable news from Camerton tomorrow.

FitzOwen sleeps tranquilly. Eleven o'clock.

Editor's Note. On May 1, by FitzOwen's express desire, he left for Camerton, intending to stay until Anne was in bed.

On May 11, Joseph was born, and "the Mother was as well as they could wish; but the child had to be sent to a person in the Village to be nursed, as Anne had not milk enough, and as the last two children have suffered so much by being brought up by hand we could not think we did the present one justice by making the experiment."

On May 23, FitzOwen died in his brother's arms.

July 12

Mrs. Skinner engaged this man's[1] wife as a wet nurse for our child, and was to pay her seven shillings a week for taking charge of it. We were induced to trust the infant with her from noticing her very great neatness and the cleanliness of her cottage—so much better than the generality of cottagers' houses in the parish. We had every reason to be satisfied with her care of the child, and found everything going on well.

The latter end of June, George Dando, her husband, hearing I was enquiring for an outdoor servant, said he should be glad to take the situation if I approved of it, but that he had engaged to cut some grass for Farmer James, of Radford Mill. If he suited I agreed to give him 14*s.* a week for his work, without fire or drink, and 1*s.* 6*d.* towards the rent of his cottage, making the whole 15*s.* 6*d.* per week.

As rainy weather came on and he was frequently stopped in his mowing by the farmer he came up to me on those days and worked in the garden, always returning to James, his employer when the

[1] George Dando.

weather held up. As I had an old man to look after my garden I let him suit his convenience in coming on my premises. This he continued to do during three weeks, the weather being very rainy. At length he told me Farmer James had put two men into the fields he had agreed to mow, and as he had broken his agreement he was at liberty to leave him.

I begged he would go to the farmer to explain his reasons. He did so, and received his money for the ground he had mowed. This is all I knew of the transaction between Dando and the farmer till he mentioned, Saturday August 4, that Farmer James had got a summons from the Justices for him to appear before them at Old Down, Monday the 6th. I supposed from his representation of the affair that, as the farmer had broken his agreement, when the business came before the Magistrates they would dismiss it.

August 6

I lent Dando my mare to ride to Old Down where the Justices' Meeting was held.

About dinner time one of the maids said Dando was come home, and that he said he thought he was to be sent to prison. I must confess I was much surprised at the termination of the affair. On questioning him as to the particulars I found that he had misbehaved himself most grossly before the Justices, saying that if justice were not done there he would take care to have it done elsewhere, and moreover that when his mittimus was making out he rode away. I told him that he had behaved in every way in so disrespectful a manner that I should not be surprised if he were very severely punished for contempt of the Bench; but his conduct appeared still more reprehensible when I heard the real state of the case. Farmer James had agreed with him for mowing and had agreed to find him work when he was not mowing, and he was therefore his servant till the object of the contract was fulfilled. He then offered himself, before he left Farmer James, to mow twelve acres at Timsbury, and on Farmer James refusing his permission he left his work and came away.

August 7

George Dando was apprehended and sent to Shepton Mallet gaol.

I then rode over to Chewton, to Mr. Kingsmill, one of the Magistrates who had committed him, to understand what might be done on his behalf. He told me that on account of his violence to the Bench, Sir John Hippisley[1] at first had ordered his commitment for three months instead of one. On my saying that I could not pretend to offer any excuse for the man but gross ignorance, but that I felt for his wife who was much distressed, he promised if the man made acknowledgement of his error he would see Sir John Hippisley on the subject.

August 8

I drove over to Shepton Mallet gaol with Mr. Holmes, and found the foolish fellow disposed to acknowledge his fault.

When Dando had signed an acknowledgement I wrote out for him I advised him very forcibly not to make any acquaintance with his fellow prisoners, as they were all kept together and some were confined for notorious crimes. He promised me he would not.

The gaoler, who by the way is very civil and apparently humane man, accompanied us around the different apartments, which are kept remarkably neat, and told us there was one man committed the day before for sheep stealing, and as the skins with the marks were found on him there was but little doubt but he would suffer death. On my asking whether I could see him, he said, certainly, he was with the others. I begged to know whether they had any Clergyman appointed to attend the prisoners. On his replying in the negative I said I should like to speak a few words to the men in order if possible to awaken some pious ideas. I accordingly was shown the (room) where the male prisoners were collected to the number of ten or twelve. The people were very attentive to what I said, and thanked me when I had done. On going into the female ward I delivered myself nearly in the same terms. Two or three cried while I was speaking. One of them, I understand, is to be tried for a capital offence, she having destroyed her baseborn child.

Leaving the gaol we gave something to the keeper for the prisoners He promised to be attentive to G. Dando, and makes no doubt on his application to the Magistrates he will be released. He says he will remit the fees, 13*s*. 8*d*. The gaoler certainly seems to discharge the duties of his station very properly, as I never saw any place more clean or the prisoners more orderly and quiet.

After my return to Camerton I went to Farmer James and procured his consent to the liberation of George Dando as soon as the

[1] Sir John Hippisley, (1748–1825), of Ston Easton.

Magistrates permit. I also called on Dando's wife, and told her I hoped he would be at home again on Saturday.

August 9

I went again to Mr. Kingsmill, at Chewton, and delivered him the letter from George Dando. He was just going to ride to Bath, but on my speaking on the subject promised to call directly on Sir John Hippisley and take measures for the man's discharge.

I heard nothing further of George Dando till Sunday, when his father-in-law, Shearer, called at my house saying that he was not returned from prison. He wished to know whether I had any objection to his calling on Mr. Kingsmill, to know whether the Order had been sent for his release from prison. I said, "certainly not," and lent him my horse to go.

Between 9 and 10 o'clock at night Dando came to my house after his release, and I understand from Shearer that the order was signed by Sir John Hippisley and Mr. Kingsmill on Thursday, and retained by the Justices' Clerk, Mr. Mills, till his own fee, 3s. 6d. was paid. Therefore if Shearer had not gone the poor fellow might have been confined a week longer. Certainly these things ought not to be, and the Magistrates should take care that their agents act in conformity with their wishes, for Dando, had the order been sent to Shepton, would himself have paid the fees to the person bringing it, and all reasonable expenses.

Dando seemed very thankful for the part I had taken, and quite sensible of the folly of depending upon his own knowledge of law.

I have no manner of doubt his having been to prison will be construed very much to his disadvantage by his malignant neighbours, therefore it is my duty to countenance and support him against their malicious tongues. Indeed it is probable I shall not escape my share, and they will attribute my exertions to far different motives, as the week before he was confined, a near neighbour of Dando's, of the name of Burge, having quarrelled with Dando's wife respecting a little dog she keeps at the cottage, which came into his garden, said—No wonder she was so proud, as the Parson gave 8s. a week for the keep of his child and two guineas a leap to herself.

When Dando mentioned this to me on the Friday previous to the Justices' business I rode down to make every enquiry and get, if I could, sufficient evidence to punish the man, but on going there could gain nothing from the neighbours, though some had heard mention made of the two guineas, but did not hear my name at all. The man denied having mentioned me, and was ready to swear he did not; the woman on the other hand was equally positive as to what she told her husband.

What a place we live in!

At the conclusion of Evening Service I spoke to my servant, George Dando, who during the sermon had sat with his legs up at full length on the seat in Farmer Burfitt's pew, and fell asleep. He denied having been asleep, but said nothing uncivil. Collings, the Churchwarden, being present I told him I should take some steps to have that pew restored to its original form, Burfitt having had it altered during my absence from home without either my consent or the consent of the Ordinary, as this was the second instance of improper behaviour I had had occasion to notice since it had been an enclosed seat. On leaving the Church, just by the Porch I spoke again to Dando respecting what I had told Collings, and seeing his brother, standing near at hand, who last Autumn had behaved with still greater impropriety in the same seat by sitting down when he ought to stand, etc., I then said to him also that I would have the pew altered in order to prevent such impropriety in future. He immediately in the most insolent way began to tell me I had no right to notice what he did, I had better attend to myself; that he did not wish to come to Church, and very seldom was there; that he cared nothing for me, that I myself was a scandal to the profession. On my desiring him to hold his tongue and not insult me, he nevertheless still continued to make use of the most disrespectful language two or three times, employing very low aggravating expressions such as, There was plenty of parsons in Hell and I might go and join the number, that he no more cared for me than the t — d beneath his feet or the —— I repeated if he continued that kind of conversation I would put him in the Ecclesiastical Court for brawling in the Churchyard, he said he cared as little for the Ecclesiastical Court as he did for me. I begged the Churchwarden to notice those words in particular, and desired him and his two brothers who were with him to leave the Churchyard, which after a time they did, but making use of the same kind of aggravating language their brother had done. The occasion of my speaking to him in the first instance was briefly this; he came into Burfitt's pew with Burfitt's niece about the end of the first Lesson; as soon as they entered I observed them laughing two or three times, which drew my attention; instead of standing up when the Magnificat was read, Collings kept his seat, notwithstanding I looked at him indicating my displeasure at his not doing as the other part of the congregation did. He stared at me with the greatest insolence, and continued sitting after the second Lesson. I had occasion to pass by the pew, in which he was, to perform the Service of Baptism. I then said to him I expected he would stand up as the others did, to which he replied he should do as he thought proper.

On coming out of Church he waited for me in the path leading to my house, made use of the most insolent language, saying he should always do just as he chose when he came to Church—that he should sit or stand, just as he thought proper; that a Clergyman had no right to notice what he did. I told him it would be much better he should stay away, if such were his sentiments.

George Dando, my servant, afterwards came up to my house saying that he was much concerned to have witnessed such abuse, that in his life he never had heard anything like it; that when I was gone Collings said he wished to provoke the Parson, if he had only hit him he would have knocked him over the wall.

August 27

Having experienced a gross insult from Collings the preceding day (Sunday) in the discharge of my duty, I went to Wells and saw Mr. Parfitt, one of the Proctors of the Court, with whom I left my complaint in writing. I also spoke respecting the conversion of two sittings in the Church into a pew, which had been done some time back without my permission, and which pew had twice been the occasion of the ill behaviour I complained of.

Parfitt said he would attend to what I said and send Citations when the Court was to meet, it not being term time. The apparitor only delivered one Citation to Farmer Burfitt respecting the pew, to make his appearance in October. Collings, who in my opinion is the most reprehensible, for saying before my people at my Church Porch he neither cared for me nor the ecclesiastical law, I should hope might be made to apologize for his conduct before the Court, for if this open disregard of clerical authority be unnoticed I can have little prospect of doing anything hereafter with the rude, un-civilized race of beings over whom I have the misfortune to be placed.

I met Joseph Goold. He said he felt very much hurt because I brought forward circumstances which had happened three years ago relative to the pew; that it was very wrong in me so to do, and that I did it merely for the sake of contention. I replied it was no such thing; that I should not have noticed anything about the alteration had there not been two instances occurred wherein persons had misbehaved in that pew who had no business to set there; that I understood he had gone to joint expense with Burfitt, but that neither he nor Burfitt had any right to make the alteration without first procuring my leave. He replied that I must recollect his having spoken to me on the business during the time he was Churchwarden, and that I had given leave. I said that was every way false, that I well remembered when speaking to Burfitt and asking him why he did not attend his Church more frequently, that he said since he had been at his new house he had no seat, and he could not bear when he came to Church, sitting with the bitch Elizabeth Cottle. I reproved him at the time for speaking thus of one of my servants, and said there should be no further obstacle on this head, accordingly I had part of my own pew in the Chancel taken off in order that my female servants should be in quiet, and they have set there ever since.

Goold, finding he could not effect anything by his pretended recollection of circumstances, changed his ground and said that previous to the alteration of the seats there had been a sitting for the Churchwarden, and that he had the pew made for the accommodation of the Churchwarden for the time being. Seeing the art and subterfuge of the man I had to deal with I finished the conversation by saying I was fully convinced in my own mind I had never given any kind of permission for the erection of a pew.

Some desultory conversation intervened whilst speaking on the subject of the pew, and Goold told me (which by the way he has frequently done before) that things would go on much more quietly in the parish if I did not take them up too warmly, or in other words put myself in such passions. To this I answered I was ready enough to acknowledge I was frequently angry, but the fault was with those I had to deal with as much as with myself; that when they did everything to insult and provoke me, flying in my face on every trivial occasion, and, what was worse, when they even offered insults to the Deity, whose Minister I was, by the grossest misbehaviour in the sacred house of God, I then could not but take warning; that I knew my own disposition sufficiently to assure him that if my parishioners had taken half the pains to please me and to discharge their several duties they would never have had reason to complain of the warmth of my temper, but as it was, with the continual insults I was exposed to, it was not possible for me to be at all times myself, that to be calm under present circumstances one must be deaf and blind—at any rate possessed of less feeling than I had.

This was the substance of my conversation with Joseph Goold.

December 20

This day was buried James Britten, of the Parish of Camerton. He was born there of poor parents in the year 1740, and continued through the whole course of his life working at or near the place as a day labourer or farmer's servant. He brought up a family of children whom he supported without ever applying to the Parish for assistance; his weekly pay of seven shillings per week, which fifty years ago was the common allowance of a working man, he never desired to have increased, and though when the coal pits were worked and much more considerable pay was received by those around him he never applied to his employers for more than he had been accustomed to receive four years ago. I had occasion to employ him in digging potatoes, and was so much pleased with his industry, contented disposition and constant attendance to his religious duties, I occasionally had opportunities of rendering him some little assistance.

Finding him getting more infirm I told him to come to the Parsonage whenever he was out of employ and I would find him in work, or if I had none I would give him some trifle, but such was the diffidence of the old man he never made any application, neither would he ask any pay from the Parish till I urged it so strongly he at length consented, and at Easter 1807 he procured an allowance of 1*s*. 6*d*. per week, and this was all he ever received as constant pay, but by working on the roads whenever he was not prevented by the rheumatism he added somewhat more—probably 4*s*. per week to this moderate stipend, but he was perfectly contented and never once murmured; when prevented from working he was always uneasy, and felt uncomfortable at setting without employment.

In the Autumn of 1810 he dug up half an acre of potatoes in the Parsonage Field; when stopped by the rain or his tormenting complaint, the rheumatism, he never failed on Saturday night when he received his pay to make the exact deductions for the time he had not worked. Indeed I never saw any man more exactly and conscientiously honest. Every Sunday he dined at the Parsonage for upwards of two years, and I never at any time saw the least difference in his manners of disposition; always grateful, modest, unassuming, it was with difficulty one could get him to make any little want known, so fearful was he of giving trouble.

On Sunday, December 16, having missed him in his usual place at Church, I knew he must be ill. On going down to the place where he lodged I found him suffering with a violent headache. He told me he had got wet on Wednesday and sat in his wet clothes which gave him a violent cold, and half his head seemed dead; Mrs. Skinner sent him down some cordial which he could not take.

On Monday I went to him, and found him speechless. Monday night he died.

I have made these memoranda, as it is a pleasure to record the merits of one worthy man amongst so many of a contrary character. I verily believe he was in every sense of the word religious, sober, honest, fully prepared to quit this world in firm confidence of a happy resurrection to a better state. Often and often has he expressed his wishes on this head to me, and said most happy should he be if the Almighty would please to take him before he got too infirm to work, as he knew not what he should do without some employment, and he could not bear to think of being a burden to others.

At his funeral, on the 20th instant, I could not help saying to the bystanders after he was put in the grave that I believed the most honest man in Camerton was gone, and I knew not where to look for his equal.

I determined in memory of this good old creature to put up a gravestone with an inscription to this effect:

Here lieth James Britten
who was what every true Briton should be,
An honest, Good Man,
he died December 17, 1810. Aged 70.

Reader
Mayest thou both live and die as he did.

1811

BEFORE tea this evening it being nearly dusk, I went down into the village. Passing by Amos Heal's house I saw his wife standing at the wicket and said, "Mrs. Heal, it is nearly two months since I mentioned to you about that place before your door. Of a dark evening a person might break his leg as he walked along the footpath; I shall insist upon having the hole filled up;" that not long since I had fallen with one leg into it; that if it were not done I would represent the nuisance to a magistrate, and they would be fined. She said she cared not what I did; that I always had a spite to her, and a great deal of abuse in which her daughter joined. I said it was true I had often occasion to speak to her for misconduct in keeping a disorderly w — — house; that she, during the time she had washed for my family had entertained many of my *bad* servants and did all their commissions for them, procuring gin at the public-house and everything which was bad. She said that it was true four or five times she had got gin for one of my servants who was still in the house, but that she had not for others; that with regard to her's being a w — — house, there was not a more regular family in the parish. On my asking how it happened that her daughter, who was standing by her, had had two bastards if she did not encourage her to do what was wrong? She still denied that any men came to the house, or ever had been entertained. I said it had been represented to me by my churchwarden some time since that he knew three men at one time who were accustomed to be received by her daughters in her house, and I had other sources of information which convinced me this was true; that Mr. Stephens, whose the house was, if their conduct were represented to him ought doubtless to turn them out of their cottage. She said she could get a house anywhere, and continued repeating a deal of abuse, saying I had frightened her so much she was quite ill—her daughter joining in the clamour. I said I could not help thinking they were both in liquor, and told them so; they said that was perhaps more my own case. I then left them. I could have said much more on the subject, but it was in vain to think of exciting any feeling of shame in persons so wholly depraved as they are.

This evening Reynolds, bailiff at the coal pit, and his brother called on me saying they wished to speak respecting an occurrence which had lately happened in the parish, which was the most iniquitous thing that could be imagined, as a woman at the new pits had sworn a rape against a young man, son to the underground bailiff, who was herself a common prostitute and had often before encouraged his coming to the house, and now, because she happened to have the foul disorder, and he had left off visiting her, had laid this information against him, and moreover said the young man had given it her; that Mr. Else, the Justice's Clerk, had been there Tuesday and taken her deposition, on which Mr. Purnell had committed the young man to Ilchester where he was gone; that the colliers at the New Pit were so much afraid of the malicious disposition of the woman, mother to the person who had sworn the rape, that they refused to work, lest she should cut the rope and endanger their lives; that they therefore wished me to draw up a memorial stating the iniquitous character of the person who had sworn against the young man, in order that the transaction might be known. I replied I had heard an account of the business from Heal, the Parish Officer—that I knew nothing of the parties myself, not even knowing them personally; but, as the examination of the parties had been taken before a magistrate, that magistrate was the most competent judge of what might be done; that on a capital offence, such as rape, the oath of an accuser was quite sufficient for the conviction of an offender; that I was sorry the colliers of the pit had refused to work on the occasion; that if I were in their place, the bailiffs', I would laugh them out of their foolish determination by asking whether such a number of stout, fine fellows would not be afraid to meet twice the number of Frenchmen, would suffer themselves to be frightened by an old woman; that it was not probable she ever entertained the idea of cutting the rope, even if she had formed so malicious a design there were plenty of people about who would prevent her carrying it into execution. After they left me I went to Aaron Heal, Parish Officer, to state I thought it improper for the parish to take any steps for the removal of the woman, especially as I heard she was then ill with the bad disorder, and in a course of mercury; that if she caught cold and anything happened to her, he, as Overseer, would stand in an awkward predicament; that it would have the appearance of joining a party against the woman. It was therefore my advice, as one of the parish, not to refuse giving her proper relief as long as she continued here, and that I doubted not the parish of Clutton on her removal would indemnify us. Heal sent to Burfitt's for the Bath paper, and I read the advertisement which stated that the rape had been committed on a young woman of the name of Challinger by a collier of the name of Aslip; that he had taken her into the mill house of the coal pit and effected his purpose, her cries not being heard on account of the noise of the water; that the man had been committed to Ilchester by Mr. Purnell. Heal related many circumstances which, *if true*, will, I should imagine, speak strongly in favour of the prisoner on his trial. I heard from Joseph Goold that the rope once was cut at the coal pit, by which a man of the name of Parfitt lost his life. Indeed I remember some years ago having heard two twists of the rope at the Lower Pit were found cut, but in time to prevent any accident. What a diabolical method of revenge. What a nefarious race!

April 6

I was going to call this morning on William Goold, Jnr., to ask whether he would pay the composition for tithe for this last year, as he had promised to do it on Monday and had failed so doing. Saw Joseph Goold in his garden, asked him when he meant to pay his tithe; he said, some day next week. I mentioned his brother having failed, and said I was sorry to take legal steps to get my dues, but must if I could not without; that I was tired of asking the tithe payers for money. He said he hoped I should not do that, it would be better to meet as we used to do and have a dinner, when the farmers would meet and everything would be settled in an amicable manner. I said that time was gone by, for I never could with comfort set down with people to eat with them who I knew would pervert every word that I said and do me every injury in their power behind my back; I was well aware there had been a regular combination against me; that I very much wished they would act openly like men and let me know what they had to say to my disadvantage, and then I should know with whom I had to deal, but all underhand dealings were beneath the character of Englishmen. I begged to recall to his memory that though the Living had been bought under the idea of my making a considerable rise when I took possession of it, yet I had made no augmentation for three years; that it was from this period I date the ill will my parishioners have conceived against me as their Rector.

Goold pretended to be very civil, said he would endeavour to get his brother to settle what was due to me. He then entered upon the business of the woman who had sworn the rape, as he was employed as constable to take up the poor man. He said she had kept company with the man for a year previous to the time in question; that they sent the mother out of the way to buy some beer when he had connection with her; that on the mother's return, so far from making complaint, she locked the young man into her house, not letting him return to his father though two persons were sent for him there, and many other circumstances which I cannot recapitulate, calculated to do discredit to the testimony of the accusers, who, he said, no more valued an oath than speaking the most trifling thing. I said I feared that was too much the case everywhere now, but that Truth would stand, and those who attempted to establish anything by falsehood must in the end be the sufferers.

Memorandum. I have not spoken to this man excepting on business since his insulting me, and perhaps had better not have done it now.

William Goold afterwards, going on his old courses, was put into prison for debt, where he continued for some time; his wife and children, who were staying at a house belonging to old Goold at Radford, were to be pitied, and I called upon them occasionally. She was the daughter of old Benjamin Rossiter, and deserved a better fate. When he came out of prison it was considered all his debts were liquidated: of course I lost my money.

Respecting Mrs. Brimble and Evans

On going through the village in my way to Red Hill I saw old Mrs. Brimble, of Tunley, in a violent rage with one of the colliers opposite Goold's house, swearing and making use of the grossest language. On my speaking to her (after a while) she went away, and one of the bystanders said that he had rather at any time fight with the stoutest man than hear the abuse of that woman, it was enough to frighten anyone, as she made use of such words as no one ever heard or could believe. Indeed I made a memorandum when her daughter was married to Parfitt on my first coming to Camerton of the scene which was transacted in the church, to this effect: The daughter being with child and near her time, the Overseers wished to unite the parties as soon as possible, but when the man came to the point he refused having her unless they gave him two guineas, which I told them they were by no means authorized to do. During the delay which was occasioned by the persuasions and threats of the Parish Officers and the obstinacy of the man old Mrs. Brimble went up to her daughter, who was crying in a seat in the church, and said, "If thou dostn't ha he I will put a whittle in thy droat" she replied, "I'll ha he, but he wunt ha I." It was so ridiculous I could scarcely keep my countenance, yet I was obliged to put a stop to such conversation, and was going from the church when the man, Parfitt, said he would consent to the union.

N.B. The fellow was afterwards committed for theft at Bath, and was supposed to be connected with a set of horsestealers living in Gloucestershire; indeed at Tunley there exists a most nefarious colony of wretches who ostensibly gain a livelihood by taking coal on half starved horses and asses to Bath; this Mrs. Brimble and a younger daughter daily being on the tramp with a brother of the former called King Evans, another brother was shot some years ago near Bristol by a gentleman's servant whom he attempted to rob, and a third, going by the name of Quaddy Evans, lately deceased, was tried for sheepstealing, and got off from transportation through the interest made for him by Mr. Stephens when he was Sheriff for the County. But it had been better for society if he had gone, as he continued his depredations to the last, even when he was so infirm from sores in his legs that he could scarcely put one foot before another. To shew the depravity and hardness of heart of this unfortunate wretch, Quaddy Evans, I will just relate what I myself was witness to not long before he died: He was accustomed to hobble up to my Parsonage and complain that he was starving, which I believe sometimes was actually the case, as the two shillings a week he received from Dunkerton Parish was frequently spent in drink immediately he received it. On these occasions I used to give him some bread and cheese and any scraps there might be in the house, which he ate lying down in front of the railings. One day whilst he was in that situation he told me he should not long trouble the Parish or anyone else, as he was sure he should not live a fortnight; that he had spent the last night near the Coke Pit fire, and his legs were so bad and full of sores he could scarcely creep along. I asked him, as he thought his end was so near, whether he had prepared for the state he was to enter into: that he must appear before the Judgment Seat of God. He replied, God was a merciful God, and he hoped would receive him. I said it was very true, but to those who were rebellious and forgetful He would assuredly punish at that dreadful day. He said he had suffered enough here and there was no need he should suffer more hereafter, he was sure it was enough to be punished as he was. I said in all likelihood he had been punished through his own vices, and perhaps had to thank himself for the sores which he complained of, the poverty to which he was reduced, and the coldness he complained of his fellow creatures to relieve him; they knew what a sad fellow he had been and treated him accordingly, and if it was true and he did not sincerely repent his misdeeds, and implore the forgiveness of God and the mediation of a Blessed Redeemer he would only exchange this state of torment for a worse, and if with all the suffering he complained of he still continued to pursue his wicked courses it was a sign his mind was hardened instead of being corrected, and that I must tell him, if he did not repent and with sincere sorrow acknowledge his evil ways, he would be condemned to lasting torments in Hell, and what would he do then? "Why," said the hardened wretch with a frown and diabolical cast of countenance, "*I must do as the rest do*."

N.B. Both Parfitt's father and brother were hanged.

April 9

Charles Dando came to settle his tithe this day, he paid me seven years arrears for a field called "How Trees," which he had hitherto withheld on pretence of paying it to Dunkerton. This plea he had employed so long that I insisted upon knowing whether Mr. Munton actually received for it, and found he did not. Finding Dando very civil and ready to pay without further difficulty I did not enlarge on the subject, but in conversation I asked him what was the reason I never saw him at Church. He said he would tell me the reason; that he conceived I had not acted right towards him, therefore he had not come to Church. I answered that was indeed a most foolish reason to give, that because he was offended with his clergyman he should give offence to his Maker, but I was happy in having an opportunity of hearing what this offence was; I well knew that my parishioners had been set against me, and had said all manner of ill of me behind my back. I was now glad to find one who would in a manly manner tell me in what I had offended, therefore I should with patience listen to what he had to say. He begged I would remember having received a guinea when his child was buried, that he thought it a hard case because that with property in the Parish, he then happening to live out of it, he should pay any fees for burying. I said I was astonished to hear so frivolous a cause of offence: that it was a general rule, and I had given orders to the Clerk to receive a guinea for breaking the ground from everyone who did not live in the parish, and accordingly he must submit to the general rule as well as the others. He replied it was not the money he cared for, but he conceived I had taken a spite against him and had shewn my dislike by making him pay the fees. I replied that, as for spite I never entertained any, had I conceived cause for offence I should have called upon him and come to an explanation, that, as in the instance he mentioned, offence was taken for no reason whatever, if persons were so prejudiced it was impossible to live comfortably together; but I again advised his coming to Church, which he said he would do.

Memoranda respecting a conversation with a Methodist, called Green, living in one of the cottages at Bridge Place,

July 18

Whilst walking my usual round in the village Sunday evening in order to see things were going on quietly I saw this Green, who is a very staunch Methodist, standing at his door reading a book out loud as I passed by. I stopped for a moment to hear the subject on which he was haranguing in this public manner. When he saw I stopped he said he was looking over a book of instruction for young people to see whether it had a catechism in it, as he wished to find it there. I said I was very glad to hear him say so, as I thought it was proper that all young people of the school lately instituted at the Meeting House should be instructed in the Catechism, as it was the ground work of religion, and that John Wesley himself, the founder of Methodism, always recommended it to his followers. He replied, to be sure John Wesley had recommended many good things, but there were other things of much importance to be attended to besides what he had mentioned. I said, from what dropped from him, I must then suppose alterations had taken place in the doctrines of the Methodists since John Wesley's time. Certainly, he said, there were some alterations. I said I also had observed them myself. John Wesley recommended his followers to go to Church, and receive the Sacrament at stated periods; both these injunctions were rarely complied with at present, and I did not know how any number of persons professing to be the disciples of Christ could neglect so important a command and abstain from the Communion. He said he did not himself abstain from it, and had received it in my Church. The conversation then took quite a spiritual turn, when he strongly insisted on the efficacy of the Spirit in working immediate conviction and enabling men to preach the gospel although they had originally no idea of being called to the ministry. Knowing that this man himself had set up for a *pray-er*, though he had not arrived at the honour of a *preacher*, I told him that many who set up for teachers, even in this country, could not speak their own language, much less that of another country. Then he said, "I suppose you will deny there is such a thing as the gift of repentance," indeed, he continued, in a sarcastic manner, "I can easily suppose you know but little about this gift." Not heeding his insolence (for he began to be nettled when he became entangled in the argument,) I continued, "religion is not that easy thing you think it to be. When you have committed a fault you must be sorry for it. God will give his assistance that the grace of repentance may grow and increase if it be your wish and you fervently pray for it, but the labour and efforts must be your own." He concluded by telling me I was myself quite blind as to repentance, and was sure I knew not what it was. Finding he began to be insolent, I thought I had better leave him before he said anything to irritate my feelings. Accordingly I quitted him, after an hour's conversation.

August 2

This morning my servant, George Dando, said he wanted to go into Bath as his wife was summoned before the magistrates owing to some dispute with a neighbour, and had thrown water in her face. I told him I could not very well spare him as I had company, and if she was so violent she was able to take care of herself and his appearance, as he was not present at the time of the dispute, could be of no service. However, as he promised to be back in the course of four or five hours, I let him go. He went off about ten o'clock, and did not return the whole evening. Next morning about breakfast time his wife and father-in-law came to say he had not been at home all night, and they made no doubt he was then off with a servant who used to live with me, with whom he had kept up an improper connection in Bath, and that she was with child by him: that he had been very idle and good for nothing of late, never coming home to his wife till 12 o'clock at night, lying about at the alehouse, and lying with Captain Boyce's servants. I said I had no conception of this, that he had appeared to me quite different, and I had hopes he might have been a steady servant; but really I now was fully convinced that nothing in Camerton could be good. The man by going off had acted certainly in the most ungrateful manner to me as I had ever been kind to him, but what was worse he left his children. I further said I feared his wife, by her ill humour had in the first instance made his home uncomfortable; that that was no excuse for his leaving his children, and I could not but think the man who committed a robbery on the highway was not so guilty in the eyes of God as he who deserted his children, as he introduced them into the world they had a demand upon him for subsistence. I was very angry at this fresh instance of depravity, but it is in vain to think of finding anything like principle amongst this hardened people!

August 4

On going down to Hillman's, the Clerk, before Morning Prayers, I saw a person dressed in black going through the village, and asked him civilly whether he was going to preach at the chapel. He replied in the affirmative. I said the reason I took the liberty of speaking to him was that I wished to ask him a single question, which I thought it my duty to do, and as it was from the best motives I was sure he would not decline giving me an explicit answer, I then asked him whether it was a doctrine preached at his chapel that repentance was the immediate gift of God, and that conversion was also miraculous? I then explained briefly my conversation with Green, and shewed how dangerous would be the error if the ignorant were to believe they were to wait till they were converted, and that no efforts of their own were of any avail till that period arrived. He answered me he never taught such doctrines, was equally aware with myself of their pernicious tendency, but of late many Calvanistic tenets had been propagated which misled many. I said it behoved him certainly to endeavour to counteract them, as they would be so very prejudicial, as there would be an end of the little morality at present retained amongst the lower orders if these were to obtain. He agreed with me, and we parted.

November 13

A person from Bath, of the name of Lavinia Purnell, was buried, who was sister to Amos Heal's wife, the washerwoman, and I find had been a very unfortunate woman. When quite young she lived as servant with Farmer Emery, of Durcot in this parish, who seduced her, and a discovery being made by his wife of the connection she got into service at Bath, where he still kept up the intercourse, and got her two or three times from good situations, pretending that he was her uncle and had need of her services at home, thus preventing her gaining an honest livelihood when she was herself disposed to do so. At last she became quite a lost creature, and was brought to an untimely grave. Having been informed of these particulars, and meeting Farmer Emery a few days after her funeral, I said to him, "Farmer, you ought to have been chief mourner at the funeral we had the other day!" "Why so?" said he. "Because you had more reason to *mourn*," I replied, "than any that were present." I then let him know I was not ignorant of what was past, but it had no more effect upon the man than if I had spoken to a rock.

N.B. Once, after Emery had received a slight paralytic stroke which drew down the corners of his mouth, I spoke to him on the warning which had been given him of the uncertainty of life. I told him he stood on the brink of a precipice, and might be pushed over in an instant. At this time, and this time only, did he shew *any signs of compunction*. He promised amendment, and even made an effort to come to Church the following Sunday. But not many weeks after, on my speaking to him again on the road to Bath from whence I was returning of the course he was pursuing, he said, "Why do you talk to me about these things? look to yourself!"

Memorandum. Emery was afterwards obliged to leave his farm, and is now reduced to the greatest poverty, driving coal horses to Bath for his support. Of all the people I have ever met with he seems the most hardened.

William Gullick's wife, and Hannah West

I was going through the village and met this woman, Gullick, in a most ragged state. On entering into conversation with her why she does not come to Church, and appear more tidy, she said although she did not go to Church she did not go anywhere else, for she hated the Methodists and thought them a false set of people. I told her it was not well to find fault with others whilst she was so much to blame herself in neglecting her duty; that she was getting an old woman, in the course of things she could not expect to live long, and if she made no provision for a future state how dreadful would be her departure from this world. She then began to make the usual excuse of not having sufficiently good clothes to come to Church in, and this I overruled by saying God did not attend to what was of the outside (although she might certainly dress more tidy than she did), but to the inside. She then said she got old and infirm. This I told her was but a poor excuse, for she was able to walk up to Mr. Purnell's two or three times a week with meat, and I had frequently seen her walking quite as fast as I could, and I desired her to direct her steps towards the Church on a Sunday; that I observed her husband came more than he used to do, and as she had no children to attend to at home there was nothing to hinder her coming. She promised she would be better in future.

I went to visit *Hannah West, of Red Hill*, who was a sad, reprobate character, and having when drunk fallen from a horse on which she carried coal to Bath, had fractured her skull and it was not expected she could live. I found her in a very bad state indeed, both from pain of body and compunction of mind. She said she was sure she should die, and what was to become of her? and cried and groaned most bitterly. On my speaking to her very seriously on her notorious neglect of all religious and moral duties and the danger of putting off repentance to the last, she said if God would permit her to live only a few months longer she would be quite a new creature, she would not swear nor drink again, indeed she would sell her coal horse and not drive coal again to Bath, for that was the way she got into liquor, stopping at public-houses by the wayside and falling into evil company. The second visit I made her I found old Evans of Tunley who, hearing she was not expected to live, paid her a visit. I thought it a good opportunity to admonish him on his going on, as not a day of his life passed without his returning drunk from Bath, after having sold his coal. I said, "You see what a situation this woman is in by a fall when in a state of intoxication she has fractured her skull, and the same may happen to you tomorrow or any day, and you may be killed on the spot and hurried into eternity with all your unrepented sins on your head. The man seemed so much struck with the apprehension of death, which he saw as it were so near, and from the accident which occasioned the woman's sufferings, which he knew he was himself continually exposed to, that he actually shed tears, and made me a firm promise to come to Church and be more careful of his conduct. The woman, contrary to expectation, got about again; but instead of selling her coal horse and abstaining from drink, etc; she got worse than ever, and indeed threatened to kill her husband with a knife, and was so violent with her neighbours that they complained to me they could not live near her. As she was in the poor houses at Red Hill I spoke to the Overseers, who threatened to turn them out if they did not live more peaceably. Her husband soon after built himself a hovel in a piece of ground near their houses, where I understand they go to reside sometimes, and would, I suppose, altogether if they were forced from the poorhouse.

Old Evans came to Church the Sunday after I spoke to him, but then left it off. I should not be surprised if he actually meets with his death by a fall from his horse some night on his return from Bath.

November 28

I quitted my house at Camerton to accompany my dear Anne to Clifton; her cough and oppression at the chest having so much increased, I became very anxious to procure her the best advice in my power, and a warmer and drier situation than the Parsonage before winter set in. We took lodgings on St. Vincent's Parade near the Well House, and immediately sent for Dr. Garrick a physician we had heard highly spoken of.

1812

EDITOR'S NOTE. *In 1811 Skinner's infant daughter Tertia, aged three months, died of consumption, and when his wife became ill, his mind was full of apprehensions, both from what he had witnessed in FitzOwen's case, and from the rather discouraging tone of the doctor. He sought distraction as usual in long walks, in viewing the antiquities and sights of the neighbourhood, and in making careful descriptions and sketches of the points of interest in the Cathedral and Churches of Bristol, and had intended visiting the whole number besides the Catholic Chapels and Meeting Houses of various denominations, but his wife began to need the whole of his attention. Every moment was now devoted to her, except when he went to the market or for a walk on the Downs.*

As winter passed into spring they moved their lodgings nearer to the Down, as she could no longer bear the fatigue of getting into a carriage.

NEVER did I witness such perfect resignation; not a sigh, not a murmur escapes her. The loss of our infant she bears with unshaken fortitude; indeed, she told me she daily offered up her most grateful thanks to the Almighty that He was pleased to take it to Him, as should she herself be taken from me, there would be less anxiety on my mind.

All her thoughts, which have anything to do with this world, are now directed to me; she declares that the only wish she has to live longer is that she may continue to console me, and when she thinks how desolate I shall be, if left alone amidst the ill-disposed people of Camerton, without any friends to whom I may confide my cares, or who may soothe my mind when too much irritated by their misconduct, she feels indeed most wretched, and hopes and begs she may be spared.

As the days drew on and hope waned, her great desire was that she may be permitted to continue till June 17, our wedding day. But it was not to be, and the end came very soon. Here is the story of the last hours.

I hinted that Susan had better sleep in the next room in case she should want her in the night. Looking at me, she said, "John, you have all along been my nurse at night, and I don't want any other.

I dare say when I get to sleep I shall have as good a night as usual."
I went to bed about twelve, and she slept pretty tranquilly after
taking about fifteen drops of laudanum. About two I gave her some
soda-water, and she seemed to sleep again; a little after she awoke,
and began to cough. Finding that she did so with more difficulty
than usual I supported her head, and she breathed her last without
a sigh or a struggle; for, on ringing the bell for Susan, thinking she
had fainted, she never stirred more, and when her sister Harriet
came into the room she was quite dead. In compliance with dear
Anne's injunctions, Susan alone was with her to perform what
was requisite. I went out for two hours as soon as the day began
to dawn on the Down; returning, I visited the corpse in order to
satisfy myself that every proper attention had been paid, and to
bid farewell to all that was earthly of my dearest friend, and having
given directions to Harriet about settling a few trifles that were
owing at Clifton, and written a letter to Mr. Holmes informing him
of the event, I got into a chaise and returned to Camerton.

On May 15, Mr. Stephens and Harriet accompanied the hearse
from Clifton to Camerton, and I attended her remains to the grave,
Mr. Barter performing the service. Although I had endeavoured to
prepare my mind for this occasion, it entirely overcame me, and on
the 20th, my friends leaving me and taking little Laura with them,
I was quite alone; but still the Comforter was with me.

EDITOR'S NOTE. *In Camerton Churchyard stands a small altar tomb,
bearing on its east side the following inscription:*

Hic Jacet
Anna Skinner
obiit
A.D. MDCCCXII
Tu secura jaces
Nobis reliquisti querelas
Praeisti hospitium dulce
Parare tuis
Vale sed non in aetern.
Vale charissima Anna.

June 28

Joseph Aslip was buried this day, aged 22. This was the young
man against whom a rape had been sworn by a prostitute of the

name of Challinger, and who had in consequence been committed to Ilchester, where he stayed in gaol some weeks, but afterwards was released without any trial. He had caught a sort of typhus fever, which at this season was very prevalent in the village, and just before he died I was sent for by his mother to attend him. On going to her house in Collier's Row I asked where the sick person was, thinking I should have to go upstairs to his bedroom. "No," she replied, "you need not go up, he will come down to you." I had no idea of his being so ill, and to my utter astonishment they brought him down wrapped up in a blanket, and when they seated him in the chair I thought he would have died on the spot, as he could not articulate a single word, and had such a guggling in his throat as though in the very agony of death. On my asking him if he knew me he nodded his head as much as to say he did. I then begged he would give some sign if he could understand me if I prayed by him, he again nodded assent, and I read some prayers in the Office of the Visitation of the Sick. He leaned his head on the table, and the guggling still increased.

Being much affected by what I saw, and finding I could be of no further service, I left him. He died in a short time after I quitted the house; so he must have been, as I suppose, dying when they brought him down stairs. What ignorance in the parents to think the merely having a clergyman at that time could be of the smallest benefit!

There were six or seven people ill at the same time, and two children died of it (typhus). When I attended them I was in the habit of carrying camphor in my pocket and rubbing my hands with it, so I escaped infection. But to shew the insensibility of the colliers even in their own danger I will just mention that, on my speaking to the neighbours after young Aslip's death, telling them they ought not only to abstain from going into the house where the corpse was, but to fumigate their own residences with tobacco and whitewash the walls, but not all I could say had the least effect.

One of the women in the same row, wife of J. Parfitt, soon after sickened, as did two children. She, I thought would have died, her throat was so bad and her fever so high. Mr. Flower who attended her, having given orders that such a medicine was to be taken directly and that her husband was to go over for it to Chilcompton, he absolutely refused to do it, notwithstanding his wife was so bad, and I had to get another messenger.

How is it possible to work upon the minds of such a hardened set of people!! If even the fear of death before their eyes cannot operate on them to consult their own interest, how can anything I say respecting a future state be expected to have the least influence?

In the summer of 1812, one Sunday, William Collings, the Overseer, came to the Parsonage saying he wished I would go to Redhill, for Coward had been endeavouring to hang himself, and he thought he would do himself a mischief, he was in so low and melancholy a state. I went there immediately, and never saw a poor wretch so completely miserable. He said something came across him sometimes which made him think he could not bear to live any longer, and that he must make away with himself. I told him that "something" was nothing more than the suggestions of an evil conscience: that the devil put it into his head in order to make him his for ever, but there was still time to save himself from the threatened destruction. He said he was so miserable he could not bear to live; but I begged him to consider what would be his state if he rushed headlong into the presence of an offended God and Judge; that the torments of mind he now experienced did not amount to the thousandth part of what he would be doomed to feel in another world. I urged him therefore to break off immediately his connection with that bad woman, who seemed to have him entirely under her power, and would be the means of driving him to destruction: that I was authorized to say from Scripture that if he was sincerely sorry for the past, and was determined to lead a new life, that he might yet save his soul. I worked much upon him, and he appeared more composed.

I then spoke some minutes to Sarah Summers, telling her that she had to answer not only for her own crimes, which indeed had been great, but for those of that poor wretch whom she had almost driven to desperation: if he had destroyed himself could she have had one easy moment after? She said in the most hardened manner, "Why, if the man chooses to come up here I can't help it, I don't encourage him to do so, do I Betty?" turning to her grown up daughter, who is now as bad as herself. The daughter answered in the negative. I said she might depend upon it, if anything happened to the man through her I would see her punished in this world, and in the next I could answer for her sufferings being beyond what heart could conceive or tongue relate.

Coward in the course of a week was quite composed, and went to get work somewhere in the neighbourhood of Bath. He afterwards was sent back to Camerton and starved himself to death, having first confessed he had committed every devilry.

George Purnell was buried this day, aged 71. He was found dead near the coke pit, where he had laid himself down to sleep the night before. I had all along imagined he would not die in his bed, as he was of such a restless disposition; always upon the tramp, like the poor wretch, Quaddy Evans, he had lived by pilfering and stealing, and, like him too, had a most miserable end.

About six or seven years ago, after he had lost his wife, who died of a dropsy, I occasionally called at his miserable cottage at Dagland. One day I found him lying in bed with no other covering than an old horse rug, and no shirt. He said, not having anything to make a fire with, he thought it best to lie in bed the whole day; that the two shillings a week he had was not enough to support him. His cottage, which was in a ruinous state, afterwards fell down, and I found Purnell one evening in my glebe field sleeping under a haystack, and on my asking what he did there, thinking he was going to steal the hay, he said he had no place to stay in, and had been to the Overseer two or three times, but could not get him to find him a bed.

I spoke to the Overseer, and he told me he had sent a bed up to Red Hill, but the people who were in the house refused to let him come in, he was so very dirty.

Purnell told me if he could sleep in the hayloft at the public-house he should be quite satisfied, and a bed being put there he continued there a few days during an illness he had, and I went to him, mounting a ladder on the outside; indeed it was a work of danger, for the floor of the loft was made of hurdles which were nearly rotten, and it was dangerous to tread unless on a rafter. The boys and drunken colliers drove the poor wretch from this place by pelting in stones, one of which hit him on the leg and hurt him much. He then took to his wandering course again, and died, as I before stated, near the coke pit.

He was in manners the exact counterpart of Evans, yet might have done very well had he been tolerably useful, having been brought up as a gentleman's servant and was an excellent gardener, but so idle and dissipated he would stick to nothing.

1813

JUST before the licencing day in 1813 Jacob Balne called upon me, said he had a request to make with which he hoped I would comply, which was to set up a public house in the parish at the house then occupied by Skeates; that he had the consent of all the farmers in the parish, and had been to Mr. Stephens at Windsor, who also approved of it, as did Mr. Purnell. He then shewed me a list of names signed to a petition stating, that as the population of the parish was considerably increased, it was necessary to have another public house, there being only one in the place—they recommended Jacob Balne as a fit person to fill the office. I replied that it was a matter of astonishment to me that the farmers could set their names to such a falsehood; that most of them I had heard complain of their servants being too much at the public house. Therefore where they had reason to complain of the nuisance it seemed madness to increase it; that instead of one there were already two in our small parish, for I considered the Red Post the same as Camerton Inn in our Parish, and I knew the abuses so well that were carried on in both houses, that instead of having another it was high time to apply to the magistrates to take away the licence of one or both of them. He replied that he well knew that there were bad goings on and disorderly meetings, but if he kept a public house it would be very different, for, being a constable, he could preserve order and see that all things were proper and quiet. I replied that I would never consent to another being licensed, and should if he persisted in his intentions, most certainly attend the meeting of the Justices and state my objections. After having endeavoured to persuade me by much talking to alter my resolution he left me, not over and above pleased by my refusal.

May 6

In the middle of the day, after Vestry, on my way home I observed William Goold standing idle and unoccupied with some of the colliers, and immediately said to him it was a shame he did not get to work, as the Parish had of late been obliged to contribute towards the maintenance of his wife and children; that if he did not settle to anything I would speak to the magistrates and have him committed, in reply he said something very impertinent, and I left him. In the evening of the same day I saw Joseph Goold, and spoke to him on the subject of his brother's being unemployed. "What do you talk to me so much about my brother for?" said he in the most insolent manner, "if you have anything to speak say it to him, not to me; I have nothing to do with him." I said I conceived he had, and was the properest person to speak to. After a repetition of what he had before advanced, delivered, if possible, in a far more insolent way and rather in a menacing style, he said I had no business to interfere with him as I had done of late; that he was sure I would do him some injury if I could, but that he would put it out of my power. I replied, if he meant that I wished to punish him for his insolence and ill behaviour in many instances he was perfectly right, and that he might depend upon it that I would not let the next opportunity slip, as I had done before in many particulars. During this conversation I had walked to the top of the street returning to my own house, he followed close to my side, now and then as he walked brushing against me. I turned back again, thinking he would leave me, instead of which he continued following me down the street again, abusing me in the most insolent manner, calling me by my surname, as "No, no, Skinner, that won't do," and making use of every aggravating expression. At last I stopped and told him if he again brushed against me in the manner he had done before I should consider it as a blow and would return it with interest, or my words, I believe, were I would knock him down. He replied he should desire nothing better than that I should strike him; indeed his whole behaviour was calculated to provoke me to do this, not merely through the expressions he uttered but the menacing attitude into which he put himself. In the course of his exclamations he said "d — — you, who cares for that?" and "I'll be d — — d if I mind it," on my telling him I would note down those oaths, and that he should pay for them, he said he could afford to pay a couple of shillings as well as I, and that if I wanted a pencil he would lend me one, etc. Returning again homewards, on passing his house he went to his own gate, calling after me and making use of some expressions the meaning of which was "I might go to H — —", or "I should go to H — —" I then came home. This was about eight o'clock in the evening, or it might be later.

I heard Goold had been drinking at the public house. Indeed, he spends the greater part of his time there every day, and his brother, William, when he can get a shilling is generally there too, leaving his

children without bread to put in their mouths. I had him summoned
the Friday following before the magistrates, where he was fined for
his two oaths, which money, when demanded of him, he threw
down in the most insolent manner imaginable.

June

I attended a poor man at Cridlingcot of the name of Samuel
Buchler, who lingered many weeks in a consumption. During one
visit that I paid him I saw a person in his room of the name of Bush,
a collier working in Camerton pits, but who had recently taken upon
himself the office of instructor to his associates. On my proposing to
read some prayers to Buchler, Bush said, "Do you not think we can
offer up ourselves some prayers to God for this our sick brother?"
I replied that those I was about to read to him were far superior to
any I could substitute instead, neither did I think if he were to take
upon himself to utter whatever came into his mind that it would be
either as good or efficacious as what was composed for the purpose
by better and wiser men than ourselves. He replied, "Aye, but if the
Spirit of God gives us utterance it is better than all the learning of
men, that the gift of God was superior to all human attainments and
beyond all books, that book learning was a mere dead letter without
the Spirit enlightened it". I told him it was impossible to expound
the Scriptures properly without a considerable share of learning,
as even the translations of the Bible and Testament, being made
from other languages, it was necessary to consult the originals for
the proper meaning of many passages. "What," he exclaimed, "do
you say, Sir, that the Bible is wrong?" I said mistakes had occurred,
and it was thought necessary to know where those mistakes had been
made in order to avoid building erroneous doctrines thereon.
Although silenced he did not seem convinced by what I said. However, he knelt down and joined in the prayers I offered by the bed
of the sick man.

June 27

I breakfasted this morning with Warren, who pressed me so
much to preach I could no longer decline doing so; especially as he
had one of my sermons by him. I find no inconvenience as to the
exertion, although in the morning I had a return of the spitting of
blood, which for sometime past has so constantly attended me.
Farmer Salmon's wife (Emery's daughter), who came to live at

Durcot Farm with her husband when Emery quitted it, on my speaking to her one day on the subject of her never coming to the Church, said she was so nervous that she could not bear to be where there was a number of people, that her head became so giddy she seemed as though she should fall down, and then gave me so lamentable account of her nervous headaches, etc., etc., that I really felt for her, and began to prescribe a regimen I myself had pursued many years ago under similar circumstances. I told her to get up early and use regular exercise, to bathe her head and take a glass of cold spring water in the morning on rising and going to bed, and when she felt the sinking she complained of to take some bark in port wine. Bark, she said, did not agree with her, but thought a glass of port wine, if it were good, might be of some service. I said I would send her down a bottle to try, which I knew to be perfectly good, which had been in bottle upwards of eighteen years, and accordingly sent her some of the wine got from Mr. Holmes's cellar. Not many days after this James Widcombe's wife, to whom I had given some port wine in an illness which seemed to tend to a putrid fever, on hearing that I had sent a bottle to Mrs. Salmon told me she had brought on all her nervous complaints by drinking, and doubted not would finish the whole of what I gave her at a sitting. This, on a little enquiry finding to be pretty nearly the case, of course I saved my old port for better purposes in future.

September 9

Jane Webb, a miserable old woman at Cridlingcot, who had been supported for a time by the parish to which she belonged in a manner as scarcely to give her the necessaries of life, was this day interred at Camerton. I had visited her occasionally, both when she lived at Red Hill and afterwards at Cridlingcot, and scarcely ever saw such indigence and ignorance united; her bed seemed only to be a collection of rags thrown up into a heap, and all her furniture an old stool. Her daughter used occasionally to attend her, but I believe did not behave as she ought. One day when I called on her she said that she had had a wonderful vision which affected her very much, and related it to me nearly in the following words: That she thought the end of the world was come, for she heard great noises and saw everything in a blaze; that she saw a number of people going along a broad road and she went with them. At last she came to a small wicket, where she heard some music and singing, and knocked there for admission, but a hoarse voice said that place was not for her. She was very sorry she could not get in, but going on further she saw another gate, which she went into, and heard loud noises and saw great fires blazing up, and there she saw a man whom she knew tied by the heels to a branch of a tree with his head downwards, and some ugly-looking people were taking flaming brimstone in an iron ladle and pouring it into him, laughing and making great sport all the time, and that some of them were going to seize her and do the same to her, which had so frightened her that she awake and had been miserable ever since, for she was sure she was going to hell when she died. I found the poor creature had been talked to by the Methodists, and because she could not say she was sure she was to be saved they told her she was on the broad way that leadeth to destruction, and their descriptions of the narrow wicket, etc., had wrought so powerfully on her mind as to produce the above mentioned dream.

1814

EDITOR'S NOTE. *Of necessity the Antiquities are not very prominent in the published extracts of the Journal, but how large they loomed in Skinner's own mind is shewn by some words he wrote on August 13, 1839, when preparing his volumes for the British Museum.*

"By way of introduction to the contents of the ensuing volumes I think it necessary to remark that the early bias my mind received for the study of antiquities may be attributed to my casual acquaintance with Antiquaries, especially with the venerable Mr. Graves, Rector of Claverton, near Bath, who had a good collection of Roman coins, many of them found in the immediate vicinity. This communicative old gentleman used to point out to me the Belgic British earth works on Claverton Downs, and the large settlement of the same people on Hampton Downs, and also the Roman vicinal road leading from Bath to Farleigh and across the downs to Marlborough, and having engaged me to execute two or three commissions in his favourite pursuit when residing at Oxford by consulting the Bodleian Library, I became soon enlisted in the learned corps. Moreover when I subsequently was staying with my College friend, Mr. Dawson Warren, the Vicar of Edmonton, after I had taken my first degree, I was introduced to Sir James Lake, who resided near the place, and through him to Mr. Gough at Enfield, who presented me with several views of Castles in Wales executed by Boydell when a young artist, which excited a strong wish in my mind to visit them to extend my researches with respect to topography and antiquities in my own country.

The following extracts show Skinner engaged on one of his most useful archaeological achievements—the discovery and safeguarding of the famous chambered tumulus at Stoney Littleton, a mile and a half from Wellow. He first heard of it when he was taking part in the uncovering of the tesselated pavement of a Roman Villa at Wellow Hayes, but his mind was then so occupied by the works of the Romans, he was not much inclined to divide it by examining those of the Britons. Consequently he thought no more of it until he visited it in a walk with his friend Warren, who was staying with him at Camerton. The

Barrow is described by Skinner as a burying place of oblong form, 107 feet in length and 54 feet in extreme width, having something of the appearance of a ship. It stands on the side of a sloping field called Round Hill Tyning. They took a lantern and entered it by two holes. These openings were made many years before by a farmer, who, on removing some stones from the top and sides of the barrow to repair the roads, discovered several vaults filled with bones. The place attracted the attention of the villagers, and many people entered and took away what excited their interest. A blacksmith from Wellow took home a skull, in which for a long time, he kept nails. A fox took shelter there when pursued by hounds, and was followed by the huntsman who threw down some of the covering stones in order to expose him. Such was the state of the sepulchre when first he inspected it with Warren. Skinner then obtained permission to examine it properly, and brought the matter before Sir Richard Hoare.[1]

On May 23, 1814, Sir Richard and his brother Peter, Mr. Crocker and Mr. Russell Skinner, assembled at Camerton Rectory for the purpose of exploring the tumulus. The next morning after breakfast Skinner drove his brother and Mr. Hoare in his car to Stoney Littleton, while Sir Richard and Mr. Crocker rode on horseback.

May 23

Our new visitors expressed themselves very much pleased with the object before them, both coinciding in opinion as to its remote antiquity.

On examining the interior, Sir Richard thought from the appearance of two upright stones like pillars at the south-west end of the passage, against which a large flat one reclined, that this might have been the original entrance. I accordingly desired the workmen to clear away the outside earth in order to ascertain whether this were the case. In so doing they turned up some small fragments of red and brown pottery, which evidently had been in the lathe. This for a short time seemed to stagger our opinion as to the high antiquity of the tumulus; but as the unbaked pottery we found in the interior was evidently of the rudest materials and workmanship, we were inclined to suppose the other might have been thrown in at a subsequent period when the mouth of the sepulchre was finally closed, which a short time after we had sufficient inducement to believe was actually the case. In the course of an hour's working the men were

[1] Sir Richard Colt Hoare, (1758–1838), of Stourhead, the celebrated antiquary.

enabled to take away the flat stone which leant against the two uprights and covered the mouth of the sepulchre, which we entered by an aperature about 3½ feet in height and 2½ feet in width, a large stone of upwards of 6 feet in length formed a kind of lintel over the doorway. Having given the men directions to clear out all the earth so as to make an easy approach to the entrance, and after Mr. Hoare had made a sketch of the premises, we returned home to an early dinner."

May 24

Sir Richard left us after breakfast for Stourhead, and I rode to the sepulchre at Stoney Littleton to see what progress the men had made in digging away the earth at the entrance. I found they had not been idle, and moreover was agreeably surprised by a discovery of two walls constructed of small flat stones (similar to those employed in the interior to fill up the vacant spaces between the larger ones), spreading outwards from the entrance towards the hedge of an adjoining field, thus leaving an aditus before the mouth of the vault, but of what dimensions we have yet to learn, as I have no permission to grub the farmer's fence, and shall perhaps find some difficulty in procuring it.

As I had fixed for going to town on Monday following, I paid off the other labourers, leaving only one Wellow man in charge of the premises till my return, with directions to examine the south-east end of the carnedd by sinking down into it, to ascertain for a certainty whether there were any cists or vaults beyond those we had explored, also to fill in the opening we had made at the side for the same purpose, and cover over the passage according to its original form before the stone had been displaced by the farmer at its first discovery. I also wrote to Sir Richard, mentioning the further discovery of the walls, etc., and to Mrs. Leigh, saying it was open for her inspection, if she wished to see it before it was closed.

On my return from Town after a fortnight's absence, I went to the tumulus and found the man had done as I desired, and gave directions for closing the mouth of the sepulchre with a large flat stone and a fence to be made around the aditus.

In less than a week after this was done, Weston (the man who had been left in charge of the performance) came to acquaint me that some riotous colliers had assembled there on the Sunday, and, finding the entrance closed, had broken the stone and found their way into the sepulchre, taking away a great many of the bones, etc. As I could get no evidence of the people who committed this wanton mischief I must be content to put up with it, and yet it is very mortifying, after all the trouble and expense I have been at in order to reinstate and preserve this interesting remains of antiquity, that my intention should be thus frustrated. Sir Richard wished to set up a memorial cut in stone at the entrance to the vault, indicative of the time we visited it, but I dissuaded him from so doing, as it would only be defaced by the mischievous rabble in the neighbourhood."

May 25

I mounted my horse and rode to the Barrow in order to see what the labourers had done since I was last there. As it rained hard on my arrival at the spot I found them all three safely housed in the interior of the Sepulchre, but perceived they had not been idle, as the whole of the roof was secured in the manner I directed, and a space cleared at the northern extremity of the Barrow in order to facilitate the approach to any friend to antiquities hereafter. I desired Weston to fill in the vacancies on the surface of the Barrow, and to continue daily there to prevent mischief till it is well secured.

The middle of July I accompanied Warner[1] to the sepulchre, and was concerned to perceive some mischievous colliers had forced away the large stone I had ordered to be put up to secure the entrance, and taken away some of the bones. Warner wished me to persevere in opening the ground beyond the hedge, to see how far the walls extended, but unless there were some security against the visits of the lawless inhabitants of the neighbourhood, who seem to spare nothing either human or divine, it is very disheartening to do anything which we may so soon have the mortification of seeing destroyed; but if Mr. Hanbury Tracy were to feel an interest in preserving this remain something further might be done, but at the distance I live from the spot I shall not under present circumstances attempt it.

October 23

My brother and self accompanied Dr. and Mrs. Scobel, their son and daughter to the sepulchre, some of the stones from the sides had been pulled down in the centre of the vault, and I fear the place will soon be reduced to the state it was in two years ago if some

[1] Reverend Richard Warner, 1763–1857, vicar of St. James's, Bath.

decisive steps are not taken for its preservation. The whole party expressed themselves highly gratified with their visit to the tomb.

June 11

Susannah Heal, daughter of Aaron Heal, a farmer before mentioned, was buried this day; she had lingered many months in a consumption, which illness she supported with great patience, and was perfectly prepared and resigned to her fate. She was only seventeen when she died, and has changed a wretched situation on earth, I hope and trust, for a glorious one in heaven! Indeed, I have never attended any person at Camerton who seemed so sincerely impressed with the power and consolation of religion to cheer the gloom of death. Miss Holmes, who was staying with me at Camerton during her illness, was very kind in her attendance, and on going away left a pound note for me to purchase any little comforts she stood in need of; indeed, what rendered her last moments more peculiarly distressing was the sale of all the furniture in the house, her father having spent everything and was obliged to quit his farm. This sale took place just before she died, and the thoughts of what was to become of her good-for-nothing parent seemed to weigh heavy on her mind to the last.

Memorandum. Heal borrowed £2 of me to pay for the funeral, which I afterwards forgave him as he had no power to pay it, being reduced to the situation of a common labourer. Such is the end of drunkenness and unprincipled conduct.

1815

OWING to a very severe cold I could not attend the Vestry. Mr. Purnell was there, I understood, and a few farmers. After looking over the accounts of Lippiatt, the Overseer, for the last year, they dispersed without nominating Overseers for the ensuing year, or Churchwardens. Three days after a set of drunkards met at the public house and appointed Lippiatt to the office at a salary of £15 a year. The persons who agreed to this nomination were Gibbs, Snook, the two Widcomes, Reynolds and Collings, the agreement was drawn up on a paper to which the above-mentioned signatures were affixed. Both Gibbs and Widcome, Junior, positively affirm and say they are ready to swear they did not write their names. On hearing of the transaction I told them that the appointment of Lippiatt at such a place was not legal. Lippiatt afterwards got it inserted in the Poor Book that the nomination was made at Vestry, and obtained some signatures by calling on some persons who signed their names at their own houses, though the preamble stated it was at Vestry.

When he afterwards called upon me for my Rates I declined paying him on the ground that he was not the Overseer, not having been appointed at Vestry. He told me he would make me pay, I might depend on it, and accordingly got a Warrant from the Magistrates in Bath for my appearance to show cause why I refused my rate. I went there and mentioned to Mr. Clarke, who was in the Chair, my reasons for refusing to pay Lippiatt, viz, that he had been appointed by a drunken set at the alehouse and at a salary of £15 a year, which I should never agree to, Mr. Clarke said that the nomination at the alehouse was highly improper and every way illegal, but as Lippiatt had been appointed to the office of Overseer by the Magistrates since that, who had the power of nominating whom they chose if the Parish did not, he was ipso facto Overseer, and I must pay the rate, but with regard to the salary of £15 per annum I was authorized to appeal at Quarter Sessions against such an appropriation of Parish money without my consent.

Memorandum. Lippiatt was afterwards excessively insolent to me, saying he would manage the Parish without consulting me, and would take good care that he was paid for his trouble also.

May 22

Not seeing my servant, Bush, waiting at table this day, my friend Burrard[1] being on a visit with me, I asked one of the maidservants where he was. She said, "in the kitchen," On sending to speak to him he came into the parlour, I then said, "what is the reason you do not wait at table as usual?" he replied, "Not today, sir." "Why not today?" "Because Miss Gibbs is there."

Miss Gibbs the governess that day dined with us, and as there had been a quarrel between himself and wife with her he had declared he never would wait on her as long as he stayed in the house. I told him, as he chose to disobey my orders, he should leave my service immediately, and accordingly, having given him a draft on my banker for the money due for his wages, I dismissed him after dinner, and his wife soon after went away.

Memorandum. Bush and his wife came to live with me in June 1813, on Mr. Barter's recommendation, and I gave them forty guineas a year, besides many perquisites. The first year they conducted themselves exceedingly well, and never since I have had a housekeeper have I been served better; afterwards I saw that they considered their interests too much, and my expenses increased much more in housekeeping than they ought to have done. When Miss Gibbs came as governess to the children, who also engaged to take charge of the housekeeping, they immediately became dissatisfied, thinking she would be a check upon their proceedings, and it ended in their going away.

In the winter of 1815 I saw a black come to my Church, and one day took an opportunity of speaking to him as to his country and reasons for coming into our neighbourhood. He said that he came from the East Indies, having lived with a master in Bombay who had some large plantations of sugar canes; that his master and family wishing to come to England, he accompanied them in a large ship, which was wrecked off the island where Bonaparte was now gone to, and his master and a great part of the crew drowned; that he and the remainder were picked up by a Bristol trader and carried to

---

[1] Rev. George Burrard, Rector of Yarmouth (I.O.W.), brother of Sir Harry Burrard-Neale whom he succeeded to the Baronetcy.

Bristol, and that having none to recommend him to service, he had come to work in the coal pits. I did not think his story hung well together. In the first place the large plantations of sugar canes in Bombay rather surprised me, in the second place a shipwreck off St. Helena, where the water is of such depth all around the island and no shoals or currents, seemed very improbable, but the most improbable of all was his having been picked up by a Bristol trader in that latitude and carried to the Port of Bristol. The natural conclusion I formed was that he had invented the story of being an East Indian Black in order to prevent people supposing that he had come from the West Indies, which I conclude was fact, and that he had run away from his master on landing in England.

However, as he told me he was employed at the coal works I did not like to question him more closely, but telling him that if he behaved himself well it would give me pleasure to befriend him, so our conversation ended. Afterwards, on speaking to White, one of the singers, respecting him, he told me they did not know exactly what to make of him, and it was a joke among the colliers having a Black, as the bailiff had once said he did not mind taking anyone to work but a Black; at last they had got even one of them. I found afterwards that his introduction to the parish was owing to Thomas Bush, the methodistical collier, who thought that it would be a great feather in his cap if he should convert the Black as St. Philip did the eunuch. Smallcomb told me that he once in his pretended zeal offered to take off his shirt and put it on the Black, which was all a stage trick to gain the attention of his associates; but the Black, instead of being a dupe, shortly after showed that he knew a trick or two as well as those who played their legerdemain upon him, for in the middle of February, 1816, he decamped from his lodgings, taking with him all the money he could collect out of his host's stock, which he made off with, but being taken on the road to Bristol was committed to Ilchester Gaol to take his trial for theft.

An account of the sad catastrophe which occurred during my absence from home, in December, 1815, to Frances Heal, an unfortunate girl belonging to Camerton.

I had received several complaints against this girl as a common prostitute, as she was accustomed to entice the younger colliers and lead them into all manner of mischief; indeed some of the appointments were made near the Coke Pits, and I was requested to go down some evening and put a stop to such but I conceived that it was the duty of the constable to represent it to the magistrates, and the magistrates to check it, but I did not interfere in an open manner. However, I spoke very seriously to the girl herself at different times, and just before I left home had a particular conversation with her at Red Hill before her mother, showing the danger she was in if she persisted in such a course of life as heretofore. She then promised amendment, and said that she would attend her church and behave better in future. On my return home at Christmas I found that she had been buried by Mr. Boodle,[1] and the particulars of her death are nearly as follows: She had gone to Bath in company with some local bargemen, and it is supposed was thrown into the river by one of them on account of an old grudge, but this was not traced home, and the coroner's inquest merely returned that she was found drowned in the Avon. Thus the poor wretch was taken off in the midst of all her unrepented transgressions. The mother has been a very indifferent person herself, and has, I fear, rather encouraged than checked her daughters in the conduct they have pursued.

[1] Rev. Richard Boodle, Rector of Radstock.

1816

A WOMAN of the name of Lucy Heal came to attend her daughter of the name of Nash to her churching. Both of them were Methodists of the most enthusiastic description, indeed Heal about two years ago openly declared that she had frequent communications with Jesus Christ. On my going to ask if she really had affirmed as above stated she declared to me it was very true, and that Jesus Christ frequently appeared to her and conversed with her in her cottage. Having endeavoured in vain to convince her of the folly and wickedness of such an assertion I left her with marks of great disapprobation, but happening to come out of church and walking together towards the Parsonage I again asked her whether she had had any further communications or visions, she replied, "Blessed be the Lord, His manifestations were very frequent, to the great comfort of her soul, as they assured her she was in a state of salvation, and that all her sins were forgiven her. I told her that this was impossible to be known upon earth, that it was very dangerous doctrine to believe in a remission of sins and certain acceptance with God before the judgment took place. I told her it was my duty as the clergyman of the parish to declare to her that these opinions were erroneous, and also the visions that she pretended to were no other than delusive dreams, since Christ did not now manifest Himself on earth, and that visions and miracles had long ceased —I might say many hundred years. She exclaimed with astonishment that the operations of the Spirit were now as strong as ever; that I had only to go to Radstock to see how powerfully the Lord worked there, that the man who had broken his back in the coal pits was a living example of the operations of the Spirit, and proclaimed as the Spirit gave him utterance. I repeated with some warmth that it was gross ignorance to believe in operations of this kind, and if she only attended to her Church, instead of those self-taught teachers who took upon themselves the office of expounding the Scriptures without making a proper distinction between the ordinary and extra-ordinary operations of the Spirit that it was her own fault, but that I would assure her that I did not believe that it would be admitted as an excuse at the Great Day of Judgment to have run to the errors having the power by their attendance on their regular teachers in Church to know better.

February 16

On going down to the village to visit Mrs. Hillman who was lying ill, Joseph Goold's wife spoke to me and asked whether I had heard of the extraordinary meeting of the Methodists which took place last night at Lewis's house. She said that she understood that it was one of the most extraordinary that had occurred, since they were all crying and bewailing their sins, and continued in that state until 11 o'clock at night. I replied that I was sorry to hear that they had suffered their feelings to be worked upon in such a manner by the ignorant and designing; that it would be much better for them to come to Church to convince their reason and understanding, instead of suffering themselves to be misled by the heats of a disordered imagination. On leaving her, as I returned towards the Parsonage, I saw Bush and Hill going into the cottage of Hall, who lives about 100 yards from my house. Supposing what might be the object of their visit I also went and asked Mrs. Hall who with her two daughters was listening to them (the latter of whom I had taken some pains to instruct at the Sunday School), whether they were about to be converted to Methodism. Hill replied that they wished not only to convert them but everyone in the parish of Camerton, which they trusted in Christ they should do ere long. Bush then declared with great vehemence that Christ had begun the work, and could not leave it unfinished. I told them that it would be much better for such ignorant and uninformed persons as they were to attend to their own business as colliers and leave me to direct the souls of my parishioners which were committed to my charge; that it was my business and office to do so, and that they had no place or pretence to take that office from my hands. They both at once declared that Christ had sent them to perform His work, and that they would do it in spite of all opposition, and that their object in coming to Mrs. Hall was to pray; that with regard to the conversion I alluded to that it was their duty to save the souls of as many poor wretches as they could, for unless they were born again it was impossible they could enter into the Kingdom of Heaven, that our Saviour Himself had said so, and if I contradicted that I contradicted Scripture. I replied that that text, like so many others, had been wrested from its true meaning and import, which shewed the necessity there was for a well-educated instructor to explain the proper meaning of the Scriptures; that those who took on themselves to instruct others, without being instructed themselves, incurred a great share of responsibility, since they not only continued in ignorance themselves but prevented many of their companions from learning their duty; that our Saviour had declared that it were better for a millstone to be tied around their necks and that they should be thrown into the sea than to offend or otherwise misled the weak. They then broke out in the most violent way, saying that I with all my learning had never converted one since I had been in the parish, and that instead of being able to assist others by my doctrines I was in the greatest need of divine assistance myself; that if I had only been with them yesterday I might have shed tears too and been pricked to the heart and perhaps converted also, so powerfully did Christ work amongst them. I said that if I shed tears it would have been to have seen so many deluded by presumptuous imposters; that as there were two meeting houses licensed in my parish they had no right to assemble in this manner in private houses, that it was my duty to prevent it, and they might depend on my making a proper representation to the magistrates on the subject. They replied that they knew I had no power to prevent them meeting at each other's houses, and Hill said as he paid rent for his house he had a right to call in as many neighbours as he chose to pray with, and would do it in spite of *any* magistrate; that the magistrates, if they were only reasonable men, would approve of what they did for the conversion of souls; but even if they should oppose it, as I did oppose it, they did not care, they must attend to God rather than man and would continue to do so. Bush continued, if they did not pray in their houses they might in the fields, and that there would be plenty to follow them there; that the work of God was now begun, and would not be hindered by any opposition; that lately at Bristol 500 were added to their Church, and that ere long Methodism would be universal. I asked him what he meant by *their Church*. He said any congregation of the faithful, that it was not a building of stones like that out there (pointing to Camerton Church, for he was then standing in Hall's garden,) but any place wherein the word of God was properly taught and expounded. This was the substance of the conversation which passed between us but a great deal more was said in direct terms relative to the success of their cause and the depression of the Church. Having again in a serious and solemn manner warned them not to persevere in their meetings at private houses, as being contrary to the law, and having again heard their defiance as to my inability to prevent them, I returned home.

N.B. I forgot to mention that during our conversation Bush declared he wondered I could oppose them as I always did, as none of the clergy in the neighbourhood did, for they had meetings at Radstock, at Mrs. Hall's sister's house, sometimes till one o'clock in the morning on weekdays and Sundays, and that Mr. Boodle never said anything about it or gave them any interruption or even noticed it, neither did Mr. Barter.

After dinner I again called on Mrs. Hall and gave her a solemn admonition not to be misled by the presumptuous pretensions of these men, and exhorted her to attend constantly her Church. Her husband who was present, having returned from the coal works, seemed to accord with me, but she seemed fully determined to attend their meetings, saying her father and some of her family had saved their souls by following these doctrines, and she thought it very hard she might not save her own soul in the same way. Finding how weak reason is when employed against fanaticism in this instance, as I have found a hundred times before, I left her cottage mortified, but not deterred from exerting myself as far as possible to oppose the evil to the utmost of my power.

Memorandum. Hill, when I was remonstrating with him on his presumption, made quotation from Acts VIII, 23 where St. Paul reproves Simon Magus. The very same quotation was employed on a similar occasion some time ago by another Methodist of the name of Green when I was endeavouring to convince him of his errors. Quare, do they suppose that they are in the light of the Apostles, gifted with the Spirit, and we, the clergy, like Simon Magus, wish to purchase it for money?

February 22

Mrs. Hall, as I was passing by her cottage this morning, called to me and said that she was very sorry such a disturbance had taken place with Tom Bush and Will Hill, that her husband had been so angry with her she did not know whether, if he were worked up more against her, he might do her a mischief; that she was sure she did not ever want to see Bush or Hill come into her house; that it was not for the sake of praying with her, but with a determination to insult me. I asked her how that could possibly be, since they could not suppose that I should come into their cottage. She said she knew that that alone was their object to provoke me, for they had said as much, and she knew that there were some who would kill me if they could; that they had been setting up reports about her and Bush when they came with Smallcombe's wife in the waggon from Bath; that for her part she could declare that she did not know whether he were a man or woman, that her daughter had to go to Bath on business before the magistrates about those who stole Farmer Gibb's turnip greens, and she thought it her duty to go and take care of her, that as to what other people had to do with Bush it was nothing to her, she knew him to be a bad fellow, and had sent him word never to darken her doors again; that it was a very hard case such stories should go about respecting her, and I could not blame her for feeling as she did and wishing to clear herself; that the people of Camerton had nothing else to do but to tell lies and make mischief one with another; that if I knew all that they told of me I should be of the same opinion; that I was anxious enough to find out the story they told of me and the nursery maid, therefore I could not wonder at what she did in her own case; that she believed that there was not so wicked a place as Camerton anywhere, and that she thought it would all sink one of these days. I then told her, if she altered her mind with respect to going to hear Bush I hoped she would constantly attend her Church, and make her family do so likewise, and I would answer for it she would not miss of salvation if it were not her own fault.

March 3

Isaac Burge, William Powell and Hibbert had been drinking at Gay's, at the Red Post, from two o'clock till nearly six. They then were returning to Camerton by Whitebrook Lane, and met Robert Paine's lad as they came out of the Red Post with a can in his hand, he having been to get some beer for his father who lived in Whitebrook Lane, Isaac Burge and Powell drank up the beer, and afterwards kicked the can all the way down the road to near Jacob Richardson's house, where he saw them. Robert Paine went into Bath to get summonses for the offenders. He said Joseph Balne was at the Red Post yesterday evening, who said he should have the people bound over to keep the peace. Robert Paine, he said, had got the summonses from Mr. Page, the Justices' Clerk, at Bath, for he thought it would be of no use to go to Mr. Purnell, it being his house.

Memorandum. This Isaac Burge is the person who robbed Mr. Stephens's garden about three years ago and the grape house, but the business was made up for £1 7s.

Joseph Goold, of the New Pit, was there the same day from nine o'clock till four in the evening, and quite drunk.

William Turner, who married Hannah West, was also there the whole day, and so drunk he lay the whole night upon a dung heap near the Red Post.

Peter Richardson was also there till five or six o'clock in the evening.

Jacob Richardson told me all these particulars coming to the Parsonage on purpose.

N.B. This complaint of Gay's public house, and the one from Joseph Parfitt respecting the Camerton Inn, shows the mode of proceeding on a Sunday in both places and calls aloud for the interference of the magistrate, but so long as such a fellow as Jacob Balne is constable of the district, whose business it is to enquire into such things and to represent them, but instead of doing so endeavours to shield the offenders, fearing the licenses of the publicans will be taken away, so long will all these disturbances continue.

Another occurrence happened about this time which shews the disinclination, or rather I should say the supineness of the magistrates of the Bath Forum division in exerting that authority which rested in them for the purpose of restraining vice and immorality. A Camerton farmer, of the name of Sainsbury, had been into Bath, and continued drinking until a late hour in a public house in Holywell with a collier of the name of Maine, and was returning home much in liquor with Maine behind him on horseback, when Maine's wife, who had come in search of her husband, met them, the woman being very angry with her husband at finding him in such a situation, as he had sent his coal cart home under charge of a little boy, after some expostulation pulled him by the coat whilst the horse was proceeding, and the saddle turning round, both Sainsbury and Maine fell off. Sainsbury declares that the woman, when he was lying on the ground, took up a large stone and beat out four of his teeth. He accordingly had a warrant for her, and the parties appeared before the magistrates who, declaring it was an indictable offence at the sessions, took no further cognizance of it. Quare: Are not the magistrates obliged by virtue of their office to prevent the licencing of these disorderly public houses, from whence so much evil arises?

Whilst my friend Burrard, was staying with me, we saw two fellows handcuffed pass by in front of the parsonage accompanied by Langford, the butcher, and Weeks, the tything man of Timsbury. They said that they had apprehended them for sheepstealing, and were going to take them before a magistrate to get them committed to prison. They were brothers, of the name of Bassett, the elder, nicknamed Fudgee, who was well known in all the public houses of the neighbourhood as a singer and a drinking bad fellow, and the younger brother had lately returned from transportation. It seems they had stolen a sheep from Farmer Collings of Camerton, not long since, and left the skin behind in the field where they had killed it. The skin indeed of this second was not found, but the butcher says he can swear to the head as being his sheep. I only hope they will suffer as examples to the rest, as they are much connected with the clan at Tunley, and I have understood have carried on their depredations on the property of the farmers for a length of time without being detected.

I walked with my brother after Church up Whitebrooks Lane with the intent of visiting the Red Post to see if any drinking was going on there after the recent complaint I had received from Richardson. I preferred going up the lane instead of taking the plantation road, as I was accustomed to do on former occasions, which gave the people who might be assembled a good opportunity to seeing me before I got to the house, which enabled them to get out at the back door and hide themselves in the outbuildings, but by going up this lane we came direct upon the house, and that so suddenly as almost to preclude the possibility of their getting away without being perceived. As we proceeded thither we saw Jacob Balne and his son, who were in a field belonging to him close to the road side. I accordingly accosted him and informed him of my intentions of visiting the Red Post, as I had heard a great deal of drinking had been going on there of late, especially the Sunday before; that it was his duty to notice these irregularities and represent them to the magistrates. He said he had heard something of the kind himself and had spoken to Gay on the subject before, but I found that the business between Payne's boy and Burge and Powell, who had drunk up the beer and kicked the can as before stated had been compromised in the usual manner in order to screen the irregularities of the landlord, Gay, from the magistrates. Balne on going with us was witness to some persons being there assembled, amongst whom was his own brother. I then spoke to Gay, telling him that I conceived it to be my duty to notice the mismanagement of his house on Sunday, which was contrary to the conditions on which he held his licence; that the order of the magistrates, which he ought to have printed in his house and which I had blamed him before for not having put up against the wall, prohibited any beer being drawn, excepting for travellers, and that his licence was in danger of being taken away if he acted contrary to these regulations. He told me he knew that Jacob Richardson had informed me of it out of mere spite, because he had once put him into Court for some money he had owed him. I told him that this was not the only time I had had occasion to speak on the subject, and that it was very general; that a person of my parish who was now dead, and had brought on his death by drinking, had informed me that the Red Post was the ruin of his body and soul; that frequently when he had intended to come to Church he had been drawn away by the enticements that had been held out to him at this house. Jacob Balne then joined in the conversation and said those things ought not to be, that Gay should not draw liquor on a Sunday except for travellers, and that it was contrary to the orders of the magistrates. He then spoke something to his brother about being there, and both Gay and his wife promised to keep better order in future. On leaving the house I told Jacob Balne to mention the circumstances which had occurred to Mr. Purnell, for that he, both in his capacity of magistrate and of owner of the property, should check such irregularities in future. Indeed I am so fully convinced that the public houses are the occasion of most of the evils which occur in this neighbourhood, for they not only encourage the squandering of money in the weekdays, and all kinds of rioting, fighting and blasphemous conversation, but do away all respect of the Sabbath, and convert a day of rest into a season of depravity.

This breach of the Sabbath was in France the forerunner of the Revolution, and I doubt not will be attended with very serious consequences to this country if the laws be not put in force to prevent the violation of an express command of God, and one indeed so replete with kindness and benevolence to the race of man, especially to the lower part of the community in this parish. The sacred ordinance of a rest from labour seems to be entirely disregarded for the bailiffs of the coal works without scruple employ it in repairing any accidents which might have occurred in the week, in cleansing out the boilers of the steam engine, etc. Several times I spoke to Goold on the subject saying I wondered how he who pretended to be so religious a man could answer it to his conscience to break one of the express commands of God. His reply was that he conceived works of necessity might be performed on that day, that our Saviour Himself had said so. I said it was true that any work that was necessary for our sustenance and the relief of our fellow creatures, or as an immediate prevention against accidents might be performed, but that any business that might be as well performed on the Monday as on the Sunday, neither the laws of God or man would allow. I also mentioned the same to Reynolds who succeeded Goold, and on my threatening to lay before the magistrates any notorious breach of the Sabbath he said he would be careful not to permit any work to be done but what was absolutely necessary. But I know the same things are done as heretofore. Indeed, if we trace the evil still higher, we shall find that the influence of Mr. Stephens in times back and Mr. Purnell at present has contributed much to encourage an indifference among the farmers, their servants and dependents of the observance of the Sabbath, which not all my sermons from the pulpit nor conversations in private can prevent. Mr. Stephens, when he resided in the parish never attended his Church nor set an example deserving the imitation of his parishioners. Indeed his freedom of discourse on the subject of religion was calculated to confirm rather than to reform their errors. He made no distinction as to abstaining from his usual occupations on that day, but would sometimes walk about the plantations with his gardener Laws, marking trees which were to be cut down, and once indeed, having instructed his workmen to fell some trees, which had been marked, on the following day, and on one replying that it could not be done on that day as it would be Good Friday, he instantly said, "What's Good Friday to me? d — — — Good Friday," and the workmen did accordingly proceed in the work. Having heard that they were engaged in cutting down the trees, I went to them before Church in the morning and told them that I thought it very improper to work on that day. They said they thought so too, but as Mr. Stephens had ordered them they did not like to disobey their master. I asked, if he ordered him to put his little finger into the fire and hold it there whether he would do it, and if he would refuse to injure so small a member in the service of his master for a short time only how could he venture to risk the burning of his whole body for ever? He said it was very true, but as they had undertaken to do the job they must perform it. The people employed were the two Widcomes, Harris and Hiscox, and they had first of all an intention of cutting down one of the oaks close to the church, but I begged them to defer their operations till after the service was concluded.

Memorandum. This was the Easter of 1813, and Mr. Stephens had expressly come over from Bath to give directions for a great fall of wood.

Mr. Purnell of Woodborough, never now makes his appearance at church. He used at my first coming to the Living to attend once a fortnight, when the sermon was in the morning, but he gradually has left it off entirely, and very seldom sends his servants thither. How can it be expected that the farmers should be more attentive when they see persons of education and magistrates think so lightly on the subject, and how can the colliers and workmen think there is any harm in spending the Sabbath at the public house, when they are frequently employed on works of labour on that day for the benefit of the coal proprietors contrary to the express commandment of God?

1817

I LEFT Camerton this morning at eight with my two children, Laura and Owen, in the car. We arrived at Warminster about twelve o'clock, the distance from Camerton being sixteen miles, but the first part of the stage heavy on account of the cross roads and hills. Warminster is a flourishing town celebrated for its market for grain, being in the midst of the corn country. Whilst the horse was baiting we called upon Mr. Griffith, who superintends the school under the patronage of the Marquis of Bath, as I wished to inform myself of his terms, etc., having for some time past had an idea of sending my boys there, preparatory to their going to Winchester. He gave me a card of his terms, which are there stated rather under £50 per annum, but I suppose with etceteras will be £60. Mr. Hoare's two eldest boys, who have been there for some time give a good account of the treatment they experience; as to their proficiency I have no opportunity of judging.

May

Correspondence with Mrs. Jarrett[1]

I wrote as follows to Mrs. Jarrett soon after Mr. Stephens's death, hearing it was her intention to visit Camerton, offering her every accommodation the Parsonage could afford when she came there, as all the furniture had been sold at the Manor House.

Mrs. Jarrett's reply from Holbrook, Ipswich

"Your obliging letter was forwarded to me from this place, and should have received an earlier answer but that I had hurt my right hand. I am even now not very well able to write, but I will no longer delay thanking you for your hospitable offer of accommodation, but which I must decline with many acknowledgements for your polite attention. I am not quite determined on going to Camerton in October, but if I do I trust my business will not detain me above two mornings, and I shall probably sleep at Bath. Whenever I visit Camerton I hope that I shall find yourself and family in good

---

[1] The Lady of the Manor, widow of Herbert Newton Jarrett, Esq., of Golden Grove, Jamaica, daughter and heiress of James Stephens, Esq., of Camerton House, 1783–1830.

health. My aunt is now in Warwickshire, or I am sure she would desire her best compliments and thanks.

> Believe me, Sir,
>> Your obliged and humble Servant,
>> ANNE JARRETT."

When the monument was put up in the church, to the memory of Mr. Stephens, Mr. Fry thus addressed me through motives best known to himself.

"Rev. Sir,
May I beg the favour of being informed if any fee is due to you for erecting the monument over Mrs. Jarrett's servants' pew in what is called the aisle, and if so what is it? Mrs. Jarrett having understood that you are about to have the Church painted, she will be obliged by your getting her pew painted in the same manner and colour you may approve, and I will pay the expense."

In reply to Mr. Fry's application I sent the annexed letter to Mrs. Jarrett on May 22, 1817.

"On my return from the Isle of Wight, where I have been staying nearly a month, I found a note from Mr. Fry asking whether any fee was required by me for the monument which is about to be erected in the Church. I have not the most distant idea of making any such claim; on the contrary it will at all times give me the greatest pleasure to offer every assistance and accommodation in my power to you or your family while residing at Camerton. After the monument is put up I will endeavour to see your orders executed respecting the painting of the pew. I wrote to Mr. Carew of Crowcombe Court mentioning the dilapidation of the monuments of the Carews, and received a very polite answer saying that if the Chapel was retained by the family on the sale of the estate he will not hesitate making the necessary reparations, and begs to be informed on this head. As I am unable to do so, I have not yet replied to his letter. Perhaps you or Mrs. Stephens may be able to inform me, and I will immediately write on hearing from you. Since you were at Camerton I have been busily engaged in prosecuting my researches in the eighteen-acre field, when it was fallow, and my labours have been attended with success, as we discovered the foundations of a large building, which was undoubtedly Roman from the number of coins and pottery found near it. The coins are all of the Lower Empire, and lead one to suppose that the date of the building was about the time of Constantine, 1,500 years ago. I have already made one report to the Antiquarian Society, and purpose sending another when the removal of the farmer's crop permits me to extend my researches in the field, as the stones will be removed. After my plans are taken, I shall be obliged to you to permit me to employ some of them at the Parsonage, as I have in contemplation to make an addition of two rooms and heighten the roof over the kitchen for as many garrets."

Fry, the steward, thinking that I had set my heart on carrying on the researches, and that he could not give me more pain than by putting a stop to them, persuaded Mrs. Jarrett that it would injure the ground to dig it up, and shortly after orders were given to prevent my digging any more on the spot, notwithstanding the farmer wished me to continue, as he was handsomely paid for the permission and was conscious by turning up the black soil, which lay two feet deep, it was greatly benefiting the ground. I must own the unjust steward gained in this instance more than in any other the first object and wish of his heart, which was to pain and worry me.

July 18

Mrs. Jarrett, who arrived at Camerton with her aunt, Mrs. Anne Stephens, and is now resident at Sopers, the Bailiff's at the Coal Works, in order to direct the repairs at the Manor House, drank tea with me this evening. In the course of conversation she apologized for not having answered my letter, as she was in daily expectation of coming herself to Camerton; that the Chapel of the Carews had not been reserved by that family; that if any little trifling repairs were wanting to the monuments she should not mind having them done, but would not go to any expense beyond what was absolutely necessary, as she thought they were very well as they were; that with regard to the stones I wanted for repairing my house, she thought it would be much more convenient for me the getting them nearer at hand, as there would be plenty to spare at the Great House, and she knew that Mr. Fry wished to employ those I had dug up in the eighteen-acre field for some buildings on the farm; that she understood that the farmer grumbled at my having them dug up, as it drew a number of idle people to the place and spoiled his crops. I replied I could not conceive how the farmer should say this, since I had offered him every indemnification for the injury he might sustain, and that moreover, in order to prevent the shadow of complaint, I had offered to rent that part of the field facing the Fosseway, where the Roman remains were discovered and pay him double the rent he gave for it, as I was anxious to prosecute my researches, and eventually it would be beneficial to the soil to dig it over thoroughly and to remove the stones which were near the surface. Mrs. Jarrett said she was agriculturist enough to know that digging deep did not always improve the soil, since clay was frequently turned up which might be better left where it was. I asked in a joking manner whether she remembered the fable of the man who left a considerable sum of money to his eldest son and a field to the younger, telling him that if he dug it over carefully he would find a treasure, which he did, and it returned to him such ample crops as fully recompensed him for his trouble. "Aye," said she, "you know that is but a fable. I am of a contrary opinion, and like things to remain such as they are and not go in search of treasures. I understand that Farmer Gibbs is of the same opinion too, and does not like to be disturbed, which is pretty much the same case with us all." Playing upon the word, "treasure," I replied she did not know what greater riches might be discovered: that I would shew her what I had already met with, which, as Lady of the Manor, were of course at her disposal. I then brought in the drawer containing my coins which were found in the eighteen-acre field, and asked whether she would like me to put up any for her or her aunt, which they both declined. Mrs. Anne Stephens, on looking over the list of coins, saw the silver one of Vespasian mentioned, and asked whether it was found with the rest in eighteen-acre field. I replied in the negative, since it was discovered by a man making a hedge in Mr. Purnell's ground facing the Red Post. "What, they bring them all to you?" I replied, Yes; that I rewarded those who bought me any coins, as they tended to complete the series I was forming, and every coin was more or less interesting to me on that account: that I had it in contemplation to write a history of Camerton; that I could already prove that the Romans were residents here upwards of 400 years, as coins had been found from Augustus to the later emperors. She said that it might be very interesting to me, but she did not see any good in the study of past times, that the present was quite sufficient to interest her. I said that perhaps she was not fond of reading history. She answered,

No, that a History Book or a Grammar she could never bear. From this conversation I was perfectly assured that Mr. Fry had been using his influence with Mrs. Jarrett to prevent my carrying on my researches in the eighteen-acre field. If Mrs. Jarrett is illiberal enough to be guided by him in this matter of course I can have but little hope of deriving much satisfaction from my new neighbour, for although she may have no great goût for antiquities herself, yet certainly it is not well to interfere with the views of another in this respect, when they cannot be attended with any possible detriment to herself. Notwithstanding her refusal to contribute to my amusements, she borrowed the drawings I have taken at Camerton in order to shew them to Miss Dutton on her return to Twickenham. It was her intention, she said, to reside at Camerton in the summer months, and have a house in Town. In the course of the evening while talking about the Reynolds, late bailiffs of the coal works, she said what a rascal was John Reynolds; that if it had not been for him the other might have done very well, but the uncle had involved him in every kind of difficulty by his knavery, and had even threatened his life, but how shocking it was they should die so near together. I could not forbear saying that of the two I conceived the nephew was far more culpable; that the uncle when first he came to Camerton appeared a steady, sober man, but his nephew by his conduct in embezzling money and even stealing it from the box in which it was kept, involved his accounts so that he could never bring them to balance properly, which was the occasion, as I had heard, of his conniving at some frauds which were practised, and not being able to support his reflections had taken to drinking. I had always understood that he was only a book-keeper under his nephew, that he was the agent of the Coal Company. Indeed, I could bear witness myself to the licentiousness of William Reynolds' conduct, as he spent most of his time in the alehouse, or in setting the people to fight, or in coursing, fishing or shooting, when he ought to have been occupied in the business of his employers; and as to religion he had not the most distant idea of it, for I had attended him once when he thought he was dying, and could therefore speak from my own knowledge on that head.

July 25

On my return from Mr. Barter's, while passing J. Goold's I saw him busily employed in building an outhouse to the end of his dwelling. On asking him whether he had spoken to the steward for some wood to finish the paling as he intended, he said, no, he had not himself, but his wife had the other evening mentioned it to Mrs. Jarrett as she was walking by, who returned for answer that they had better apply to Mr. Skinner for wood, as she had understood he had ordered the palings to be made, he was the properest person to finish them; that she did not know what right any person had to order things to be done at Camerton but herself. This surely is very early to declare her sentiments, if she listened to the tittle tattle of the common people she will have enough to do. In the first place I never ordered the palings, but only approved the plan when Goold mentioned it to me of thus enclosing the plot of ground before his door in order to give a better appearance to the cottage, and I assisted his neighbour, Ashbourne, with some wood to carry on the railing in order to make the place complete. Surely I should have thought Mrs. Jarrett would have felt pleased at any improvements made in the place. The village footpath I gravelled from my own house to the Rossiter's cost me £10, and the whitewashing of the cottages was done by my persuasion, and some at my expense, and if these are offences against the Lady of the Manor I fear that she will meet with frequent occasions of displeasure, as I shall not refrain from inculcating neatness in the habitations of my parishioners through apprehension of offending her, as I conceive it is more connected with their orderly living than she is aware of. She is, I fear, a silly woman, at any rate she must be a very imprudent one to lend herself to such a low fellow as Fry, who wishes to instil high ideas of authority which she must be daily disappointed in.

July 28

My brother Russell, the four children and myself went this day on a visit to Mr. Hoare,[1] at Southfield, he in the Frome coach and the rest of the party in the car. We found all his numerous family at home, and yet found sufficient room in the house. The day proved very fine, and he has just cut the grass in front of his house.

July 29

After breakfast I drove with my brother to Shepton Mallet, in hopes of seeing a collection of paintings and antiques in the possession of Mr. Taylor, a linen draper in that place. Unfortunately he was

[1] Mr. Peter Hoare of Southfield House, brother to Sir Richard Hoare.

from home, which disappointed us in the principal object of our visit. However, we found some interest in calling upon Dr. Coombs,[1] the Catholic clergyman, who walked with us to the Nunnery established in the town; we were admitted to the Chapel and outward apartments, but did not see any of the ladies. They have a very comfortable house and extensive grounds. A daughter of Mr. Hart, who lives at Camerton, within these last two years has taken the veil there. The superior, I believe, is sister of Mr. Weld, of Lulworth.[2] The road from Shepton to Southfield in many parts is interesting. I understand the Roman road runs near a large clump of trees in the parish of Cranmore. At Doulting they dig freestone, and supply the neighbourhood for miles round with the article, if I mistake not, the church tower of Camerton with some of it. The distance from Southfield to Shepton Mallet is about ten miles.

July 30

As my brother has never seen Stourhead we set off after breakfast for that delightful place, taking the two girls with us, and some cold provisions to eat in the grounds had the weather permitted, but after we had made a tour of the house and gardens we found the clouds so threatening we thought it better to dine at the Inn. Sir Richard Hoare was not at home. We got back to Southfield in time for tea.

August 2

After breakfast we took leave of our hosts, and returned to Camerton to dinner, to meet my mother who came over from Bath in order to take leave of the boys, who were to go to Warminster School on the Monday.

August 4

I drove Laura and Joseph in the car to Warminster, Owen rode on horseback. As it was Visitation Day I did not see the elder Mr. Griffith, but left the boys in charge of his brothers, and returned with Laura to Radstock where we were engaged to dine with the Boodles.

August 5

Sir Richard Hoare and his brother Peter came over to Camerton this morning. The day was so very warm we did not move after their

[1] Rev. William Henry Coombes, D.D., a native of Camerton.
[2] Thomas Weld, Cardinal, of Lulworth Castle, 1773–1837.

arrival and spent the evening in conversation, chiefly on antiquarian subjects.

August 6

After breakfast we went to the eighteen-acre field, as Sir Richard Hoare wished to see the Roman edifice which we had discovered in the spring, the field being now cropped with barley we could not extend our researches. We rode to Hallatrow in order to visit the British encampment on Highbury, and returned home by Timsbury. Dr. Warren came on a visit from Town, and joined us just before dinner.

August 7

Sir Richard Hoare and his brother left us soon after breakfast on his return to Stourhead. He has been spending a month at Bath, and has derived considerable benefit from the waters, but I am sorry to say his deafness increases.

August 8

Warren occupied the morning *in meditations*. After dinner I drove him to Stoney Littleton Barrow, and thence to Combe Hay, where we drank tea with Mr. Gardiner and his family.

August 9

Warren spent the whole of the morning nearly in meditation on the bench in the upper walk. In the evening we strolled about the premises.

August 10

Warren preached at Camerton in the morning, as I was engaged to do duty for Mr. Barter at Timsbury. In the evening he also gave a sermon, and the Methodists were highly gratified. After tea I drove him into Bath, as he was engaged to return home by one of the early stages next morning.

August 12

Having been invited by Mr. Sherston, of Stowbury, near Wells, to spend a few days with him I set off this morning with Mr. Baker, his son-in-law, in the car, taking my servant, William, who rode his horse. We arrived there some time before dinner, which gave me an opportunity of walking over the grounds, which are well wooded, commanding fine views of the Cathedral, city and surrounding country. After dinner Miss Sherston and her sister, Mrs. Baker, gave us some delightful duets on the piano and harp. Captain Sherston is a good mechanic, and shewed me an excellent lathe; at present he is busily occupied in completing a musical clock.

August 13

I made some sketches before breakfast of the figures outside the Cathedral. Afterwards I was introduced to a curious character residing in the city, usually denominated Conjuror Paine. He had, I find, a hand at everything, electricity, magic, turning, carpentry, collecting fossils, gardening, doctoring, and moreover he is a book collector. I purchased one off him, denominated the "Silver Bell," written about 150 years ago, and a fossil, for which I paid him six times its value. I afterwards went over the Cathedral, escorted by Mr. Sherston, and spent some time in the library. If I lived in the neighbourhood it would be a pretty constant attraction.

August 16

After breakfast, having taken leave of my kind host, the ladies accompanied Baker and myself to Penhill, a conspicuous eminence in the neighbourhood of Stowbury, commanding most extensive views of the country. Here bidding adieu to my companions, who returned to Stowbury, I pursued my road to Camerton and got home to dinner.

August 20

As I had by letter appointed to meet Mr. & Mrs. Charles Warren and Miss Sandham at Warminster on their way to my house in order to escort them to Longleat and Stourhead, we left Camerton this morning at twelve, Russell and the two girls being in the car, and young Edward Boodle, who I invited to join the party, on horseback. The day was remarkably fine, which induced me to stop at Philip's Norton to take a sketch of the old house, now used as an inn, which I should imagine from the style of the windows, etc., was built in Henry VIIth's time. On arriving at Warminster we found our friends had arrived the evening before, and were waiting for us at the Bath Arms.

Breakfast was over before eight, and we drove to Longleat, taking the boys with us from school. Owen mounted the pony instead of Edward Boodle, and by so doing exposed himself to a tumble off as he was opening a gate, but without sustaining any injury. The whole of the road from Warminster to Longleat House is truly interesting, and the approach thither through the great gateway very imposing. Immediately on our arrival at the mansion, although the Marquis and his family were at breakfast, we were permitted to see the apartments usually shewn to strangers. The Hall is particularly striking, and the family portraits arranged in the Saloon and other rooms for the most part well executed, but of course not so interesting to others as the parties they concern. A Lavaterist would not say much in favour of the countenance of Sir John Thynne, who built Longleat House, but his works at least declare, in spite of his features, he had a magnificent turn of mind, assisted by considerable wealth, to enable him to complete so grand a pile. The library is a comfortable room, but in no respect comparable to Stourhead. Leaving Longleat about eleven, we proceeded straight forwards through Maiden Bradley to Stourhead. On arriving at Stourton village we put up our horses at the inn and walked directly to the house. Hearing that Sir Richard Hoare was at home, I went into his room, and was glad to find him looking quite well. He asked me to meet him at Mr. Lambert's on the 15th of next month, when he promised to shew me the lines of several British villages in the neighbourhood of Warminster, also he said he would accompany me to the British remains at Heytesbury. Having requested Sir Richard to permit me to shew my friends the drawings of Durer's in the sitting room and also the library, I returned to the Saloon and accompanied them to both rooms, with which they were much gratified. We then made a tour of the grounds, which far surpassed the expectations they had formed, and they were unanimous in giving this place the preference to Longleat.

Passing through Warminster, I called on the Boys at School and spent a couple of hours with them. I continued my course to Frome and thence to Mells.

Only three Clergymen were assembled on my arrival; viz Mr. Rogers of Berkeley, Mr. Richardson of Farley Castle, and Mr. Williams of Cameley; afterwards five others arrived.

Our conversation turned generally on the state of the Church during the authorized efforts of the Dissenters and Methodists to undermine it, since, it can be considered in no other light, when we read the opinions of Scott in a late decision and observe the unqualified licences which are granted to the ignorant and imposing candidates for popularity, I fear it will be found too late that this liberty will eventually bring about the same scenes as were witnessed in this country in the times of Charles I, the first and canting Oliver, but if the Magistrates of this country do not think so and if some of the leaders in both Houses of Parliament are perfectly indifferent to religious concerns, and like Gallio care for none of these things; without being gifted with Prophecy I may affirm that either they or their children will one of these days have reason to repent of their supineness and indifference.

Mr. Rogers appears to be well read in divinity and a good scholar. I only wish our Meeting were better attended and more systematic. If a paper were to be written against each meeting on the leading subjects of the day and read, as we used to do in our Literary Meetings at Oxford, I think it might be better than delivering our crude opinions on such important concerns without sufficient consideration. For myself I find I am more inclined to be a listener, than a speaker, and this I fancy is much the case with others of the party.

Mr. Skurry, of Orchardleigh, seems to be a quiet man but rather prolix in delivering his sentiment. I continued at Mells until seven o'clock, and then returned with Boodle and took tea at his house before I went home. I found my Mother expecting my arrival at Camerton.

November 18

Mrs. Jarrett spent a few days at Camerton in order to see the repairs going on. She purposes coming to reside in the spring. Farmer Gibbs told me he had some conversation with her respecting my digging in the eighteen-acre field, and that she told him that I was perfectly at liberty to open as much as I pleased if I would move away all the stones, and level it by the spring when the ground would be wanted for sowing, but after that she hoped that I should not want to extend my researches.

1818

AFTER dinner Anna and myelf went up into the Upper Walk into the field. The men found ten coins, and a small image carved in stone about a foot long, perfect except the head. Afterwards they found part of a head, an ear, they also found an iron ring and two other pieces of iron, but no pottery.

June 24

Respecting John Harris, the parish clerk

On my return from Town at the latter end of May it was mentioned to me by John Rossiter and Joseph Goold that the Clerk, Harris, had received from Mrs. Anne Stephens a one pound note, which he was commissioned to deliver to the ringers, and that instead of doing so he had kept it himself. They also mentioned other circumstances highly injurious to his character, and they moreover said that if he continued in his office as clerk that many of the farmers had declared that they would not attend their Church. I represented how highly disgraceful it would be to themselves if they continued in this resolution, for although they might quarrel with Harris and might not be pleased with what he did, yet it was no reason why they should quarrel with their Maker. Rossiter said that Gibbs, Dando, Sainsbury and a number of other farmers had said they would have the business looked into. I said that if they made a proper application to me as Clergyman of the Parish, and stated their reasons for disapproving of Harris, it was my wish as well as my duty to inquire into it, and they might depend on my dismissing him if he were found faulty to the extent they represented. I thought that the best method was for them to meet at Vestry and calmly investigate the business, and then make their representation to me in writing, and they might rely on my seeing proper justice done. They accordingly called a Vestry for the following Thursday, which I did not attend, being engaged to leave home on a little excursion to the lower part of the county. On my return they presented me a paper, on which it was stated in general terms that they did not think John Harris was fit to be Clerk, and they conceived they ought to nominate another. Now, as they did not enter into any particular statement of their accusation against Harris, I thought it unjust to have him condemned without a hearing.

Besides, as they took upon themselves in the wording of the paper the power of nominating a fresh Clerk, which I conceived from the custom of the parish to be in the trust of the Rector, I declined to have anything to do with the resolutions of that Vestry, and told Rossiter if he would with Gibbs, the other Churchwarden, and some of the farmers draw out a paper and state the specific objections to Harris I would have the matter examined properly before them, for no man ought to be condemned without a fair hearing. A day or two after Gibbs and Rossiter called on me and said, as perhaps they could not word the paper in a manner that would meet my wishes, they requested me to draw out a form which they might give their signatures to. I accordingly wrote in pencil a form, which was afterwards copied by Rossiter's brother on a strip of paper, and signed by them.

Another reason for my wishing to have the requisition of the farmers written on paper, instead of a mere verbal statement, was to prevent if possible their flying from the charge hereafter, as they have not infrequently done in former instances, leaving me to bear all the onus of the investigation and the blame of undue interference. Accordingly on receiving the paper on Sunday, June 22, I desired a meeting might be called for Thursday at eleven o'clock, and requested as many of the parishioners would attend as possible. I also spoke to Harris, telling him I expected that he would be there to answer the charge against him, as he professed to be innocent of all intention to retain the money. He said that it was all spite and malice in John Rossiter.

June 25

We met in the Church at the time appointed, and to prevent undue altercation between the parties I thought it best to put down on paper the questions I proposed and the answers which were given, and afterwards to sum up the whole to the farmers and take the opinion of each in turn as to the guilt or innocence of the accused. I accordingly began by addressing Harris as to the crime of dishonesty, and said that the Parish wished to be satisfied as to his conduct, and put to him the questions. Having heard Harris I desired him to go out of the Church for a little, as I wished to enquire of the ringers what had passed between them and himself. They affirmed that he had said nothing about receiving the money, "although my Father tried him on the subject." "How did he try him?" "Harris asked him whether he would go to Radstock Church to ring in the evening. Father said it would not do to go there without having something to drink, and he had no money—thinking this would be a fair opportunity for him to mention what he had for us, if he meant to pay it."

I then asked James Widcombe whether Harris had told him of his having the one pound note for the ringers. Widcombe replied that he had as a matter of course the day after; he did not seem to make any secret of it, and that it was his firm belief that the man never meant to keep the money, but it would have been better if he had paid them immediately, as it would have prevented all that had been said about it.

I then requested Harris to leave the Church, and told them that, as it was my wish to leave the decision entirely to them, without any kind of bias on my part, "I shall decline giving my opinion on the subject till the last, when I assure you I will deliver it in as candid a manner as I am able."

In due course Harris was sent for, and I told him that as he had been acquitted by the majority of dishonest intentions in withholding the money I should not proceed any further in the business as it concerned his office as Clerk. Still, I conceived it my duty to mention to him I felt very unpleasant sensations in my mind which I wish could have been removed, and if he wished to regain a proper place in my regard he must in future be very careful of his conduct; I hoped that Harris would remember the lesson.

After some desultory conversation respecting Lypiatt, our former Overseer, who is now in gaol, and the money he carried to account as paid to Mr. Williams, the attorney, which is still due, and respecting Snook of Sheephouse, who embezzled £30 of the parish taxes which is to be collected over again, the meeting dissolved.

Although in my own mind I am fully convinced of the Harris delinquency, I should have been very awkwardly situated if it had been necessary to turn him out of his present situation, for I could not have appointed one of whom I have a better opinion to discharge the office. I might not have met with another so good. If he takes warning from this exposure things may go on better in future. Still, it is very difficult to regain lost confidence.

August 11

I returned from the Isle of Wight, where I had been staying about five weeks, and found the schoolroom for the girls, which had been prepared under Mrs. Jarrett's direction, nearly completed, also the gallery in the Church which I had ordered to be enlarged two rows for the reception of my Sunday School boys is now finished, as I have given up the weekly school I supported under the direction of Ruth James for the instruction of poor children under ten years of age, Mrs. Jarrett having taken the management of the girls under her immediate direction, and the £10 a year I used to apply to this service, which is derived from the tithe of the gardens, is henceforth to be spent in forwarding the education of the collier boys on Sundays. Mrs. Jarrett having engaged a married woman as Schoolmistress for her girls, I mean to see whether her husband be qualified to take charge of the boys and accompany them to Church every Sunday. I had at first intended offering this charge to Harris, but since the late investigation am not at all satisfied with his principles.

Great depredations having been committed in the gardens and orchards of the parishioners I proposed a meeting of the farmers Sept. 2, at Vestry to enter into a subscription to employ men to watch of nights. Only three attended, and nothing was done. I offered to subscribe a one pound note, and Mrs. Jarrett an equal sum if the subscription became general.

December 12

We walked up the hill above the Parsonage, and found the dark soil prevail in most of the gardens, and where it had that appearance we met with quantities of pottery. One of the cottagers told us they had picked up several pieces of money in time past, some copper and some leather stamped, and he believed his daughter had a silver coin upstairs. On my requesting to see it she brought it me, and I found that, instead of belonging to the Romanised Britons as I expected, it was of the reign of Henry III, and I purchased it. If I recollect rightly we have no English coin older than the reign of Edward I, so this will be an acquisition.

December 31

I had agreed to pay Farmer Young eight pounds for leave to dig on two acres of that field till he wished to prepare it for his crop, and in the course of my examinations had nearly dug up the ground within the foundations of the buildings, but there might have been about quarter of an acre of the outside which I did not have dug up. When he came over about a fortnight since to receive his eight pounds he told me he expected me to dig up the whole of the two acres, and to leave them in such a state that he might put in his wheat crop without ploughing. When I remonstrated with him and said that the eight pounds were in lieu of all such labour and meant as a compensation for any loss he might sustain in not occupying the ground with a crop, and that if I had not dug on the spot he still would have received sufficient compensation, he became very impudent, and said that I should not again dig on his ground, for unless I made it better worth his while he would not give me leave, so I fear there will be a stop put altogether to my discoveries in that quarter, as well as in the eighteen-acre field which Mrs. Jarrett will not have examined again. It is really very distressing to be thwarted in these pursuits. I had great amusement in these you know, and it turned my attention to other objects than the people around me, whose bad conduct only vexed and irritated my mind. Now there will be but little sugar to take the bad taste out of my mouth.

The school, I fear, will not go on near so well now she (Miss Alton) and Miss Jarrett are gone. Occasionally I call in and find all in confusion, no regularity about the hours of coming or of instruction, the children under no kind of control from the schoolmistress; in short, instead of improving, they seem fast going back. My dinner to the boys was given the day after Christmas Day. As Smallcombe and Hester as well as the Clerk dined with them there were about 100. They dined in the schoolroom. As there was a gentleman with me from Bath, who had engaged to return by the mail. I could not leave him to attend to the dinner myself, but the boys and Stone went, and from their acount the whole party appeared satisfied and happy. On Sunday whilst I was in the parish one of the boys came up to me and thanked me for his dinner, saying how good it was and that he had plenty, but about twenty of the boys he said, had gotten no plum pudding. On my asking how this was, as I understood there was plenty for all he replied: 'so there was': that he heard 'there were eight large puddings, but only four were distributed among them.' On making enquiry of Harris, the Clerk, who cut up the puddings, he said only three were devoted to the boys, the fourth was retained for the party who dined after the dinner was concluded. On speaking to my cook I find eight very large puddings were made and sent to the school. They must have been, I imagine, very large, since I find in the grocer's account 22 lbs. of raisins and currants charged, and not 2 lbs remaining. So much for parish histories. I wish they were as sweet as the plum puddings, and not so heavy.

1819

AT HALF past seven this evening, when I was reading in my study, I heard Mrs. Jarrett's voice and that of her son at the front door, who were endeavouring to find the bell. On going downstairs I waited in the hall till William had opened the door, and then lit them into the dining room, where my brother was writing. On being seated Mrs. Jarrett apologised for the unseasonable hour, but said she came on business, and had brought her son with her as it was very proper he should be initiated into things of this kind, as he was to have an estate of his own. She then said that she was very sorry to find that there had been an altercation between Mr. Fry and myself, and that I had made some very severe reflections on him in public which she thought I was called on to explain to her, as he was not only her agent, but also on her recommendation agent to the Coal Works; that she understood that my language had been very high, but I was not aware perhaps that Mr. Fry came of a very good family, at any rate as good as her own, which I might judge was that of a gentleman as she had conceived him a fit companion for herself and children, and should always have a high regard for him as she had known him from infancy; until she was informed for a certainty of any misconduct, to obtain which information was the object of her visit to me. I requested to hear what accounts she had heard of the conversation betwixt Mr. Fry and myself. She said they told her I began it by asking him how he dared let Mrs. Widcombe have her bees? and had moreover learnt that I made use of some term like rascal, although it might not be immediately that. I replied that she had been rather misinformed in both these particulars; that I had not said "how dare you," but asked whether Mrs. Widcombe had the bees by his authority as she told me she had, and that he had said it was a lie as great as any Old Gibbs was accustomed to tell; that with respect to calling Mr. Fry a rascal, I did not say that, but told him that there had been a system of rascality going on for some time in the parish, and that I should do all I could to oppose it, and that when Mr. Fry inquired if I made any allusion to him I had said, "if the cap fits put it on." I then told Mrs. Jarrett she herself must be aware that there was a system of rascality going on, more especially

117

in the Coal Works, that there was Goold, then Reynolds and Soper who had all turned out great knaves, and that these were all friends of Mr. Fry's, and that he had even taken her and her aunt, Mrs. Anne Stephens, to Reynolds' house, which I considered at the time was rather a singular thing. She said that it was (by) her own wish that she had gone there, and that she had no acquaintance with the Reynolds, having never seen either of them in her life, as they were not in the house when they were there, and that the only part of the family she had ever seen was the back of the head of Reynolds' wife.

N.B. This seems a strange assertion, as at the time she and her aunt were there I know that spirits had been brought from Bath by Fry's order, and that the Reynolds as well as some farmers who had come to pay rent had got excessively drunk.

I told Mrs. Jarrett, moreover, that by this time she must be assured that Soper was not a bit better, neither was old Goold who preceded them. She said that was very true, there had been no honesty among the bailiffs ever since the Coal Works had been established, and that as to Soper, Mr. Fry thought him so very dishonest, although he was his own brother-in-law, as to say he deserved to be hanged. I said that notwithstanding all these people had been upheld, the same as in a late instance Mr. Fry would have upheld Widcombe. She asked, in what manner? I replied that though Mr. Fry seemed outwardly to be against him, and pretended not to know where he was, yet to my certain knowledge he had had communication with him on Sunday, August 22, in Bath. She said, if he had it was by her order.

N.B. It is a singular thing that Mrs. Jarrett, who was at Twickenham, should have given orders to Fry to see Widcombe, who was then playing hide and seek, and had driven off his stock for the purpose of defrauding his creditors, which of course she must have been informed of. This very confession of hers was a clear indication that it was her intention to support the fellow at that time, and I verily believe for reasons best known to herself she would have done so now had I not made so steady a stand against her. From a recollection of these several circumstances I told Mrs. Jarrett she must be convinced it behoved a few honest people who were remaining amongst us to oppose to the utmost this system of rascality, otherwise there would be no living in the parish. She replied, "Who do you call honest people? I know none." "I know one honest one, I hope," I replied, laying my hand on my breast, and hoped she was one too. She said she was not a man, therefore had nothing to say on that score. I replied, Yes, but she was, for in Scripture it is said, speaking of men, "Male and female, created He them." She said, admitting there were two, who were there besides? She knew none. My brother said he believed I had a good opinion of old Stephen Rossiter; she replied she knew he was not better than the rest. Young Jarrett said, "Why, there's George Cottle!" "Yes," said Mrs. Jarrett, "but he is not one of the farmers." Mrs. Jarrett then renewed her first conversations respecting what allegations I had to bring against Fry, as we had been, she said, wandering very far from the business. I told her that there were certainly many things that I had been informed of to his disadvantage, but did not think it quite proper to communicate them to her when her mind seemed so prejudiced in his favour. What I had heard was through the report of others, who perhaps, when called upon in a legal way to substantiate the facts would not do it through apprehension of offending her if she was so favourable to Mr. Fry, and then I should be left unsupported; that if Mrs. Jarrett wished for a fair and proper inquiry, and would permit me to consult her account books, and would herself impartially listen to the evidence which might be brought forward, I then would pledge myself to render her every assistance in my power. She said with regard to her account books she knew they must be right as she was able to add them up herself, and with regard to the Coal Company's books she had nothing to do with them. Besides, she did not think it incumbent on her to take an active part, she had only to listen to the allegations made and to decide if they were of sufficient weight or not.

N.B. After her underhand support of Widcombe I had little reason to trust to her impartial decision, and considered that I should be but exposing myself to considerable difficulties if I took upon myself to repeat what I had heard; but I told her that it was not only here, but I had heard others speak of Mr. Fry not in the most respectful terms in his own country; that when I was with Sir Richard Hoare last year in the lower part of Somersetshire I fell into conversation with a Mr. Spencer, formerly of Wells, who said he wished Mrs. Jarrett was acquainted with some of Mr. Fry's proceedings, or that he had an opportunity of communicating them to one of her friends who might inform her of them. Mrs. Jarrett and her son seemed very anxious to learn his address. I said I believed he lived at Mark, so I suppose she purposes waiting on him. Our conversation was protracted until half past nine, when Mrs. Jarrett and her son rose from their seats, and my brother and myself accompanied them to the garden door, where Mrs. Jarrett stopped, and said she wished I had mentioned any circumstances I had alluded to, as her mind was left in a state of great uncertainty. I replied that if she would lay aside all prejudice, and would calmly enter into an investigation of the business with me I would, as I said before, render her every assistance in my power, but it was unreasonable for her to suppose that I should take the whole responsibility and onus on myself. She said she should consult her pillow upon the subject, which was her best counsellor. I then wished her good night and was going to return with the candle indoors, having in the absent state of my mind been so engrossed in the subject we had been talking on as to forget to open the door. I did it then and walked towards the Church, lighting her with the candle, and as I stopped again to wish her good night, shook her by the hand, saying that I hoped that conversation I had had with her would not be the cause of coolness among ourselves; that it was equally our interest to oppose the wrong doings that were going on in the parish, and that if I had spoken my mind freely upon some points it was because I conceived it my duty so to do; that I should be very sorry if it was the occasion of any quarrel between us. She replied, "No Sir, I do not mean to quarrel; that is neither lady-like nor Christianlike." She and her son then proceeded on, and I returned to the Parsonage.

October 26

I left Camerton this morning in my car for Stourhead, having engaged to spend a few days with Sir Richard Hoare.

October 27

I was up at eight, and spent a couple of hours in the library before breakfast; Sir Richard came in soon after I went there, and presented me with Avebury, his last publication, also a printed plate of the route of the Roman road from Bath to Marlborough; he was so obliging as to say he was much pleased with the iter I had sent him, which he had gotten Crocker to transcribe, not being able to make out my writing. I showed him my plans of Camalodunum. He said he conceived I stood upon strong ground, but he would read Tacitus himself, without any comment, and would then give me his opinion.

Mr. P. Hoare and Mr. Hayes during our conversation after breakfast on the subject seemed fully to coincide in my ideas of its having been at Camerton; Temple Cloud having been in its neighbourhood, its vicinity to the country of the Silures and its being in Britannia Prima seemed to be conclusive arguments. Mr. Crocker called on me after breakfast, and begged I would look at the Mausoleum, Sir Richard had just finished for himself and descendants. Mr. Hugh Hoare, Sir Richard's brother, dined here in his way from Devonshire, and proceeded to Town the same night.

October 28

I called on Mr. Crocker before breakfast, and visited with him the Mausoleum in the Churchyard, which is now nearly complete under the direction of Pinch, the architect of the new Church of Bath.[1] A vault of considerable dimensions, arched over with brick, contains twenty-four receptacles for coffins, twelve on each side, arranged in tiers, the flooring is well paved and descended by several steps. A large stone is appropriated to cover the mouth of this vault. Near it is a plain Gothic edifice, intended to contain a sarcophagus now making at Florence. The worthy Baronet, instead of being depressed by these operations, finds a pleasure in overlooking the workmen, and walks down to the Churchyard two or three times a day. Indeed he met me there and explained to me what kind of sarcophagus it was to be, also mentioned that he had taken the design of the edifice in a great measure from the porch at the Parsonage House at Bremhill, which is of course paying a great compliment to Bowles's taste. Should he survive Sir Richard, I do not know a fitter person to write his epitaph, but I hope that finale will be far distant. After breakfast Mr. Conybeare, formerly Saxon, now Poetry Professor at Oxford, and Mr. Selwyn, his friend, called at Stourhead to visit the library, which Mr. Conybeare had not before seen. He seemed much struck with a manuscript, or rather a collection of romances, of the Middle Ages, which seems to be in good preservation, one of them called "The Brute," from its recording the old legend of Brutus settling in Britain, another "The Grail," describing the adventures of King Arthur's Knights in search of the sacred vessel used by Christ at the Last Supper.

I find Sir Richard has published a work on ancient inscriptions, which I must endeavour to procure. Dr. Conybeare gave me a polite

[1] St. Mary's, Bathwick.

invitation to visit him at Bath Easton next week, when he promises to dig into the ancient camp called Salusbury, above the village, Mr. Selwyn, his friend, resides at Kilmington, above Stourhead, and was formerly tutor to Lord Ilchester, which nobleman married his wife's sister. He is esteemed a clever man and a good scholar, but has apparently wretched health. After these gentlemen quitted the library I conducted them to the exhibition of British remains in the room below stairs, where Sir Richard has cases made for the reception of all Mr. Carrington's collection, in which they are exceedingly well arranged, forming perhaps the most extensive museum of the kind in Europe. All the urns and other vessels are placed on shelves, inclosed by wire lattice work, which gives a full view of them but prevents their being handled; the brass spear heads, beads, trinkets, stone celts, flint arrow heads, wet stones, etc; are separated in different drawers in a cabinet.

Whilst the party were engaged at cards Henry Hoare endeavoured to give me a lesson at chess, but I proved so dull a scholar that I soon gave it up. I only wish that I had learnt the game heretofore. Mrs. Henry Hoare's little girl I saw could play it much better with her cousin. She is an elegant child, and will I dare say make a figure in life; but it is unfortunate that as she is an only child that she was not a boy, as the estate, I should suppose, is entailed on the male line.

October 29

After breakfast I was greatly surprised to see Mr. Spencer ushered into the room. I found he had been with Mr. Crocker, and then walked up to pay his respects to Sir Richard. He told me that he had heard from his wife that Mrs. Jarrett had written to ask him whether he had said anything to me respecting Mr. Fry. I explained our conversation; he said he would inform her of quite enough respecting him; that he had been dismissed from all his other employments on account of mal-conduct; and that years ago he had taken the liberty to suggest to Mr. Stephens that he had better get rid of him, but he should not be foolish enough in his reply to Mrs. Jarrett's letter to commit himself, but would wait upon her some day and mention quite sufficient in a few words to convince her he was not deserving the place of trust he stood in, in respect to herself. Mr. Spencer, I afterwards understood from Mr. Crocker, has been to Town in order to procure a patent for converting the peat of the moors into bark, having, as he says, discovered that it is equally efficacious in most complaints. It seems a wild scheme, and I was in hopes, as his speculations have hitherto proved so truly unfortunate to himself and family, he would have continued satisfied with his last acquisition of property and gone on quietly in his profession, but he is a singular character, I believe. After Mr. Spencer was gone Mr. Hoare and myself walked around the gardens and met Mr. Henry Hoare. It was too wet for his shooting today, but yesterday the keeper and he killed forty-three couple of rabbits; he says the pheasants are much thinned owing to the dry weather in the summer, which destroyed many of the young ones. The lake is covered with wild fowl, and some wood cocks have been shot, which seem to be indications of an early winter. I hope it may, as it will be more healthy for the country.

October 30

I left Stourhead after breakfast, the weather being unfavourable for an excursion in an open carriage, as it rained all the way till I arrived at Radstock, where I was engaged to dine, and I was completely soaked. However, with the assistance of Mr. Boodle's wardrobe I was enabled to make a change of clothes. I did not get home until eleven o'clock.

November 8

Today, we were instrumental in relieving a poor woman from much distress. This person we found had been sent to change a five pound note, and whilst crossing the field had just discovered she had dropped the four one pound notes from her hand, the change of silver and halfpence still remaining in her basket. Of course we endeavoured to assist her in the recovery of her volatile treasure, but as the wind was high, conceived they might have blown already to a distance; but, by good fortune, on casting my eyes to the end of the field I saw something white lying on the grass, which I desired William to run after, and which proved to be the identical notes. The poor creature received the lost treasure with the greatest joy, as may be supposed, for as she was a pauper her employer might have suspected her honesty had not the money been forthcoming.

November 11

I walked into Bath after breakfast with my brother, called on Mr. Cruttwell and gave him directions to write to Dando, and proceed against Gibbs if he did not pay the money he was indebted to me. I am sorry to perceive he has mislaid the documents I intrusted him with but hope he will find them, otherwise it will be difficult to proceed in my suit. I then visited Mr. Fortescue in Pulteney Street, and was highly gratified in looking over Mr. Fortescue's sketches in Savoy. I walked also to the new Church at the end of Pulteney Street, which they have disfigured most wantonly by erecting a lofty flagstaff, like the mast of a vessel, in no respect according with the style or intention of the edifice.

1820

Excursion to Wellow with Mr. Cranch

THIS veteran Antiquary came over to Camerton on the evening of Shrove Tuesday after my dinner in order to speak respecting the intended plan of examining the villa at Wellow. He expressed himself very ready to take charge of superintending the workmen, in case we can provide a sufficient sum to commence operations, but at present we cannot insure a subscription above £30, and it would be folly to begin unless our funds are £50. Sir Richard Hoare has promised £10, Mr. Wansey £5, myself £5, Mr. Duncan £1, and from some of the people in the immediate neighbourhood I might perhaps get £10 more, but unless Mr. Barrett can procure subscribers in Bath we shall not advance a step. Cranch thinks two workmen might be sufficient to be constantly employed, and so I think they would; but then his own expenses must be taken into account, which would not be less than £1 10s. a week. I am very anxious to set the business agoing, but cannot without more active coadjutors.

After breakfast we left the Parsonage with the design of visiting the spot. I pointed out to him the quarry facing the Red Post Inn where graves have been found dug in the rock, and the field adjoining called "Great Stowborough," where we discovered the year before last foundations of buildings, Roman pottery and coins. Just as we approached the entrance of Wellow we met a group of gipsies, who were preparing to decamp from a piece of waste land they had occupied near the roadside. A little child which was tied to the back of an ass, surrounded by a variety of tent equipage, being very clamorous, drew our attention to it. On enquiring of its mother whether it ailed anything, its cries were so piercing, she replied that it ailed nothing more than it always had done from the time of its birth, as it was unfortunately an idiot, and although seven years old was not near so large as its brother who was not four: that it was accustomed to make that horrid yelling, and was so importunate for food it would regularly eat a small loaf a day and not be satisfied. We visited the Hayes where the villa stood, and Mr. Cranch became fully a convert to my opinion that not one half was laid open when

Mr. Leigh employed labourers about ten years ago. At present I perceive the field in tillage, which will postpone our operations till the autumn, not but what the site of the villa might be examined, as that is never put in cultivation, could the idle colliers be restrained from trampling down the corn when the pavements are again laid open for inspection. We visited the cottage of Zebedee Weston, a labourer I employed when about the sepulchre at Stoney Littleton four years ago, with whom Cranch became then acquainted, and wishes to secure him for his future operations. Skirting the valley, we ascended the heights and got on to the Ridgway, where, after having put the old gentleman on his road to Bath, I pursued my route homewards. The day was beautifully clear, and I never enjoyed an antiquarian iter better."

March 8

Having engaged to dine with Mr. Boodle at Radstock I left home immediately after breakfast; the day being beautiful I enjoyed my ride exceedingly.

I dined and slept at Boodle's, and early the next morning proceeded to Timsbury, having engaged to attend Mr. Barter and Captain Parish to the nomination of the County Members at Wells.

Arriving there, found a large meeting of the Country Gentry, and heard some speeches from Sir Abraham Elton, Colonel Horner, Mr. Lutterel, Sir Thomas Lethbridge, etc., and then signed my name and address of *Condolence and Congratulation* to His Majesty in the Chapter House, where a large body of the Clergy assembled. Sir Thomas Lethbridge afterwards appeared on the hustings, and I suppose will be returned with Mr. Dickenson—Mr. Gore-Langton,[1] who is in Paris, having declined the contest. I hate public meetings, but on the present occasion when the country seems so agitated, I thought it my duty to go there. There was no appearance of republicanism or of radicalism, as it is now termed, but the whole was conducted with great decorum.

The Sheriff, Mr. Napier, is, I understand, great nephew to my predecessor at Camerton, Mr. Prowse. He spoke much to the purpose when called on, and discharged his office very properly, although it must have been with no small inconvenience to himself, being on crutches through the gout.

We dined at Wells, and returned in the evening to Timsbury where I slept, and went home next morning.

[1] Mr. William Gore-Langton, 1787–1828, of Combe Hay.

My eldest daughter Laura, having met with the same accident her dear mother did nine years before, namely, the rupture of a blood vessel, I determined on removing her as soon as possible to put her under Dr. Garrick's care at Clifton.

Accordingly I left home this morning, having borrowed Mrs. Jarrett's carriage, as being easier than a chaise, in which my housekeeper accompanied her, and I proceeded on horseback. We passed by Temple and Whitchurch, as the road was not so rough in that direction although farther about, arrived at Clifton at 3 p.m. and consigned my dear girl to the care of her Aunt Holmes, now residing in Portland Place. In the evening Dr. Garrick came, but did not order bleeding again, which I imagined he would, and was very apprehensive on Laura's account as she has so great a dread of it. On the whole she is better than I could have expected after the Journey.

Laura passed a pretty good night, and her pulse is not near so full, but there is certainly too great a quickness, and her cough is troublesome at times. After breakfast I took a walk to Long Ashton. When I returned home I found Dr. Garrick had called, and thought Laura better. In the evening he called again after she was gone to bed, and told me he thought her pulse rather quick, and that he must have recourse to bleeding if it continued so.

I went to the College and heard a good sermon from the Dean, Dr. Beck, but badly delivered, found it very cold, and not being well perhaps made it appear more so. I attended Evening Prayers at Clifton; the new Church is just beginning to appear above the ground a little to the north of the present edifice, large vaults are made beneath, which I suppose will return a great profit from the subsequent interments. Dr. Garrick thinks Laura better, but still talks of bleeding. I found myself so unwell I went soon to bed, having a considerable degree of fever.

Dr. Garrick when he called on Laura prescribed a medicine for me, which was serviceable, and I found myself better on going to bed. Laura still continues to amend, and has a good appetite although she is not permitted to take any animal food.

Finding myself better this morning, I took a ride after breakfast over the Down. The dock constructed at Sea Mills is in a ruinous state, nearly filled with mud formed by the deposit of the thick waters of the Severn; a crowd of people were busily employed on the spot in purchasing coal brought from Wales, for which they pay seven pence a bushel—as cheap as I purchase it at the Camerton pits, which must be a great advantage to the poor in the vicinity.

After breakfast this morning, as dear Laura seemed better, having passed a good night, I mounted my horse in order to return to Camerton; my own cold being very indifferent, and a great inclination to fever, I conceived it best to return home and to nurse myself for a few days.

J.S. to L.S.

"Many thanks for your letter, which was very welcome as it assured me of your being better. I will say nothing on the subject of bleeding, I am *almost* as *sore* on that particular as you are, as I would fain have my Laura copy the firmness of a Portia than be a poltroon, for there are so many occasions in life, my dearest girl, to try one's fortitude it is a great misfortune not to exert it when it is requisite; but away with a grave lecture which I do not relish giving any more than you in receiving. Miss Hoskin is arrived, I understand from the Boodle's, and they wished Anna to dine and to spend tomorrow at their house with her, but I thought it as well not to break in upon her occupations, and therefore declined it. I believe, being Easter Tuesday, the Club walked at Radstock, and there will be a great uproar on the occasion. I had a curious wedding this morning at Camerton, Widow Wilcox, who has five children, some nearly grown up, gave her fair hand to a lad named Sparks, who cannot be more than nineteen: a pretty Spark he must be. However, as the parties seemed themselves most happy I had nothing further to say than, "Thank you" for the half-crown I received for doing what not a million half-crowns will ever pay me for undoing. Pray write to me when you feel inclined. This half-crown will pay the postage of several letters. I have heard nothing of the boys for an age. I suppose they would have no objection to the draft I am now sending you. I wonder what they would do with it.

April 9

Having heard from Joseph Goold that James Widcombe had been seen secreted at Farmer Gibb's at Homehouse Farm after having driven off his stock from Camerton, and that he had been seen at his father's at Wick Lane, and from John Rossiter that two of his heifers were in Chick Meads, a field belonging to Joseph Balne, I sent a message by Joseph Goold to Balne desiring him to execute the warrant he had for his apprehension: that he returned for answer that he did not know that he was in the neighbourhood. As £5 reward had been offered for his apprehension Widcombe thought it necessary to decamp to London, leaving his wife and children in a lodging in Holloway, the parish paying 6s. a week for their support. Having continued there a few weeks he returned to Bath, where, meeting my servant William, he said, "How are you going to Camerton? I have seen Jacob Balne, and shall shortly come back again to you." On William's mentioning the circumstance to me on his return I thought it so great an instance of hardened impudence that I immediately wrote a note to the constable, Jacob Balne, to apprehend him. As he did not attend I wrote a second:

"Mr. Balne,
Your not coming this morning to Camerton obliges me to write again. Widcombe, I understand, was yesterday at Camerton; what is more, I hear you saw him in Bath on the morning of the same day. As you have a warrant for his apprehension for the embezzlement of the parish money it was your duty to have executed that warrant. If the man is not taken into custody immediately the blame will consequently rest with you, and you may depend on my having an ample investigation of the subject if you permit him to be longer at large."

April 24

Jacob Balne came in the evening and excused himself for not having called sooner, saying he had been obliged to go to Norton Fair. He denied having seen Widcombe in Bath, but promised to take him immediately, which he did shortly after. The Overseer, Hicks, accompanied him before the Magistrates, and he was committed to Shepton Gaol on a charge of having embezzled £50 (£5 he owed me, also upwards of half a year's tithe) belonging to the Parish; but the amount was considerably more. A few weeks had not elapsed before his aunt, Sarah Purnell, spoke to me as I was going to Church, and begged that I would interest myself about getting him out of prison. I told her I could not possibly do so, as I thought that he had behaved himself in so rascally a manner that he ought to suffer for it. Not long after William Kimbury, his brother-in-law, who had first informed me of his knavery in taking my pocket-book and notes in the Church, made a similar request, saying that he thought that he had had sufficient punishment for his offence. I told him I thought by no means, and that so far from conducting himself as he ought, that he had told them in Shepton Gaol that he was not going to stop there long, and that he had never written any apology for his fault or expression of contrition for it. Kimbury said he was sure he must be sorry to be kept away from his wife and family. I told him that had it not been for his wife's extravagance in various particulars he might not have been there: that she persuaded him to do many of the dishonest acts for which he was then suffering. A short time after this I received a letter from Widcombe saying he was sorry for what he had done, and wished me to use my endeavours for his liberation. I had previously written to him, and to Pitman the gaoler, requesting him to inform me how he had conducted himself in prison, as I had heard it reported his behaviour was so riotous he was obliged to be double ironed. Not receiving any answer from Pitman I did not take any steps for his benefit, but wishing myself to inquire concerning what I had heard I procured an order from Sir John Cox Hippisley to admit me to Shepton Gaol, of which the following is a copy:

"Mr. Pitman,

You will admit the Rev. Mr. Skinner to see J. Widcombe, and shew Mr. Skinner the state of our wards. J. C. Hippisley.

As you may not be well enough yourself, let a turnkey allow Mr. Skinner."

I did not avail myself of this permission till I had again written to the gaoler through the older Harris, who goes to Shepton, requesting him to write if he had anything to say respecting him. Not receiving any answer I no longer thought it necessary to interest myself about him. However, on his wife's calling at the Parsonage a short time after saying she was going down to see her husband in prison and asking if I had any message to send, I told her I had nothing to say to her husband, but to tell the gaoler I wished that he would reply to those questions I put to him in my letter. I gave her half-a-crown, as she told me her goods in Holloway had been seized for rent, and her children were starving. I found afterwards on enquiry that the woman had been turned out of her lodging on very different grounds, namely, that of having brought home a young man to sleep with her, and having gone in his company to the Red Lion on Odd Down, leaving her children without anything to eat. I certified myself of the truth of this report by going to see the person with whom she lodged, of the name of Sims, who told me that was the reason why he had locked her room, and that the father of the young man who had been at the Red Lion with her had separated them at that place. I afterwards spoke to Old Widcombe, his father, asking him if he had heard of these particulars. He replied in the affirmative, saying that he had all along known that she was a great deal the worst of the two, and had been the cause of leading his son into dishonest practices.

April 26

I was prevented going to Clifton Wednesday as I intended, but having heard more favourable accounts from Miss Holmes of dear Laura I felt the disappointment less, and this morning after breakfast I took the direction of Farmborough to Clifton, where I arrived in the middle of the day. I must confess that I was much struck at seeing the dear invalid so much thinner, and as she had been obliged once again to undergo the operation of bleeding, I fear my apprehensions were but too well founded. But God's will be done! I dined and spent the evening with her in Portland Place, and returned to Bath Hotel to sleep. Notwithstanding the advanced season there was a hard frost as I walked thither at 10 o'clock, and the wind from the Down was as cold as in winter.

April 27

I called on Mr. Garrick immediately after breakfast, and as he pressed me much to take a family dinner with him and his wife I did not decline the invitation, as I wished for an opportunity of having his candid opinion respecting my child. I spent the remainder of the morning with dear Laura. Dr. Garrick's dinner hour was not before six. I was punctual to my time, but the Doctor's engagements were such I did not see him till nearly eight. However, I did not regret the delay, as I enjoyed a very rational tete-a-tete with Mrs. Garrick, formerly one of the Miss Tudways of Wells. After dinner, when the lady had retired, I asked the Doctor his candid opinion about Laura. He said with a great deal of feeling that he was fearful that neither air nor medicine would be of any real service to her; that he had never been able to lower her pulse in the least, and that as the cough still continued and the expectoration rather increased she must naturally get weaker. Although this entirely coincided with my own opinion I seemed as though I had rather not have heard what I requested to hear.

April 28

On conversing with the apothecary who attends dear Laura, and asking him whether he thought she could bear the journey without suffering any material inconvenience, he assured me he thought it might prove rather beneficial to her than otherwise, but recommended my taking it as soon as possible, since she was getting weaker every day. I asked him whether she might not take something more nourishing, even if it were only to give her strength for the journey without fear of the renewing of the spitting of blood. He said, "certainly, she might venture to take either fish or chicken," and there was no further apprehension on that head, and as a low regimen had been tried in vain he conceived that she might for the future be indulged in what she was most inclined to take. I then spoke to dear Laura herself, and asked if she would not like to visit her grandmother. The dear girl said she should of all things like to see her grandmother for a few days, but added, "I shall come back again to your aunt when I am stronger, and then go upon the Down again as I used to do." Arriving at my mother's at six o'clock, she approved in every respect of the removal of dear Laura, and said that she would let her have two of the most airy apartments in the house, which would be requisite as the hot weather came on.

May 1

At sunrise this morning the Down facing my window was thronged with people. At first I could not imagine the cause of their assembling so early, but on recollecting the custom of the country to collect in this manner on May Day the wonder ceased. The revellers were accompanied by a band of music, and parties of children were dressed out for the occasion. I could not help reflecting on the contrast to their merriment and the sad depression which hung over my spirits at the moment; but I have had my days of enjoyment also, and do not repine. After breakfast having procured an easy carriage and good driver, I ordered him to be in readiness by eleven o'clock. When the hour arrived the carriage was punctual to the time. I assisted Laura into it, and the servant took her place by her side, while I followed on horseback. We arrived at my mother's at three o'clock, dear Laura having borne the journey better than I had expected.

May 4

I took a walk before breakfast to the top of Banner Down over which the Fosse passes, but found but little interest in those pursuits which used most to interest me.

May 11

I had forgotten this was my birthday, but dear Laura remembered it and purchased a penknife for me as a present for the occasion. Anna procured me a smelling bottle with salts to relieve my headaches.

May 12

Attempted to employ myself, but find that everything has lost its former relish, and time is now quite a blank on my hands. In the course of the day I attempted to read part of the "Monastery," the last and most absurd of Walter Scott's productions; it is derogatory to his character as an author to have sent it into the world.

May 13

Every day finds Laura weaker, and the profuse night perspirations contribute to reduce her very rapidly, but not a sigh nor complaint does she utter, although her bones begin to wear the skin, and her deafness increases so that it is with difficulty she can hear what one says to her. I ever knew her to be of the most heavenly disposition, but could not conceive such perfect patience and resignation in human form. She told her grandmother the other day she hoped she should be always patient and give as little trouble as possible. She continues still to read the Lessons and Psalms for the day to herself, usually having her small Bible and Prayer Book on her bed. I read prayers once to her, but she found it so difficult to hear me I perceived it distressed her, and shall not repeat it without she particularly desires it, as indeed it is most distressing to myself. I know not how I shall support this last blow. I have borne up against the malice and injustice of mankind with fortitude, but on this point I am most vulnerable and weak. Yet the loss alone is mine. The dear angel will be removed from a bad and troublesome world before she has smarted from its baseness and ingratitude. I had looked forward to the comfort and consolation of her estimable society to smooth the remainder of my days.

May 14

I cannot look upon her but with a degree of veneration.

May 15

I stayed in dear Laura's room, sometimes endeavouring to amuse her with cutting out things in tamarind stones. I received a truly friendly letter from Mr. Hoare.

May 16

When my horse comes tomorrow I shall be able to take some exercise, which I begin to find absolutely necessary both for my health and spirits.

May 22

The dear sufferer every day gets weaker and weaker. I cannot see any comfort in leaving the house to take my rides as I intended.

May 23

I pray that the last may not be painful; the heat of the weather is most oppressive, I fear it will add to the suffering. I hear she still continues in a doze; the silence of the chamber above me is worse now than when I used to hear her so often cough. I wish to hear that sign of her being here. Yet why should I wish her to be here? I have long bidden my farewell.

May 24

Laura died at seven o'clock this evening. God's will be done.
Poor dear, at the very last she preserved the natural benevolence of her disposition. Sunday evening, not being able to sleep and

finding two servants attending her she said how sorry she was for all the trouble she had given them, and calling for her purse she gave Mrs. Treherne nine shillings, and afterwards three apiece to the other servants.

I desired her books, which she daily read to be carried into my room, and I shall retain them as my constant companions. The Bible and Prayer Book, also a little book of devotions, had been nicely papered by the dear girl, when lying on her death bed, thus indicating the ruling inclination of neatness and propriety even to the last.

Another instance of her charming delicacy I cannot but record, which has just come to my knowledge: one of the females who came to lift her up in bed, only a day or two before she died, had been taking a glass of wine, which my Mother had given her, thinking it necessary at that time; when Laura smelt her breath she exclaimed, "You have been drinking some of the wine; pray never do that, it is very improper for a female, and a servant to take wine"; on the reason for so doing being explained to her she was perfectly satisfied.

May 28

It rained the whole way to Camerton and of course my spirits were more than usually depressed. On passing the turnpike at Odd Down, where the car was stopped when the horse had run away with Laura and Owen about four years ago, I could not help reflecting on the fortitude the dear girl then showed, not being ten years of age, although the distance was upwards of half a mile and several coal carts were in the road, she neither screamed nor attempted to jump out, but sat quiet till the turnpike man put to the gate, which the mare attempted to leap and broke the upper bar, also its jaw . . . I passed a dreadful night, not being able to command my feelings— all appeared such a blank . . . I strove in vain for some comfort during this afflicting night, and found none till, quite wearied, I got to sleep.

May 29

Laura's body was laid to rest with her mother. How glad I was when the masquerade was over, and I was left to myself. What is all the pomp, the parade of external mourning? . . . Alas! my mourning is not that of gloves and scarfs . . . How willingly would I have lived in poverty and parted with everything, could I but have retained

135

this one treasure. But God's will be done; I am selfish, I am weak, but I am not murmuring.

May 30

I was up at six and went to see the grave, which was properly turfed and the superfluous earth removed. Often have I before visited the spot where dear Anna was laid; how often shall I now visit it?—till the time it opens to receive myself.

May 31

This morning I felt a painful satisfaction in examining dear Laura's cabinet which I had given her for her coins and collections, also in looking over the contents of a little box which she had with her all the time she was at Clifton and Bath. In the cabinet everything was placed with the greatest neatness, the coins and shells arranged in boxes and drawers.

In one of the drawers I found a pocket-book with several affectionate memoranda. The Journals she kept from the time she was educated at home; and it will be a lasting memorial of her capacity and intelligence; since she was able to learn so many different lessons, in Latin, Italian, and French with perfect ease to herself; and continue her work and drawing as amusements.

That part of the Journal relative to the keeping of her birthday, so affected me, I put down the book; but shall request my brother to transcribe the whole.

There was a funeral in the Evening of a child, I attempted to perform the ceremony, contrary to the persuasion of Boodle, but could with difficulty get through it: how presumptuous to depend on one's own strength!!

August 17

I could not help thinking how differently this morning was to be spent by myself, an obscure individual, on the desolate heights of Mendip, and the Queen of these realms in the midst of her judges in the most splendid metropolis in the world. Yet when half the number of years have rolled away which these tumuli have witnessed how will every memorial, every trace, be forgotten of the agitation which now fills every breast; all the busy heads and aching hearts will be as quiet as those of the savage chieftains which have so long occupied these hillocks.

I attended the Vestry at twelve. Messrs Purnell, Day, Hicks, Jacob Balne, Weeks, Old Widcombe, Fear and Widcombe's sister present found their object was to release Widcombe from prison on the payment of a sum of money by his relatives, and that Mr. Purnell had called the Vestry, or rather ordered it to be called, on this account. Fear began by saying he was ordered by his employers the proprietors of the Coal Works, to endeavour to procure the liberation of Widcombe, as the expense of 6s. a week incurred by his family during the time of the confinement was such an addition to the Poor rate they wished to save that money. I asked whether the proprietors of the Coal Work had been properly informed of the causes for which Widcombe was detained in prison, namely, perjury and felony; if they had been, I should think they were too respectable men to wish for his liberation on account of the paltry sum of six shillings a week.

Jacob Balne denied he was guilty either of perjury or felony, that he had brought up his accounts with the acknowledgment of his being indebted so much to the Parish, and had sworn them as being correct. I replied I did not wonder Mr. Balne stood out as the advocate of Widcombe, since he had favoured him from the beginning, and had not only neglected to apprehend him when a warrant was issued against him, but had taken care of his cows in his own field, which he had driven off by night in order to avoid his creditors and make restitution to the Parish he had so grossly cheated. Balne and the Overseers must have been aware that Widcombe made false entries of monies paid to the Poor in distress: he had set down to Perry, the tailor, thirty shillings as advanced in distress, not a farthing of which he had received; and several other instances might be discovered by applying to the book, which the Overseer ought to have brought with him.

Widcombe's sister then came forward and said she and her husband were ready to advance £10 now, and pay two shillings a week till the debt was liquidated if the Parish would consent to his liberation.

Some of the farmers then talked of putting it to the vote. Mr. Purnell said but little, but I clearly perceived he favoured the wishes of the majority. Farmer Day alone said he thought his conduct had been so rascally he was better off where he was. I replied we had suffered so much from knavery in the parish that I thought it was a good riddance to get quit even of one. Old Widcombe and his daughter accused me of being hard hearted. The latter especially said I ought to shew mercy if I expected mercy. I replied that a private offence against myself I might pardon, as I freely did his stealing my seven pounds out of the pulpit when he was clerk, but his taking the bread out of the mouths of the poor I could not look over, nor did I wish such a fellow ever again to come amongst us.

September 8

I had engaged to dine with Mr. Purnell to-day ever since Sunday, and began to dread the trial I should be exposed to should the conversation be renewed respecting Widcombe, as I could not but speak warmly on a subject so palpably iniquitous, especially in a Magistrate. Fortunately for me Mr. Ireland, from Frome, came to spend the day, which enabled me to send an excuse. I accompanied this gentleman, who is a mineralogist, to some of the quarries in our neighbourhood, and gave him those specimens from my collection he most approved of. After dinner we looked over Shakespeare prints, with which he seemed much interested.

September 9

A party from Timsbury, consisting of the Miss Palmers, Mr. Johnson, and Miss Harding from Bath, came to an early breakfast. I afterwards attended them to the Wellow Pavement, which I had opened for them to see the patterns, and to the sepulchre at Stoney Littleton.

September 10

Mr. Johnson did duty at Timsbury. I called in the morning on Mrs. Harding, Bacon, junior, Mrs. Sotter, Rossiter and Harris, and was not sorry to learn my conduct respecting Widcombe was approved by the poorer orders; however, it may subject me to animadversion from the farmers. After Evening Service buried a child who had died in the measles which are now very prevalent in the parish.

Other efforts followed, which had the support of Mrs. Jarrett, to obtain the release of Widcombe, but the Magistrates determined that, as by the commitment Widcombe had to continue in prison until the money was paid, they had no power to liberate him.

September 16

After an early breakfast I accompanied Dr. and Mrs. Haggard to Camerton. I was in hopes that they would have spent this day and the succeeding Sunday at the Parsonage, but as they were anxious to attend the Cathedral service at Wells and visit Cheddar on their way thither, and I could not pretend to offer anything equivalent to such grand sights in my retirement, they accordingly left me about one o'clock for Cheddar, and I proceeded to my study. This day's post brought me a letter from Mr. Clutterbuck of Bradford, saying that Gore-Langton could have no objection to the opening of the pavement at Wellow, as he had promised Sir Richard Hoare, but as he was expected home himself in the course of ten days he thought nothing had better be done till his arrival. I hope this permission will not terminate in the same manner that one did respecting the map of Wellow, which I was promised a sight of several years ago, but it was vox et praeterea nihil, my application having been rendered abortive through the great man's great man, alias his steward: ita est et ita erit—like a true Antiquary I only wish I had nothing to do with the Moderns or they with me!!! I wish entirely to forget the present scene and mix altogether in the transactions of past times.

September 17

As Mr. Johnson is at Timsbury and kindly took charge of the Church for me I had only service at my own.

In the evening I buried one of White's children, who died of the measles; this is the second one who has fallen a victim to this complaint within these few days, and I find it very prevalent in the neighbourhood. The mother seemed so much affected I gave her some wine.

September 18

This being the day appointed for our Quarterly Clerical Meeting at Mells, I attended it; about the middle of the day we mustered eleven, and we spent a pleasant evening together.

September 19

I was occupied the greater part of the morning in selecting and packing up the original Journals from which Russell has made his copies, for Mrs. Wm. Skinner, as she is at all times so much interested in my pursuits I am sure she will make a proper use of them; and in case anything should happen to myself and the collection I have made for these last twenty years, it is satisfactory to know that all traces will not perish with me. I also put up some sermons written and preached on particular occasions, and several pages of poetry which Russell transcribed for another work, with the Manuscript Journals I had given to my dearest Laura, also some little tokens given to the dear girl. It was a melancholy morning to me, and recalled in full force those feelings I have been so anxiously striving to overcome.

September 20

I was up nearly as soon as it was light to transcribe the memoranda I have made respecting Baden Hill, in order to take them with me to Warner's, as I am anxious to stir him up to prosecute his researches in those parts.

Our party at tea was joined by Colonel Birch, of the Life Guards, whom I have not seen for twenty-five years. I was with him at Cheam, and afterwards knew him at Oxford, so we had much conversation respecting past events. As his memory seems to be most tenacious he recorded many circumstances which had entirely escaped my recollection respecting Gilpin,[1] and the present Chancellor of the Exchequer, Vansittart,[2] who, he says, was considered at school as a good poet; as I was very young when I went to Cheam, and Vansittart at the head of the school, I have very little recollection respecting him. Birch, being several years older, of course had better opportunities of knowing this. He also mentioned a circumstance I had entirely forgotten respecting myself, which was, when I had to undergo flagellation I always made a point of shewing no expression of pain, which induced Gilpin to exert himself more strenuously in the service. Whatever might have been my conduct in those days I am sure since I have been so schooled it would be no wonder if I had actually become callous to all sensation, which, alas! is not the case. Birch was rather too minute in some of his old Cheam stories, but he seems an open hearted and, I hear, is a benevolent man, therefore the ladies would not be too severe on him. Such is his veneration for old Gilpin, his first master, that he has given £50 for a small book of his drawings. It was nearly ten when I left Warner's, but the moon being nearly full I had a pleasant ride home.

[1] Rev. William Gilpin, Sen. headmaster of Cheam School.
[2] Nicholas Vansittart, 1766–1851, 1st Baron Bexley.

After Church I visited Mrs. Gullick, who has, I found, been some time unwell from a bad confinement. I heard respecting the Methodists, of whose Society she has been a member, that the numbers of the leaders are decreased in our parish from forty to sixteen, but that they are endeavouring to recruit, and, in future, that every Friday evening is to be employed as a meeting through the district.

There were twenty-eight stayed Sacrament; the collection £1 11s. 6d. The lessons for the morning respecting Shadrach, Meshach and Abednego, and in the evening respecting Daniel, particularly struck me at this present time, when each of us may be exposed to a similar confederacy. Surely the translation "and the fourth was like *the* Son of God" is erroneous, the definite article being used instead of the indefinite article, especially as it is mentioned just after that the Lord sent his angel to deliver them; Indeed it is clear that it ought to have been "and the fourth was like a son of God."

Before I mounted my horse I visited Harris, the clerk's wife, who is very ill in the measles, and wished for wine, which I could not give till she had seen Mr. Crang; there is also another woman I saw in the course of the day ill of the same complaint, and, I fear, dangerously so, as she is a weak consumption habit. I have never known the measles so prevalent as at this time.

Having visited the two invalids, Mrs. Harris and Heal, I mounted my horse and took my usual course to Wellow. I believe the animal is now so used to the road she would go forward to the spot without my guidance. As the day was very stormy and there was little to do on the ground, I rode home by three o'clock. I understand a woodcock was killed yesterday by a gentleman I saw on the Wellow Hayes. This is remarkably early for their coming over, and indicates a severe winter; indeed, three or four days ago I noticed a large flock of grey plovers, and another of larks. I found a letter from Mr. Clutterbuck, Mr. Gore-Langton's steward, mentioning Mr. Gore-Langton's return to England and his permission to continue our researches; if I had delayed the opening till this time it would have been hardly worth while to have begun it, as it is we are full late should the winter set in, as I expect it will.

After Church I visited the sick, found Mrs. Heal in a very weak state with a violent pain in her side. I desired her to send for a blister to my house, which I had ordered for my own use, but I hope I shall not have immediate occasion for it.

October 19

I had intended visiting Wellow, but on paying a visit at Radstock was persuaded to dine there; as the weather was very misty little could have been done as to our researches at Wellow. I returned home before dark. The schoolmistress called and wasted nearly a couple of hours, so that little progress was made in my drawings.

October 22

I was very unwell the whole night, and in a strong fever. However, I persevered in doing the duty twice, but could eat nothing, the fever being accompanied by a sore throat.

October 25

I took my breakfast with Dr. Holland at his mother's, No. 14 Bladud Buildings, Mrs. Holland, daughter of Lord Erskine,[1] was of the party, at the breakfast table also was their son, Erskine, a fine lad about fifteen or sixteen.

When the ladies left the room we had some conversation respecting the present proceedings against the Queen. I find he is entirely of opinion that the Bill will not pass, but thinks there will be a modification as to her establishment, etc., etc., in this country; but it strikes me that half measures will not succeed, and the country will not be satisfied with any other verdict than Guilty, or Not Guilty. If her conduct has been such as has been described she merits degradation, but if not, and undue means have been used to bring her name and character into discredit, she ought not only to be acquitted but the authors of such arts should suffer for their malignity. A few weeks, perhaps a few days, may determine the grand question, which has so long exclusively occupied the public mind. Dr. Holland has by many been supposed to be the Dr. Holland who accompanied the Princess having originally been the physician but on his marriage with Miss Erskine went into orders.

[1] Thomas, 1st Lord Erskine, 1750–1823, son of the 10th Earl of Buchan, and Lord Chancellor.

October 26

I sent for Mr. Crang, the Apothecary.

November 2

I had a great many visitors. Mr. Crang says I am going on very well and desires me to discontinue the calomel, which I am very glad of, as I have a great dread of this medicine, and already perceive it has affected my gums and teeth.

November 10

Mr. Barratt from Bath called this morning, and having mentioned his design of visiting the operations at Wellow I could not help accompanying him. Not being able to continue longer on the spot as the day turned off very raw and cold, I took leave of my companion and returned to Bath by Combe Hay, and pursued my way across the Hayes fields which are to the west of the ground in which the pavements were discovered. I have for some time past conceived that there was a range of habitations along the side of the hill, nearly parallel to the one under our examination, and am now convinced I was right in my conjecture, since the fields now being fallow indicate several divisions of enclosures; white lyas and pennant stone, Roman brick and pottery, the Ridgeway Road running from Eckwick on the summit of the ridge of down and connecting these habitations with those on the Fosseway as far as Clan Down, so in fact the tradition of an extensive town stretching from Wellow in that direction may be substantiated in the course of our examination. In the field adjoining the Ridgeway Road to the south east of the clump of trees on the top of the Ick, or where Farmer Ponting's ploughman informed me he had found so many coins formerly whilst ploughing, I clearly noticed different places on the height where habitations had been erected. An unexpected gleam of sunshine breaking out beneath the dark clouds showed all the distances to the greatest advantage. From a boy attending sheep in an adjoining field I learnt that the interesting spot above mentioned is belonging to White Oxmead Farm; probably I may hereafter be able to extend my inquiries in this direction, also if we make good this link we shall be able to prove to a demonstration there was a line of habitations extending along the Ridgeway which traverses the Dunum from Twinney to Clandown, a length of six miles, the most extensive Roman remains without any doubt to be found in Britain.

I rode to Radstock intending to have proceeded from thence to Wellow, but was persuaded to sleep there, or rather, I should say, to lay awake the greater part of the night, the people being so very noisy in their rejoicings for the *Queen's acquittal* that it was impossible to close my eyes. *Posterity* (if any men of calm reason remain among *posterity*) will look back to the proceedings of these last six weeks with astonishment, and think it hardly possible that such things should have been *said* and *suffered* in the most enlightened and best informed country in the world. The plain state of the case seems to be this; a person and his wife, not agreeing in sentiments or manners, by mutual consent separate, and by mutual consent agree to follow their own inclinations. The female after a while goes abroad, and is guilty of some freedoms and lightness of behaviour in her domestic transactions, which *her servants* are required carefully to examine and, if called upon, to record; the husband in the meanwhile follows his own inclinations at home. The only tribunal which had any right to feel offended or to give judgment for this moral evil was a tribunal far above all *human* influence. Yet this said tribunal not only minutely inquired into each of these secret acts of one of the parties concerned, but had all those secret acts brought before the face of the world, acts which might have passed unnoticed even by the servants themselves unless they had been instructed to spy them out, and which were of that kind and description that even when permitted ought never to be *named*; yet these disgusting and most offensive descriptions were not only encouraged but listened to day after day by the nobles and bishops of the land by the patterns of honour and religion, and not only listened to but published for the perusal of the people from one end of the kingdom to the other. Mr. Wilberforce foresaw the danger, and strove, anxiously strove, to prevent the deluge of filth and obscenity from spreading over the country. Surely it was an infatuation which prevented them attending to his wise admonitions. These are sad signs of the times; and yet see the populace rejoicing in the midst of these pestiferous events, guns are fired, huzzahs resound, bonfires are made, and they rejoice with a savage joy, and wherefore? before the power which kept the people in control has been compelled to manifest its own weakness. Alas! these are but the beginning of sorrows. England, my country, I love thee greatly, but when I see those evils coming on thee which countries as great as thyself have experienced I cannot but tremble at thy fall. These were my waking dreams at Radstock. May I lie low when these things actually do take place.

I did duty twice today. Dined with Mrs. Jarrett at the Manor House, having three times before been prevented accepting her invitation, I did not decline it, but I had rather not leave home on a Sunday, there was music in the Evening.

Mrs. Jarrett having lent me one of the fashionable novels called "Guy Mannering," I read it, or rather ran it over. It may be want of taste in me to think differently from the generality of people, but I cannot see with their eyes in these matters. The novels I have chanced to meet with, written by the same Author, possess few attractions beyond others of the same stamp. The Old proverb of "Get a name and go to sleep" is here sufficiently verified. If Walter Scott be the Author I am sorry, since he is fitted for greater things; if he suffers his name to be lent to them I am sorry, since they are an unseemly appendage to his other works. But if he is making a fortune by that is another matter. Peter Pindar's Razor-selling Jew little cared whether his instruments cut, if they only were purchased; but enough of novels.

The day being unpromising, I staid at home writing letters. Mrs. Boodle called, and reminded me of a half kind of promise I made last week, to go to the Old Down Ball tomorrow; so much was said about it, I was obliged to consent, but had much rather occupy myself with the Ancients, if I might be permitted to do so, but in these days if a man retires from the herd, they will turn upon him and butt him to pieces.

In the evening I corrected what Russell last transcribed for me, to be written over again.

I was engaged the whole of the morning settling accounts. I find the people of the Parish are still in my debt £312, a greater part of this sum, I fear I shall never get; however I must take some steps to insure payment in future, otherwise it will be impossible to go on.

I may exclaim with the Psalmist, "Woe is me—I have long dwelt among those who are enemies unto my peace".

Oxford Iter

I set off in the Oxford mail, which took me up at Grosvenor Place (Bath) a little after eleven, and whilst the horses were changing at Cross Hands I made the best of my way to the camp at Little Sodbury, which is so perfect a specimen of Roman castrametation. Proceeding to Tetbury, or the Tadbury of the Britains, where we again changed horses, and from hence to Cirencester. At Cirencester we dined. I trust I may be able to spend a day or two in this neighbourhood on my return; as the evening closed in I could make no observations on the country lying between this town and Oxford. At Farringdon, where we changed horses, they were ringing very merrily, preparatory, as the people informed us, to Christmas, but I am induced to think the favourite topic of the queen's triumph, as it is styled, had some share in it. It was nearly ten when I got to Oxford, and I immediately went to Exeter College where Mr. Johnson, one of the Fellows, was expecting my arrival, as I had promised to visit him when he was in Somersetshire, and he had procured apartments for me in College belonging to one of the Fellows who was absent. Sorry was I to find the spirit of insubordination had not subsided, and a grand riot was at that time going on in the streets, the towns people having openly insulted the gownsmen and pelted them with stones, insomuch that the Vice-Chancellor was obliged to be summoned to read the Riot Act. I understand that one of the Proctors before this had been struck by a radical and had his gown torn, and the clergy insulted by name. These are sad times! It was nearly twelve when I got to bed.

I was up before eight, and wrote my Journal. Afterwards took my breakfast with Mr. Johnson, who accompanied me to the library, garden, etc., of the College; he gave me also a key of the library, that I might take what books I wanted to my room, which I availed myself of. An old schoolfellow, named Rigaud, formerly of Exeter, but now married and living in the city, called upon me. I find he is assistant mathematical professor, also gives lectures on natural philosophy. We had some conversation respecting old times.

Afterwards I walked with Mr. Johnson up Heddington Hill to Joe Pullens tree, and returned to Oxford by a new walk made from thence along the fields. Dined in Hall, and afterwards went to the Common Room. In the evening we were summoned into the town, the gownsmen being assembled in great numbers to avenge the attack made on them by the radicals. We saw a crowd of gownsmen, chiefly undergraduates, passing in a compact body along Broad Street, into the Corn Market; several masters of arts and proctors were endeavouring to disperse them and send them back to their different colleges, which they did not seem much to relish; there was also a party of constables, with thick bludgeons, to act in case of necessity. There did not appear a large body of townspeople assembled, but I heard occasional hissing and cries of "Caroline," also, "now go to it." All authority of the proctors these radicals set at nought, one of them not only collared a proctor last night but kicked his shins at the same time. Indeed the Clergy more especially excite their animosity, and whenever they can find two or three stragglers they do not fail to abuse them, and even to strike if they can do so with impunity, but they are at heart so cowardly they will not contend with numbers. What will be the end of all this God only knows! but I clearly perceive it is not confined to Oxford, but the same spirit is universal through the country.

December 1

I accompanied Johnson to the castle, but we did not examine the interior. From hence we walked to Christ Church, passed the quadrangle and traversed the avenue towards Magdalen. I was sorry to notice some of the fine elm trees are beginning to shew the effects of old age, and in the course of a few years I should apprehend the beauties of this noble walk will be defaced. Having made a circuit of Magdalen walks we returned up High Street to Exeter, stopping by the way to look at the building going on at Hart Hall, which, when complete, will be called Magdalen Hall, as the society will be removed to this place. The streets were quiet, but I noticed a reward of twenty guineas offered for the discovery of the person who assaulted and violently beat the Hon. Mr. Barrington of Oriel. Another gentleman, of Trinity named Philips, has also been a great sufferer; but the man who attacked him has been taken up, and proves to be a servant of Dr. Barnes, of Christ Church. It is in contemplation in several of the colleges to send the young men home before the usual time in order to be out of the way of such outrages; indeed, as the spirit of the gownsmen has been roused, it will be difficult to restrain it from breaking forth.

The Rector of Exeter, Dr. Jones, called on me and invited me to dine with him Sunday. I dined in Hall, and met there Mr. Nicols, of Balliol, sub-Librarian of the Bodleian, also Rigaud, whom Johnson had asked to dine with him. The Rector also was of the party, and after dinner we had some interesting conversation on pursuits connected with my own in the common room. Mr. Nichols, who sat near me, has promised to shew me a manuscript of Tacitus, also all the old editions of the same author, so I look forward for much information. After tea we went to the music room, which was quite crowded, Miss Stephens,[1] from Town, having been invited as a performer at £35 an evening. Some very interesting music and Scotch airs were performed, and it was nearly eleven when it was concluded.

December 2

After breakfast I went into the Bodleian to consult the ancient editions of Tacitus. Mr. Nichols, the sub-Librarian, very obligingly brought me a manuscript copy, the only one in the Library, which probably was written about the fourteenth century. On leaving the Library I took a walk along the parks beyond Wadham College, which I perceive has been much improved in appearance since I was last in Oxford by taking in a small court in front, the walks from the parks have also been extended along the Common Fields to a considerable distance. This work was performed a few years ago, I understand, when the poor wanted employment, and must be of considerable advantage to the gownsmen as a gymnasium after the hours of study. Being engaged to dine with one of the Fellows, who had a large party, and the Rector, Dr. Jones, I was not able to arrange my transcripts taken in the morning as I had intended. The subject of the Queen formed the principal topic of conversation; in my own humble opinion one of the most dissatisfactory which can be adopted, and one of the least calculated to excite pleasurable or improving ideas; I wish it were entirely washed by the waters of Lethe from recollection. Of one thing I am sure, it will never find

---

[1] Catherine Stephens, 1794–1882, later Countess of Essex, well-known singer at Covent Garden, 1813–22.

sufficient interest in my mind to induce me to take any part in the conversation when it is on the tapis.

I was up as soon as I could see to dress, and went to chapel with Mr. Johnson, who I find is sub-Rector of the College. The first Lesson was read by one of the undergraduates from a brass stand in the area of the chapel. It would certainly be advisable amongst the several Professors in the University to have one established for elocution for *reading*, as I perceive this necessary attainment is as little attended to as ever, and is of more consequence to the community at large who are to receive instructions from the pulpit than can be possibly estimated. An unlearned man with a tolerable voice and proper emphasis will command more attention from a public audience than the most deep read scholar without this simple and easily attainable qualification. After breakfast I accompanied Johnson to St. Mary's Church, and heard a most excellent discourse delivered by Mr. Russell, a Fellow of Magdalen, on the text, "Grieve ye not the Holy Spirit." The church at St. Mary's I found very cold, though well attended. I sat on the seats appropriated to the masters in the body of the Church.

The Service concluded, Mr. Johnson walked with me to the bottom of High Street, but the day being raw and uninviting we returned soon to our rooms. At two we again attended the sermon at St. Mary's, which was delivered by another gentleman of Magdalen, whose name I could not learn. It was by no means equal to the discourse I heard in the morning, the arguments being trite and the style very inferior.

At five we dined with the Rector of Exeter, who has an excellent house fitted up in the quadrangle, and I spent a pleasant evening there.

Having been engaged to dine at the Rector's, and meet some ladies who were going to the music room, we were there at five, and in the concert room before seven in order to secure good places. The selection I did not altogether so much admire as on Friday. However, Miss Stephens was very powerful in several songs, especially that of "The Horse and his Rider shall be both thrown into the Sea." During the evening I was introduced to the Vice-Chancellor, whom I remember having before seen at Claverton, when on a visit to old Graves. He invited me to dine with him next Friday, with Mr. Johnson. It was past twelve when I got to bed.

December 5

I was up as soon as it was light and wrote my Journal, and afterwards took my breakfast in the bursar's room, where Mr. Johnson had some friends, amongst them Mr. Buckland, Professor of Mineralogy, who has visited our coal pits at Camerton and the vicinity. His opinion respecting the different beds of this vegetable matter is that it was done by a succession of deluges depositing these wood plants, etc., etc., of the country, the lightest parts being uppermost, the sand and heavier clay subsiding; that the marine strata imbedded over the vegetable was a continuation of the same process to the tops of the highest hills. After breakfast I continued in the Bodleian till three o'clock, making extracts from Dion, etc., then visited the crypt of St. Peters.

Having spent half an hour on the spot, I called at New College on Mr. Barter, the sub-Warden, but he not being in rooms I got the porter to accompany me to the chapel, which I never visit but with fresh satisfaction. The painted window by Sir Joshua Reynolds has certainly great merit; indeed the whole of the building is deserving of a more particular attention than I could bestow upon it. The evening being very dark and gloomy, and the time admonishing me to return to Exeter to dress. At five I walked again to New College, being engaged to dine there with Barter on the Gaudy or Founder's Day, which I was glad of having an opportunity of witnessing, as no gownsman who is not a Wickamist is permitted to partake of, but a general invitation is sent to them throughout the University. On going into the Hall I was much struck with the improvement it has undergone within these few years in the fitting up the interior. Barter having introduced me to the Warden, Dr. Gauntlet, I was placed near him at the head of the high table, accommodating, I should suppose, upwards of forty members and their guests, with a profusion of good things on the surface. As Mr. Buckland, of Corpus, had been a Wickamist he was there, and sat next to me. I was also introduced to a Mr. Shuttleworth[1] and Mr. Knatchbull, the latter Fellow of All Souls and cousin to Mr. Knatchbull of Babington. After dinner the grace was sung in the Hall by the

[1] Philip Nicolas Shuttleworth, 1782–1842, Fellow of New College and Warden in 1822; later Bishop of Chichester.

choristers and musical men attached to the College, and was very fine. We afterwards adjourned to the Common Room, where a table was covered with an excellent dessert, which extended the whole length of the room, a most comfortable apartment lighted by a chandelier containing four large globular lamps. The Warden and sub-Warden, as at dinner, sat side by side at the top of the table, and I was placed near Barter. I found the evening very pleasant, as I was left at full liberty to do as I chose as to wine, and the catches and glees were sung by members of the college and Mr. Johnson, Fellow of Magdalen, and were performed in the highest style, amongst them as a matter of course there was Dulce Domum and Omnibus Wickamisis. At half-past nine the company separated, and I returned to Exeter and accompanied Mr. Johnson to the Common Room where the feast of the Gaudy was concluded by a plate of oysters. This sumptuous living is very well for a few days, but would not exactly suit me for a constancy.

December 7

A little after one o'clock, having previously made an engagement with Johnson to walk to Iffley, we set out on the excursion, and were more favoured by the weather than for some days past. A little beyond Magdalen Bridge we passed a curious little church called St. Clement's, standing between the two London roads, the turnpike house built so close to it as to have the appearance of being part of the edifice itself. I could not help recalling the scenes of past times, when, some twenty-seven years ago, I walked slowly along this same road after having lost part of one of my fingers by the bursting of a gun whilst snipe shooting at Iffley, my companion, Stackhouse, having gone forwards to tell the surgeon, Grosvenor, to attend my arrival in my rooms. How different are my pursuits now to what they were then; an old church or a Roman pavement have more charms than any shooting or boating of which I used to be so fond. I am very thankful I still have sufficient health and activity to follow my other pursuits without inconvenience. The Church at Iffley certainly surpassed my expectations, and I do not hesitate in giving it the preference to any building of the kind I have seen. I only regretted I had not more time to bestow on the sketches I made. The interior of the church also possesses considerable attractions, but I could not pretend to make any sketch during so cursory a visit, and was obliged to content myself by taking the font, which is exactly similar in form to that of Winchester Cathedral, but without any ornament or sculpture. Having done as much as I could during the half-hour we stayed at Iffley we retraced our steps to Oxford, and, accompanied by Mr. Buckland, visited the gasometer, an apparatus for lighting the university. I find they consume on an average six tons of coal a night, which would be good custom for our pits if they were in our neighbourhood. On inquiring what was done with the tar when extracted from the coal, which at Bath is sold as paint for outdoor work, I found that, not being able to procure a proper sale for it in the neighbourhood, Dr. Kidd,[1] who is a great chemist at Oxford, has put them in the way of extracting still more gas from the tar, which will be as profitable as though they got a shilling a pound for the remainder. The coal is supplied from Bitton, between Bath and Bristol, and delivered at a guinea a ton. When examining the apparatus I was introduced to Dr. Kidd, who invited me to attend this lecture room tomorrow. I understand he is a very intelligent man, and a good scholar.

Our time had been so much occupied at the gasometer we were obliged to hurry back to dress for dinner.

December 8

After breakfast I went to the Radcliffe Library to meet Dr. Kidd who promised to shew me the laboratory and anatomical room at Christ Church. He was very clear in his explanations of the several subjects he submitted to my notice. The doctor also shewed me some chemical experiments in the laboratory in melting some small grains, a preparation, I believe, of lead. It produced a most beautiful vapour of a violet colour. Not being at all a chemist I could not enter into the process he next shewed me, of extracting different fluids from coal. The anatomical room contains human skeletons, also those of animals, and a numerous collection of different parts of human bodies preserved in spirits.

We dined with the Vice-Chancellor at Pembroke College, and met a large party, amongst whom was the Rector of Exeter and Dr. Williams, the botanical professor, Dr. Hall afterwards shewed me a very good collection of prints; there were also in the dining room two or three good portraits, one of Dr. Johnson exceedingly well

[1] Dr. John Kidd, 1775–1851; Regius Professor of Physic, 1822; Keeper of the Radcliffe Library, 1834.

done, though I understand it is a copy, also a print of old Mr. Graves, formerly of this college and a friend of Dr. Hall's.

December 9

I walked with Mr. Johnson to Godstow, passing through the village of Wolvercote. On arriving at my rooms to dress about half-past four I had an hour to spare, as I did not go to the Rector's of the college to whom I was engaged till nearly six o'clock. There was a large party of the heads of the university, that is the Vice-Chancellor, Provost of Oriel, heads of St. Johns, Jesus, and St. Alban's Hall, both the Proctors, and Mr. Michael Angelo Taylor,[1] who was very amusing the whole evening and occupied the chief post in the conversation. I remember this gentleman at the Installation of the Duke of Portland on account of the splendid diamond button he sported on the occasion. He was at one time a great favourite with the King, when Prince of Wales, but is not so just at present, and opposes most strenuously the whole of the measures against the Queen. It was past twelve before I got to bed.

December 10

This being the day appointed for preaching a sermon in Exeter Chapel in commemoration of the founder of the edifice, who left a bequest for the purpose, the service was not till ten o'clock instead of eight. Mr. Dalby, one of the Fellows, was the preacher, his text, "My house is a house of prayer." After the sermon the Sacrament was administered to the whole Society, not only gownsmen but the servants of the college, the Rector, Sub-Rector and two of the junior Fellows officiating in conveying the sacred elements to the persons, who continued in their seats.

I dined in Hall, the Rector being present, afterwards went into the Common Room till the chapel bell summoned us there. After the service I went into Johnson's room, and spent the evening with him.

December 12

I walked for an hour in the parks, but the day was damp and unpleasant. At half-past five I walked with Johnson and the Rector of Exeter to Corpus College, being engaged to dine with Mr. White-head, one of the Fellows, and met there Dr. Kidd, Mr. Buckland, Dr. Lawrence, Professor of Hebrew and Canon of Christ Church,

[1] Michael Angelo Taylor, 1757–1834, Whig politician.

Dr. Cotton, Librarian of the Bodleian, and several other gownsmen. I spent a pleasant evening, and did not get to bed till nearly twelve.

December 14

Occupied the whole morning in Johnson's room taking the sketches of the College Library, part of the Schools, Radcliffe's Library and St. Mary's, as seen from his window beyond the college garden. Although my time has been much occupied in more weighty concerns I find there (are) already nineteen sketches in my portfolio of Oxford and immediate vicinity, and I hope if the weather permit to enlarge the collection before my return to Bath and Camerton.

Dined with Mr. Dalby, another of the Exeter Fellows, a pleasant, sensible man who has, I understand, several friends and connections in the vicinity of Frome and Bath. Mr. Buckland was of the party. As we purposed setting out soon the following day I returned to my rooms at ten, and arranged for packing up my things.

December 15

I was up as soon as it was light, and occupied myself till breakfast time in taking some farewell memoranda of the College in whose walls I have experienced the greatest hospitality and kindness. After breakfast I called upon the Rector pour prendre congé. This gentleman's very obliging attentions I shall ever recollect with the warmest sensations of regard. At half-past ten, the chaise being at the college gates, Mr. Johnson and myself set off at a rattling rate for Woodstock.

December 18

Arriving at Cirencester we stopped to dine. Fain would I have devoted a day to this spot, as was our original intention, and then have walked along the Fosse to Bath, but the state of the weather and the roads prohibited the execution of the plan. At dinner several Oxonians, who had been outside passengers, joined our party, and so silent a meeting never did I witness. I understood from Johnson that this is now the usual mode with the gentry of that seat of muses not to open their lips to a stranger. This may be very prudent perhaps, but it certainly is not very entertaining. They did not observe such continence with respect to the several articles set before them, which they did not disdain opening their lips again and again to devour. On arriving at my mother's I found the whole party had gone to the play. I therefore occupied myself till bed time in writing my Journal and penning in the sketches I had taken.

December 20

Mr. Johnson and Mr. Holland dined at my mother's. The latter I found was one of the taciturn Oxonians I had met at Cirencester, but as this was only an esprit de corps it was entirely laid aside with the atmosphere of Bath. My boys arrived in the evening from Twyford.

December 21

After an early dinner I returned to Camerton in a chaise with my boys, found all well, and was pleased to learn that the workmen at Wellow had met with one hundred and five coins during my absence, also a variety of other articles.

Editor's Note.

In addition to Oxford, Skinner paid occasional visits to London. He records the following amusing incident when travelling from Bath in the York House Coach.

Our places were taken overnight in the York House Coach, which left Bath at six in the morning. We had a pleasant drive, the day being fine, to Marlborough, where we stopped to breakfast.

One of our fellow travellers was an Officer just returned from Ireland, another was an intelligent young man who had been abroad and seemed to have made classical observations on what he had seen at Rome, etc., but a third companion was of a different cast—vulgar in his manners and gross in his person. He declared, speaking of the Catholics, that in his opinion the Pope of Canterbury was as bad as the Pope of Rome, that both alike—a humbug; that every man ought to profess his own religion without the assistance of the Priest, and he would in half an hour settle all the differences between the Catholic and the Protestant, if it were only left to him, he would take away all the loaves and fishes about which they were quarrelling, and appropriate them to the uses of Government; that what had once been given by the people to the Church the people had a right to take away. I thought it necessary to say something to shew the fallacy of the arguments of this disciple of the Liberal School, both my companions joined in corroborating what I said, and the man sat sulky and surly till we got rid of him, much to our satisfaction, at Newbury—

I could not help reflecting on the opinion of the common people respecting the Clergy, and on the bad influence of those liberal opinions, as they are called, when put into the minds and uttered by the mouths of such low, unprincipled fellows as the one I have here had occasion to mention.

December 24

Did duty twice, and called upon some of the people; the typhus fever, I am sorry to hear, has made its appearance in the Village.

December 25

The Winter seems to have set in with unusual severity; the day before yesterday the boys picked primroses, and it was mild as in April; today it is insufferably cold, and there is every prospect of a hard frost. I walked round (the Parish) from Red Hill to Tunley, from thence to Cridlingcot, to distribute a portion of the Sacrament money, which amounted nearly to four pounds, there being upwards of forty communicants.

December 27

Mr. Johnson and myself took a walk along the Fosse beyond Radstock, in the morning. After dinner I accompanied him to the Old Down Ball, which was fully attended; I joined the agile throng, although my dancing days are over, yet in these times, it is necessary now and then to shew oneself to the gregarious herd, lest they invade one's sylvan haunts and gore thé stricken deer; indeed I had another inducement which was to meet Mr. Hoare and his family, whom I have not seen since their return from Wales. Henry Hoare accompanied us back to Camerton; it was past four when we got to bed.

December 28

Henry Hoare and myself set out to walk to his Father's at Southfield, preferring this mode, to that of going in the Car this cold weather; in our way, calling on the Boodles at Radstock, Mr. Boodle and his brother accompanied us with their guns as far as Kilmersdon. I took a shot en passant, in order to see whether I had forgotten to point a gun, and was the death of two larks; and we stopped a few minutes at Mr. Knatchbull's at Babington, as Mr. Hoare said he probably might meet us there on his return from Sir John Hippisley's, where he had slept, it was past four when we arrived at Southfield.

Mr. Hoare accompanied me after breakfast, on my return as far as Mr. Jolliffe's[1], we there separated, and I proceeded the shortest line by Writhlington to Camerton, meeting in the way, the woman I had sent home with my clothes; the distance she will have walked when she got home, cannot be less than twenty miles. I found the boys who came in the morning from Bath awaiting my arrival. After dinner I went into my Study, to compose myself and my Sermon, against the ensuing day, but although I kept a blazing fire, it was impossible to get warm.

On rising this morning, I found myself so hoarse I could hardly speak, and with great difficulty got through the Service; a bad beginning for the New Year.

[1] Thomas Samuel Jolliffe, M.P., 1746–1824, of Ammerdown.

1821

SKATED a couple of hours at Bengrove to teach young Jarrett and Owen, who for the first time put on skates.

Skated three hours after breakfast, then occupied the remainder of the day in drawing things brought from Wellow. Mr. Boodle, his mother and brother called and made us promise to dine with them tomorrow. I shall be heartily glad when Old Christmas limps away; now forty-eight of them passed over my head, I find, non sum qualis eram, in other words, it becomes daily more difficult to relinquish what I really like and engage in what I do not like, but not meaning actually to hermitize, must occasionally do as the rest do.

Preached a Sermon in Course as to the Preparation in Lent: visited the sick; and found myself heartily tired, having had a great deal of occasional duty; namely a Funeral, the administration of the Sacrament, and a Baptism, independently of two services and the visiting several sick, amongst whom Joseph Gould's wife, who seems in a very low nervous way.

I had intended riding to Southfield to call on Mrs. Hoare who has been for sometime an invalid, but the rain coming on prevented me. Occupied the morning in my map of Britannia Prima and Secunda, and the evening in reading.

I rode to Kilmersdon in the middle of the day, to sign a petition against the Catholic Claims; met the Rural Dean, Mr. Williams, and six other Clergymen; all signed the Petition, as several of our Division had done before at Frome; but Mr. Cookson of Writhlington did not choose to put his name for reasons best known to himself.

I staid at home the whole morning for the purpose of attending a Vestry called for the purpose of liberating Widcombe, who is in Shepton Gaol for embezzling the parish money. Mr. Fry attended on behalf of Mrs. Jarrett, and I requested to know whether he was authorised in taking any part in the Vestry, as he paid no rates in the parish, neither had any residence in it. He replied that he was perfectly qualified to draw up the resolutions and to put them to the vote, although he might not vote himself, yet Mrs. Jarrett would. I said I should protest against the Vestry as altogether illegal. About eight persons signed their names to the vote for the liberation of James Widcombe. Mr. Day and myself disapproved the measure; Mrs. Jarrett, being called by Mr. Fry, signed her name to the resolutions, and delivered a splendid oration, which clearly evinced the influence under which she acted. I entered a protest, and wrote a letter to the Chairman of the Magistrates saying that I should be ready to state before them my reasons for opposing the resolutions. This letter I gave to Mr. Day to deliver on his going into Bath on Saturday.

I did Morning Service at Radstock for Mr. Boodle, Mr. Burrard officiating for me. Mrs. Jarrett her son and daughter called after at the Parsonage, and asked the Burrards to dine with her on Easter Sunday, as they did not decline going, I was constrained also to consent.

I performed the service and administered the Sacrament at Radstock; Burrard did the same at my Church, and collected £3 7s. 0d. I read prayers in the Evening at Camerton and dined with Mrs. Jarrett.

Attended the Vestry to elect John Rossiter, Churchwarden. Hicks and Weeks were there, the former tolerably civil, but the latter much the reverse, doing all he could to provoke me when I taxed him with the impropriety of his conduct in having advised Widcombe to take the step he did and afterwards to wish for his liberation in opposition to all honesty and justice.

May 1

Accompanied Mr. Johnson and the young Jarrett to Wellow Pavement and Stoney Littleton sepulchre. Cottle had found two coins which I gave to my companions. Young Jarrett stayed till ten o'clock. It appears that Mr. Fry is no friend of his, at least he says so, sed haud credo quod dicit.

May 3

At seven I accompanied Captain and Mrs. Scobel to a Ball given by the gentleman of the Amicable Society at Old Down to the neighbourhood. Dancing continued till midnight when there was a supper, Catches, and Glees, etc., till three o'clock, when dancing recommenced, and we did not get home till five o'clock. I only danced two dances with Mrs. Scobel.

May 11

Having engaged to shew young Jarrett the beauties of Stourhead, we left Camerton at six and passing through Mells had a comfortable breakfast at the little inn at Nunney, after visiting the remains of the Castle. Sir Richard was not at home, but I showed my companion the interior of the interesting Mansion; we then walked around the gardens and visited the greenhouses, with which Jarrett seemed highly gratified, the great number and variety of the geraniums surpassing everything of the kind he had seen before. After our walk we returned to the inn to take luncheon and remounting our horses about five o'clock, rode along the roads to Alfred's tower which we climbed to the summit, the evening unfortunately proving hazy. Resuming our steeds we trotted home at a good pace and spent the evening with Mrs. Jarrett and family.

May 13

I did duty twice at the Church walked after dinner to Cridlingcot and called on several cottagers.

May 18

The morning proving clear and beautiful after the heavy rains of yesterday. I accompanied Mr. Richardson[1] on his return to Farleigh as far as Wellow: in our way thither speaking of the difficulty of procuring my arrears and the conduct of Sainsbury who engaged to

---

[1] Mr. Benjamin Richardson, Rector of Farleigh Hungerford.

pay £2 a month to Cruttwell in order to liquidate his debt and had not paid a farthing. He said such a man ought to be made an example of, for the sake of others, and persuaded me to let him inquire if there was any chance of arresting him to procure payment. I told him I should certainly feel no repugnance in making him smart, since his behaviour had been so improper. Still I did not like the idea of sending him to prison if he could not pay the debt, as I am afraid there were several creditors besides myself. He said he would ride over to Twerton and make enquiries and let me know the result at the Visitation.

May 20

I did duty twice at Camerton as our Bells are now taken down in order to prepare for the reception of the new peal from Town, the people were called to church by striking against the largest bell, which was suspended for the purpose from a beam in the belfry. John Boodle attended evening prayers and dined, but went away at seven as I wished to have the rest of the evening to myself.

May 28

Three new bells for the Church came from London, and were taken, by permission, through my new road thither.

May 31

After breakfast I rode to Timsbury and called on Mr. Barter and rode with him to Priston to see the new Parsonage House building by Mr. Hammond, who has succeeded Mr. Hunton in the Living. It appears to be erecting on a large scale and will of course exceed the estimate. We may truly say the Clergy in this neighbourhood are by no means sparing in expense when repairing or rebuilding their residences.

Within these few years a new Parsonage has been built at Timsbury, another at Dunkerton, another at Radstock, one at Writhlington. Ditto at Midsomer Norton, and my house at Camerton has not cost me less than £1,000 in repair.

June 1

This being the day appointed by the Archdeacon for his Visitation at Frome, I drove thither immediately after breakfast. Whilst driving by the lodges of Mr. Champneys[1] at Orchardleigh, melancholy reflections crossed my mind at the fate of its possessor. Certainly he has acted very improperly, but the weight he has to sustain has been much increased by the little minded rabble, who delight to tread to the dust a falling man, especially a superior.

The Visitation was well attended.

June 3

The bells all being dismounted, there was some difficulty in collecting the people, which was done in part by sending around the different houses, but several not receiving the summons, did not come in the morning, thinking from the circumstance of having no bells that I was engaged in doing duty elsewhere. Neither was the Church better attended in the evening on account of the rain, which was violent and almost incessant.

Memorandum. I find that White and some of the Singers assembled at the Camerton Inn were so riotous and contentious in their cups on Saturday night, that some were disqualified from appearing at Church on account of black eyes received in the affray; as the School sung in their stead, I shall employ them again next Sunday, and if the disorder be repeated, dissolve the Band altogether.

Widcombe wrote and expressed great contrition. The letter is accompanied by a few lines from Pitman, the gaoler at Shepton, stating that of late his conduct had been very orderly and proper, and that it was his belief he would, if released, return with advantage to society. I resolved to visit Shepton the following day, as I thought what Widcombe said might be true.

June 4

I mounted my horse and proceeded to Shepton, taking the line of the Fosse through Stratton. I perceived while passing that village that the Catholics settled at Downside House are building themselves a Chapel, apparently of large dimensions, attached to the house. What can be their object in enlarging their place of prayer, unless they have expectation of filling it? Had the Bill passed it would have afforded them greater facility, but as it is they will not be so tardy in their exertions so to do, as the Rector of Stratton, Mr. Tardiff,

---

[1] Thomas Swymmer Champneys of Orchardleigh House prosecuted the vicar and Churchwarden of Frome Selwood in 1808 to establish his hereditary right to appoint the sexton/sacristan [a relative]; he won the action.

will be slow in his endeavours to prevent them. The head and fellows of this College wear caps and gowns similar to the fellows of our universities. I am well aware of the indefatigable perseverance of these people; I well know their principles respecting us are unchanged. I know what had been done, and can anticipate what will yet be done by encouraging such sparks and fanning them into flame which, if it comes into contact with a combustible rabble, may yet renew the horrors of a St. Bartholomew's Eve or reillumine the bonfires of Smithfield.

On arriving at Shepton I immediately proceeded to the gaol, and was admitted to the gaoler, Mr. Pitman. On mentioning my wish to see James Widcombe he was introduced to the room, and I was quite shocked to see him fall down on his knees on coming in at the door. I begged him for God's sake not to employ that posture to any but to God alone, and to stand up. He said he was so sensible of the great injuries he had done to others, and to me in particular, he could not be too humble. I told him with respect to myself I freely forgave him, and should have visited him sooner and had procured an order for that purpose, but delayed coming on account of information received that he had conducted himself disorderly in prison. . . . Widcombe with many tears declared he would never fall into the same crimes he had done before, and that he prayed to God to forgive him, and he would in future do everything to compensate for the evil he had done if he were only liberated from that place of confinement.

Having given Widcombe a small sum for present use he left the room with every expression of gratitude, and I believe him sincere. Pitman asked what method I proposed pursuing to procure his liberation. I said I believed it was in the power of the Parish, if all were unanimous, to procure a rate off the debt. Pitman then took me round the several wards of the prison. In some felons were confined double ironed, in others debtors, in others persons for small offences. All lodging apartments and courts of the ward were kept so clean it was really delightful to see them. Many of the prisoners were engaged in works for the benefit of the prison as masons, blacksmiths, shoemakers. Five boys about the age of fifteen, who were confined for stealing wearing apparel, had profited so much under the direction of an instructor they were able to read and to repeat verses from the Sacred Writings, and say their prayers with great propriety. Indeed, the whole I saw convinced me of the great benefits to be derived from the internal regulations of our gaols, converting a temporary punishment into a lasting advantage, since many will receive such instructions, both as to manual and spiritual occupations, as will render them better men and more valuable citizens for the remainder of their lives. But in order to uphold this salutary discipline and instruction it is absolutely necessary that due authority be vested in the Overseer of the Gaol. Mr. Pitman seemed to be apprehensive that the charges now preferred against Mr. Bridle,[1] at Ilchester Gaol, might pave the way to insubordination in other prisons, and possibly it may. These human philanthropists who encourage the murmurs of inferiors against those in authority are not aware of the mischief they are doing.

June 5

After dinner we walked to the lower Coal Pits, where we met Mrs. Jarrett, who speaking of Widcombe, said she was his greatest creditor, as he owed her upwards of £100. I mentioned what the man had told me the day before, that he conceived if everything was settled after the sale of the hay, etc., there would be money over to be divided amongst his creditors. Mrs. Jarrett said it was a great lie, and that she could prove the contrary, that nothing was coming to him, that nobody had to do with her accounts, but Widcombe might see them. I replied that he had a right to do so, also his other creditors might require a statement from him of the assets. She said those who had money owed to them on bond might, but the Parish had no right.

Whitsunday, June 10

Got up early, wrote a sermon and preached on the Communion Service, which I also administered. Afterwards called on Mrs. Anne Stephens (at the Manor House.)

June 11

The Club walked to the Church through my grounds; but I had permission asked in form, to prevent a claim being established to have a public road. I should have gladly preached to them had their conduct been better than it has been of late but really they are incorrigible.

---

[1] Wm. Bridle, Gaoler and Governor dismissed from his post on being found guilty of certain charges brought against him by a prisoner in 1821. Published his defence Feb. 1822.

I called on Charles Dando of Cridlingcot, having heard there was an execution in the house, as he owed me upwards of £50. I fear there is but small chance for my money. I found him surrounded by duns, crying drunk! Mrs. Dando, who is a very well behaved woman, seemed much distressed. I begged her to keep her husband from liquor, as I was well aware, instead of raising his spirits it would have the contrary tendency; she said that was too true, that the following morning after he had taken too much, he was almost driven to despair.

I said I much wished to speak to him in his cooler moments, not as a creditor, but in my profession as I felt how necessary it was he should look only to that support which would not fail him; a support far beyond the world. The poor woman said she found it requisite to put on the best appearance for her husband's sake; but when she reflected on her large family, and the distresses which awaited them, it almost went beyond her. I said I would make a point of calling shortly again, but in the interim wished to speak to her husband at the Parsonage by himself, and again urging her to use her influence to keep him from liquor, I left the house.

I walked into the village before breakfast, the people are now all healthy, and the Colliers in good employ, most of them having a joint of meat for their Sunday's dinner. The new bells are now complete, and I heard them for the first time this morning: the Parish are to pay £92, independently of the old ones, which are to be recast.

As my boys were to come to Bath from Mr. Bedford's School at Twyford in the course of the evening, I determined on spending the day at my mother's.

After tea we drove to Camerton, as I had despatched my Mother's servant for my car in the morning. The boys were highly delighted whilst running over the premises before they went to bed. I am not yet too old to forget the sensation of the first day's return from School.

I drove Charles Warren in the car to Philips Norton, the boys accompanying us on horseback. Being in very good time, I made three drawings of the Old Inn, originally, I should suppose, a family Mansion, about the time of Henry VIII, but the present occupier gives it a much higher date, as she said, her Grandfather, a Clergyman had told her it was 800 years old.

This being the day appointed for the King's Coronation [George IV], it was ushered in by the ringing of the bells in all the surrounding Parishes, as well as our own. Two sheep were dressed for the Colliers at Camerton, and beer was supplied at the expense of their employers. The evening passes off without rioting or accidents in my Parish, but a man at Paulton was severely hurt by the bursting of a gun.

Having learnt that Charles Dando of Cridlingcot was killed by a fall from his horse whilst riding from Bristol, I walked to his house to enquire after his family. My anxiety on their account was soon relieved, as I found them sitting round a large table, regaling themselves, without any apparent emotion. Strange it is that the mind should become so callous and indifferent in the midst of the severest trials: their apathy at least, spared me the painful task I had anticipated in my walk to an expected house of mourning, therefore I had no reason to feel distressed on the occasion.

I was summoned this morning before six o'clock to bury Charles Dando, as the Clerk informed me his corpse had been brought to the Church by his son-in-law and friend, in order to avoid its being arrested, a writ having been sued, and was expected to be executed by persons brought for the purpose. After the grave was dug (for it had not been finished by the Clerk, who expected the funeral at one o'clock) I performed the ceremony, and I must say, with a considerable degree of mental sensation; knowing the whole career of this unfortunate man: the ruin he has entailed on his family; and what is still more dreadful, the dark prospect of retribution in another world. I could not but feel considerably affected, and after the Service was concluded, I addressed the bystanders, begging them to reflect on the serious warning that was held out to all of us to prepare for death; that we might not be taken away unprepared, as was the case of the poor creature we had just committed to the ground. They seemed to be very serious, I cannot but hope it may have its due influence. May it work for good, yet alas! like the moths which flutter round the candle, we see our associates destroyed around us, and madly rush upon the same destruction ourselves.

July 28

I was up early, and commenced writing the sermon I have for some time been reflecting on, respecting the awful departure of Charles Dando, on the text "Let us eat and drink for tomorrow we die." I had ever made a point during the whole of my Ministry, not to be personal in my sermons, and therefore should not mention any names or particulars, but I conceived it my duty not to let slip this solemn opportunity of impressing the necessity of reformation, lest we should be cut off suddenly, and it be too late.

July 29

I preached to a crowded audience, so great indeed, the Church could not contain them. They were for the most part attentive to the discourse, which spoke of Death and Immortality. I must say, I was not a little hurt at the total want of all propriety in the people after the Service was concluded, since instead of returning quietly to their respective homes in order to reflect on the subject I had taken so much pains to impress on their minds, and which had so fully occupied my own, they banish at once all serious reflection by a merry peal! This barbarous interruption to self communion however, I soon put a stop to in person, and gave orders to the Clerk to bring the Key of the Church in future to the Parsonage, as soon as the service was concluded. Alas! my labours in the Vineyard, I feel more and more convinced are of no avail: when I look for good fruit the grapes still continue to tart, they set my teeth on edge. Truly may it be said Society is now out of joint; what with Methodists, Catholics, Colliers, Servants and Attorneys, all domestic comfort is estranged: may better prospects brighten upon me.

August 21

Having promised last week, when the two Conybeares were at Camerton, to spend a couple of days with them at Bath Easton, and take Owen with me, I drove thither after breakfast this morning, stopping for an hour with my Mother at Grosvenor Place. Mr. Conybeare then accompanied me to Mr. Wiltshire's at Shockerwick. Mr. Wiltshire was from home, but we were indebted to his Sisters for the sight of four excellent pictures by Gainsborough in the Saloon and Drawing Room. Two are landscapes with Cattle, which for transparency of colour, might rival Claude; and the other portraits, a full length of Quin, most beautifully executed, the second, a fine half length of an old Clerk of Trowbridge. I have always been a great admirer of Gainsborough, but think these quite Chef d'oeuvres of his pencil. After enjoying this treat of modern production, we ascended the hill to the back of the house, under the escort of a servant, to examine the works of the Ancients.

September 1

It being a fine day, Owen and myself rode to Woodborough to call on Mr. Purnell, thence to Radstock, where we dined with the Boodles, and returned so as to save our light in the evening.

September 2

I performed duty at Camerton in the morning. Afterwards did duty at Timsbury in the Evening when I gave the same discourse on the subject of Naaman, the Syrian, having composed one for the purpose. Owen and myself dined at the ancient Manor House with Miss Palmer, her brother and Aunt, and took a walk before tea to the high hill beyond the house, called Timsbury Slade or Slate. As the horizon was remarkably clear, we were able to observe to the greatest advantage, the extensive prospects of this magnificent Panorama.

September 3

This being the day appointed for Owen's going to Bath on his way to Winchester School, I wrote letters to Dr. Gabell[1], Mr. Bedford, to little Joseph, to my Mother and Russell to send by Owen. After he was gone I spent some time in my study reading and writing the Journal of the preceding days. I had intended accompanying my boy to School myself, but not knowing how Mr. Barter might be circumstanced as to his return to Timsbury, and moreover, being unsettled in my Servants, etc., etc., etc., I thought whether to continue

[1] Henry Dyson Gabell, D.D., 1764–1831; Headmaster of Winchester College.

home, my brother (Russell) accordingly took upon himself the charge of introducing Owen to his former School fellow, Dr. Gabell; my best wishes go with him: were it not for the unfortunate impediment in his speech that he labours under, I would entertain no doubt of his passing through the School with credit to himself and to his Master; as it is, I shall be very anxious to hear how he is able to retain his situation in his class, as when at Mr. Bedford's at Twyford, he was much indulged with the privilege of writing any word he could not readily express; but this mode must not be allowed in a large School. I missed my young companion at dinner, and during the evening.

September 6

I was much concerned to hear in the course of the morning that Mrs. Scobell's house was burnt down at Hallatrow.

September 8

I received a letter from Owen, at Winchester, which by no means is satisfactory, as he complains of the impediment in his speech being so great as to prevent his saying his lessons, or keeping his place in his class; but I hope after he has been settled awhile, he will be more comfortable, as to himself, and in a few weeks, I shall be able to ascertain whether this obstacle will prove a bar to his passing through a public school, as I propose he should do.

September 10

I had intended riding to Mells, it being the day appointed for the Clerical Meeting; but the weather was so rainy in the morning, I gave up the idea of it, and occupied myself in reading Caesar's Commentaries, and some of Horace's Epistles.

September 11

Mrs. Clarke, the schoolmistress, called upon me after dinner to speak respecting her child who was to be christened next day. She told me she was sure that Mrs. Jarrett had promised to stand godmother to her child and that the youngest Jarrett was to be godfather, but she believed that the butler's wife, Mrs. Dilly, would answer for her, and that young Jarrett would answer for himself. I asked what age he was as I should not like him to stand under the age of fourteen, as it would be a precedent for all the colliery boys offering themselves on similar occasions. She said she did not know exactly his age, but could ask Mrs. Dilly and could let me know.

Having learnt that the people were anxious to bury Hester Nash immediately after Church in the evening, which was the time appointed to christen Mrs. Clarke's child, I went to speak to the mother about it. She told me she had enquired about the age of young Jarrett, and found he would not be fourteen till November, but that Mr. Dilly, the Butler, would answer for him as proxy.

Returning from their house I saw Harris, the Clerk, up in his plum tree gathering his plums. I told him I thought he had better take another time for doing that than Sunday morning. The Sunday before that I had seen him walking up the village with a great sack of bran or some kind of grit upon his shoulders.

William told me this morning that Hester, when returning from the Red Post with my newspaper, had been turned off the Plantation Road where she was walking, by the younger Jarrett, who first asked her if she was of Camerton, and upon her reply in the affirmative and that she worked for me, he told her that she had no more business in that road than she had in his mother's parlour. On my going to Hester to inquire into particulars she confirmed the above mentioned account. I then walked with my brother to speak to Mrs. Jarrett on the subject but on passing through the Churchyard, seeing she was engaged with the company who were walking with her before the house, we did not speak to her, but I wrote the following note on my return home:

"Madam,

My brother and myself intended to pay our respects to you this morning, chiefly on a matter of business, but on perceiving as we passed the Churchyard you were engaged with company we did not wish to intrude at that time. The fact is, having learnt from the person I sent to the Red Post this morning for my letters that your youngest son had warned her from the premises, I feel very anxious to know whether it is your intention to exclude me from the use of the road to the turnpike in the manner I have been accustomed to, or whether there has not been some mistake in what she told me or in what your son said to her. A line on this subject will much oblige."

Mrs. Jarrett in reply:

"Sir,

I am sorry any circumstance should have prevented my having the pleasure of seeing you and Mr. Russell Skinner to-day, and still more sorry to find there has been any mistake concerning your servant going along the Coach Road, and I beg to say that now as ever you and yours are most perfectly welcome to the use of that road. Upon enquiry I find that my son, Stephen, did speak to your servant, for which he deserves to be severely punished, and I am extremely angry with him for so doing. He says he did not know her to be your servant, and had often heard me complain of the mischief that is done to the woods and plantations, and also say that I must in future endeavour to prevent it by warning the people off. He thought to assume a very improper authority in this case. I hope you will be so good as to accept this excuse."

September 15

On going out of Church this morning I wished to give a letter I had received from Mr. Parfitt of Wells, to Weeks the Churchwarden respecting some returns that ought to have been made of the repairs of the Church, and which had been directed to me. Weeks, who had gone out of the Church before me, was in the field above Mrs. Jarrett's house, when Harris called him to say I wanted to speak with him. On my going to him and delivering the letter he looked at it and turned it about in his hand, and then said. "What is all this about? It is not directed to me," I told him if he read it he would know what it is about, and that as he was Churchwarden it behoved him to attend to it. At a Vestry next day Weeks asked me what was to be done respecting the letter. I told him I supposed it alluded to the repair of bells and belfry, which Gibbs had an injunction to get done when he was Churchwarden, and I recommended him writing immediately to Mr. Parfitt saying that the Parish would be ready to do what was necessary in the business, and only hoped they would stop proceedings. I also told him that the late Churchwarden had been ordered to get a table of affinity to put up in the Church. On his asking what that was for I said that it was to prevent people marrying within the degrees of consanguinity there prohibited, and it was the duty of the Churchwarden to present them. Someone remarked (I believe Mr. Day) that Farmer Hicks would then come under that law, as he had married his wife's sister, and also old

Gibbs for having married his niece. Weeks replied that could not be, for he was never married to her. I also told Weeks and wrote it down on paper, that he was to obtain a Proclamation against swearing, at Cruttwell's, and to pay him for the parchments that had been bought for transcribing the registers on.

September 17

On my speaking to Harris the Clerk, about not bringing back the Church Key to the Parsonage yesterday, after service, as I had given him positive order to do, and that if he did not obey my orders I would dismiss him from his situation, he replied, he did not care if I did so, that it was no great matter to him; that I had dismissed him once before and might do so again if I chose, saying I had never given any orders. I told him the reason I had dismissed him before was for being impudent, and that his tongue would get him into the same mischief it then did. He replied he was flesh and blood as well as myself, and if I spoke to him he should answer me. I said I perceived he was of the Radical School, and he might see whether that School would profit him. I would not permit that kind of insubordination as long as I had any authority. During the conversation I mentioned that he would be sorry for the part he had taken, that I ought to have dismissed him about the money he had neglected to pay the ringers, and I had other complaints made which I had not attended to, but I should not be surprised if there were some truth in them, namely, that some of my tools had been seen in his house. He then was in a violent rage, and wished to know who told me so, that he would compel me to bring them forward, that his character should not be taken away in that manner. I note down particularly the conduct of this man, as it is entirely of a piece with that of James Widcombe when he gave up the Clerkship, and I am certain I shall hereafter find that this fellow had been doing something very wrong, and had rather make a shew of quitting his office on account of what he may call a quarrel with the Parson, than be dismissed from it in a more public manner. So much for the moderns.

September 18

Mrs. Jarrett asked me whether I would not ride with her and her daughter to the Ploughing Match at Old Down; I accordingly did, and afterwards dined with her. Mrs. Jarrett said that we had misunderstood each other she believed, respecting the boys' Sunday

School; that she had never wished to interfere; and that she understood, for some reason or other, I had given up my attendance. I said that the present cottage was by no means a convenient or proper place for the purpose, and in consequence I had wished to see it put on a different footing; that as our population, owing to the Colliers, had increased so much in the course of these few years, and since the Church was not of sufficient size to accommodate all the Parishioners, I thought by stating these circumstances we might procure a sufficient sum of money from the fund established for the purpose of augmenting Churches, and be enabled to make an addition to our own of equal dimensions to the Carew's Chapel, which might not only accommodate all the boys' School, but be supplied with seats for the Farmers, leaving the body of the Church and the Gallery open to the Parishioners and the Colliers. That £100 I thought, would be sufficient for this purpose as the Windows would serve again, and the materials of the outer wall; that a small stove for warming the place in Winter, and freestone for the Arches might be an additional charge; but these could be dispensed with if the sum we received were not sufficient, or be added to by private subscription. She said she approved of the plan much, and should be very ready to lend it every assistance in her power.

After dinner, Harris came and made his excuse, pretending he did not understand, that he did not know that he was to bring the key when they were to ring for a Wedding, I again told him that it was his duty to bring the key at all times to the Parsonage as soon as the Service was concluded: that my displeasure was not merely on this account, but for his insubordination and insolence. He then promised he would never do so again and went away; affording another instance of an ineffectual struggle to produce something like order, without any prospects of accomplishing it; but it is not merely in the microcosm of this Parish that the lower orders are striving to supplant their superiors, the whole kingdom is exactly in the same situation, and in the course of a few years, the contest will be waged, not by abuse and oaths, but by swords and staves; but sufficient for the day is the evil thereof.

September 26

Having engaged some workmen to open a Tumulus on the hill to the south of Radstock Church, I went thither after breakfast and directed them. It was nearly six o'clock when our operations were over, and having paid the men for their labour, as well as the Victuals and drink they had (which remuneration generally falls to my lot, as a kind of appendage to the name of Antiquary) I went to Mr. Boodle's to dinner, and must say, I found far less to interest me in his Parlour than I had done in his Parish; sed de nihilo sit nihil; one may make something of a Barrow, but it requires a second Swift to extract anything from dry broomstick.

September 29

Mrs. Jarrett wrote to me for the character of William Keates who left my service a few days before, and having been tampered with, and the prospect of higher wages—she having offered him £18 a year, instead of the £10 a year which I thought quite sufficient as he was just out of his apprenticeship.

September 30

To my surprise I first heard that Mrs. Jarett had hired my servant William, but on a little consideration my surprise ceased. She wrote a note, and kindly recommended one of her coachman's relations to supply his place. This would be living rather too neighbourly. I understand well enough this intended kindness. What a world we live in!

I preached on the Gospel, No man can serve two Masters. I will myself endeavour to serve one, and wean myself from the world as much as possible. Had I been prosperous or brought forward in any public situation, it would, I fear, have made me presumptuous. Now I am kept low enough, God knows, for I have been trampled upon even unto the ground; but I will jump again more elastic from the tread. Si Deus nobiscum quis contra nos?

October 3

I find one of my female servants has entangled herself in a village connection, of which I clearly perceive the object. The man has no intention of marrying her. How often have I warned my servants from forming any acquaintance with the people around me, as it is sure to involve them in mischief. Indeed I have made it a rule when I hire a servant to state my dislike of their going into the village, but promised in lieu of it to permit them at stated times to go home to their friends, or occasionally to see them here. However, as I am about to change the whole set it is of no great consequence to myself.

October 4

I spoke to Mary and said she must make up her mind to drop all connection with Cottle while she continued in my service or leave it immediately; she is likely to become the tool of the designing set, with whom I have had so much to do, but she would not take heed.

October 5

Cottle, to whom I wrote yesterday to come to the Parsonage to know whether he had any serious thought of marriage, never made his appearance, and I am perfectly satisfied I am not wrong in my conjectures concerning him and his employers. I find the connection has been going on upwards of three-quarters of a year: time will discover the plan and arrangement.

October 7

I had two services, two Christenings, two Churchings and the Sacrament at Camerton. Collected £2 9s. 6d. I am happy to find I can now perform these additional services without inconvenience to myself, which I could not do a year ago.

November 4

Mrs. Jarrett, who was not at Church, being indisposed, sent a message by her son that she wished to speak to me, on going to her house she informed me that she had determined to dismiss Clarke the Schoolmaster, and his wife who took care of the Girls' School, from the house they occupied: that she could not bear having such disturbances and quarrels kept up in the parish as had been of late; that she knew and could prove that Clarke was a liar, a swearer, a thief, and that his wife had taken a false oath respecting Harris's wife before the Magistrates, and that therefore neither one nor the other was fit to superintend the school. In reply I said that I was sorry the quarrel had gone to such lengths between the Harrises and Clarkes. I did not pretend entirely to exculpate the latter, but with respect to the former I thought them the more to blame, since I myself endeavoured to persuade Harris to pay the tithe to Clarke and save all unnecessary trouble, but he would not do so: that the summons for Clarke's wife respecting the saucepan, which she had alluded to, I believe was revenge for having been obliged to pay the tithe. Mrs. Jarrett said she certainly would dismiss the Schoolmaster and his wife from their present residence, and should give orders for them to quit in six months and remove them from the parish, as they were likely to become a large and expensive family. She also said she thought it better for me to put a stop to his being a Schoolmaster at once. I replied I could not think of doing this, as I had maintained a Sunday School ever since I came to Camerton, and should not like to set it aside even though it were not conducted as I could wish; that if the plan were adopted which I had recommended of building a proper school house, or of enlarging the Church for the purpose, I would pledge myself to superintend it or to see that the scholars were properly taken care of. Mrs. Jarrett then asked what objection I had to the present place. I answered I had before stated my objections, which I thought could not be remedied. In the first place the cottage was too small for the number of boys who might be sent there, in the second the family residing in the house occasioned serious interruptions in the case of illness or the woman's confinement and in the third—it was not regulated according to the forms of other schools, which made it as difficult for a master to know what was required of him as for the scholars to know what was expected from them. Mrs. Jarrett then said she could never consent to having any connection with the National School: she had learnt from very good authority that it would give the Government some hold upon her property, which she would never consent to: that with regard to the enlargement of the Church, she thought a gallery might be carried along the nave, which would answer all the purposes of giving room. She had an objection of making the school in the Church, as I first proposed, since the boys would be continually doing mischief in the Church and playing about in front of her house. I said this might be easily remedied by having the entrance to the schoolroom on the south side of the Church, so that the boys would not at all come in front, and that they would both come and go to the school along the new walk I had made without being the smallest inconvenience to herself. This plan she said demanded further consideration.

Gibbs and Weeks behaved most shamefully in every respect during Widcombe's confinement, and injured him even with his wife as was reported. Charles Dando, another friend in Widcombe's prosperity, during his licentious career was killed by a fall from his horse, July 22, 1821. By him I lost £61, besides what was due for the last half-year £76 more. By Gibbs I lost £26, by Widcombe upwards of £15. Weeks afterwards spent part of the money he had collected as Churchwarden for recasting the bells, and it was not without the greatest difficulty that he was compelled to refund what he had spent. So true it is that by the company he keeps you shall know a man.

I was occupied after breakfast for a while in perusing Dr. Moysey's Charge to the Clergy of his Archdeaconry, and Mr. Baines[1] the Catholic Priest's reply to those parts he conceived reflected on his Church. I must confess I found little to approve in either composition. The first being written too loosely for publication, and the latter far too personal and abusive. More than once he openly accuses the Dr. of Falsehood and slander, and at the same time makes some round assertions which with greater justice, must implicate himself in the same censure. The times are strangely out of joint, but I cannot think that polemical controversies will mend them. The truth Mr. Baines for a certainty proclaims, namely, that all the dissenters are against the Church. Still I cannot think the Catholics are less so.

Respecting Feare, the Bailiff of the Coal Works, who wished to make it appear as though the Rector of Camerton required tithe for their gardens after having been paid for them by the Proprietors of the Works, in order to make him unpopular in their eyes.

Clarke, the Schoolmaster, to whom I had given the tithe of the gardens as his salary, called to say that Mr. Feare had forbidden the colliers to pay their accustomed composition for the tithe of the grounds they occupied, under the plea that they were included in the composition of £30 paid by the Coal Company. I went immediately to Feare's house and shewed him my tithe book as drawn out by Cruse, the surveyor, in 1807, wherein the gardens are reckoned separately from the other grounds occupied by the Coal Company, and as such had paid tithes for several years past. On asking Feare whether he acted on his own authority in giving notice to the colliers or on that of his employers, he told me on his own. I then asked on what grounds. He said he had been informed by Mr. Soper the composition of the farm occupied by the Coal Company included all the gardens. I asked if he conceived Mr. Soper's intelligence to be correct why did he not act upon it immediately that Soper turned out of the works nearly three years ago, and said that if Clarke, the Schoolmaster, received any detriment in the collection

[1] Reverend Peter Augustus Baines, D.D., 1786–1843, later a Roman Catholic Bishop and founder of Prior Park College at Bath.

of his dues from what he, Feare, had chosen to report I would bring an action against him for damages. The man seemed disposed to be very insolent. One of the under bailiffs said that he was ready to pay his dues on my shewing him the separate entries, and some of the colliers also said they were ready to do so, but did not like to pay twice over. A man standing by said that it was a great pity there were either tithes or taxes. I replied that it was necessary there should be such paid, and the poor had much less to complain of in these respects than those above them. The man continued he knew no use of parsons. I then told him there was some use in striving to prevent people being as bad as himself, that though some might not attend to their exhortations to do what was right, others did, but if all the world were left to go on as they pleased things would be much worse than they were at present, which indeed was bad enough. I am more and more convinced that undue influence has been exerted of late by setting the common people against me, but these are only the tokens of the times and clear indications of a decline.

November 22

Being engaged to meet Feare before the Magistrates to prove my title to the tithe of the colliers' gardens, which were originally taken from the farm, I went to Bath soon after breakfast. Sir Robert Baker and Mr. Clarke, the Mayor, were the only magistrates present. On producing my Tithe Book the magistrates told Feare he had no plea whatever in withholding from Clarke the dues which I have given him, and asked him his motives for so doing. The man replied he wished to see Mr. Skinner's agreement with the Coal Company, and that was the reason he desired the men to withhold their payments. I said his reason was to set the colliers against me and render unpopular a measure which I intended for their good, as Clarke, the Schoolmaster, had his tithe for keeping a Sunday School to which all the colliers might send their children. On leaving the Hall I told Feare I was convinced that he meant to set the colliers against me: that it was most impolitic his so doing, since I had always been very careful to advise this body of men to be obedient to the agents employed to superintend them, and that I well knew the evil of stirring up sedition among so numerous a class of men, and that even when they made their just complaints against some of the late bailiffs who had defrauded them I still recommended their obedience for the general benefit of society. He said he was sure he had never meant to set the people against me, and should not in future induce them to withhold their dues.

December 21

Mrs. Jarrett called, and seemed to make such a point of my dining at her house to meet Sir Charles Rich I did so. Music and cards occupied the evening, Mrs. Jarrett gave me a card for a Ball and Supper she had fixed for the second of next month, and invited all her acquaintances,—Timeo Danaos et dona ferentes, but as I have no reasonable excuse for non-attendance, fit sicut petitur.

December 24

The day being rainy I was principally occupied in attending to lessons with the boys. Owen I set to translate a work on Greek Antiquities, which was published about a century since in one of the German Universities, and seems a very useful little treatise. I was glad to find he was able to do his task without difficulty: he is moreover improved in his hand writing, which is somewhat the more extraordinary, as I find they never have any instructions in writing at Winchester. Joseph is giddy, but does not want abilities. I set him to translate the first Chapter of the Selecta e Veteribus concerning the nature and attributes of GOD, and I purpose his continuing his translation into English every day; as Latin exercises and repetitions form so great a part of the business at School, it is necessary to attend to the writing of English which is best learnt by translating from the best Latin and Greek Authors.

Towards the middle of the day when it cleared up, I sent them to take a ride on Clan Down.

December 25

I performed a Morning Service, and afterwards rode with the boys on Clan Down for a couple of hours. After dinner we went to Mrs. Jarrett's, as the young people had prepared some Christmas sports, Snap Dragon, etc.

December 28

A very rainy day, and all the country inundated. Mrs. Jarrett and family spent the evening with us at the Parsonage.

December 30

Still very miserable weather. I performed duty twice at Camerton. My text to-day, at the conclusion of the Year, "So teach us to number our days, that we may apply our hearts unto wisdom".

1822

I CALLED at Mrs. Jarrett's at breakfast time to ask whether I could accommodate her with anything for her party, to which all the country are invited; so true is the old adage, if you pipe you will not want dancers. In the present age they are all merry dancers, from the Ministers of State to the Country Parson and apothecary: no sooner is the sound of music heard than all are on the alert. We must not say like those engaged in Holbein's Dance of Death since that would be ominous.

When skaters glide over the smooth surface of a still, deep pond perhaps it might detract from their satisfaction if they bore in mind that one small aperture might let in the grim tyrant. Singular cogitations on the eve of a ball! but I had rather commune with my own heart in my chamber and be still than join in the uproar I am about to partake in. These caustic reflections having been shaken off, I accompanied Mr. Hoare's two sons and young Newman, who had all dined with me, at eight o'clock to the Manor House, and found about thirty people assembled. The number soon increased to upwards of eighty. Having procured my young friends partners I sat down to view the exhibition of quadrilles and country dances: a just epitome of the progress of life, the young and active were all bustle and animation, shewing off themselves to the best advantage, anxious to please and to be pleased, whilst those of middle age like myself who had retired from the crowds were content to be spectators only. I could not help smiling to observe some of my brethren of the cloth paying close court to a certain baronet who lives not far from Ston Easton, because he had a Sir (a vox et praeterea nihil) placed before his name. If these Reverences had the same title before their own it might prove equally imposing on the multitude. I was highly amused at this moving picture, this microcosm in a nutshell; it reminded me of the anthill recorded in the Rambler, each striving to be thought something and somebody like the Lady Ant with the white straw in her mouth.

At one time I entered into conversation with a good rational man, a brother clergyman, who seemed to enjoy the passing scene as much as myself; I may indeed say we were both highly entertained. I did not join the dancing parties but I had ample food for ears and eyes, and in my turn, I doubt not, produced a similar supply for tongues.

At twelve, supper was announced, and a grand display exhibited in an upper apartment. The Landlady of Camerton in appropriate costume! her voice and unique expressions occasionally being elevated above the hum of the eaters of tarts and cheesecakes, chickens and cold fowls. The dancing recommenced after supper, and I longed to get home, but as my companions were engaged in dancing I sat down to a card table with Mr. Knatchbull and played two rubbers, after which it being five o'clock, the company began to disperse, and, having wished a good evening to the Lady of the Mansion, we walked to the Parsonage, the clerk, Harris, officiously lighting us home in order, I verily believe, to hear what remarks might have been made by the company, and report them at headquarters. How unpleasant it is to have been dragooned into distrust, but I cannot help feeling as I do after what I have known and do know.

The day being very rainy and unpleasant I therefore went into my study for an hour, and afterwards took some exercise with my turning lathe; the young men then looked over some of Boydell's Plates of Shakespeare's Plays. As they were fatigued after the exertions and short repose of the preceding evening the whole party went to bed early.

January 10

I rode—to Timsbury, and called on Mrs. Palmer, and Captain Parish;[1] dined and spent the evening with the latter and met an intelligent man, rather a rarity in our parts.

January 12

I rode to Meadgates; in my way through the village, met Mrs. Jarrett, or rather she called after me, as I had not observed her whilst standing at the door of Farmer Keel's house. She said, she wished me to bear in mind that Clarke, the Schoolmaster was to leave her house at Lady Day, as she was determined to keep him no longer, as he was a liar, a drunkard, and a thief. I replied, even if it were as she said, it would be difficult to find a better at Camerton. —In order to grasp at too much authority, this virago will defeat her own ends.

[1] Capt. John Parish, R.N., J.P., 1778–1837.

January 20

I performed duty twice at Camerton. Mrs. Jarrett I find continues her plan of coming only once to Church, and it seems to influence the people, as there is a fashion in religion, as well as in other matters.

February 3

I called at the Manor House with the boys after Church, who took leave previously to their leaving home. Mrs. Jarrett "cum fronte simulate," but as the old epitaph says, "her smiles I court not, nor her frowns I fear;" but I must confess she is somewhat an obstacle to professional exertion and will I fear continue so.

February 11

Mr. Barter called before dinner; he told me, Mrs. Jarrett had agreed to let the Methodists put in two fresh Lives in the Meeting House: and afterwards forgave the sum they stipulated to pay: the transaction was conducted with Bush of Midsomer Norton, whom she went over to hear preach at Red Hill. I am convinced she follows the same policy as her father, in encouraging these people, and that from no very praiseworthy motives: but time will shew.

February 13

After my walk to visit the Glebe House and new Barn I had some conversation with Clarke, the Schoolmaster who said he was about to leave the house he occupied of Mrs. Jarrett according to the notice he had received, and wished me to lend him my cart to take his things to Cridlingcot, which I of course did. I understand that Mrs. Jarrett's butler's brother's wife, whose husband is servant to her son, is to be placed in the house as schoolmistress in the place of Clarke's wife. Indeed these people have been hardly dealt with, as far as I am able to see; the woman was attentive in her superintendance of the girls, and the man, with proper over-looking, might have done as well for me as another schoolmaster. He had his faults, but not those glaring ones Mrs. Jarrett represents. The man told me there would be no peace in the place so long as Mrs. Jarrett listened to every idle tale that was told her. He seemed to intimate that the Cottles, and Fear, the bailiff of the coal works, had great influence with her, but most of all her servant, Dilly. But this is all folly. If I listened to it I should be as bad as she. So far I feel very sore. A school, which I myself established under the idea of instructing the colliers' children on my first coming to Camerton upwards of twenty years ago and which I have supported at my own expense, owing to the interference of Mrs. Jarrett is now entirely laid aside, since I have no place to put a schoolmaster in nor a house for the children. However, I have the satisfaction of knowing, although my endeavours have been frustrated, *I still have endeavoured.* Mrs. Jarrett told Mr. Barter that I had said Clarke should continue schoolmaster in opposition to her, and that I would give him my Glebe House to live in. I am inclined to think she magnified her own suspicions into realities, but it is every way false that I ever said so, or had any such idea, as my Glebe House is appropriated to the use of the person who takes my tithe, and independently of this I could not get any scholars unless Mrs. Jarrett permitted the parents to send their children, as they were mostly her tenants. It is an absurd idea that I should keep a school in opposition to her. Surely, if any improvement were made in the parish she would derive more benefit from it than myself, if we consider ourselves alone. The real motive of all that has been done or thought is this: Mrs. Jarrett cannot bear a divided authority; her disposition like that of Catherine of Russia, is truly despotic.

I am sick of the vineyard it is my lot to cultivate. Whatever plants are put into it die away and wither, and without I could cultivate others in my study, which do yield me fruit, I could not exist under such a continual state of irritation and disappointment.

February 17

There was a Wedding here just after breakfast after the established custom of the Parish; that is, a little out of season. Mrs. Jarrett and her family were at Church morning and evening; but we did not speak. I walked round the Parish after Service, in order to see they were quiet—I feared there might have been some disturbance on account of a Show brought from Bath Fair; but I can do nothing, as there is not a single person in the Parish on whom I may depend for assistance in the discharge of my duty, and the preservation of order, and Mrs. Jarrett will find she is ill advised, to lower my legitimate authority amongst the common people.

March 4

Being engaged to attend a clerical meeting at Mells, I set off soon after breakfast purporting to visit Mr. Hoare on my way, arrived at his house at Southfield at eleven and continued with him till two, when I proceeded to the meeting. It was thinly attended, there being only the Rural Dean, Mr. Williams, Mr. Richardson, Mr. Hoblyn, Mr. Ireland, Mr. Sainsbury and myself. I am inclined to think it will dwindle away; Mr. Boodle and Mr. Edwards mean to withdraw their names. Returned to Mr. Hoare's to drink tea, and to sleep.

March 5

Mr. Hoare accompanied me after breakfast to Nunney to call on Mr. Ireland, and to Marston to visit Mr. Mead. I cannot say the situation of Lord Cork's[1] house possesses much attraction, as it looks over a flat expanse formerly marsh, from whence it derives its name. In ancient times it formed part of the great Forest of Selwood. We met Lord Dungarvon, eldest son of this nobleman, who is, I believe, unfortunately subject to epilepsy. From thence we continued our walk to Frome, and attended a sale of books, which went off very dear apparently a bookseller's job. I called to ask the price of three Chinese paintings, but could not get the owner to fix any, they being curious indicia of the manners of that singular people. I offered two guineas for them, which was not accepted. We returned to Southfield to dinner, and I slept there.

March 6

A very rainy morning. However, I was obliged to return home, Mr. Hammond, of Priston, having engaged to dine with me. On my way from Southfield I stopped for an hour at Mr. Hoblyn's at Whatley Parsonage, who directed me a short cut across the fields to get into the Mells road, but the brook in the Murdurcombe valley was so swollen by the rain I could not get my horse through, and was obliged to go around, which lost much time. Near Babington I met Mr. Knatchbull who told me he had been to Camerton to ask me to dine with him on the following day: indeed he had previously written a note which I did not receive. Mr. Hammond dined, and spent the evening with me.

March 7

I dined at Babington, and met Colonel A'Court,[2] Messrs Paget,[3] Coney, Gooch, and Hoare of Southfield, played at cards and slept there.

[1] 8th Earl of Cork and Orrery (1767–1856) of Marston, Nr. Frome.
[2] Ancient family, formerly Lords of the Manor of Rodden; kinsman to Lord Heytesbury.
[3] John Paget of Cranmore [1761–1825].

After breakfast Mr. Knatchbull showed us an ancient bed which belonged to the Hungerfords of Farleigh Castle, the bedposts supporting an oak canopy are very massive, formed of the same material and carved in rather tasteful manner. He also exhibited quantities of the same sort of carved work, chiefly collected from an old mansion in the vicinity of Shepton, a great deal of Old china purchased by the late Mr. Knatchbull, with other curious articles occupying a room above the coach-house. Having taken leave of my obliging host (who is what a country gentleman ought to be, kind-hearted and willing to make himself serviceable to those around him) I returned to Camerton. The rain continued to fall fast the whole way, so that I was quite wet through when I arrived.

I had the unpleasant intelligence at breakfast that Bull's son had broken his neck and one of his ribs in the pit the evening before. I visited him after Church, and found his limbs paralysed in consequence, and there seems but small hope of his living, indeed under such circumstances it is hardly desirable. The poor creature was surrounded by women, who came out of curiosity, I fear, rather than with a wish to comfort him. Whilst I was reading to him the apothecary arrived, and as he was obliged to perform an operation I left him, promising to return after Church. After Church I went again to the poor man, and found his house crowded as before. I took the liberty of recommending them to disperse and leave him quiet, but I suspect that, being Methodists, a kind of prayer meeting will be held in order to ensure, according to their ideas, the poor sufferer a passport to heaven.

I heard the children say their Catechism before Church, and afterwards walked to the poor man, Bull, who had been lingering the whole week in great pain. He was evidently dying when I saw him. I read the 23rd Psalm and some of the prayers, but he could not enter into any kind of conversation; it will be a most happy release when it pleases God to take him. The Methodists have been constantly with him; but in this instance I think they have been of service.

I walked to Mr. Boodle's where I took an early dinner and afterwards strolled with him and the ladies to the new Coal Works in Hewish, the valley leading to Kilmersdon. On our return we visited a poor man of Radstock parish, who had his back broken in the Coal Works in the same manner as Bull, who has lately died, but this man did survive the accident nearly seven years; the whole of the extremities are paralysed and without feeling, and one of his hips dislocated; he can only continue in one position, namely, lying on his back, and has of course no occupation to beguile time but that of singing. What imprisonment can be equal to such confinement as this?

I drank tea and slept at the Boodle's playing the accustomed game of cards as a substitute for conversation.

I composed a sermon on the subject of sudden death and the necessity of habitual preparation, as another man of the name of Cromwell lost his life during my absence by the rope coiling round his body in the Coal Pit, which killed him instantaneously. I walked after tea to see his Widow who is a poor helpless creature near her confinement. The man is to be buried tomorrow.

I was interrupted in my studies by Parochial concerns: Joseph Goold, I yesterday heard, after spending his time and money in Bath for two days, returned home, beat, and misused his wife in so dreadful a manner, that she left the house, having intimated that she should destroy herself: I was applied to by J. Rossiter and Farmer Collins, and immediately sent Smallcombe in quest of the woman: also wrote a letter to her father at Frome, stating the deplorable situation his daughter was in, and the danger of her being driven to some desperate act, in case he did not protect her. This morning I learnt that Mrs. Goold had walked all the way to her Father's and that he had received her, and promised to write shortly to me on the subject.

This being Good Friday, I performed Service in the morning, at Camerton, and in the evening at Priston, and visited a poor man, dying of a consumption.

April 6

In the course of the morning, having received a very imperfect account of agistments from Day of the Home Farm, I wrote him the following letter.

"Sir,

I am sorry so much unnecessary trouble is occasioned both to you and myself, by misapprehension of the business between us. The time you specified for my settling with you yesterday (Good Friday) is not generally appropriated by the Protestant Church to secular purposes, although the common people sometimes assume the liberty of performing their usual occupations on that day.

> I remain, Sir,
> > Your obedient servant,
> > > J. SKINNER."

N.B. Mr. Day is a Catholic.

April 7

I did duty at Camerton in the morning, and administered the Sacrament, collected £3 3s. 0d., in the whole, Mrs. Jarrett's family attending.

Goold's wife came back from Frome, and he left her in a sad state, and went himelf to the Public House; I gave Keel's boy sixpence to go and fetch him back.

April 20

As I wished much to have an interview with Mrs. Goold's Father at Frome, in order to explain the actual state of his daugher, and endeavour to arrange something for her future benefit, I rode thither after breakfast. The old man spoke very rationally, and indeed feelingly on the subject, saying he had already advanced Goold upwards of two hundred pounds in money; besides giving clothes and provisions: that he was convinced he would spend every farthing he could lay his hands upon, and begged I would take charge of two pounds, to give his daughter five shillings a week. I told him I could myself advance that sum, and could settle with him when I came to the Visitation at Frome; still I feared his donation would be of little service, unless it was bestowed on some proper person to look after his daughter, since if the husband got it, she would derive no possible benefit; and under present circumstances, she was not in a situation to take care of any money herself: that she was quite unable to direct herself properly; But I hoped if her mind were kept calm, she might still recover, and urged strongly his receiving her again; but both he and his wife seemed decidedly against this, however, I may be able now that I have introduced myself, to do something in future.

I called at the Manor House, Mrs. Jarrett having expressed a desire to have some particular conversation. She began by saying, she supposed I had remarked that there was something on the tapis between Mr. Gooch[1] and her daughter; in fact they were shortly to be married; and as of course she was much interested to retain her daughter near, she had a proposition to make, which she hoped I should not feel offended at, even if I did not agree to it: if I had any thoughts of leaving home for a time, or indeed if I wished to relinquish the Living altogether, on a fair equivalent to be given, she should be very glad to treat for the same; she well knew I had met with much uneasiness from the people of the Parish, and thought it might tend to my future comfort if I resided elsewhere: she wished to prevent all unpleasant feelings between the Farmers and myself, and would, as before stated, enter into any arrangements on the subject I might approve of, if I would relinquish the Living altogether, so that Mr. Gooch might be presented to it, she would make it worth my while. I replied that was entirely out of the question, even where I so disposed, it would not be in my power, without incurring simony; neither could Mr. Gooch take preferment on those terms, without equally offending.

I might say, the misconduct of the people had made me so uncomfortable, that I should have no objection to leave them at any rate for a time; that the only way in which this could be effected, was by appointing Mr. Gooch my resident Curate: letting him the Parsonage whilst Mrs. Jarrett herself might have a lease of the Tithe, but I could not make up my mind to any arrangement on this head, without consideration: that I expected Mr. Peter Hoare at Camerton, and would talk over the business with him, as a person whom I might safely consult, and on whose advice I might rely. Mrs. Jarrett then said, she hoped I would state my terms, etc., in writing, before Tuesday as she was then going to Town.

I returned in order to receive Mr. and Mrs. Hoare at the Parsonage, they came from Southfield about five o'clock. On opening the business

[1] Rev. William Gooch, d.1876, a Canon of York.

to Mr. Hoare, he agreed that if I had really made up my mind to withdraw from my Parishioners, under present circumstances, he did not know but he should advise my so doing.

April 28

As Mrs. Jarrett had commissioned her son to ask me to dine, on the plea of meeting Mr. Gooch, it being fixed they were to leave home on Tuesday; I went there at six o'clock. Mrs. Jarrett very gracious. Upon my admiring some gooseberry wine at dinner, she turned to the Butler, and ordered him to send half-a-dozen to the Parsonage the following day, which I did all I could to decline, under the old feeling, Timeo Danaos et dona ferentes.

May 24

As we had agreed over night to visit Stanton Drew, I drove to Radstock to breakfast; we afterwards proceeded on our way in the car and Boodle's gig, taking cold provisions with us. Passing beyond Hallatrow, we stopped to visit the Cascade, and make sketches. Thence we proceeded through Temple Cloud to Clutton. Continuing along the Bristol road, we had a most beautiful and extensive view of the country in the vicinity of that City. About ½ mile to the left of the turnpike, having put up the horses, we walked to the Circles at Stanton, through the fields, and I had the satisfaction of seeing the whole party took an interest in examining them. When the Country in the vicinity was covered with wood, and the white robed Druids stood in solemn silence, each one by his stone of power in the centre of this gloomy recess, the scene of course was more impressive; fancy alone can now portray the picture.

Having finished our observations, and made sketches for the ladies, as memorials of the interesting spot, we returned to Stanton-wick, to partake of the cold repast we had brought with us, which was augmented by some eggs and bacon and diluted by excellent cyder, doubly estimable during the excessive heat of the weather. About five o'clock we left our Caravansary, and drove to Hound-street Park, in order to visit the magnificent seat of General Popham.

Although upwards of Thirty thousand Pounds were expended on the Mansion and grounds, not many years since, the whole is going fast to decay; there being no inhabitant on the premises, not even a person to open the windows. The noble piece of water is covered with weeds and long grass; thistles and nettles cover the walks: I can only regret these things as a passing traveller; but to those who reside in the vicinity, the blockade of such a residence as this must be severely felt, especially when all this money collected on the estate is compelled to flow into other channels. The evening was in every respect beautiful, and the setting sun one of the grandest I almost remember to have witnessed. We arrived at Radstock a little after nine highly gratified by our excursion.

June 5

Before breakfast I sent my servant, Heal, to see whether the coal barge I had ordered to be prepared to convey the ladies to Combe Hay was ready. All being arranged according to my orders, the party arrived about ten o'clock and went almost immediately to the canal. To screen them from the sun there was an awning carried over the centre of the vessel and a table and chairs placed beneath. As all Mr. Boodle's children and two nurses, with the man-servant, were of the party from Radstock we mustered fifteen on board. My horse, under the direction of a man from the coal works, towed us along. We first visited the head of the canal at Paulton Basin, and returned thence through Camerton and Dunkerton to Combe Hay. Having explored the beautiful grounds, etc., we partook of our cold collation under the shade of the elm trees near the cascade, and in the cool of the evening proceeded homewards. Passing the "Swan" at Dunkerton the Camerton band came on board and played marches and Scotch airs the whole way home. The music and the dressed-out coal barge attracted multitudes, who followed our course along the banks of the canal and lined the bridges under which we passed, which gave a novel appearance to the scenery and a pleasing termination to our rural fete. On quitting the water the ladies drank tea at Camerton, and I accompanied them to Radstock.

June 10

I went into the field where they were tithing Day's rye grass. Smallcombe and Heal, who were appointed to take up the tithe, I had heard were dissatisfied because I did not allow them beer, and on inquiring for Smallcombe learnt he was gone to the Red Post public house, thinking if he took the opportunity of my dinner hour I should not discover it. I took the direction of the Red Post, and found him seated very comfortably with his beer before him.

However, his enjoyment was not of long duration, since I took him by the collar of his jacket and soon showed him the way to the door. He begged to go back to drink his beer, but this I did not permit him to do. Having seen him into the field I arrived when dinner was over, but I was so warm both internally and externally I had little inclination to eat anything.

June 11

On making inquiries what had been done as to tithing the evening before, and understanding that Smallcombe had left the field at six o'clock, although Day continued hauling till ten (consequently all the tithing was done by his people), I went to Smallcombe, and, after upbraiding him with his great ingratitude and insolence, dismissed him.

This man I have attended and relieved in sickness, employed him when he could not get employment elsewhere during the dead part of the year, and now because work is plenty he behaves in this manner. When I said he would doubtless suffer for his conduct before the next winter was over, and probably groan again on a bed of sickness without a friend to relieve him as I had done in his distress, instead of being called to any grateful recollection by this apostrophe he replied, many a parson might groan in hell, which was still worse. As Smallcombe took a scythe, pickaxe and shovel with him from the Glebe House, which I had no opportunity of examining, I walked down to his cottage to endeavour to ascertain whether they were his own. Mrs. Smallcombe was in the house, and immediately began by asking what business I had on her premises; that I had turned her husband off mine, and I should not come on her's. I replied I had business to visit any place in my parish; that when her husband had been so ill, and I frequently called to see and relieve him, neither she nor her husband then found fault with me for coming on the premises. She replied, if I did come then she did not send for me and never should again, neither should I ever again enter her garden. The insolence of this woman increased and her fury became so violent and her countenance so distorted she resembled one of the witches in the painting of Sir Joshua Reynolds. "You a parson, a shepherd of the flock, to come here," she vociferated, "and insult a poor woman like me (because I called her 'beldame'). You will smart for this I assure you, I assure you." Tyler's wife, a very rank Methodist, who was in the house, then began to join in the contest and asked whether I was not ashamed of myself to call such names: that I might talk about canting Methodists, but there never was a Churchman like me in a house but the Devil was there also. I then said "woman, such expressions I might make you answer for in the Ecclesiastical Court, if you were not infinitely beneath my notice." Her husband then came in and compelled her to go back to his own home, but not before she had retorted in the greatest rage, "Why, you called Mrs. Smallcombe worse; you said she was a 'Beldame.'" I asked her what she supposed was meant by that? And when I explained that it meant a scold, both she and Smallcombe's wife became more tranquil, and said they had supposed it meant something much worse.

I particularise these absurd scenes, not only because they are worth recording as curiosities but, in another point of view, they are indices of the malignity of these sectarists. Both Smallcombe and this Tyler's wife gave the same pious expressions towards the clergy: the one that parsons would howl in hell, and the other that where there was a Churchman like me in a house there was the Devil. I am heartily sick of the flock over which I am nominated and placed; instead of being a shepherd, as I told the methodistical beldame when she twitted me with the name, I am in fact a pig driver; I despise myself most thoroughly for suffering irritation from such vermin. Leaving these scenes of discord, I endeavoured to tranquilise my mind by visiting those more softened by sickness and sorrow, and to converse with those who do indeed need assistance.

On returning home to dinner I found an invitation from Mr. Johnson to join the party at Timsbury House in the evening. As my mind needed some change of idea, I determined on accepting it. I mounted my horse about six, on my arrival at Mr. Palmer's found a large party was expected: Mr. and Mrs. Barter, Colonel [? Capt.] and Mrs. Scobel, Captain Savage, Mr. James[1] and family, etc. After tea they stood up to dance, one of the ladies playing upon the piano. I danced two sets with Mrs. Scobel, formerly Mrs. James, with whom I used to dance in former times at Bath and Weymouth; sed tempora mutantur. As the evening was dark Mrs. Palmer invited me to take my bed at her house. I was glad to accept the offer, and reposed very comfortably in the Ancient Mansion of the Sambournes, without being interrupted by ghosts or goblins.

[1] William Coxeter James, Esq., J.P., Deputy Lieutenant for the county.

I walked about the premises before breakfast, and am pretty well assured there was a fortified post on the hill on which the Mansion is built. As my obliging entertainers did everything to render my stay with them agreeable, and I knew it would be tout au contraire if I returned to my Tithetakers in the Hayfield I came to the resolution of enjoying for a day longer the lively conversation of the better part of our species, and lounged away the morning in their society, and I may add, the evening too, as I took an interesting walk on a charitable errand after dinner under the direction of Miss Palmer and Mr. Johnson, who conducted me to visit a poor girl, who had both her legs lately broken by a waggon passing over them, and has supported her sufferings with exemplary patience.

I occupied my apartment in the old Mansion, having despatched a person to Camerton to inform my housekeeper of my intention, and to procure me some linen.

As Mr. James had engaged a large party to make an excursion to Nunney and Vallis, and requested me to be the leader, I left Mrs. Palmer's after an early breakfast, both her daughters being in the Phaeton, Mr. Johnson and myself on horse back: the rendezvous being at Paulton. We met there eight other carriages, and numbered twenty-six independently of servants—I must confess one quarter of the number, to me had been more agreeable. We first stopped at the gateway leading to Mells Park, where leaving the carriages and horses under the care of the servants; I conducted the Ladies to a point commanding the full extent of the water, with the bridge at the N.W. extremity; thence crossing the Park, I pointed out the sequestered dell I so much admired not long before: the day was in every respect most favourable for the distant views. Resuming our cavalcade, we proceeded through Whatley to Nunney Castle, where we stopped nearly an hour to examine the Castle and Church. From Nunney we proceeded in front of Mr. Shore's house at Whatley, and traversing the Frome Road, turned off to the left, and entered Vallis near the Farm House formerly occupied by the celebrated Mrs. Rowe.[1] My guidance was here most severely reprobated, as I afterwards understood, by those of the party who had fourwheeled carriages and two horses, on account of the difficulty of quartering: the ruts

[1] Elizabeth Rowe, 1674–1737, the poetess; b. Ilchester, buried at Frome.

being very deep; Colonel [Capt.] Scobel's gig also, in endeavouring to cross out of one of the deep ravines, had a wheel broken, and was obliged to be conveyed to Vallis Farm, the Colonel [Capt.] and his son being received by other conveyances in the rear. I had before mentioned the bad state of the road, but added, that a great deal of the most interesting scenery would be lost if the Party went round by Mells, instead of pursuing this road. I am happy to say on arriving at the beautiful little Cottage at Elm, all these difficulties were forgotten; and having obtained Mr. Blakeney's permission, the whole party shortly after sat down to an excellent repast provided by the different families who composed it: cold meats, fowls, tarts, tongues, salads, etc., abound in profusion: also every kind of liquor calculated to relieve the burning thirst, so many hours exposure to a hot sun had occasioned: we afterwards retired from the Cottage to the Cavern above the brook leaving the servants to finish the repast, and heard some excellent songs from the ladies, Captain Scobel, etc., whilst the wine was passing round: we afterwards walked up the valley as far as Fussell's Iron Works, and saw persons engaged in such laborious occupations, as would have called forth the indignation of all the British Philanthropists from Land's End to the Orkneys, if such tasks had been imposed on our brethren of sable complexion, either in the E. or W. Indies.

Our walk concluded we returned to the Cavern, where a syllabub was waiting our arrival, which I have reason to believe was composed of stronger materials than were quite suitable to the heat of the weather, and the weakness of some of the heads which had to withstand their force.

Having afterwards returned our thanks to Mr. Blakeney for the permission he had given us to enjoy his beautiful domain in a complimentary address signed by all the company, we returned home in the cool of the evening. I left the party at Kilmersdon and got to Camerton a little before ten, and was glad to exchange a hard saddle, clouds of dust, and a broiling Sun, for a soft, cool and comfortable bed.

Sunday, July 7

Thinking it probable that Weeks, the Churchwarden, and Hicks, the Overseer, might not attend Church, and consequently not know what measures to pursue respecting the collection, I sent Harris, the Clerk, to them; but it was of no avail.

I preached the sermon I had written for the occasion, and introduced the heart-rending accounts from Ireland[1] to the committee for managing the subscription. The people were very attentive, but rather a thin congregation. Mr. Purnell being present, after Church I mentioned to him my intention of sending the Chuchwarden and the Overseer round the parish to collect from house to house.

As John Rossiter, the person I had appointed Churchwarden, did not attend the Visitation, alleging, as I understood, he had never been sworn in, I asked Farmer Keel whether he had any objection to officiate. If he had not he must go to Frome on the 16th to be sworn in. He said he had no objections, but believed that the Churchwardens' accounts were in a very confused state.

After dinner I visited West's wife who is much weaker, and not able to leave her bed. The young man at Wick Lane is, I should think, very near his end, as he can only speak in a whisper and his legs are much swollen. Goold's wife much the same. Cottle's daughter I found very little altered in the three weeks I have been absent. Mr. Barter administered the Sacrament to her, as I had requested he would do.

I promised to lend her a book to read, as she said it would be an amusement to her. From hence I walked to Timsbury, and drank tea and chatted with Mr. and Mrs. Barter till ten o'clock. Mrs. Jarrett, I found, was at Camerton for three days lately, and is expected with the newly married pair this week. The budget will then be opened.

Monday, July 8

I called upon John Rossiter with a list I had made out for the Irish contribution, to which I put my name for £5. I then asked him his reason for not attending the Visitation as my Churchwarden on Friday. He replied that the accounts respecting the Bells were in such a state, and the difficulty of collecting the money so great, that he would have nothing to do with it. I answered that he had performed the office of Churchwarden in signing the briefs and other matters, and, having given no notice of his intention to decline it, and the Archdeacon not having notified me to the contrary, I had considered him as such; but, if he wished to give it up, I should substitute Farmer Keel in his place, and send him on the 16th to be sworn in. I further said that he [Rossiter] was to all intents and purposes my Churchwarden, but if he was disposed to consider the

[1] Famine in Ireland, 1822.

duties of his office as unpleasant and purposed discharging them unwillingly, I would, as I before said, nominate Keel. To this he answered that it was Weeks, the Churchwarden, he had to complain of; that he had collected some of the Bells money and never accounted for it; if he collected still greater sums and spent them, they would come upon him [Rossiter]. I said it was his duty to see that the sums collected were rightly secured; that the Parish (when I dismissed the man for his ill-conduct) ought to have been better advised than to put him in an office which would give him the power to defraud them; that they might be sure if he could advise Widcombe, after having embezzled the parish money, to drive off his stock, he could not be an honest man, and they were rightly served for their folly. I further said, it was the conduct of the Parish in these particulars that had made me determine not to attend any Vestry without I was obliged to do so, and I full well saw that they would so much increase their difficulties that ruin must ensue. He said that was certainly the case, but he was afraid to act, for if he opposed such things he should make the people his enemies, and they would injure his character behind his back.

I told the man to do his duty, and not to be afraid of what people said of him; that I always acted upon this principle, and no more minded the malevolence and calumny of the people of Camerton than I did the whistling of the wind! "But you have not got your bread to gain by it as I have," was the reply. Yet, I answered, if one is to be deterred from acting uprightly and doing justice through apprehension of displeasing knaves, there is a great chance of displeasing One whose favour we ought to be more anxious to secure.

I clearly see I cannot live longer with this people, I am so continually disgusted with their conduct; and in the situation I am placed I cannot avoid noticing it. At the conclusion of our conversation Rossiter agreed to go round with Hicks [the Overseer] to-morrow to collect the money for the distressed Irish.

I afterwards visited the three invalids. Dawson, the man in Wick Lane, seemed in a dying state, yet he was able to attend to the prayers I read to him. On returning home, and having brought up my Journal, I went to bed a little after ten.

Tuesday, July 9

The poor man in Wick Lane died in the night. After breakfast I sent my car into Bath for my two boys, Owen and Joseph, who returned to dinner. The interval till their arrival was occupied in settling accounts.

I had to pay the mowers £4, Heal £3, also Goold £3. There are altogether three mows of hay, about thirty tons. The barn floor is laid, but the doors not yet fixed; I gave orders for completing the work as speedily as possible, since I must put in a tenant by Michaelmas if Mrs. Jarrett does not rent the tythe. If the patroness of this Living could get rid of me altogether, and let her son-in-law, Mr. Gooch, step into my shoes, it would be a good stroke of policy. I am inclined to think this Lady looks with a Jezebel's eye on Naboth's Vineyard; yet, though sons of Belial might be found in abundance, thanks to our well-administered laws it is more difficult to carry into execution acts of treachery and malevolence than under a despotic government. "Je crains mon Dieu et je n'ai point d'autre crainte."

Whilst attending Cottle's daughter this morning her Mother told me that Mr. Gooch, who is to be married this day to Miss Jarrett, was expected at Camerton on Friday, that the Lady herself was not expected for a month or six weeks, and in the plenitude of her gossip she continued to state that Mrs. Jarrett, when here, was very thin and unwell; that she cried over her [Cottle's] daughter as if she had been her own; and further that when she told her that Mr. Skinner had been so good as to call before he left home, she, Mrs. Jarrett, said she had a great regard for Mr. Skinner herself, and would go up to her knees in snow to do him any good. Mrs. Jarrett expressed herself very differently to Clarke, the Schoolmaster, when she turned him from her house, screaming out, as the man described, "like a fiend": "Now there will be no more gossiping with those I hate." This certainly was a little unguarded in this politic Lady! Mrs. Jarrett reminds me of the fable of the ostrich—Sed satis, jam satis.

Wednesday, July 10

About the middle of the day the bells rang out a merry peal in consequence, I understood, of the intelligence of Miss Jarrett's marriage having been received. In the evening there was a Funeral of an Infant; and I could not help remarking how fully the tolling for the deceased had been absorbed by the more merry news. Harris, the Clerk, not being in attendance [at the funeral], I enquired the reason, and learnt he had been despatched by order of Mrs. Jarrett to carry bride-cake round the neighbourhood.

Bacon called in the evening and paid his last half-year's rent of glebe and tythe; he wished a further reduction of rent which I was not inclined to make.

As there was great shouting at the Coal Works, music playing, singing, etc., etc., which I could hear from the Parsonage field, I imagined at first that the whole populace participated in the glad tidings which set the bells aringing; but Bacon informed me the Proprietors of the Works were present at the Bailiff's, and had distributed money, on account of the discovery of a fresh vein of coal, which promises to be very advantageous. This, I think, is indeed good news for the parish, as it regards the future prospects of so many who depend on the prosperity of the mines.

Thursday, July 11

Day came in the morning and paid his agistments. There must be something wrong, but I cannot detect it. The whole of the Parks, for which I used to receive from Chichester £20 per annum when he compounded for hay, only nets me now, when fed off, £6 11s. 0d. Out of this sum I paid Day two guineas for rent of the Church Road. He informed me that the lambs would be ready to be tythed in the evening. I afterwards passed three hours in my study; then visited the sick. The boys, Owen and Joseph, rode into Bath to see their Grandmother. I therefore dined alone. After dinner I walked with my servant, Heal, to Day's farm to tythe the lambs. Sixteen came to my share; but there was a little shabby manoeuvring about the last, which was a lamb with its back broke, which Day said fell to my share. However, I must take things as I find them, I cannot yet help myself; but I must take an early opportunity of getting a tenant, as I would not have this interruption to my usual pursuits for twice the value of the Living.

The poor man, Dawson, who died on Tuesday, was buried this evening, and a merry peal succeeded, as in the preceding case. I understand that £2 are ordered to the ringers, as Dilly, the Butler [at the Manor House], asked me how I should recommend its being paid. I said, if possible, one half to be spent in beer, the other to be divided amongst them; but I feared this could not be done. I shall be heartily glad when this scene of drunkenness and uproar is at an end. No work done at the Pits, and the people are more brutified than ever.

Between eleven and twelve last night I was awoke by a jingling of bells announcing the arrival of the Bride and Bridegroom, and before I got up I was destined to be grievously tormented by a more noisy peal, and which continued the whole of the day with little intermission.

In the course of the morning I called upon Cottle's daughter, who continues daily losing strength, but very resigned. As I had administered the Sacrament to her the other day, she expressed how much comfort she had derived from it, and wished, she said, to prevail on her Father and Mother to receive it in Church, but could not.

On going to West's wife I found her much worse, and making heavy complaints of the revelling in the parish, and saying that both her husband and her Father had been so intoxicated during the whole time that it made her quite miserable. She had understood Smallcombe's son—one of the ringers—had so beaten his wife, she was quite a mummy; her husband never comes near her in his sober moments, and her Father has not been upstairs, she says, since she kept her bed.

On my quitting the sick-room, Mrs. White made a formal complaint, and wished me to speak to her husband, which I did; but with very little prospect of benefiting him. The arguments I made use of were grounded on the brevity and uncertainty of human life, and the great impropriety of behaving so riotously when his daughter was dying in the house.

In the evening Mr. and Mrs. Gooch sent some Bride-cake, with a note stating they were very sorry they did not send it before, as they thought I was not returned from Town. It was a matter of such insignificance that it was not worth thinking of. Nevertheless, the excuse is rather an awkward one, as they must have known from Dilly's wife, who went expressly from Camerton to attend the wedding, that I was come home. How open are those who are playing a part to detection!

My boys drove in the car after breakfast to fetch their relatives, the Eyres, whom I had invited to spend the ensuing week at Camerton. I was occupied the whole morning in preparing some of the sketches I had taken in Sussex and Hants, for my son Owen to set, in order to have them bound up.

Just before dinner I walked to call on Mr. Gooch, and saw him in front of the Manor House. Having paid my compliments, he said Mrs. Gooch did not wish to see anyone just yet. I then apologised for having called so soon, stating I knew it was etiquette not to visit till after their appearance at Church; but, being so near, I did not wish to appear backward in paying my respects. He said, moreover, it was not their intention to come to Church to-morrow.

I am more and more convinced I tread on deceitful ground, and must take heed how I walk! since every step is watched, and every expression noted. The young man I am disposed to think well of; but he himself is not perhaps aware of the power which influences him.

Sunday, July 14

As soon as the bells began to ring I went to the Church to request we might have no more rejoicing, as we had been surfeited with it the last week. Harris said it was not his intention to ring otherwise than to call the people to Church, unless Mr. Gooch sent to order it.

I replied that it was a general order of mine that there should be no peal-ringing on a Sunday, and that order must be abided by: that I had no idea Mr. Gooch would send any message of the kind; if he did, he [Harris] was to say what I had told him. I read prayers in the morning: very few attended.

The First Lesson, the 12th chapter of the second book of Samuel, contained the beautiful apostrophe of Nathan to David. Are there none of our neighbours coveting the possessions of others? Would there were not! But I must prevent the intrusion of such ideas.

During the evening service the Church was crowded; and the singers, who have been in a state of constant intoxication since yesterday, being offended because I would not suffer them to chaunt the service after the First Lesson, put on their hats and left the Church. This is the most open breach of all religious decorum I have ever witnessed. However, it is too gross even to excite anger: it induces *awe* at the hardened wickedness of those wretches. Though White and West could fill their houses with oaths and execrations when their daughter and wife was dying above stairs, and under the influence of liquor produced in these injurious revels forget their duties as men to their dearest connections, I was not prepared to expect so open a violation of all decency in the house of God.

There could not have been less than twelve or fourteen who quitted the Church at the same instant, thinking I should miss their aid when the Psalm was to be sung before the sermon. But I was fully prepared to go through the whole service, even without the assistance of the girls, whom I ordered to sing the hundredth psalm: O serve the Lord with gladness, and come before His presence with a song. The sermon followed. . . . The subject I selected for my discourse was the imperious call afforded by the death of our neighbours and companions to serious *reflection*, *repentance*, and *reformation*, which I more particularly alluded to in the recent dissolution of Dawson the poor man in Wick Lane, who was buried on Thursday, and the approaching fate of the two young women now dying of consumption; shewing that neither health nor strength could ensure their exemption from the general summons, which might be given indeed in an instant, without any warning, as was the case in four events still fresh in their recollections, namely, in the instantaneous dissolution of Dando, Mullens, Cromwell, and Bull: the latter only survived a couple of days after his accident.

The people were very attentive, and I found no difficulty in delivering myself with sufficient energy—the greater part of the discourse being extempore—excited by the hardened conduct of the people who had thus openly shewn disregard to religion. Their only excuse, if any can be offered in such a case, is that they were acting under the influence of liquor, which I verily believe was the case.

After dinner I walked to see the invalids, both now hastening to that bourne from which no traveller returns.

After tea, I spent a couple of hours in my study before I went to bed.

Monday, July 15

Whilst lying awake this morning, the thoughts of the preceding day and the conduct of the people in Church being uppermost in my mind, it struck me, as *vanity* operated so strongly on these musical mutineers, whether by subjecting their behaviour to the public animadversion I might not, by wounding that vanity, induce them to think more humbly of themselves, and more properly of their situation. A serious lecture I knew would have no effect, I had so often tried it in vain. I accordingly treated the subject in a more playful manner in the following lines:

LINES WRITTEN IN CONSEQUENCE OF THE ABRUPT DEPARTURE OF THE SINGERS FROM CAMERTON CHURCH DURING THE TIME OF DIVINE SERVICE, IN THE EVENING OF SUNDAY, JULY 14, 1822

> *Some merry musicians quite fresh from the barrel*
> *Last Sunday resolved with Religion to quarrel,*
> *So, quitting their seats in the midst of the prayers,*
> *Clapp'd their hats on their noddles and hurried downstairs—*
> *Conceiving by thus turning backs on the Church*
> *Both Parson and People were left in the lurch.*
> *But Parson and People had a more serious thing*
> *To attend to than hear these blythe revellers sing;*
> *The subject was Death! for only three days before*
> *To the grave, where vain mortals can revel no more,*
> *A companion was borne, once as healthy and strong*
> *As themselves, who now trip it so joyous along.*
> *Grateful feast to the worms. Alas! silent and mute,*
> *No longer exulting with Viol and Flute,*
> *They too will be laid in dark cells 'neath the sod,*
> *To corruption a prey, whilst their Souls meet their God.*
> *Of these short-lived carousers reflection may ask,*
> *Is it wisdom to barter their souls for a cask?*
> *Since not one single drop of the gallons they drain*
> *Can quench Hell's fierce fire, nor extinguish their pain;*
> *Whilst the oaths they have sworn, and vile songs they have sung,*
> *Will add fuel abundant to flame on their tongue.*

After breakfast, having transcribed these lines, with a letter addressed to Combes, the Landlord of the Inn, I called upon Feare, the Bailiff of the Coal Works, to desire that he would transcribe them and have them sent by post or some other conveyance to Combes: as he was at Church during the transaction I thought I had a right to ask his assistance. There could be no possible objection in my writing to Combes myself, but if his guests conceived that their conduct was under the observation of others, whose animadversion they had subjected themselves to, it might have greater weight. My letter to him was as follows:

"Sir,—

"As I can well suppose a great deal of interesting conversation at times takes place under your much-frequented roof, you will oblige me by making the enclosed copy of verses the subject of your next discussion: its novelty perhaps may ensure it a hearing.

"I am, Sir,

"A sincere well-wisher to yourself and guests,

"Philanthropos."

Feare, on reading the lines, suggested it might be better to insert them in the *Bath & Cheltenham Gazette*, which was read at the Camerton Inn, to which I consented on condition that my name was concealed, as I have no ambition to contribute to the papers.

Feare descanted largely on the conduct of the Camertonians, saying no parish business could be transacted, and he supposed they should lose the money the Churchwarden had collected for the Bells. I replied it was their own fault for having chosen him as Churchwarden, when I had given such proof of his dishonesty.

I afterwards visited Cottle and West—both still more languid and approaching their end.

Whilst at Cottle's, the son, who used to be an admirer of my late servant's—speaking of the conduct of the singers—said he had understood they had gone from the Church immediately to the Red Post Public House, and had determined to sing in future at the Meeting-House, where the gallery was to be enlarged for their accommodation.

I had heard that Mrs. Jarrett had been applied to by Isaac Green— a staunch Methodist—to contribute to this enlargement, but had not yet done so.

White's wife told me she had been to fetch her husband from the "Red Post" in the evening, and she saw the singers all there, and old Rogers, Father-in-Law of Dawson who was buried on Thursday, so drunk the road seemed not wide enough to hold him, or words to that effect. I mentioned that a Bill had passed Parliament,[1] which would regulate the Ale Houses better than they had been for years back, as they were the principal causes of all the evil we had to

[1] Ale Houses Act (3 George IV, c. 78), An Act to amend the laws for licensing Ale Houses, and for more effectually preventing disorders therein.

complain of. She said in truth they were Devil's Houses, and she could say none had more reason to lament them than she had.

I received a book from Barratt's to-day, which I think will be of great use to me in my Hebrew studies. It is called *Glossarium-Universale-Hebraicum*, published at Paris, 1697.

Tuesday, July 16

I was occupied for the most of the morning in my study tinting the drawings of my last Journals in order to have them bound. I afterwards visited West's wife, and found Isaac Green, the Methodist, with her, which I am sorry for, as I am sure he will not render her latter end more calm or comfortable. I read the prayers, and afterwards took an opportunity during my conversation with her to mention the fallacy of those ideas which led people to say they were certain of going to heaven; that there was no part of Scripture that authorised any such presumption; if it were indeed so, there would be no use in a Day of Judgment! since persons would be beforehand convinced of their acceptance or rejection: we might humbly hope through the merits and mediation of a crucified Redeemer that the promises proclaimed in the Gospel to penitent sinners would be completed; but to say we were sure of acceptance was a most dangerous error. To this Green replied nothing, but I perceived he by no means approved of the doctrine I used. I know he is one of the Calvinistic Methodists, and of course retains very different ideas on the subject. On my leaving the house he followed me downstairs, and said how much obliged he was for my kind attention to the poor woman! I replied there could be no possible obligation, since I only did my duty. I was happy to find her in a proper frame of mind, and only hoped they would not disturb it.

I afterwards sat a quarter of an hour with Cottle's daughter, who told me that her next-door neighbour—Rose—wished to see me, as he was declining very fast. I accordingly went, and found him in a very low state, exclaiming, after the Methodist manner, how great a sinner he had been, but hoped through the Blessed Saviour he should work out his salvation.

I said the work must depend a great deal on his own exertions; that he must not only repent of what he had done amiss, but make every reparation in his power; if he had injured anybody by word or deed, he should instantly make all the atonement possible. It was a dangerous error to rely solely on the sacrifice of Christ, unless he was disposed to make some sacrifice *himself*.

The man, I find, is a strong Methodist, and his reason for sending to me to attend him I cannot exactly comprehend, though as he mentioned his pecuniary distresses, probably this may have some weight. It was nearly dusk when I got home.

Wednesday, July 17

This being a rainy morning I was engaged in my study till dinner-time drawing. [The man] Rose expressed himself very thankful for the half-a-crown I had sent him by Owen, and found a little meat [also] very strengthening. From the observation I have made of these Methodists, they have great benevolence in their expressions to-wards each other, but I do not observe they are ready to part with their money—fully exemplifying by their conduct the lip-serving Christians alluded to by St. James, who are ready enough to say, "Be ye warmed and clothed," but give them not where-with to warm *or* clothe them. I am sure I am not uncharitable in these surmises, since daily experience convinces me of their truth. As my son, Owen, who has of late accompanied me to these sick houses, seems to feel too acutely, I shall not in future take him with me.

Thursday, July 18

I was engaged the greater part of the morning in my study, and in the glebe field overlooking the carpenters who have now nearly finished their work at the new house. I afterwards called on Mr. and Mrs. Gooch. Mr. Barter called before dinner, and asked me to dine with him on Sunday to meet Archdeacon Moysey. Henry Hoare came over from Southfield, and dined and slept at Camerton; his Father he informed me was gone to Stourhead to meet Sir John Ackland.

Cottle's daughter still continues tranquil and composed. White's daughter still getting weaker and weaker. As I returned home I called at the Manor House to request Mrs. Gooch to send some Current Jelly to her, as what my housekeeper sent was not good, and she wished to take the bad taste from her mouth.

Friday, July 19

Collins of the Mill looked at the corn I had to dispose of, and declined giving £30 for the ricks of wheat and barley. Last year

Parker paid me £40 when there were only forty acres of wheat tythed, instead of fifty. He said that wheat was now 20s. a sack, and would be still lower; that lambs were 12s. apiece; but I clearly perceived that his object was to depreciate the tythe. This man was a miller, who has been keeping up the price of bread in a very different proportion to what he talks of; thus it seems I can depend on no purchasers in this immediate neighbourhood, and if I can get the wheat and barley threshed out there will be great risque in having a large part of it stolen by the Thresher.

Returning from the glebe, Stephens, the under-gardener to Mrs. Jarrett, came to me in the field facing my house saying he had a favour to ask, which was to let the ringers give a peal, it being the King's Coronation Day,[1] and that the people at Paulton and Midsomer Norton had been ringing the whole morning. I said I was as much attached to the King as any man in the country, yet could not see how His Majesty derived any good from people leaving their work to make a noise with the bells; with respect to the ringers, they certainly did themselves much injury by frequenting the Ale Houses in the manner they had done last week, and then returning home and beating their wives to a jelly. I said, as the Parish seemed so desirous of having them rung (Mr. Gooch had given them a guinea, and Weeks, the Churchwarden, 5s. for the purpose) I would not oppose it; but I recommended their not going to the Public House spending the money they had gained in folly, which might be much better spent on their families. They accordingly commenced their ringing, and I walked in the village to avoid the jingling of the Bells.

The boys, having gone to Radstock in my car, returned in good time, and informed me they had engaged in a Cricket Match with Mr. Boodle and Mr. Flower, and that the servants were admitted in the set, which may be usual in regular matches, but I do not so much approve of my children keeping such company, and therefore I shall be more careful in future not to send them without I can myself be one of the party.

Saturday, July 20

I began writing a sermon for the ensuing day in order to make one more effort for the distressed Irish, as I find that Rossiter (my Churchwarden) was not successful in his application at the Manor House.

---

[1] First anniversary Coronation of George IV.

I was up before six to finish my sermon on the Gospel for the day. After breakfast, my sermon being completed, I walked to Church. Mr. and Mrs. Gooch, the bride and bridegroom, attended, and afterwards subscribed £5 to the Churchwarden's plate. In all he collected £6 11s. 5d. I gave notice I should preach again in the evening, and make another collection.

The girls sang both morning and evening, and much more to my satisfaction than the great Bulls of Basan in the gallery used to do, who, though never in tune or time, were so highly conceited of their own abilities they thought of nothing else the whole time of the service. If they chuse to withdraw themselves, we shall do better without them. The Churchwarden collected 8s. 6d. in the evening.

Returning from Church I rode to Timsbury, where I dined and spent the evening with Mr. and Mrs. Barter. Dr. Moysey is a pleasant and well-informed man, and seems to have a taste for antiquities. He has engaged to breakfast with me at Camerton next Wednesday, in order to visit the Sepulchre at Stoney Littleton.

The boys drove to Bath in the car and I sent in by them the total of the money collected at Camerton for the relief of the Irish—

THE ACCOUNT

Mr. Purnell	.	.	.	£5 5 0
Mr. Gooch	.	.	.	5 0 0
Myself .	.	.	.	5 0 0
Mr. Day	.	.	.	5 5
The Farmers and Colliers				3 13 2½
				£19 3 7½

which I directed my Banker to remit to Town to be at the disposal of the Committee. On speaking to Heal, who works in my garden, to ascertain the reason why he did not come to Church yesterday, when there was a christening of his child, he had no other excuse to offer than that his sister had come from Bath. I said I should not admit those excuses, I was fearful he was joined with the misguided among my parishioners who always made a point of setting my servants against me; that he would gain little by working their work. He listened without saying anything, but it was with a look of obstinacy rather than feeling. I am convinced nothing can be done with this people.

I proceeded with the drawings in my study the greater part of the morning. Captain Scobel called to say he would trace the map of the Dunum for me from the Government Survey, which offer I was happy to accept, as it will be of great service to me by enabling me to mark down with more accuracy the places where Roman and British remains are to be found. He also brought an invitation from Squire Purnell for myself and boys to dine at Woodborough on Friday. After dinner, Harris, the clerk, called for the key of the Church, saying Mrs. Jarrett and her son were arrived, and the people wished to ring. I replied, he must have recollected what I told him on Sunday, that I would not permit the bells to be made mere play-things of; if the ringers did not employ them for the purpose they were intended I should not consent to any extra ringing, and on these grounds should refuse the key.

He accordingly went away very sulkily.

As Dr. Moysey had engaged to be with me early in order to visit the Sepulchre at Stoney Littleton, I called at the Manor House and left a message stating the reason I should not wait on Mrs. Jarrett, but said I would do so the following day at twelve.

We were engaged the whole morning at Stoney Littleton and Wellow; and Cottle opened some of the pavement for the inspection of Dr. Moysey.

On leaving the place, I was attacked rather unexpectedly by Coles, the farmer, saying I had not satisfied him for the opening of it, and had been riding over his wheat; that he thought it was not at all like a gentleman to behave in this manner. In reply I said I had already given what I conceived sufficient satisfaction for every damage to the farmer before I began digging; that, as Mr. Gore-Langton had given me permission through Sir Richard Hoare, I did not conceive he had any claim on me, as the ground was filled up before his sowing; but he might depend on it, if he talked in the manner he did, he never would have a single sixpence, and if he was insolent, I should call upon Mr. Gore-Langton and explain all these particulars. With respect to having ridden over his wheat, I utterly denied it; that Dr. Moysey, the gentleman who was with me, as well as my own boys, had left their horses to be held by two of the reapers where the corn was not cut, in order to avoid the possibility of doing the least damage; neither could he, if he spoke true, affirm that a farthing's damage had been done.

The man then became more civil, and said he hoped I would consider him as I had done the other farmer.

The weather appearing very threatening, the boys and myself made the best of our way home, where we arrived completely wet about half-past four.

Dr. Moysey returned to Bath by Combe Hay.

Thursday, July 25

I was engaged in my study for a while before breakfast. Afterwards I visited Cottle, Rose, and White's daughter, and walked from thence to Cridlingcot to administer the Sacrament to Mrs. Lippeatt, she having sent to request I would instead of Sunday. I found her Father and Mother were prepared to receive it with her, also another woman whom I had not before seen, whose name I understood is Kelson. On saying I had not expected to see her, and should only administer it to the Father and Mother of Mrs. Lippeatt, who were so infirm they could not come conveniently to Church, she said she was also so infirm as to be able to go to no place of worship, and hoped I would not refuse her as she had prepared her mind for the purpose. As she seemed so much bent upon it I permitted her, after prefacing it by saying I hoped she had not undertaken so serious a duty in a light manner; that her own heart alone could determine the question.

There was something in the whole proceeding of this woman I thought so remarkable that, after the ceremony was concluded, I touched upon the state of mind which it behoved us to be in, and the scrutiny we should make of our affection toward God. If I could read the heart of this woman through her countenance, I should have said that it was very opposite to her professions. I always feel distrustful when I am sent for by these bigoted people; they undermine the authority of the Church in all possible ways, and cannot be sincere in requiring the assistance of the clergy, unless they absurdly imagine that the sacramental bread and wine is a viaticum to heaven.

Leaving Cridlingcot, I called on Mrs. Jarrett on my way home. Being shewn into the dining parlour, it was some minutes before she made her appearance; but I heard the voice in no very prepossessing tone scolding the servants about some defect in laying down the carpet in the drawing-room. On entering the parlour where I was, she began to say that her object in coming to Camerton at this time was to settle the business between us, and for this purpose she had sent for her lawyer, Mr. Fry, immediately on her arrival, and hoped he would be able to direct her as to what was best to be done; that I was well aware that, as a woman, she understood but little of the business of Tythe, and must depend upon his judgment as to the value: she could not help thinking that £450 was a great sum for the income of the Living, and she hoped I would have no objection to see Mr. Fry to speak on the business, or appoint a person on my part so to do.

In reply I said that when the proposition of renting the Tythe and the glebe land had come from her, my friend, Mr. Peter Hoare, was staying with me, and we had spent some time in making the calculations I had according to her desire forwarded to her, and this calculation was considerably below my present receipts. It remained with her to consider whether it suited her convenience to give that sum or not. She said she could do nothing without consulting Mr. Fry: that the statement I made of my present receipts might be quite correct, and she doubted not they were so, but it behoved Mr. Fry to see my tythe book, in order that he might calculate whether she could with safety to her own interest close with my offer. She then began to state that Mr. Gooch had informed her that if the Bishop licensed him to the curacy, he had a right to demand a sum proportionate to the population; and as Camerton was estimated to contain upwards of one thousand inhabitants, that the salary of the curate would be rated at least at £100 per annum.

If Mrs. Jarrett had been serious in her ideas of renting the Tythe, she might have settled the business with me herself; as she was well aware I should not permit Mr. Fry to have anything to do with my concerns: perhaps Mr. Fry did not inform his employer I had the power of granting a lease for twenty-one years, and that the lease would be binding on my successor for that period? This apparent treaty between Mrs. Jarrett and myself would have done me an incalculable injury had I not been provided for taking up my tythe, as I doubt not, at Michaelmas, owing to the suggestions of Mr. Fry, all the Farmers will send notices for putting out their tythe in kind; since he has doubtless told them what he has told Mrs. Jarrett, that I require £150 too much; as she mentioned she should lose that sum if she took the tythe at my present valuation, namely £450 per annum, and consequently they will be disposed to make the experiment of putting it out. Surely this man is in every sense of the word a κ᾿ κοδαίμων. I then again reverted to my first declaration, that it would not suit me to take less than the sum I had specified; that the proposition of my letting my glebe and giving up the Parsonage to Mr. Gooch had originated in her; that I never should have thought of leaving my charge if they had not, of late especially, conducted themselves in such a manner as to shew they purposely kicked at all authority; but if I continued amongst them I should exert the powers I possessed, and although an unpleasant contest might ensue, I was prepared to go through with it, and doubted not in the end I should be successful.

In reply she said she conceived there could be no great pleasure in pulling my own nose, to be on a footing with those who made wry faces; that she knew I had been very improperly treated by the ignorant people around me, and that I had felt considerable irritation in consequence; and, moreover, thought if I were to remove from the place awhile it might be better. She then said, if she did take the offer I made, she should expect, if Mr. Gooch gave up the curacy on promotion, that I should leave the appointment of another curate in his stead to herself; that it would be very unpleasant to have anyone who interfered with her son about game, and she should expect I would be bound in honour not to nominate anyone who might be unpleasant to herself. As I perceived a carriage driving up to the door I took my leave, and returned to the Parsonage.

I am afraid, from the whole of my conversation with this extraordinary woman, that there is some important business now on the tapis respecting her own temporal concerns.

Mrs. Jarrett informed me of a family event which was to take place at no very distant period, which she said would tie up her hands and prevent her doing what she should otherwise feel disposed to do if she were left free to act for herself. She enjoined the strictest secrecy as to the circumstance, which of course I shall preserve; but if she tells it to twenty other people she may possibly afterwards accuse me of having betrayed her confidence. It is after all perhaps only a *ruse de guerre*. However, it is clear she does not know exactly what to do, and under these circumstances it is better I should be on my post.

She informed me that she herself was to leave Camerton with her son and daughter at nine the following morning for Cowes, and was uncertain whether she should return immediately or not, as sea-bathing was necessary for her. The plain state of the case is, if Mrs. Jarrett, by making my situation uncomfortable, could drive me from it, get the Living on her own terms and open the way for Mr. Gooch to step into my Parsonage, her policy would succeed; but as I am not to be frightened by the opposition of the lower orders, even headed by herself, and, as I know, by letting the whole I can save myself the trouble of taking up the tythe, I am inclined to continue firm to my first proposition, and leave it to time to work out a change in the people around me.

Saturday, July 27

After breakfast I drove the boys to Bath to their Grandmother's, whom I have not seen since my return from Town. I took with me two volumes of Journals, fit to be bound up, and the bookbinder has promised to get them done immediately. I then walked to call on Mrs. Gore; found the General better than I had reason to expect, after his severe sufferings since I last was with him. We had some serious conversation, and he prayed most fervently to be released. It was nearly four o'clock before I left Marlborough Buildings, and I was wet through before I got to my Mother's.

Sunday, July 28

Last evening was so wet, I sent a person to Camerton to say we should not return till this morning.

Before Church two of the singers, White and Harper, both under-bailiffs of the coal works, called to say they were very sorry for their behaviour in leaving the Church in the manner they did, and would never be guilty of such bad conduct in future, and hoped I would permit them to sing again. I replied, on condition of their constant attendance at Church and proper attention to the service there, I would myself look over their past ill behaviour; but there was One of more consequence a thousand million times than myself, whose favour they should be more anxious to regain, and that was God. On every account it behoved them to endeavour by their future conduct to make what reparation they could for the ill they had done and the scandal they had occasioned. They promised faithfully to be more serious and attentive in future, and accordingly took their places again during the evening service.

There was no singing in the morning as the school girls were not at Church, Mrs. Jarrett having dismissed the person who attended them, and it is I find in contemplation to restore Mrs. Clarke to her situation. In the interim the girls are to have a month's holiday.

Can anything more plainly demonstrate the caprice of this Lady? and how little she is calculated to do any permanent good? A little while since the boys' Sunday School was broken up by her unjustifiable interference, and now she gets rid of that under her own immediate patronage, and is about to reinstate the woman she dismissed with every mark of displeasure a few months since. It strikes me that there are some causes for her conduct more reprehensible than mere caprice: she is aware that she has expressed herself in the strongest words of hatred against myself, and it is now her policy to pretend she is on good terms with me in order to cover the treachery of her proceedings; countenancing a party to undermine my authority, and vilify me in the eyes of the people. Surely, surely, this duplicity will not be permitted to continue; the veil will be thrown off, and she herself will be injured by the very instruments by which she intended to injure others. . . . But enough of this unpalatable subject.

Sermon.—I preached in the evening on the text: "Now I beseech you, brethren, by the name of our Lord Jesus Christ, that ye all speak the same thing, and that there be no divisions among you."

It seems to be the interest of the Methodist preachers to inculcate that they do not separate from the Church, and that it is the same thing whether the people go to their Chapel or to the Church. This artful policy has of late been extended to the Bible Societies, where dissenters of all denominations pretend a great regard for the Establishment, and for the well-educated Ministry; but this is only to lull the exertions of the more able amongst the Clergy from being directed against themselves; since it may reasonably be asked, Is it the same thing to attend the crude, undigested effusion of a cobbler or a collier, under the name of prayer, as the beautiful service of our Liturgy? Is it the same thing to have a Minister resident amongst them to visit the sick, advise the ignorant and relieve the afflicted, or to contribute at the Meeting House to a needy adventurer, who himself is greedy of the dole extorted from the hard hands of mechanics?

After dinner I called upon the invalids, and found them on the whole better. West's wife is free from pain, and on that account thinks she shall be permitted to recover. I met Hill, the Methodist, in her room. If ever there was a worthless fellow, this is surely one. How extraordinary it is that these people should gain admittance everywhere!

I was occupied the early part of the morning in discharging Joseph Goold from his situation of taking my tythe, as I found the money I thus put in his pocket was of no service to his poor wife and children, as he spent it all at the Ale House; and with respect to taking care of my interest I was from the first well aware I could trust him no further than I could see him. They had tythed in the course of last week twenty-eight acres of wheat, and I desired them to haul it into the Glebe: fearful to letting it remain in Day's field, after he had removed his own.

About two o'clock I set off in the car with the two boys and drove to Southfield, having engaged to spend two or three days with Mr. Peter Hoare. I walked a little with him before dinner, and had a good deal of conversation respecting my concerns with Mrs. Jarrett, and was glad to find he thinks I have done right to adhere to the original stipulation.

I was in the study a couple of hours before breakfast, and twice that period afterwards, in looking over Dr. Shaw's "Travels to the Levant." Some of his remarks respecting Egypt I think hereafter may be of service to me. There is also a curious dissertation on the animals mentioned in the Scripture, and on the representations given in the mosaic pavement at Proneste.

At two o'clock I walked with Mr. Hoare to Wanstrow. On our return across Cloford Common I made drawings of the four tumuli, which I imagine to have been thrown up by the Danes after a battle, but shall hereafter perhaps be able to satisfy myself on this head by excavation.

On going into the study before breakfast I was for a while occupied with Horne Tooke's "Diversions of Purley." His derivations of English words from the Anglo-Saxon are for the most part correct, but he seems to rest satisfied with the Saxon, without shewing us the source from whence they derived their particles in common with the Greeks and Romans. Had he gone to the originals he would sufficiently have accounted for this identity in all primitive particles. Some of his remarks, however, I found so pertinent, and the information conveyed in the notes more especially, so much connected with the investigation I am engaged in, that I determined on making extracts. Accordingly, after breakfast, I commenced operations, and I continued writing till two o'clock. Mr. Valentine dined and spent the evening at Southfield.

Thursday, August 1

I was as usual in the study before breakfast, continuing my extracts: the day proving very rainy. Afterwards, when it held up a little, we drove to Camerton without the soaking we anticipated.

I found on my return that Heal and his assistant had secured the tythe wheat in four windmows, so that it has suffered no detriment from the rain.

Friday, August 2

I sent to enquire how the invalids were, and, hearing no material change had taken place, persevered in my intention of driving to Bath after breakfast, as I had promised to visit General Gore on this day when I last saw him. On my arrival at Upland House, Claverton Hill, I found my Mother was again suffering from the gall-stones, but better than she had been. General Gore was so indifferent he could not see me, but I learnt from Mrs. Gore he was considerably weakened, and dozed away a great part of his time. She herself seemed far from well.

As she was anxious to make enquiries about Sion Hill School, kept by Dr. Allen, for her nephew, John Page, I walked there with Owen, and found everything most satisfactory in appearance, his terms only fifty guineas a year including everything, whereas I am paying upwards of eighty for Joseph at a preparatory School.

Owen and myself got back to dinner. My Mother so much better that she joined with the children in playing a pool at Commerce.

Saturday, August 3

After an early breakfast I took leave of my son, Joseph, and went in the car to meet the Southampton coach, by which he was to be conveyed to Romsey, and thence in a post chaise to Twyford.

Soon after my arrival home Mrs. Dilly came to say that Joseph Goold's wife was so dreadfully burnt, they did not think she could live; that her husband and daughter having left her by herself locked into the cottage her clothes had caught fire, and if they had not been extinguished by the fortunate intervention of a person on a visit at Mr. Keel's, the house probably had been burnt. Immediately I wrote to Mr. Crang requesting he would come to Camerton without delay, and also to Mrs. Goold's Father, requesting him to see his daughter —perhaps for the last time. I had previously despatched my house-keeper, Mrs. Williams, to do what she could for the poor sufferer. On going there I saw her, and indeed a most shocking spectacle did she exhibit, surrounded by women; her exclamations were, "Why do you not help me, I say? Why do you not help me?" The force of the flame had been most prevalent on the chest, which seemed almost burnt to the bone; her hands also were dreadfully injured, and the poor creature at first felt so much disposed to gnaw them that they were obliged to tie her hands behind her back. Joseph Goold had been sent for from his accustomed haunt, the Ale House, and seemed to me to be in no fit state to give directions. Mr. Crang arrived before tea, and said there were small hopes of her getting over it.

Sunday, August 4

I heard the first thing this morning that the poor creature had been released about four o'clock. The women who were with her say she repeated her prayers two or three times, and counted the hours as they struck, apparently without much suffering. To herself indeed it is a happy release; but as to her Father and Husband, by whose unpardonable neglect the fatal catastrophe arrived, I cannot say I hope they may not feel, indeed I trust they *will*, and that acutely too, for their gross misconduct. This is another instance which forcibly proves the bad influence of our Poor Laws, in checking that ὀργή or natural affection which ought to bind a human creature in a more especial manner to his kindred; or perhaps I should better express myself by saying they offer an excuse to the ill-disposed and self-interested for not performing the duties which are required of them by natural ties, and which they could not dispense with through fear of incurring the hatred and detestation of their fellow creatures, unless this, the excuse of the Parish being obliged to provide for its several members in distress, were afforded them. A strong case in the present instance might be made out.

The woman conducted herself in every respect, as far as I can judge, with propriety, till her husband's ill conduct induced her occasionally to drink more than she ought to have done, in order to keep up her spirits; but she was far from being an habitual drinker, as it was her endeavour, by keeping a shop, to gain a livelihood for herself and children when her husband was dismissed from his employment. Her Father, a man in easy circumstances, often advanced money for the shop, but Goold's extravagance prevented these aids from being of the service they might have been, and at length he refused paying any more of his debts. Be it as it may be, the daughter was not the offending party: she was dutiful, obedient, and careful of her children, and was not a partaker in her husband's extravagance, the money he expended being usually on his own gratifications. Owing to ill treatment, affliction, penury, and perhaps other causes, the poor woman gradually fell into a low way, and no proper medical aid or other necessary assistances having been administered, at length she lost her reason.

I had applied to her Father in the first instance by letter, afterwards called upon him myself at Frome, and represented the state in which his daughter lay, moreover stating that if she had but proper assistance and proper persons to look after her, she might—possibly— recover; but all I could gain was the promise of a weekly allowance of five shillings.

On a further application for her removal to a proper place of confinement he sent me a rude answer to my letter, saying it was the duty of the Parish to see to this, and that he would only contribute what he said he would in the first instance, namely, five shillings per week.

I then tried what I could do by employing Goold in my tythe field, in order to put some money in his pocket, as he told me his wife was in absolute want of the common articles of clothing. On enquiring I found his wife was not benefited one iota; indeed, sometimes she has been left in absolute want of food, as Goold spent most of the money he procured at the Ale House or in Bath. I dismissed him from my employ.

He then said he should compel Hicks, the Overseer, to send his wife to a proper place of confinement: that, as he could not maintain her the parish should. Mrs. Jarrett having told me she would pay eighteen-pence weekly, over and above what the Parish might do, should she be sent away, I said I would add another shilling so as to make it half-a-crown, and this with the five shillings which the Parish ought to give and the five shillings the Father agreed to pay, would go towards her maintenance. I moreover promised to make another effort with the Father to complete the farther sum which might be required, and then send her either to Hindon, or to Dr. Fox's at Brislington, who only received fifteen shillings a week when Tyler was sent from Camerton thither. I wrote to her Father, but received no answer, and in this state things were when the accident happened.

It is evident from the foregoing statement that both the Father of the poor woman and her Husband, who were both able to have contributed to her removal to a proper place where attention might have been paid her, *both declined*, under the idea that the Parish would be *compelled* to afford this assistance. The Parish Officers on the contrary were backward in taking the onus upon themselves, knowing the Father was in good circumstances, and it was his duty to see his daughter taken care of; and that the husband was in receipt of 35s. per week, and was enabled to contribute out of that income for the purpose.

Thus it happened, between the Parish, the Father, and the Husband, that the poor creature was shamefully neglected while living, and at length came to a shocking end. I received a letter in the course of the day from the Father, stating that he was unable to come over to Camerton himself, but begged I would give directions for a decent funeral, and that he would repay me.

Mr. and Mrs. Gooch attended the evening service, and afterwards called at the Parsonage. I did not touch on Mrs. Jarrett's last note, as I consider the treaty is at an end between us respecting the tythe. It being a beautiful evening, I walked with Anna and Owen to drink tea with Mr. Barter, as he is about to leave home for Devonshire on Wednesday, and I am to officiate during his absence.

I understood during our conversation that young Stephen Jarrett had called upon him the day I had my interview with his Mother, and told him the business was all settled between us: that I was to give up the Living for twenty-one years, and go abroad. It is thus that a fatal injury may be done me by even listening to Mrs. Jarrett's proposition, since the people will think they may at any time drive me from them by a repetition of their ill conduct. I am more and more disgusted with the people around me; such a total want of feeling prevails that there is absolutely nothing to work on. If the miserable death of their companions in the midst of them fails to excite serious reflections; if the contemplation of wretchedness in the extreme, brought on by ill conduct and extravagance; if the prospect of a future state and the apprehension of punishment be of no avail, in vain do we preach—in vain do we visit the sick and the needy, no essential benefit can be performed! They seem to be exactly in the state of the brethren of the rich man described in the parable, who, if they will not attend to Moses and the prophets, will not be persuaded though one rose from the dead!

Monday, August 5

I was occupied in my room settling weekly accounts, etc., the greatest part of the morning. I then walked to Goold's to enquire what had been done respecting the Coroner, etc. No one, I understood, had been to the house. He asked me, therefore, to advance one pound to pay for the shroud, etc., which I did. On my return I wrote the following letter to the Father, and sent it by young John Goold, who was going to Frome:

CAMERTON PARSONAGE,
August 5, 1822.

"SIR,—

I must request your attention for a few minutes, whilst I repeat in a fuller manner my sentiments on the late event. My situation entitles me to speak plainly and without further preface on the subject.

When it was in your power to assist your daughter, whose sufferings I have so long witnessed, and whose calamity called upon even *strangers* to take an interest in her welfare; when, at the expense of a few pounds, you might have placed her in fit hands, and seen her properly taken care of, *You! her Father, refused to stretch out even a finger to lift your miserable daughter from the dust*; you turned a deaf ear to all the applications I made to you in her behalf; you would not take warning from the appropriate parable I repeated to you of the beneficent treatment shewn to the poor prodigal son by a far more offended parent. And yet this daughter, as far as I have been able to learn, never herself offended you; it was not she who spent your property in riotous living. On the contrary she was dutiful and affectionate to yourself, and kind and attentive to her children. If her husband had offended, if he was not to be trusted with the charge of his wife, the more it behoved you *to take her from his hands*, and put her under proper people. This Goold himself wished to have been

219

done, and urged it equally strongly with myself; but these applications were all disregarded, and through absolute neglect your daughter has perished miserably.

On your death-bed, when the money you have spent your whole life in collecting will appear mere dross, and the coveted possessions of this world will pass away like a vapour which is rolled from the hill, how keenly will it strike and agonise your soul to reflect that, for the sake of a few pieces of useless coin, you have perhaps risqued your own acceptance with God, Who has expressly declared He will render unto everyone according to his deeds.

May these recollections rouse you to make every possible reparation in your power before it is too late. The unfortunate children of your lost—I had almost said of your murdered daughter, demand your immediate care. *They have not offended.* Employ the remainder of the time God permits you to live in giving them the assistance your daughter ought to have received; and above all it behoves you, if you value your own future interest, to be careful that they receive a just portion of your property when you are no more.

I have advanced Joseph Goold one pound towards the funeral; the attendance of Mr. Crang, the apothecary, must also be paid. For these two items I consider you my debtor, as I engaged to satisfy Mr. Crang when I sent for him.

With regard to the funeral, I beg to decline having anything to do with it beyond my own professional duties. In decency some of your family should be on the spot to give directions, and attend the mortal remains of your unfortunate daughter.

I am, Sir,

Your well wisher,

JOHN SKINNER."

After I had despatched my letter I drove Anna and Owen to Priston Rectory, where we dined and spent the evening with Mr.[1] and Mrs. Hammond.

Tuesday, August 6

Having written my Journal of the preceding day I drove with the children to Stanton Drew, as I had engaged to meet Mr. and Mrs. Hammond there at one o'clock. In our way we called on Mrs. Palmer at Timsbury, in order to ask whether any of the family would

[1] The Rev. John Hammond, Rector of Priston, near Bath, 1820–60.

accompany us. Mr. Johnson, Miss Palmer, and Mr. Gardner accordingly rode thither.

After having seen the Druidical remains, we ate some of the cold provisions we had brought with us at the small Inn, and returned to Camerton at six, in time for tea, before the funeral of Mrs. Goold, who was obliged to be interred thus early, as it was impossible to retain the corpse longer above ground.

None of her family attended, nor was any reply sent to my letter.

Wednesday, August 7

Mr. Johnson, Mr. James, and a large party of ladies on horseback called this morning soon after breakfast, in their way to the Sepulchre at Stoney Littleton, whither I accompanied them, and afterwards got Cottle to uncover some of the tessellated pavement at Wellow for their inspection. I gave Farmer Coles a one-pound note, as he laid claim to some remuneration, but without justice on his side, as no possible injury could have been done him. But, as he may influence other people not to let me extend my researches hereafter in their fields, should I feel disposed, either at Twinhoe or Whiteoxmead, I thought it best to do so.

The children and myself dined with Mr. James (at Hillside, Timsbury), and returned home at half-past ten. This is the second time I have been out in the night air this week, and I am fully convinced it is very pernicious to my constitution.

Thursday, August 8

It being a rainy day I was engaged the greater part of the morning in my study. When it cleared up, we drove to dine with the Boodles at Radstock Rectory, spent the evening and slept there.

Friday, August 9

Immediately after breakfast we left Radstock, and calling at Camerton to take into the car a freight of provisions for the party who were to meet us at Farleigh Castle, we proceeded along the Wellow Road to Hinton, where Messrs. James, Johnson, Palmer, etc., etc., accompanied by a number of ladies on horseback, joined us, so that the party altogether amounted to sixteen.

After having examined the remains of the Abbey, we proceeded to Farleigh Castle, of which I made several sketches before dinner. This meal we took in the open air, having been supplied with chairs and tables from the farmhouse. Mr. Richardson joined us during the dessert, and attended us to Colonel Holton's Gothic Mansion, with which the ladies seemed to be much interested.

We returned in the evening in time to save our light to *Camerton*.

Saturday, August 10

The greater part of the morning I was preparing my sermon: the text taken from the first lesson of the service for the succeeding day respecting the Vineyard of Naboth.

Sunday, August 11

After morning prayers I visited Mrs. Lippeatt at Cridlingcot, and had a long conversation with one of the Brittens—a staunch Methodist, who said the only reason the Methodists separated from the Church was because the regular clergy did not preach the Gospel, and were so lukewarm in their devotions.

I requested him to attend the service of my Church that evening, that he might judge with his own eyes and ears whether I was lukewarm either in reading the prayers or in delivering my discourse to the congregation. This he promised to do. I also requested the attendance of his companion, a Methodist Round Preacher, which he excused himself from doing saying he should be engaged at the Meeting at the time.

I am well aware it is throwing time away to attempt converting people of this persuasion; still, we are bound to essay it.

On my return home I called upon West's wife, who is getting weaker and weaker. She requested some port wine, which I did not refuse as nothing can be done for her benefit by medicine, and it may occasionally relieve her sinking spirits.

I preached my sermon to a crowded congregation—the people very attentive. The Methodist with whom I conversed at Britten's, who I find is his eldest son, was one of the number, and stood up the greatest part of the time I was preaching.

Friday, August 23

Some of the masons and carpenters working for Mrs. Jarrett requested the key of the Church to ring [the bells], as they said she was expected shortly to arrive home. I declined giving permission, as none of them were Camerton people, and I had made a regulation that only those who rang the bells for Church should be considered as the Parish Ringers.

They then began again on the subject of the key, and told me I had no power to refuse it; that the Churchwarden ought to retain it in his possession, not me, and that he had a right to let them ring. I told them he had no right to let them ring without my consent, and I certainly should not grant it on the present occasion. They then became very insolent, and I left them.

About an hour after, hearing one of the bells strike out, I went to the Church, supposing they had procured Mrs. Jarrett's key from one of the servants, but, all the doors being shut, I called out to the man in the belfry and desired him to come down and give me admission, which he declining to do, I put my foot to the door and forced it open. I found three men there, whom I desired instantly to leave the Church, which at first they seemed disposed to resist, but finally they went down the belfry stairs, and walked into the church-yard, which they absolutely refused to quit, saying they had as much right there as myself. Dilly, Mrs. Jarrett's servant, then came, and told them his mistress desired them immediately to leave the premises. The men then said they would do as Mrs. Jarrett wished, but not for me. They then went away.

Sunday, August 25

Mr. Gooch sent before Church to say he was ready to assist me in the duty if I wished it. I accordingly called on him, and found young Jarrett also arrived. It was settled that Mr. Gooch should preach in the evening at Camerton. I read Prayers and preached at Timsbury. On coming out of Church, Mrs. Parish said, "So there is another wedding about to take place at Camerton; young Mr. Jarrett is going to be married as well as his sister." I pretended ignorance, as Mrs. Jarrett had mentioned the circumstances to me a few weeks since as a great secret. On returning home I called at the Manor House, and mentioned what I had heard to Mrs. Jarrett, fearing lest she should think I had divulged the secret she had intrusted me with. She then said it was no longer a secret, as the lady—Miss Wathen—was then at Camerton; it was impossible that the two young people should be driving about together without its being known.

Sunday, September 1

As I had engaged to perform the morning service for Mr. Cookson at Foxcote, he being ill, I went there accordingly, fully expecting that Mr. Hammond, of Priston, would take the duty at Camerton; but to my great surprise and, I may add, chagrin, I found on my return that no morning service had been performed, and that a large congregation, after waiting upwards of half-an-hour for the Clergyman, had gone home. Whatever was the cause of the mistake, I shall not be inclined to volunteer for other Churches, where there is a chance of my own being neglected.

Monday, September 2

Having engaged to accompany Mr. Boodle to the Clerical Meeting at Mells, and call upon Mr. Knatchbull and Mr. Hoare, I took my breakfast with him at Radstock. We got to Mells before two o'clock, and met only five other Clergymen, namely, Richardson, Algar, Ireland, Bythesea, and Glóssop: some discussion but no information, respecting the Marriage Act[1] took place. It seems rather paradoxical that a composition the lawyers cannot comprehend themselves should be sent into the country for the instruction of our boobies, who will be as wise after hearing it three hundred times, instead of three, as they now are, and that is saying quite enough. I returned with Boodle to Radstock Rectory to drink tea and sleep.

Tuesday, September 3

After breakfast I returned home, as my Mother, with my sister Laura (Mrs. Manningham), and my brother Russell, had promised to spend the day at Camerton. Not finding them on my arrival, I walked to Cridlingcot to call on Mrs. Britten.

I always make a point of visiting the sick when I am sent for, but never found I have been of the slightest service to the Methodists excepting through what I may chuse to give. Old Mrs. Britten and all her family are rigid Methodists, and why they in the first instance sent for me to attend them I cannot conceive. The poor woman is very near her end; she has had some port wine and pecuniary assistance, as well as received the Sacrament at my hands, but as to my conversation being of any service, I fear it has been rendered otherwise by the misrepresentations of those around her.

Wednesday, September 4

At three o'clock I called on Boodle at Radstock, and accompanied him and his lady to Mr. Knatchbull's; we found there Mr. Dickenson[2], the County Member, his wife and son; Mr. Allen, of Bath

---

[1] Marriage Act (3 George IV, c. 75), July 22, 1822. An Act for the better preventing of Clandestine Marriages; ordered to be publicly read in all Churches on some Sunday in October, November, and December, 1822.

[2] Wm. Dickinson, [1772–1837], Member of Parliament for Somerset, 1806–31.

Hampton; Mrs. Grey and her daughter, of Stratton; and the Miss Parrys.

Mr. Knatchbull said there was a bed still at my service, which I did not accept, as I thought I might be of use in attending the Boodles—there being several gates to open, and they had no servant with them.

Thursday, September 5

I called on the invalids immediately after breakfast, and found Cottle's daughter very much worse. Adam Nash's wife was with her, a thoroughbred Methodist. How strange it is these people will interfere, and thwart and pervert all the efforts of the regular clergy. Indeed, our advice is of little value. Adam Nash, the collier, himself pretends to know far more than I know, and his wife is sent to enquire after assurances, and perplex and harass a mind, as far as I am able to judge, properly prepared to exchange this state for a better. I have often thought that some of the more steady and serious among the Methodists might be of great service to the regular clergy, if they would keep within certain bounds and not be hurried away by feeling and fancy. As they know far better the private life and disposition of the poorer orders, they might give some very useful information to the clergyman when he went to visit the sick. In the Primitive Church there were evidently persons of this description under the name of Catechumens, who were of great assistance to the parochial minister. But alas! the present Methodists set up their opinions in opposition to those of the clergyman, they in fact endeavour to convert him; and look upon him as little better than a castaway if he cannot feel as they feel. On his explaining the terms of the Gospel Covenant, and the necessity of good works as well as faith towards effecting salvation, he is told by some old woman by the bedside that "Christ is all in all"! A clergyman nowadays has indeed a difficult task to perform.

Friday, September 6

I was occupied the beginning of the day at the Glebe House, looking over the carpenter's work and settling his account. I find it will cost me £50 more than I estimated, that is, £200 instead of £150; and indeed it is a very comfortable residence for a farmer with a small family. Mrs. Jarrett and her family can have no reason to complain of my incumbency in this respect, however they may disapprove of my conduct in others, since I have expended in the course of twenty-two years no less than £1,200 on the premises, and moreover recovered the almost obsolete claim to Woodborough, after a contest of thirteen years in which I expended £500, which would have been entirely sunk had I not been successful in bringing Mr. Purnell to a compromise.

Thursday, September 12

I wrote letters to my two boys at Winchester and Twyford, and then went into the village.

Cottle's daughter died last night, quite calm and composed. May every example of mortality and summons from this sphere remind *us*!

Friday, September 13

I was engaged the shorter part of the morning in over-looking the men employed in walling up the well in the glebe field, and in my study looking over some papers respecting the analysis of ancient names, which I purpose arranging.

Frapnell, the tiler and plasterer, asked eight shillings for making some little repairs in the Chancel, which I got another man to do for two and sixpence. One cannot turn on any side without imposition, and it is melancholy to think the evil is likely to increase, as we have no school to inculcate honest principles, and the School of the Coal Pits is decidedly against everything which is in the least connected with them. If this parish were the epitome of the country in general, our hour of dissolution I should fear were near at hand.

I reminded Gullick of the ten pounds still owing to me, and which he had flattered himself I had forgotten, notwithstanding he promised in writing to pay it three months ago.

Sunday, September 15

I preached this morning on the Resurrection, in allusion to the funeral of Cottle's daughter which took place after the service was concluded. A considerable number of people attended the remains. Old Cottle and his family had a post chaise. Surely they would have judged more properly to have made less of an exhibition, as it calls forth the animadversion of their equals, and stirs up envy.

Thursday, September 19

I received a note before breakfast from Bath, stating that General Gore had breathed his last. As a chaise was sent for me by the bearer of the note, immediately after breakfast I left Camerton for Marlborough Buildings. On arriving, I found Mrs. Gore more tranquil than I expected.

Sunday, September 29

I performed duty in the morning at Camerton, and administered the Sacrament. I afterwards called on White's daughter, who seems very little altered in face during the last week. She is quite resigned; and begged I would not permit the singers to sing at her funeral, as she knew they would all go to the public house immediately afterwards.

After evening service and tea, I called on Osborne and Stephens, wishing to know from them if possible what were Joseph Goold's intentions respecting his boys, whether he would consent to their being placed out as apprentices, if the grandfather could be brought to take that charge upon him. They said they did not think that Goold would part with them, as they brought in fifteen shillings per week.

I knew this pretty well before, but also knew if I spoke to Goold myself I should hear some deception.

I continued in my study till a late hour.

Tuesday, October 1

To-day I had occasion to remark some of the same evil doings amongst my servants I have before seen, and I expressed myself in terms they could not possibly misunderstand. Mrs. Williams, my housekeeper, professed entire ignorance, but I saw by her manner she was not so innocent as she pretended to be; but enough on this head!

After breakfast I drove to dine in 10, Marlborough Buildings, Bath, expecting to meet my Mother there, but in this I was disappointed, as the engagement with Mrs. Gore had been set aside.

I read prayers to Mrs. Gore and her family; also one of Blair's sermons on the "Consolations of Religion in Adversity and Affliction."

Mrs. Gore having made me a present of Jeremy Taylor's works—fifteen volumes—they were put up with my portmanteau and conveyed to my Mother's, where I dined at three o'clock, and returned to Camerton in sufficient time to save my light.

I found notices, on my return, from Hicks and Weeks, that they should set out their tythe in kind.

The evening was employed in writing till bed-time.

Monday, October 7

Having deposited as many of my manuscripts as it would hold in the Iron Chest, in case of fire during my absence, and giving strict instructions to the servants to be careful of their candles on going to bed, I left home and drove to Bath in preparation for commencing our journey to Town.

1823

SKAITED the whole morning, but at great risque of our limbs! the colliers having thrown stones over the ice.

Walked after breakfast with the boys shooting. Owen picked up in eighteen-acre field, near the Roman habitation, a small oval Cornelian stone of a brooch, with a figure rudely cut upon it.

The frost having broken up, I was occupied in my study. In the evening one of the colliers, A. Garratt, came to say his brother had broken his back in the coal works. I immediately went to his house in Wick Lane, and found him lying in a most deplorable state, the spine having been put out below the shoulder by a mass of coal falling upon him. This is the third instance within these last two years of the same accidents having occurred. I found three or four of the Methodists assembled round the bed exhorting the poor creature to repentance, as they informed him his time was but short, and he must make the best use of it. What with his bodily pains and his mental fears, the sufferings of the man were almost beyond bearing. I staid with him above an hour, and stopped the ill-judged interference of these fanatics by saying I would employ some proper prayers for the occasion, in which we might all join for the benefit of the poor sufferer: that in the state he was himself in, it was impossible for him to collect his ideas to offer up any particular prayers for himself, and by worrying his mind under present circumstances they only increased his sufferings. I then read to him, and succeeded in getting Isaac Green, the principal of the Methodists, to leave the house at the same time I did, otherwise the poor man would have been worked up to delirium.

I went to Wick Lane immediately after breakfast. The poor fellow was grown tranquil, but suffered from not having his water drawn off, the bladder being paralysed, as well as the lower extremities.

As the man seemed desirous of having Mr. Flower's advice, as well as that of Mr. Curtis who attended him as Doctor of the Club, I sent for him by my servant, and, on seeing him after his visit, found he was of opinion that an operation might be performed with every prospect of success, that is, by removing the injured bone and relieving the pressure. I was almost inclined to persuade the poor fellow to submit, but was fearful of influencing him. I paid Mr. Flower a one-pound note, as he had expressly come over on the receipt of my note.

Sunday, January 5

I walked before Church to call on the sufferer in Wick Lane. Garratt had passed a more tranquil night, but had suffered from not having his water drawn off, nothing having passed since three o'clock on Friday afternoon, when the accident happened. Mr. Curtis had been sent for, and had relieved him by drawing off the water, and would perform the operation on the morrow.

Monday, January 6

I walked after breakfast to see the sick man, and learning that Mr. Curtis was then at John Rossiter's I went there to ask whether he actually meant to have the operation performed, and when? He replied, whenever he thought proper; that I had no business to interfere, no more than any other person; the man was under his charge, and I had no business to send for another.

I said, that as I understood from Mr. Flower on Saturday, that every day's delay added to the risque of success in the performance of the operation, I should candidly tell him I would take minutes of everything that had occurred, and draw up the case, should the man receive any detriment from the delay. Mr. Curtis then said he did not care what I did, as he conceived I had no right to injure him in his business by sending for Mr. Flower.

I called in the course of the day on Mrs. Jarrett at the Manor, hoping her interference might be of service in quelling the discord among the doctors, since Curtis declared he would walk out of the house the instant Mr. Flower entered. I found it was agreed to send for Mr. Pope to meet Mr. Flower the next day to perform the operation, which was certainly the best method to accommodate the feud, as Mr. Crang, I find, is no less at enmity with Mr. Flower than Curtis. These doctors differ among themselves, but it is hard that their patients should suffer for their disputes.

I waited at home in expectation of hearing the operation was performed; but it did not take place till the evening, when Mr. Flower with his partner, Mr. Leech, opened the back near the spine, and extracted a part of the protruding bone. The man bore the operation with great firmness, but did not experience the relief I expected.

I walked after breakfast to the poor sufferer at Wick Lane, and found him quite quiet after the operation, and anxious for me to read prayers. I then went to the Red Post, where I attended the Coroner's inquest on Farmer Lippeatt, who lost his life the Saturday preceding. It seems he had been drinking till twelve o'clock in the Red Post Public House, and was so intoxicated he fell down on the floor before the landlord turned him out of the house at that hour, shutting the door in his face, and exclaiming, "Damn your eyes, you shan't stay here all night," although the man begged to have a bed some time before, which the landlord refused because he had no money, and turned him out to take his chance. The poor man walked through a gap near the public road, thinking it was an opening to go into the field in his way to Dunkerton, and fell upwards of twenty feet into a quarry, where he lay till Sunday morning, when he was taken to the Red Post, and died not long after, his breast and back being broken. The jury, attended by Jacob Balne, the constable, brought in their verdict, Accidental Death. After the verdict was returned, I asked whether I might say something to Lloyd, the landlord. Mr. Layng, the coroner, having assented, I then said although it could not be affirmed that he was immediately instrumental to the death of the poor man, yet he could not, I supposed, feel himself comfortable under the idea of having been partly so, for if he had only attended to the regulations of the magistrates he would have drawn no beer after ten o'clock; he had permitted the man to lose his reason by intoxication, and then closed his door upon him, leaving him to destruction. I further said that this Lippeatt was not a stranger, but a farmer residing in the neighbourhood, therefore there could have been no risque in offering him a bed, as he was certain of meeting with him again. I then said it behoved him to shut his door at ten o'clock, according to his instructions, and that I should see this was done. He said he had no instructions. I then turned to Balne, the constable, and asked whether the magistrates' clerk did not supply them. On his answering in the affirmative, I desired him to procure a paper, and set it up in the public house.

Friday, January 10

I drove to Bath to my Mother's in the car, or rather young Boodle drove me, and broke one of the springs—the roads being so hard with the frost. As Dr. Holland had engaged the boys with my brother, Russell, to go to the play. I accompanied them with young Boodle and my daughter, Anna. We returned in a close carriage to my Mother's. The play was, "Mrs. Cowley's Bold Stroke for a Husband"; the entertainment, the fairy tale of "Cherry and Fair Star," the scenery and dresses better than I expected.

Saturday, January 11

Dr. Holland with his son accompanied us to Camerton to a five o'clock dinner, and we passed the evening in looking over Shakespere's Prints, by Boydell.

Sunday, January 12

I read prayers in the morning; in the evening Dr. Holland performed the service, and preached a good plain sermon on the text, "So teach us to number our days, that we may apply our hearts unto wisdom"—a good subject for the commencement of the New Year. Mrs. Jarrett was present, and the people attentive; but the school children behaved themselves but very indifferently.

Tuesday, January 14

As it had frozen hard during the night, and the boys wished me to accompany them to skaite, I walked with them to the Dundas Aqueduct in Claverton valley, and skaited for four hours on a fine piece of ice where the Combe Hay canal had not been broken. Some of the Catholic gentlemen from Downside passed us, and said they had come on the canal the whole way from Camerton.

Sunday, January 19

I called on Garratt after the morning service, when I preached on the text, "In the latter times shall come those who have itching ears, and will not endure sound doctrine." I was induced to give this sermon because I have perceived the Methodists more alert than usual, having made a new gallery to the Meeting House on Red Hill, and abstaining more from the communion of the Church than they were wont to do. The singers also have ceased their attendance, and none of the farmers now are in their places at Church. Mrs. Jarrett for the sake of popularity has held out expectations to the Methodists of contributing to their new gallery; whether she actually did so or not I have yet to learn. She is a foolish woman: Varium et mutabile, says Virgil of old. I would forgive her folly if I thought she acted on principle, which I am convinced she does not, unless it be to aquire authority by any means however degrading.

> *Two leading springs the female hearts obey,*
> *The love of pleasure and the love of sway.*

Friday, January 24

The frost so intense last night I could scarcely keep myself alive; the water froze in the pot de chambre, although there was a good fire in my bedroom, and the jug in my wash-hand bason froze solid. I never experienced anything equal to this, excepting in the hard frost of 1788 when I was in Holland.

Sunday, January 26

The snow which had fallen in the night was so deep, I agreed to have only one Church, and that was in the evening. The boys amused themselves as well as they could.

Thursday, January 30

I have not read less than ten hours a day on an average for this week past, and have got through a good deal. Again very bad accounts of dear Laura [his sister].

Friday, January 31

The boys went in to my Mother's. I wished much to have accompanied them, being anxious to learn how my sister is, but could not, there being three persons dead in the Parish.

Tuesday, February 4

I was up early to take leave of the boys, who went in the car to the Cross Keys [probably Combe Down] to meet the Salisbury coach.

After tea I thought I would ask John Rossiter's wife how she was, not having seen her for several days. On my way to the house I learnt she was dead; I was much shocked at this sudden departure, and, hastening my steps, found Mrs. Jarrett and a number of women round the bed on which the corpse was laid. Thinking I intruded just at that time, I was returning home, but as the poor husband seemed in a most deplorable state I went back again to him, and in my way met Mrs. Jarrett crossing from the house, who told me she was with the woman just as she died. Entering Rossiter's house, I found him devoting himself to feelings of despair, and unable to listen to reason. Thinking that a cordial might be given with benefit under the circumstances, I returned home for a bottle of port wine, of which I persuaded him to take two glasses, also the women who were in the house. Having continued with this afflicted family upwards of two hours, and succeeded in tranquilising the first transports of their grief, I left them a little after eight o'clock, and continued in my study till prayer time, as my mind was quite worn down.

I drove to my Mother's, and was much concerned to find my sister looking so much worse than I had seen her, indeed her cough is now so frequent, and her expectoration so copious, I cannot flatter myself that she can get over it; but at present she does not seem herself aware of the danger. I promised to take my tea with her, which I did; but was very uncomfortable in seeing her so much oppressed in breathing, the room being too close, her fever also very strong.

A person brought me a note from Miss Sennett, with Anna's account for the last half year, amounting to £54. I am sure, if we are obliged to abate one-third of our incomes, that education ought to be lower in proportion, but instead of that it is increased. What I have to pay for my three children's education this half year is as follows:

Owen	. .	£62
Anna	. .	£54
Joseph	. .	£42
		£158,

besides clothes, pocket money, journeys, etc., etc., so I can hardly estimate the education of the three children, the eldest only fifteen, at less than £400 per annum. I wrote to Anna saying she might mention to Miss Sennett that the account should be settled after I had gotten my tythe, but that I could not do so just now, having overdrawn my Banker on her brother's account. My Mother informed me that our cousin, John Page, was lately dead. This is the third lad my uncle has lost: one was killed at the Battle of Waterloo.

Sunday, March 16

Very few people at Church. Not seeing Mrs. Jarrett and her daughter there, I called at the Manor House to enquire respecting them, and was shewn into the drawing-room, where I saw Mr. and Mrs. Gooch writing letters: the former apologised for not having attended to the duty of the day. I told him no apology was necessary to me, since his own conscience must tell him what was best to be done in such matters.

On calling on John Rossiter I found him much more tranquil. He asked whether the corpse might be carried through my plantation road to the Church, which of course I consented to, only stipulating that my servant should open the gate for them, to shew that the road was not public.

I preached on the subject of Preparation for Death: "The Lord gave, and the Lord has taken away." Several at Church, among whom was Mr. Purnell.

As soon as the service was concluded I called at the Manor House to enquire after Mrs. Gooch, who had quitted the Church at the beginning of the Litany, and, as her husband followed her, I was apprehensive of her being ill, but learnt there was nothing of consequence the matter. Surely the Church is too solemn a place to trifle with, as with a drawing-room, and a clergyman above all ought to have some paramount reason for quitting it. The funeral was at four; the Church crowded, even to inconvenience; several people were there I very seldom see in attendance for their own advantage. I could not help thinking of the absurdity of following a lifeless piece of clay to the Church, when they neglected to bring their own animated bodies thither. But I am weary of moralising on this untoward people; it is a hopeless case, and things must take their course.

I got into my car a little before three o'clock and drove to my Mother's, being anxious to be on the spot during the precarious state of my sister's health. On my arrival I found it was as I expected, she was much weaker and the fever very high.

Having much to settle at home, I returned thither after breakfast. Harris, the clerk, gave me part of a fibula found in the garden; and another man, a short time since, three coins of the Lower Empire found in Mrs. Jarrett's garden. Garratt is better, but no chance of recovering the use of his limbs.

Jacob Balne married the woman he has lived with so long by my persuasion this morning. I took the opportunity of speaking seriously to him. If I could influence this fellow to do what his own mind and conscience should induce him to do, he might be of use in preserving the order of the Parish.

I heard this evening some sad accounts of the Somer family, and intend to speak to the Overseer respecting them. The mother presented the Parish with four illegitimate children, the two elder daughters have each had one and the third is in a fair way to increase the number, and yet we are now maintaining the whole family at the Poor House, when the husband of the woman, Somer, is living with another person at Timsbury, to whom report says he has been married.

I received a letter from my Mother saying Laura was so much weaker, I determined going in to Bath the following day.

Having understood that the new Catholic Bishop, Mr. Baines, was to preach on the festival of the day (Corpus Christi), and being anxious to hear what he could advance on the subject of the Real

Presence, I accompanied Mr. Haggard and my brother, Russell, to the chapel [in Bath] after breakfast. I shall not attempt a description of the ceremonies employed while celebrating High Mass; sufficient is it to say that no acting during the time the chapel was a theatre could exceed what we then witnessed; yet I must also observe that to the generality of spectators the genuflections and gestures of the priests and their attendants, and the solemnity of the music must be very impressive, when the eyes and ears are lured into the service, reason is content to be passive; indeed, how few of mankind are in a situation to employ their reason in these matters.

With regard to the subject of Mr. Baines's discourse, delivered, I must do him the credit to say, in a very impressive manner, of course I suppose it was memoriter, not extempore, the delusive turn respecting corporeal and spiritual by no means benefited his argument with men of reading and reflection. Had his auditors been permitted to read on their return home the able charge of the Bishop of Durham in 1809, they would not fail to see the subject in a very different light than they do now. I am speaking of the Protestant part of his hearers, who appeared to be very numerous. The admission to the chapel was two shillings apiece for those of a different community. Mr. Day, the farmer at Camerton, who has been so intolerant with me, although claiming almost unlimited toleration, was in the gallery close behind me. As there is, I believe, a law still extant, and a considerable fine for the clergy who are found in Catholic assemblies, I hope he will not hit upon a Catholic mode of retaliation.

Were I inclined to reply to Mr. Baines's arguments, which I am in no respect disposed to do, since they have been answered over and over again, he might treat me as a heretic without mercy.

I spent the evening with my sister, who seemed much more comfortable in herself, the oppression on her chest being removed.

Thursday, June 5

While getting up this morning a little before seven, Treherne, my Mother's man, came into my room and said that dear Laura was no more. It seems that her servant, Gibson, who slept in her room, had heard her cough a little about three o'clock, and call out, "Joseph, Joseph," as though dreaming of my youngest boy. A little after six o'clock, on going to her mistress's bedside, she found her with her eyes unclosed and quite dead. It must have been quite easy; indeed I felt most thankful I was spared the pain of witnessing the concluding scene; the anticipation of evil is always more dreadful than the reality, at least I have always found it so.

I rose early and walked in the garden before breakfast. Mr. Haggard called in order to examine the papers, to see whether any particular directions were given respecting the funeral. By the Will, directed to me as executor, it appears that the interest of the property standing in dear Laura's name in the Funds is to be employed by my Mother during her life, afterwards the principal to be divided among my three children on their coming of age. I am rather sorry for this, as a little independence is a dangerous thing for young people, especially if they are inclined to be expensive on their first outset in life. However, I am gratified by this mark of regard, which, indeed, began early, and ended only with her life.

This being the coming-of-age birthday of Mrs. Jarrett's eldest son (John Jarrett, Esq.), it was ushered in by the ringing of bells as soon as it was light, great preparations having been made for this important event by the killing of an ox and the purchase of ten hogsheads of cyder, besides strong beer, spirits, etc., etc., with seven sacks of potatoes and a waggon load of bread. All the farmers, colliers, etc., etc., and their friends from the surrounding neighbourhood did their best in the course of the evening to get rid of this good cheer; dancing, music, songs, and, I should suppose, plenty of swearing concluded the feast. As I had no great goût for entertainments of this sort, I accepted Scobel's invitation to dine with him at Farrington. Before tea we played a match of bowles on the lawn before the house, and I afterwards drove home under a heavy dew.

Owing to my cold, I was so oppressed at the chest, and my voice so hoarse, I could with difficulty get through the morning service. In the evening I preached on the Gospel for the day, which inculcates reconciliation after having been offended. I may conscientiously say I have both forgiven and forgotten innumerable injuries and insults during my residence among this perverted people, for my own sake, but am decidedly of opinion it has not been the most conducive to their amendment.

As Mr. Day was shearing his sheep, I called upon him respecting the tythe, and also to enquire about the Catholic Chapel at Downside, which is to be opened on Thursday for divine service, and a sermon preached by Dr. Coombes,[1] of Shepton Mallet; the whole of the service will be performed by Mr. Baines, the new Bishop, whom I heard a few weeks since at Bath. As Mrs. Wm. Skinner seemed anxious to witness the ceremony, I might add, acting on the occasion, I at first thought of accepting the invitation I had received by a circular letter and a ticket sent me by the Prefect, and I asked Day whether he thought the ladies might be admitted. He told me, as he should see Mr. Barber (the Prior of the College) in the evening, he would ask the question and let me know the result; but on second thoughts, I gave up the idea of going altogether, as it might have a prejudicial influence with the common people in the neighbourhood, who would think they were authorised to go constantly to that place of worship if they knew their Clergyman went once: my weaker brethren I should not wilfully mislead or put stumbling-blocks in their way. Day is an artful fellow to deal with, and he once told me he understood I had been preaching against the Catholics. He might, therefore, with good shew of reason say, Why does your Priest go and hear doctrines he himself condemns?

Henry Hoare from Southfield called in the morning, and staid for dinner; his Father, I understand, is still in the North.

Owen arrived from Winchester in the evening.

After breakfast I wrote to Mr. Barber, the Prior of the Catholic College at Downside, thanking him for his polite attention in sending me a ticket for Thursday, excusing myself from attending, but asking, however, his permission that my brother, Russell, should avail himself of it in my stead. This note was forwarded by Russell from Radstock, when he went to dine there at the Boodles'.

My brother returned from Chilcompton about the middle of the day, and gave a curious account of the masquerading scene he had witnessed in the Catholic chapel at Downside. Whenever the new Bishop, Dr. Baines, took off his mitre, Mr. Barber, the Prior of the

[1] William Henry Coombes, D.D., 1767–1850, a native of Camerton.

college, kissed it, as well as his hand and ornaments during several parts of the ceremony; the sermon was preached by Dr. Coombes, on the Real Presence; on concluding it he said, "with his Lordship's permission," meaning the new Bishop, "he would bless the people." This reminds one of Swift's Epigram on the Prelate who left the altar to attend the Viceroy!

The whole party from the Parsonage, excepting my Mother and Anna, dined at Mr. Purnell's at Woodborough, and spent a pleasant evening, Captain and Mrs. Scobel being of the party, and the weather permitting us to take a stroll round the grounds and gardens after dinner. We afterwards played at cards, so that it was nearly eleven o'clock before we returned home.

Sunday, July 13

After Church ten of the schoolgirls came to be examined previous to confirmation; others would have accompanied them had the weather been more favourable. After tea I walked with my Mother and the boys to Cridlingcot, calling in the way on Garratt in Wick Lane, who has been very feverish of late. He is not able to sit up in his bed, therefore the idea of teaching him to net must for the present be given up. I left his monthly allowance with him, up to Saturday. On going to Mrs. Kimberry's, one of the female Methodists passed me without the slightest inclination of the head, but, on the contrary, with a more marked elevation of it than usual. I should not have noticed this, had not another poor deformed creature passed me in the same ridiculous attitude. I then said to the boys I was sure some greater portion of spiritual gifts had been communicated to-day in their assembly than usual! Two young men of the Methodist persuasion, with whom I entered into conversation, expressed it as a decided opinion that all religious societies had a right to expound the scriptures their own way. When I said that it was not possible for uninstructed persons to do this, one of them replied that, when they had the gift of God, all things were possible; he said there was no reason that colliers should be despised if they had the gift of God and the grace to perform His commandments. I put the question to himself whether, if he had injured any part of his body, or had any inward complaint which required judgment to cure, would he send for a regular bred surgeon to attend him such as Mr. Crang or Mr. Flower, or go to old Crow, the horse doctor at Radstock. I am convinced little is to be gained by argument with the common people:

si decipi vult vulgus. If the Government would only require certain qualifications in the ministers of the Dissenters with respect to their knowledge and principles, the mischief might be less extensive.

Sunday, July 20

A wet morning; very few at Church in consequence. After service I heard the children their Catechism and explained the several Articles, as I did the preceding Sunday. In the evening the Church very full, and the people attentive. Two classes of the collier boys attended to say their Catechism after dinner, but could not recollect what they formerly learned, and when I explained it to them they were so very ignorant and ill-behaved I did not think I could in conscience give them tickets for Confirmation. I therefore dismissed the whole—in number about fourteen, only giving a ticket to young Clarke, the schoolmaster's son, who said his very well. There were eighteen girls who passed, among them the daughter of Sarah Somer, who behaved so improperly lately, but on her promising amendment I gave her a ticket. The impropriety, not to say injustice, of Mrs. Jarrett's having dissolved the Sunday School which I established on my first coming to Camerton was never more exemplified than on the present occasion. The boys used to say their Catechism very well, and were pretty constant in their attendance at Church; the whole object of the lady in doing away with a benefit of such essential consequence to the Parish was no other than because she thought her authority was infringed by having a school to which she did not contribute one sixpence, and which had been supported by the Clergyman of the Parish for upwards of twenty years at his own expense. One need not turn to Shakespeare for a Kate, nor to Russia for a Catherine, the prototype exists at Camerton voce persona et re.

Monday, July 21

Notwithstanding the weather was very wet and unpromising, I drove to Radstock to Boodle's to an early breakfast, and afterwards took him in the car to Frome, where we arrived a little after nine o'clock—in time to pay our respects to the Bishop of Gloucester, who officiated instead of the Bishop of Bath and Wells.[1] There were about five hundred confirmed, and an impressive charge was afterwards delivered by Dr. Ryder; I mean impressive because it came from the heart. If I were disposed to cavil I might have said the

[1] Richard Beadon, D.D., 1737–1824.

worthy Bishop was carried a little too far by his feelings and fancy, when he told the young people that a number of good and evil spirits were then on the watch, either to confirm them in their good resolutions, or entice them to evil. Alas! poor human nature is of itself sufficiently weak, without the demoniacal assaults of the Angels of Darkness. However, if this personification of evil can produce more powerful effects on the minds of the ignorant, we may be permitted to employ the figure, if we can do so without exciting prejudice. Returned in the evening to Camerton.

Saturday, August 2

A rainy morning, which confined me within doors the greater part of the time. I was occupied till bedtime in composing a sermon to further the subscriptions towards the National School, having received papers from the Bishop to require exertions on that head. I was thus engaged till past eleven.

Little Joseph drove to my Mother's in the car to dinner, preparatory to his going to school on Tuesday.

Sunday, August 3

The weather still very wet, so that there were few people at Church in the morning. During the service I read the King's letter to the Archbishop of Canterbury respecting the National Schools, and declared my intention of preaching on the subject in the evening, which I accordingly did on the text: "Train up a child in the way he should go: and when he is old, he will not depart from it." In the course of my sermon I lamented that we had now no boys' school at Camerton, and indicated that it was my wish to establish one in the Parish in connection with the National School; as it is absolutely necessary something should be done of the kind, as I found all instruction had been thrown away on those colliers' sons I examined for Confirmation, who had forgotten their Catechism, and everything they had learnt, in the space of a year when they ceased to be instructed.

Mrs. Jarrett as well as Mr. Gooch were present; the former seemed to be very attentive to the arguments I employed to shew that instruction after the mode pursued by the National School, and the discipline there encouraged, was far preferable to the desultory method of instruction practised by the sectarists. After Church I called on Mrs. Jarrett, and said it was my intention to appropriate a part of the glebe field called "Tatleys," near Tunley, for the purpose of building a schoolhouse, and also a place of residence for the master; as Mrs. Jarrett said she had objections to any places of the kind being erected on her estate this would obviate the difficulty, and I hoped I should meet with her aid in supplying funds for carrying my plans into execution. She replied, it certainly was contrary to her intention to do anything of the kind herself, but, if I arranged the plans and got assistance so as to enable me to execute them, she would have no objection to contribute her assistance. I might have said the Parish had a claim on her assistance in an essential manner, since the established schoolhouse had been pulled down by her Father, on condition of building it up again if it was wanted. However, I held my peace.

After tea I visited Garratt, the sick collier, and Mrs. Kimberry. To the latter I gave twenty shillings, thirteen for her quarter's rent, and seven to procure a girl to attend her, as her weakness is now so great she ought not to be left alone. I also visited Joseph Goold, who is in a dangerous state with a violent inflammation on the lungs. He has been blooded, and Mr. Crang, I believe, thinks very unfavourably of his case.

Tuesday, August 5

We drove to Bath to my Mother's. Joseph went early this morning in the car to meet the Southampton coach at the Cross Keys, in order to go to Romsey in his way to Twyford.

Wednesday, August 6

I walked to Bath Hampton with Owen, [and] fished in the Avon, in order to instruct Owen in dapping; caught four or five dace in our walk along the river's side from Bath Hampton to Claverton.

Sunday, August 10

I preached in the morning at Camerton a sermon, pointing out the advantages of education if properly directed, and the ills arising from the neglect of it. Mrs. Jarrett, I thought, did not seem much to approve of some parts of the discourse, as I now and then noticed an emphatic "hem." However, I am too old a soldier to be alarmed at squibs!

Still the same miserable weather; all my hay which has been cut down for this fortnight past in one of the glebe fields, by this time must be reduced to the state of manure. I do not go to witness the mischief, but take it en philosophe, for a very good reason—because I cannot help it.

My morning was occupied in writing letters to Mr. Bailey, one of the proprietors of the Camerton Coal Works, to Purnell [of Woodborough], and to Mrs. Jarrett respecting their contributions towards a parochial school in connection with the National Association.

The evening proving fair, I walked with Owen to Clan Down. It is extraordinary, this wet weather, how many wasps' nests have been found in this immediate neighbourhood; no less than sixty have been taken at Camerton, and in the adjoining villages in proportion.

I preached at Timsbury in the morning, and buried Collins, poor man, who had destroyed himself in a fit of insanity, at Widcombe. Perhaps his family would have judged better to have interred him there, instead of making a public exhibition in their own immediate neighbourhood; the churchyard was crowded.

I wrote a letter to Dr. Gabell (Winchester) enclosing a draft for £56, the amount of Owen's last half year's schooling.

Owen went off early for Winchester.

I was occupied the forepart of the day in overlooking the people in the hayfield. Having seen the remainder of the hay in a fair way to be carried before night, I walked with my guests Mr. Haggard, his daughter, and Anna. We returned in time to dress for dinner. Captain and Mrs. Parish, and two ladies staying with them, and Mr. and Miss James dined with us at Camerton.

Having engaged one of the coal barges, I had it fitted up for the ladies with an awning and matting against the sides, and tables and chairs from the public-house, in which we proceeded about eleven o'clock to Combe Hay, where we visited the Mansion House, walked round the premises, and afterwards dined under the trees near the cascade. As the day was delightful, the whole party much enjoyed the excursion. I forgot to mention that Mrs. and Miss Newnham were with us; as the latter is a nice companion for my daughter, Anna, I asked her to sleep at the Parsonage, in order to accompany us the next day to Cheddar and Wells.

Wednesday, September 10

In order to have the day before us we breakfasted at seven, and soon after set out on our excursion; Mr. Haggard, his daughter, and Anna in a chaise, Miss Newnham and myself in the car. We stopped at Chewton Mendip to examine the Romanised British remains in the vicinity of the Church, and the elegant tower of that edifice, and thence passing through Priddy, drove slowly, and walked through the cliffs with which my friends were highly gratified. We dined on our cold provisions at the little inn, and resumed our vehicles a little after three o'clock, proceeding through Rodney Stoke.

While the horses were baiting at Wells we had time to visit the cathedral and the exterior of the Bishop's palace, and, having deposited my young charge with her family at Chilcompton, I returned home a little after eight o'clock, my old mare having performed upwards of forty miles without the least appearance of fatigue to herself.

Thursday, September 11

I answered Dr. Gabell's letter respecting Joseph's going directly to Winchester, and wrote to Mr. Bedford on the subject. I could have wished him to have staid a few months longer at Twyford; but as he might not secure a vacancy, I thought it better to accept at once Dr. Gabell's offer. I visited Mrs. Collins whose child is very ill, and naming it by her request.

Friday, September 12

I walked to Radford to see Mrs. Collins; the child is still alive, and the poor woman in the greatest distress, it being an only child, and given to her after having been married eleven years without any. She does not seem to bear up at all; but who can reason against the feelings of a parent over a dying infant? You may tell her whatever is is right, but that is but poor consolation. I repeated to her the excellent moral inculcated in Parnell's "Hermit." The poor woman listened and cried; well might she have replied with our immortal bard, "Oh, who can hold a fire in his hand by thinking of the frosty Caucasus?" or in the words of Job to his friends, "All this I know as well as ye."

I was much concerned to hear that Captain Savage (of Midsomer Norton House), while shooting on Wednesday, had lost his thumb by the bursting of his powder horn. I immediately mounted my horse on my return home to enquire after him, and found from Miss Palmer that all was going on well.

Sunday, September 14

I called on Mrs. Collins; the child is better, and, I hope, will do well.

Sunday, September 28

I found Mrs. Jarrett had arrived at Camerton, but she was not at Church in the morning. I walked before evening service to Cridling-cot, and saw Mrs. Kimberry, who is on the point of death, but capable of listening to the prayers I offered up for her. After evening service I called on Mrs. Jarrett, who, more sua, was wonderfully gracious: "Il volto sciolto i pensieri stretti." But I will not touch on this subject. I spoke respecting the school, and my disappointment in not receiving assistance from the Coal Company. She said she had reason to believe they would give five pounds per annum towards the schoolmaster's salary, and perhaps the same sum towards the building, and advised my writing immediately to the National Association to see what assistance they would afford. I am fearful the onus will lie upon me, the same as I have hitherto experienced in the subscriptions to antiquarian research.

Sunday, October 5

I preached at Camerton in the morning, and administered the Sacrament; in the evening there was a Christening, Churching, and the funeral of Mrs. Kimberry. I felt so much exhausted by the exertions of the day, that I went early to bed.

Monday, October 6

I was busily occupied this morning in correcting some of the Journals, which I am sorry to see have been transcribed in too great a hurry by my brother [Russell]. About the middle of the day Mr.

Peter Hoare and his lady, with Henry and his brother, arrived at the Parsonage. I had asked Mr. Knatchbull to meet them at dinner, but he was engaged. The evening was passed in looking over books of prints, coins, etc., etc.

After an early dinner Mr. Peter Hoare and his family left us for Southfield, excepting Henry, who walked with me in the plantations. As we passed by Mrs. Jarrett's gate we saw that lady, who called to us and invited us to tea. I said my young friend and myself had determined on a long walk, and therefore declined her polite invitation; she said, as her tea hour was seven o'clock, it could not interfere with our walk, unless we chose to do so in the dark. She mentioned that two of my parishioners, Mrs. Gullick, my late tenant's wife, and a woman of the name of Padfield, were on the point of death, and this with a kind of air as though it conveyed a reproof for my not having visited them. I told her it was the first information I had received of their being ill; I accordingly determined on seeing them immediately. On arriving at Gullick's we found the family in a sad state, the poor woman being just dead; the children, seven in number, crying around their father, and the female relatives bustling about the deceased, who was upstairs, did not attend to comfort them. Finding that talking could afford but little consolation at that period, I desired one of the women to get some beer from the public house, of which I gave half a glass to each of the children and a glass to Gullick, and was glad to perceive it acted as a cordial, and they became more composed. Having staid nearly half an hour, therefore, we went next door to Gullick, and found the poor woman Padfield very bad with the dropsy, and anxious to have prayers read to her, but there being no prayer book in the house I told her I would call next morning. The husband said he had *nothing to speak against the prayers of the Church, as they were very good.*

Returning home, I wrote a note to Mrs. Jarrett excusing myself from drinking tea, as I felt really unfit for company and cards, which I suppose would have accompanied our evening's conversation, as two old ladies and Mrs. Anne Stephens were staying with her.

Henry Hoare accompanied Heal to Day's farm and saw the tithing of the grazing lambs, and then proceeded home. I walked into the village and called at Gullick's, where the family were all at dinner. The sorrow of the children is vehement at first, but soon wears off; the poor man will feel it much more, because he will find his own comfort so much connected with his loss. But happy is it that people in the lower ranks of life are not possessed of the same sensibility as their superiors; certain am I that all things are conducted on a much more equal footing than they appear to be at first sight—if enjoyment be less, privation is in proportion.

Friday, October 10

I found on getting up this morning that my outdoor servant, Heal, was not come to make the cyder; on going after breakfast to enquire respecting him, his mother said that she had some to make herself, and it was very hard that he should not assist her, as she could get none of the colliers to work for her. I said it would have been very easy to ask leave; that I had it in my power to punish him for leaving his work in this manner; that the week before he had left his work twice without even saying he was going; and if I went to Mr. Purnell I made no doubt he would grant a warrant, but I should not trouble myself to do so, but immediately get another person to finish my cider, and should have no further need of his service. The woman gave a kind of insolent smile, and said I was at liberty to do as I chose. I accordingly called at the Hopyards to speak to John Cook, and he promised to come to-morrow.

Sunday, October 19

I preached in the morning on the text, "Teach us to pray, as John also taught his disciples," shewing that a form of prayer [was] given us by our Saviour Himself, and pointing out the great loss the Methodists sustained by turning their backs on the Church Liturgy; in short, it was my duty to tell the people of my parish plainly that the doctrines taught at the Church and meeting house were not the same; that the prayers of the Church of England were composed by the best and wisest of men. The combination of the Catholics, Methodists, and Dissenters of all descriptions against the Church and State is now too openly proclaimed to be mistaken, and it was the duty of my parishioners to attend to me as long as they could be improved by what I delivered. Mr. Purnell, who was at Church, accompanied me to the Parsonage, stating he had a little business to settle. On arriving there he said he had called during the week, and found I was from home; that he had brought a stamp receipt, which I could antedate, for £15 he was indebted to me for the half-year's composition for Woodborough. I replied I could not think of ante-dating any paper of a Sunday especially, and begged to be excused from so doing. I therefore put up the three five-pound notes which he had laid on the table, and the stamp, and said I would call on him after breakfast on Monday morning, when we might settle the business. He is a strange man—very ignorant, certainly, and I apprehend has but very unstable notions of religion. Mr. Purnell has never received the Sacrament, excepting when he was to qualify himself for a magistrate, and I am sure in other respects—sed verbum sat sapienti.

Tuesday, October 21

I walked to the Glebe house after breakfast, and spoke to John Cook on the subject of his going there. I told him candidly I had met with so much dishonesty and deception from the Camerton people, I was almost determined never to employ one of them again in my service; however, I would give him a trial to Lady Day. I then hinted at his wife being too fond of dress, saying that young Widcombe would have been now in prosperity had it not been for the mis-conduct of his wife in the first instance, which influenced his own. The man listened attentively, and replied I should never have reason to accuse him of dishonesty, and he should endeavour to do every-thing to shew his gratitude. I agreed to pay him eight shillings a week till Lady Day, as the house is fully worth two shillings a week more; indeed, he paid as much for the one he now occupied. I moreover gave him the crop of potatoes in the garden, which is fully worth five pounds, so that he begins his career under easy circumstances as far as respects myself, and I only hope he has no old debts to liquidate.

On driving into Bath I had a note put into my hands from Mrs. Gore, from which I understand she is about to be married. The step is rather precipitate, but I hope it will turn out well.

Thursday, October 23

In the evening I drank tea with the Barkers. I find Mr. Barker[1] has put my large battle-piece on new canvas, and purposes doing so with the altar piece of Noah's sacrifice. I promised Miss Barker to have a

---

[1] Benjamin Barker the younger, 1766–1838, landscape artist, brother of the celebrated Thomas Barker, of Bath.

proper book made to insert some elegant paintings she has lately finished.

I drove into Bath, [and] I walked to the gasometer on the Bristol Road, where a balloon was filling under the direction of a Scotsman of the name of Graham. I do not think the thing itself would have had sufficient attractions to draw me from my way, unless Burrard had agreed I should meet him there. On my arrival, having paid a shilling for admission into the timber yard where the aerial vehicle was suspended, we continued nearly an hour in the open air, most of the time under a heavy shower of rain, till the signal was given and the gigantic ball ascended—the wife of Mr. Graham being his companion du voyage. Owing to the thickness of the atmosphere, the globe was soon out of sight; the course it took seemed to be over the Crescent, but there are so many currents of air it was impossible to determine where it would steer. For my own part I feel but little interest in these exhibitions, this being the third I have witnessed: the risque is certainly too great, and the benefits to be obtained too small to meet with encouragement from any but the inconsiderate vulgar.

Roused to more active exertions by the account of an almost unheard-of piece of barbarity in a Christian country. A collier of the name of Hodges came to inform me that James Evans, an infirm pauper, who has been a long time in a crippled helpless state through rheumatism, in the Camerton Poor House, had actually been left for ten days in his filth, so that maggots had bred in his flesh and eaten great holes in his body. Trusting that this account was not altogether as bad as represented, I sent some refreshment by the man who related it, and almost immediately followed him to the scene of misery. Two women I there found employed in washing his things, and, notwithstanding they had cleansed the object, who is almost childish and unable to help himself, from the nastiness in which he had been so long wallowing, the stench was intolerable. Finding Mr. Hicks, the Overseer, was from home, I spoke to Mr. Fear, the Bailiff of the Coal Works, and begged he would have an eye to this poor man. I also promised one of the women I would give her half-a-crown to attend him till Hicks returned, and then I would myself see that he did his duty. I have before understood this person is hard upon the poor. I afterwards visited poor Garratt, the collier, who is, I fear, in a dangerous state from a stoppage of water, which Mr. Flower does not seem able to remedy. Poor fellow, his sufferings have been extreme; it will indeed be a happy release if it pleases God to take him.

Friday, November 7

Mrs. Hicks, the Overseer's wife, called after breakfast to exculpate herself and her husband from any charge of neglect which might be brought against them on account of James Evans, by endeavouring to lay the whole of the blame on Mrs. Mitcham, a poor woman who used to assist the people in the Poor House; but I think this is nonsense, since Hicks never gave any additional allowance to this woman for so doing, and besides the woman has not strength herself, being aged, to attend on so helpless a being as Evans, and lift him from his bed when he needed it. I pointed out all these circumstances, and moreover said, if the man had died through neglect, the blame certainly would have lain at her husband's door, and it would have been a very serious thing for him to have answered before the Magistrates of the County.

Saturday, November 8

Poor Garratt, the collier, died this morning, also Evans, the miserable creature in the Poor House.

Sunday, November 9

After service I called on Garratt's wife in Wick Lane. From her account he could not have suffered much pain, as the mortification must have taken place, I conceive, shortly after I had seen him. I really believe the poor fellow was in every respect prepared to undergo the change from this troublesome state to a better; if patient, suffering resignation and firm confidence in the just dispensations of Providence entitle us to the rewards of a future state, this humble, unostentatious Christian will receive them. Oh, that all were such! I preached in the evening on the text, "Now abideth faith, hope, charity, these three; but the greatest of these is charity." I never wish to appear the least personal in my remarks from the pulpit, but I thought the occurrence last week entitled me to make the distinction between works of actual benevolence and Christian charity, and mere professions. Hicks, the Overseer, and his family were present. Instead of thinking they were preached at I hope they will apply to themselves the general ideas contained in my discourse, which, indeed, we all should attend to more than we do in our dealings with our fellow creatures. May I be more on my guard in future, and imitate the pattern set before me of forbearance and resignation. Even the uninstructed Garratt was my superior in this respect.

Saturday, November 15

The weeks pass rapidly, and I cannot produce any satisfactory employment of my time, which weighs on my mind. I hope I may be able to live a little to myself, but, under the circumstances in which I am placed, if I do not enter into society I shall be excluded altogether. Well may I exclaim, "Ubi lapsus, quid feci? sed spero meliora."

Tuesday, November 18

Mr. Flower, the apothecary, in compliance with my request, sent his bill for medicine, etc., for the collier, Garratt. It amounted to twelve pounds, but as his operation on the poor man had not been attended with success, he said he would take half the sum. I wrote a letter to Mrs. Jarrett, who had promised to go half the expense with me, enclosing the bill, and stating I thought the Parish ought to pay one third, which would bring our division to two guineas apiece. I drove to Priston [Rectory] to dine with Mr. Hammond, a little after four o'clock. We did not go into the dining-room till half-past six, and had an entertainment better suited to Grosvenor Square than a clergyman's home—French dishes and French wines in profusion. I hope such feasts will not be repeated often, or I am sure I shall not be one of the guests. I drove home at eleven o'clock.

Sunday, November 23

On going to the Church before Service, I found Joseph Goold had gotten a tombstone to be erected to the memory of his wife. On reading the inscription I perceived it was there stated that a beloved sister had caused the stone to be set up. What a satire on poor human nature! the husband who, when the woman was alive, treated her with every kind of brutality, and left her to perish through his neglect, endeavours to make his atonement by a monument, and the sister who employs the epithet "beloved" to the poor creature, who was burnt to death when she was incapable of taking care of herself, never once assisted her as a sister should have done during her mental infirmities, nor pleaded with the father that she should be properly taken care of; but now, for the honour of the family, goes to the expense of a memorial, bedecked with full-faced angels and humbug hour-glasses. I would have remitted Goold the fee for putting up the monument if he had permitted me to add only these words at the bottom of the stone: "Mirabile dictu! Codex carnifex floreat."

After Church, J. Rossiter and Feare stopped to speak to me concerning the allowance of the old people, which I had before mentioned to them as having too little—twenty pence not being at all adequate to the expenditure of a person incapable of doing work. They agreed with me in opinion, and Feare had spoken to Hicks, the Overseer, on the subject. It was agreed by us that in future the old people should have two-and-sixpence a week. I moreover [stated] that I expected the poor books to be brought every month Sunday as they used to be, that I might inform myself of the actual state of the poor.

I attended a Vestry in the Church respecting the poor. Garratt's widow requested the Parish would continue the five shillings she received weekly for herself and two small children, saying she would contrive to pay one-half the house-rent if the Parish would pay the other. It was therefore agreed to let her have five shillings.

I read a sermon in the evening to the servants, as I was accustomed to do in times past.

Tuesday, November 25

John Goold (my servant) went to Chilcompton with a draft for Mr. Flower for Garratt's bill, £6 6s. 0d., and to Oakhill to settle the brewer's account there. The evening was spent in my study.

Thursday, November 27

Visited the Red Post, where the unfortunate man, Lloyd, seems dying from the same cause his wife died before him, namely, excessive drinking. The man himself seems in a sad shaken state, and probably is at times wandering in his ideas; the apparition of Lippeatt, who lost his life by falling into the quarry a few months since, had been seen by him; also a certain gentleman in black, by the colliers denominated the Devil, had made him a visit in his bedroom. These are of course, the inventions of the vulgar; but he cannot be here long, as his appetite has entirely failed him, and there is every indication of a speedy dissolution. Alas! the wages of sin is death.

Sunday, November 30

Having previously engaged to do duty at Wellow for Mr. Gardener, who is from home, I drove there after breakfast, taking the Red Post public house by the way. The man, Lloyd, is somewhat better, but never can last long. I found Mr. West smoking and drinking there; on my telling him it was contrary to the regulations of the Magistrates to be in a public house during the time of Church Service, he was disposed to kick against their authority, but became more submissive when I spoke firmly to him.

Thursday, December 4

I received a bill of £8 15s. 0d. from Cruttwell, the lawyer, absolutely for doing nothing. This is the second time I have paid him the same amount for merely writing letters to the tithepayers, without taking any further trouble. I certainly shall freely express my sentiments.

Sunday, December 7

I preached in the morning on the Advent. Mrs. Jarrett with Miss Fry, daughter to the steward, and Mr. Purnell were present. I mention the latter gentleman as I have not seen him for a long time. I walked with him half up the plantations hoping he would have recollected something respecting his promised assistance to the Parish School; but he was silent on that head.

Monday, December 8

I drove into Bath after breakfast, to be in preparation for the great event which is to take place the ensuing day.

Tuesday, December 9

After breakfast Russell and myself walked to Walcot Church; Mrs. Gore and her sister preceded us in chairs. Having witnessed the union of Captain Campbell and Mrs. Gore, we returned to my Mother's to dinner. The happy pair drove to Clifton, having partly promised to spend two or three days at the Parsonage on their return from that place.

Wednesday, December 17

Having gotten my feet wet in crossing the brook in Smallcombe Valley, a severe cold was the consequence. I felt it coming on before I went to bed, and I could scarcely read prayers to the servants, I was so hoarse, and my cough was very violent.

The boys came over from Bath for their [Christmas] holidays, having been with my Mother since Monday.

Saturday, December 20

I took some James's Powders[1] on going to bed last night, which somewhat relieved me. I have left off meat and every stimulant.

Monday, December 22

Somewhat better this morning, my chest being relieved and my cough less violent. Mr. Barter called after breakfast, and said that, hearing from Mr. Hammond I was unwell, he came to see me. He moreover said he had spoken to Mr. Crang, the apothecary, to come and pay me a visit the following day. I told him I should have sent for him myself had my pulse continued full, but I was sure there was no need of bleeding now.

Tuesday, December 23

Still better: I attribute a great deal to James's Powders—an excellent medicine, acting as a sudorific, and to living low. Mr. Crang called in the middle of the day, and said my pulse was rather low than otherwise; he advised me by no means to think of doing duty on Christmas Day and the Sunday following, and promised to send me some drafts.

Wednesday, December 24

Smallcombe's son came to me to say he wanted to be married to-morrow, as his banns were asked out. I desired the servants to tell him I could not do so myself, neither could Mr. Hammond, and that he ought to have given a longer notice. However, as the man was very pressing, I wrote a note to Mr. Boodle, who promised to come over in the morning [from Radstock].

Owen reads the prayers to the servants at night, and I think it will be of service to remove the impediment in his speech, to make him read occasionally out loud.

[1] A famous eighteenth-century patent medicine.

I cannot say my sleep was disturbed, but my waking hours certainly were by the ringing of bells about seven o'clock announcing the joyous day, when half the Parish at least will be drunk.

Mr. Hammond performed evening service; and there were no less than six christenings.

I was occupied part of the morning in reading in the Hebrew Bible.

Smallcombe, who was married Christmas Day, and whose wife was brought to bed the same day, sent his child to be named, as they are fearful it will die.

1824

SIR Richard Hoare having invited me to attend the Annual Meeting of the gentlemen engaged with himself in examining the Antiquities of Wiltshire, I left home this morning at twelve, taking with me a report of the Antiquities of Camerton, also a letter addressed to Sir Richard, requesting him to present this communication to the Antiquarian Society. The road to Stourhead was so much impeded by snow I could not take the usual course through Mells and Nunney as I wished, in order to enable me to call upon Mr. Peter Hoare, but I was obliged to strike off from Kilmersdon to Buckland Down, and so on to Frome. On arriving at that place my mare was so much fatigued by the drift on the road, especially between Radstock and Kilmersdon, I was constrained to stop for an hour to bait. During this time I saw Mr. Champneys (of Orchardleigh), who was just returned from Stourhead, who told me that with four horses to his carriage he had been scarcely able to reach Frome from thence, and recommended my taking a cart-horse as leader to the mare. Knowing Mr. Champneys had rather what the French call a façon de parler I did not take all literally, and accordingly pursued my way as I intended, and found no very great difficulties to Maiden Bradley, but was constrained to move slowly beyond this village as the roads were much less taken care of—I mean by removing the snow, which had fallen so deep as to equal the tops of the hedges.

However, a track had been cut out for the coal carts passing to the pits for a supply of that commodity, more than ever necessary at this trying time, which I was enabled to proceed on, though at a foot's pace. I never remember to have experienced anything like the cold whilst driving from Maiden Bradley to Stourhead, and my nose and ears were so much affected I hesitated once or twice whether I should not dismount and rub them with the snow, according to the Russian recipe; our delays were such, it was nearly six before we arrived at Stourhead. I say "we" because I had taken my servant with me by desire of Sir Richard, as his party was larger than usual. I found dinner was over; but the worthy owner of the mansion left the company to see proper care taken of me, and after a hearty meal on a smoking hot beef steak I joined the party in the dining-room,

257

consisting of Lord Arundel of Wardour, Mr. Merick, Mr. C. Bowles, and Mr. Offley; Mr. Wansey had excused his attendance on account of the weather. On comparing notes I found my difficulties had not been unique, since Lord Arundel, who had four horses, had been upwards of three hours in coming from Wardour. After coffee we had a rubber of whist, in which I came off a gainer of 7s.—much beyond my expectations, as I so seldom play, and my antagonists were experienced men. Sir Richard, being so deaf, finds a relaxation in having his evening rubber; he was my partner, Lord Arundel and Mr. Merick were opponents.

Tuesday, January 4

I was downstairs a little after eight, and in the library in order to make references. Mr. Offley soon after joined me, and Mr. Charles Bowles, of Shaftesbury, who is engaged in one of the Wiltshire Hundreds, as well as Lord Arundel and Mr. Offley. Mr. Wansey, who has his part assigned him as I have before mentioned, did not appear. These gentlemen, I find, are principally engaged in tracing the descents of the landowners in their different districts, which they are enabled better to do by consulting the records and topographical accounts so admirably arranged in Sir Richard Hoare's collection. Indeed, I believe there is not a library in the kingdom so well supplied in these subjects as that at Stourhead, since not only all the public documents of Domesday and the Tower, but every private collection is so admirably arranged that Sir Richard can put his hand on the minutest book at a moment's notice. As my beat was not that of topography, I got to the folios of ancient times, and made extracts from Seneca, respecting the deification of Claudius and Pliny, respecting the distance of Camalodunum from Mona, also respecting the quantities of lead, which he describes to have been found in Britain more than in any part of the Roman territories. I had previously taken notes, but wished to refer to the originals. After breakfast we resumed our stations in the library, and I soon perceived my associates, although their pursuits were in a different beat, were not less eager than myself after antiquarian game, and we occupied the first part of the morning without any kind of interruption till we were summoned to take refreshments in the dining-room, after which Lord Arundel, Mr. Bowles, and myself took a walk through the snow to visit Mr. Howarden, the Catholic priest settled at Stourton; for Lord Stourton, when he parted with the estate to Sir Richard

Hoare's ancestors, reserved to himself an ancient mansion called Bonhams, in which a priest had constantly resided in order to administer to the spiritual necessities of the Catholics in the neighbourhood. Unfortunately Mr. Howarden was from home, but Lord Arundel showed me the Chapel attached to the house, which seemed in a very dilapidated state: I find it is in contemplation to build a new one. . . . If all Catholics were as devoid of bigotry as Lord Arundel there would be nothing to fear, indeed not only that, but a union might be effected without the smallest difficulty, for I have not yet heard an opinion fall from his lips which the most orthodox might not agree in: this cannot be termed art or management in a man of his lordship's rank, although it might bear that appearance in a Jesuit. I am decidedly against the Catholic claims, taken as a political measure; still, where there are such liberal-minded men who are excluded from a participation of what the most worthless and irreligious actually do enjoy, it then assumes rather an injurious appearance. The priest at Bonhams takes pupils; we saw several children on the premises, who receive instruction, some as preparatory, I suppose, to the ministry. Let us calmly ask the question, Are not these likely to become as good citizens and subjects as the puritanical levelling Methodists and Presbyterians? But enough of this. We called on our return on Mr. Crocker, to look at the plan he had lately taken of the camp at Hamden Hill, near Montacute. It was here that I felt a great chill, occasioned by wet boots, and could not recover any warmth the whole of the evening, which was concluded by a rubber of whist as the preceding.

Wednesday, January 5

I passed a very restless night, and had the mortification to find my cold and cough as bad as it was after quitting Stourhead two months ago; I therefore determined to confine myself to the library, as the best latitude in all respects during this astonishing cold weather. The morning was engaged in making extracts from Diodorus Siculus, there being a most splendid edition of that author, with a Latin translation facing the Greek. I was fully occupied in making extracts from Diodorus the whole of the morning, excepting half an hour spent in looking over a recent publication on the Antiquities of Colchester, which Sir Richard put into my hands; unfortunately the author, in his anxiety to prove this to have been the Camalodunum of Tacitus, makes the Romans engaged in forming walls around the station of the colony, on their immediate settlement on the spot, entirely militating against what the historian states, that the occasion of their surprise and defeat by the Britons was because they had no walls or fortifications. The whole seems a flimsy production.

Thursday, January 6

I made extracts this morning from Ptolemy's Geography, who speaks of Camalodunum of the Brigantes and Camelodunum of the Trinobantes, with the places in the immediate neighbourhood of both.

Friday, January 7

This morning was principally devoted to examining the monkish Annals of Atford. . . . My cold had so much increased, and my cough so troublesome, I had very little pleasure in my studies this morning. However, I was determined not to be unemployed.

Saturday, January 8

After breakfast I took leave of my kind host, having ordered a chaise from the inn: being fearful of encountering the eastern blast: and sent home my car by my servant. Changing horse at Frome, I called on Mr. Hoare at Southfield, and got home, though not without some difficulty, about four o'clock, the roads being a sheet of ice; my cold very indifferent, and I went to bed early—not without dread of the duty of the following day, my chest being very sore with coughing.

*   *   *

Sunday, July 4

The evening service having concluded I walked afterwards about the premises, and am much pleased to see everything in such order, which speaks well for the servants during my [late] absence. I read prayers to them about ten, and purpose assembling them regularly in the morning, as soon as I am a little settled, as well as in the evening, as it may easily be done by fixing eight as the constant hour for breakfast and requiring their attendance a little before. John may then contrive to be indoors with the rest.

Monday, July 5

My hay is got in pretty well, also the tythe clover, in quantity about seven tons. Before I went to bed I amused myself with the Roman

Missal, which I bought in Town, and which I can read with tolerable ease; it consists of extracts from the Psalms, in Latin, and prayers to the Virgin and Saints, some of them in old French. From the characters employed I cannot think it less than four centuries old; several leaves have been taken away, which renders it less valuable in the eyes of a collector, but it answers my purpose very well as forming a link between the MS. of Ulpian and the black letter book Warren gave me. I feel the comfort of returning to my quiet habitation: pray God it may continue so.

Tuesday, July 6

As it rained for several hours after breakfast I occupied the greater part of the time in study, putting my books to rights on the shelves, and arranging my Journals when taken from their repositories—the iron chests.

Saturday, July 10

Mr. Richardson who endeavoured, but in vain, to effect an accommodation between Farmer Day and myself, came after breakfast, and asked me in case there was any likelihood of coming to terms with Day, what was the ultimate I should be satisfied with? I told him I would not take less from Day than I expected from the other Farmers: That I meant to raise their tithe ten per cent at Michaelmas and should expect from him in that proportion. Richardson said, he thought as there was more arable than pasture I ought to have six shillings an acre! When he was gone to Day's Farm, Collins, of Radford Mill, called to know what he was to pay me for some ground he had taken of Skeates, and to occupy at Cridlingcot. I told him that it was my intention to raise ten per cent at Michaelmas, but he might settle on the same terms as Skeates did then. From something that dropped respecting the opposition I have experienced from Day and others in tithe matters, and hints of what I might further expect, I was induced to reply that I was well aware that a system of opposition had been made, and underhand arts had recourse to injure me, by those very persons who ought to render me respect and even assistance to keep order in this disorderly place; but the time would come when we should understand one another better, and speak face to face: hitherto to use a vulgar simile, they had kept me confined like a cat in a sack, and every coward had kicked and pinched me without the least possibility of my making any defence;

or indeed, properly seeing who were my adversaries: but when the mouth of the sack was opened, some of the personages had better look to themselves! Mr. Collins said he was sure he was not one of the description I hinted at; I said, *I hoped not*, but I could not quite forget a conversation I had with this person, who is Nephew to Bush, the Arch Methodist of Midsomer Norton, when he told me he believed there were as many Parsons in Hell, as there were tiles on the roof of the house he then pointed at. With respect to tithe, he said, he should be ready to pay an advance of ten per cent, if the others did so; and he then left the Parsonage.

Richardson returned in a couple of hours, and said that Day told him he conceived his tithe was not worth £90 per annum; indeed Mr. Skinner once offered it him at £80. (It is fully worth £116 to rent) of course there can be no kind of composition with this person: therefore we must proceed as heretofore; and I told Day whom I met in the Hay Field, when Richardson went away, that as we thought so differently on the subject, there was no likelihood of adjusting matters.

I then gave directions to my Attorney, Maule, to file a Bill in the Exchequer, which he did.

Mr. Samuel Day, son of Mr. Day, who rented a farm of Mr. Smith at Foxcote, and had some property of his own at Anglesbatch, took the Home Farm at Camerton, Lady Day, 1819. Mr. Samuel Day is a Catholic, and has been accustomed with his family to attend the Chapel in Mr. Coombes' House at Meadyeates in Camerton parish for several years before he came to reside at the Home Farm, and was well acquainted with Mr. William Henry Coombes, now Dr. Coombes, a Catholic priest now residing at Shepton Mallet. It was this gentleman, namely, Mr. William Henry Coombes, who was present at the setting out of old Mr. Coombes', his uncle's, tithe at Meadyeates, in 1807, and gave my titheingman so much unnecessary trouble. From this circumstance I am inclined to think Mr. Day entertained the same determination to harass me as a Protestant Clergyman immediately on his coming into the parish. At a Vestry held the 12th of August, 1819, he so far prevailed on the farmers as to consent to the monthly parish meeting for considering the state of the poor being altered from the Sunday to the Monday in each month. This measure he carried entirely in opposition to my wishes and in fact against the established custom of the parish and, I believe, of the law of the land by prevailing on the people present to set their signatures to his requisition entered in the vestry book; but this was not long acted upon. It only shews what influence a single Catholic may have when admitted to power even in a Vestry. Day moreover employed his influence in the first instant in screening Widcombe, the Overseer, who had embezzled £96 of the parish money, because he found him connected with Fry (Mrs. Jarrett's Steward), and a fit instrument to oppose my authority; but after I had detected his knavery, and he was lodged in prison, the wily Catholic took a contrary part, although I have my doubts whether this was not a Jeu de Theatre between him and Fry. At the termination of the year he had compounded for, namely, March 24th, 1820, Day came to the Parsonage. He said he would not agree for the farm he held the ensuing year at the same terms, or in other words he was resolved on setting out the produce of his farm in kind, and it being so determined to be done Day still continued his hostility to me, and took every opportunity of shewing it, so that I had fully determined to keep out of the way of meeting him; but at the Vestry called by him as Way Warden, July 26th, 1821, which I attended, finding that he had rated me £100 *for the tithe of his grounds* when he had refused to rent it of me for that sum, I expostulated with him on the injustice of his conduct, and found him so insolent I was more and more confirmed in opinion it was best to keep out of his way as much as possible, notwithstanding my receding from the Vestries might give him a lead and influence in the parish, and which I was well aware it would eventually be directed against myself.

Tuesday, July 13

Having spent three or four hours in my study looking over my new purchase, "Dugdale's Monasticon," I drove to my Mother's; the weather insufferably hot, with an appearance of thunder. I found both her and my brother (Russell) nearly convalescent, and the boys quite well; Owen very much grown, being nearly as tall as myself.

Friday, July 16

Mr. B. Barker, the painter, has entirely completed his obliging undertaking respecting my two paintings, the battle piece and the still more ancient picture of Noah's Sacrifice, which, now it is removed or rather translated from the old canvas in its newly gilded frame, makes a very respectable appearance. The subject is certainly executed by the hand of an ancient master, but whether Titian was that master, as Mr. Barker supposes, or not, better connoisseurs must determine; at any rate both paintings will make a conspicuous figure in the Parsonage.

It was agreed that a dancing master should attend the lads at my Mother's house twice a week, and they are to drive in (from Camerton) to take lessons. I also wish them to improve in writing this vacation, as these things are not attended to at a public school. Could French be added to the list of acquirements during their leisure time, it would be very desirable; but we must not strain the bow too tight at first. In the evening I went with the children to the brow of Hampton Down to see Graham ascend in his balloon from Sidney Gardens.

Wednesday, July 21

My boys drove in to Bath this morning early to take a second lesson in writing of a Mr. Lewis, who professes to instruct his pupils in a good running hand in six lessons for a guinea; each of my boys is also learning dancing of a Mr. Saunders, who comes to Upland House and instructs my daughter, Anna, at the same time. Neither dancing nor writing are at all attended to at a public school, and yet they enter more into the common usages of the world than either Latin or Greek. I wish I could also add French to the acquirements of the vacation; but, as they are very good boys, I do not like too much to break in on their time.

Friday, July 23

I spoke to Cook respecting taking charge of a Sunday School after Michaelmas, for I have been arranging it so that he may have the same salary I used to pay the former master, Clark, who has been dismissed by Mrs. Jarrett, about £11 per annum, which will be a comfortable addition to his income; and he is fully competent for the task, as he both reads and writes very well; and now the Farm House is enlarged, from fifty to sixty boys may be accommodated with ease. I shall speak to my servant, John Goold, to assist, and as I shall attend constantly myself we may bring the whole, I trust, into some order and regularity before Christmas. At any rate I am sure of one thing, it will not be done at all unless I take the whole business on myself, as my neighbour Purnell and the proprietors of the Coal Works, I am sure, had rather the lower orders should not have this advantage, if their sentiments were really known. Possibly I may hereafter get a little aid from Mrs. Jarrett, when she sees it in good training, as I have her promise in writing. Unless she were first and foremost in the business, and possessed the whole and sole authority as to who were to be admitted and who dismissed, etc., etc., she would never cordially lend her assistance. As I shall endeavour to excite emulation by prizes among the scholars, five or six pounds will be requisite to dispose of in this manner, besides the books. John will derive benefit as to his own spelling and reading by attending the classes.

I continued in the hayfield till quite dusk; my chest much better, and my cough gone. This I attribute to living on a vegetable diet and fruit for the most part, which keeps the bowels open without the aid of medicine. I only take one glass of wine and toast and water at dinner, and very little meat: some days none.

Monday, July 26

My servant John contrived to break the knees of my favourite mare by driving her up a place which was never intended for a cart to pass, and thus throwing her down on her knees. I have had her nearly five years, and there never was a more sure-footed animal in the world. I rather would have lost all my hay than this should have happened. I could not help saying a Somersetshire boor treats a horse like a part of the cart he drives him in.

Wednesday, July 28

I find I have no leisure for study, and shall not therefore attempt it while the boys are at home: "Non semper arcum tendit Apollo."

Thursday, July 29

The boys wished me to fish with them in the brook near Wick Lane, which I did, but finding the trout did not rise to the fly I left them shortly after; they continued fishing till nearly dinner-time. In the cool of the evening I tried the fly and grasshopper, without success, and being fearful of the damp near the brook returned before the evening closed in. I did not send for the servants in to prayers, but after I had read them to the boys went to bed; indeed, I felt very uncomfortable at John's conduct, who ought to act with more regard to my interest.

I made arrangements about the Sunday School with Cook and his wife, and desired them to assemble the boys who were willing to attend on the ensuing Sunday.

I spoke to Cook about the Sunday School, and got a list of the boys already coming, which amount to 33. I desired they would be there by nine o'clock next Sunday, when I purpose attending with my boys, to examine how far they have learnt, and divide them into classes. I should suppose we shall begin with fifty, which will be quite enough for the present. Cook will be appointed to the first class, my servant John Goold to the second, and Cook's wife for the younger children. I have desired the boys, Owen and Joseph, to purchase some small cards when they go next to Bath, and write on them, "Camerton Boys' School." These will be given every Sunday to the boys who behave well, and are regular in their attendance; if they do what is reprehensible, they will forfeit a ticket, or more, in proportion to their faults. Half-yearly the number of tickets each retains will be taken, and everyone who possesses twelve will be entitled to a book as a reward. I expect to bring them shortly into good order, at any rate I will make the effort, as I am fully assured of its importance. They were a very nice set of children who came to-day, none above twelve years of age, and some not above six. I shall purchase the necessary books, and have everything ready by next Sunday.

I went to the Glebe House a little after nine and, notwithstanding the rain, found 39 boys assembled, also a lad from Radstock, whom Boodle lent me as a director at the first arrangement of the school, as Cook knows nothing of the business of instruction as now carried on. I divided the boys into three classes; about twenty can read in the Testament, thirteen in the spelling book, and the remainder have just begun to spell.

I then walked to the Hopyards to visit the younger Bacon, who lies dangerously ill of a liver complaint. I read a portion of the prayers contained in the Communion Service, and had a good deal of serious conversation. He, poor man, prays for quiet, which he is not likely to obtain in his present residence, as his wife's mother, Mrs. Harris, is a noisy reprobate woman. I found Bacon very weak and struggling for breath, but his room was very close, so I persuaded him to open the window a little. He seems very resigned.

Monday, August 16

My boys engaged to attend young Newnham and Langford fishing in the brook; their two companions, with young Peter Hoare, came to breakfast: the whole party went afterwards to fish in the Cam. On my return I found the lads had had good success with their fishing, but young Newnham only caught one, as he thought it cruel to use a worm, and only fished with paste. I really believe he is an excellent young man, although he may in some instances carry his ideas too far.

Friday, August 20

Having heard that young Tyler was killed by a stone falling on him in the Coal Pit last night, I went to the house and found his body had been brought home and was laid in the cottage, but was very properly covered up, as it was much disfigured. His wife, who is far advanced in pregnancy, did not seem much afflicted.

Saturday, August 21

I continued the greater part of the morning in my study, writing and arranging my papers respecting the ancient history of Camalodunum, which I wish my brother to transcribe anew with the alterations I have recently made; I also set the map of the district traced by Captain Scobel for me, on calico, in order to render it portable, as a pocket map, that I may mark down the Antiquities in every Parish with some degree of certainty, and notwithstanding the objection which Sir Richard Hoare once made while alluding to these several events: "Oh, Skinner, you will bring everything at last to Camalodunum; be content with what you have already discovered, if you fancy too much you will weaken the authority of real facts," I shall be inclined, if health permit, to persevere in my undertaking.

Sunday, August 22

I preached this morning at Camerton, and I found in the course of my sermon I could with great ease to myself make allusion to passages connected with the subject of which I treated in the Lessons of the day. I feel convinced that with a little practice, I could express myself without any kind of hesitation; not that I ever mean to adopt extemporaneous preaching. I afterwards walked to Timsbury across the fields. In my way I stopped at Tyler's house at Daglan, and was destined to see the exhibition of the mangled face of the poor collier as he lay in his coffin. Surely the lower orders cannot have the same feelings as we have, otherwise they could take no delight in exposing what ought with the greatest care to be concealed, or in visiting what must convey sensations of horror rather than those of satisfaction. I dare say the cottage has been thronged the whole of the morning.

Monday, August 23

In the course of the last week the tame pigeon died, which my children have had for nearly eight years; one of the servants trod on his foot by accident, and I suppose otherwise injured him. Owen and Joseph prepared a grave, and asked me to give them an inscription for his tombstone, which was as follows, cut on the white lias:

> *Hic jacet in Tumba*
> *Formosa Columba*
> *Thomas vocata*
> *Dolore humata.*

For their faithful dog, Myrtle, they also prepared a monumental record to be placed over his grave, commemorating his attachment and the catastrophe which occasioned his death, in these words:

> *Hic jacet Myrtelis*
> *Canis fidelis*
> *Cum sit venatus*
> *Plumbo necatus.*

These are trifling things in themselves, yet if they tend to encourage feeling and affection, ought to be attended to in the education of young people.

Tuesday, August 24

The melancholy occurrences of the last week cast an inexpressible gloom over my mind. I will again aver, if we are to judge of the signs of the times: what with Joanna Southcott, Prince Hoenloe [Hohenlohe], the Priest Carrol, and the followers of the ambitious adventurer John Wesley: the minds of men will not be permitted to expand, but Novelty will continue to be the food of ignorance, to the exclusion of all wholesome provision—sed eheu satis!

Sunday, August 29

I preached on the subject of Confirmation in the morning, shewing that even those who could not read might easily join in the excellent Liturgy of the Church, and have the rules of their duty towards God and towards man properly explained to them if they only constantly attended their Church; that to those young people who were about to take upon themselves to answer for their Christian profession it was doubly requisite, and I purposed explaining the promises made for them at the time of their Baptism, which promises, now they were come of sufficient age, they were themselves bound to perform. I should also enlarge upon the ceremony of Confirmation, established in the early ages of the Church and continued to the present time, and I hoped my hearers would bestow their attention to what I was enabled to deliver to them. The people were very attentive.

My two sons officiated at the Sunday School in my stead, and reported well of the general behaviour of the children.

Friday, September 3

I rose at six in order to breakfast with the boys, and it was the last time I had to see them before they went to school.

Sunday, September

I walked to the school before Church. I was sorry to observe the children did not attend at the appointed hour, not more than a third of the school being assembled; but Cook and his wife seem very careless and indifferent about the whole concern, and I fear I shall have to part with them.

Monday, September 6

I received a letter from Owen, announcing safe arrival at Winchester. I then prepared for going to Mells, it being a quarterly meeting of the Clergy, and had proceeded as far as Ammerdown when a violent thunderstorm overtook me and completely wetted me through, so I was constrained to return home. I dined on poached eggs and bacon a little after four, and retired to my study, where I spent as useful an evening at least as though I had executed my first intention of spending it with my clerical brethren.

Wednesday, September 8

About the middle of the day I called on Bacon at Meadyeates, and sat an hour with him. During our conversation he remarked how much evil communication was carried on in the gaols, where persons, for small faults comparatively, mixed with those who were incarcerated for crimes of greater magnitude. He had been sent to Shepton on a charge of poaching, although at the time he certainly was not guilty, having been found merely with a dog following at his heels in a grass field, without a gun, and on the footpath. (Mr. Bampfylde was the magistrate who had his mittimus signed), yet this man was sent to prison, and during his confinement associated with sheep-stealers and horse-stealers, and was made acquainted with all their tricks. I also learnt from him that one of the Camerton people, of the name of Crocum, has stolen a horse; and it is supposed he will be in danger of his life as this is not his first offence, and his father was hanged for the same malpractices. Bacon seems very sincere in his professions—that should it please God to restore him he will be quite a different being; but I fear he will never get about again.

Saturday, September 11

I dined at Mr. Purnell's (Woodborough). After dinner we played at cards, which I have had more than my share of lately; and the evening being very stormy Mr. Purnell offered me a bed, which I was glad to accept.

Sunday, September 12

I returned to my parsonage before breakfast. I then rode to the Glebe School House; the boys were assembled in good order, but Mrs. Cook pays no attention to them now, John Goold and the Radstock boy having the principal management, and there are too many of them for these to take care of.

I preached my concluding sermon on Confirmation, although not one single candidate has yet offered. The Church was well attended; Mrs. Jarrett and her son, Stephen, were there. I called on them after service, and had *a very gracious reception*; but I must be on my guard, for every word is noted down that passes the door of my lips when I am in company with this lady and her promising son, otherwise I shall have cause to regret having uttered anything before them.

Stephen Jarrett called after dinner. I had seen him in the morning, when I went to the Glebe Farm, shooting at a pheasant, which he wounded, and it fell in my twelve-acre field. He did not see me. I asked whether he had any sport, and said I believed he had hit the bird he shot at, as it fell in my field, and that some of the shot came pretty close to me! He said he did not see me: that he had killed a cock pheasant, and begged I would not mention the circumstance, as he should be subject to a fine of £10 for shooting before October. He then admired the painted glass in the Parsonage windows, saying they must have cost me a great deal, and as they were fixtures he supposed they must go with the Parsonage, as I could have no power to remove what had once been put up. He then said that he supposed *he* should have the advowson, as it was not mentioned in the writings which gave his brother the estate, but that he should not present Gooch to it, as he should insist on the clergyman's residing; that for himself, although of no profession, he had a great regard for the interests of the Church. He then asked whether I meant to bring up my son, Owen, in that line. I said, "No"; that he intended studying law. "Oh! then he will have a silk gown, like our undress gowns; indeed he may be taken for a gentleman commoner, and I should be happy to shew him any civilities at Oxford." I know not which to admire most, the ignorance or impudence of this puffed-up young man. To speak to a clergyman respecting what he himself designed to do with his preferment after his death is what rarely occurs, but the looking forward to that event, even as to the disposal of the glass in his windows, is mean and contemptible in the extreme. But from a briar one does not gather mulberries.

I have not attempted any regular course of study connected with the main work I have in hand, but many hours I lie awake in the night have been occupied in comparative etymology, and I trust I am now quite perfect in that system which, I have no manner of doubt, will one of these days throw great light on primitive language. Although life and all its concerns hang but lightly on me, I still should wish to be spared till I have completed this work I am anxious to bequeath to posterity. To me indeed study has been a shield and safeguard against the evils of life, for when I find myself ruffled either by the knavery or ingratitude of my fellow creatures I retire to my books and to my private meditations, as a hermit would do to his cell, where the storm may blow hard above me but I do not longer heed it. How ardently do I desire to devote the remainder of my days to the acquisition of true knowledge by tracing the bountiful providence of the Almighty through His works, to elevate my thoughts and expectations to a more perfect stage of existence without any alloy of misery. But enough on this head. Happier is the country clergyman in his closet than the bishop in the House of Lords or the Archbishop at the Coronation.

Saturday, September 18

I walked up to the Glebe and saw the stadling prepared for the barley, and the two cart loads they had taken yesterday evening placed in a heap near it. I asked Cook whether he had received notice for tithing to-day. He answered in the negative, but said he supposed he should when the dew was off the grain. While we were conversing Day's wagon passed the lane in front of my premises to go into the field, and I asked whether there was any of Day's barley tithed since yesterday evening. To which he replied no, as he had no notice, he had not gone into the field thinking they would not haul till the dew was off. I then walked into "Stanley's" field where the barley was cut, and saw there was none set up in cock for tithing. I then said I should not consent to take the tithe unless the cocks were entirely separate and distinct from each other, for if my men only took it up with a pitch and no rake I must be a considerable loser. On looking over the half line of barley that had been left the preceding evening as well as that they were then doing I found it had not been properly divided, consequently that I had not received my full share. On pointing out this to the carter he said he had told the people to separate it. I then said I knew not what Mr. Day's religion taught him, but mine instructed me to do unto others what I should expect them to do unto me, and that Mr. Day, if he were in my place, would not wish his tithe to be set out in this manner.

As I wished for two witnesses to see the state of the barley and hear my determination not to tithe it in that state, I directed Cook, to fetch my servant, John, meanwhile the carter sent for Mr. Day. The people in the field, in number from eight to ten, continuing to rake up the barley just in the same manner as they had done before.

On Day's coming into the field he walked up to the wagon near which I was standing, and said to the carter, "What is all this about?

Why do you not go on hauling?" The carter replied, "Mr. Skinner objected to the tithing of the barley." Day then said, "You go and tithe it, never mind what that fellow says!" The carter accordingly got some boughs and began tithing the wake. I said I never would abide by such tithing, as the cocks were not separate from each other. Day said, "Never mind him, go on." He then called a little boy in his service and said, "You go and walk round each cock, that will be sufficient." The boy then scuffed away some of the barley with his feet, Day doing some of the others himself of the first line where the boughs had been already placed. I told him that would never do, as the cocks were still not divided and some of the barley still touched. He said it was false, that they did not. I immediately went up to him and asked him what he meant? that anyone might see they still touched. The air of the man was in the extreme menacing; he put his face quite up to mine, shaking his head. I again asked what he meant by saying it was false; that it was he who spoke false in saying so, and it was easy to prove the lie. He said he was not so much a liar as myself. I was scarcely able to restrain myself from striking him. However, I did not, and stepped aside, saying, if I were his equal I should very well know what to do with him, but it was beneath me to take notice of such a mongrel. He asked me what I meant by mongrel, I replied a low-bred fellow who would insult his superiors, knowing he could do so with impunity, but he would not do so to his equals, for they would probably chastise him. He said he did not know what I meant by low bred and his equals; that his father and mother were honest people and as good as mine, and as for himself he was in every respect my equal. I said he did not shew he was such: that I scorned to play mean or dirty tricks such as he was in the habit of doing, and which in the end he would suffer for, as he might depend upon it I should have legal redress. He said I had been talking about that for five years, and he was ready for me whenever I chose to begin. I said that my religion taught me to do unto others as I would have them do unto me, and that this was the best law, and if he had proper ideas of religion he would keep it: that mine was not a religion of tricks. He said, coming up to me in the most insulting manner again, what had I to say about his religion? I was not to bring his religion to reproach. I said I by no means meant to do so, but it might have taught him to do better than he did. Meanwhile the carter went on tithing, and the women continued raking up the barley in the same wakes as heretofore. I desired my servants to leave

273

the field with the cart, saying that I should not take up the tithe under such circumstances. When Day heard this he called out to one of the women (Garrett's widow) and said, "You go and see whether his name is on the cart, perhaps he will hereafter deny it was his cart." The expression of his countenance at this time was more aggravating than the words he spoke, and he walked up to me shaking his head, and, as I looked angrily at him, he called out, "You need not make those ugly faces, they do not become you" endeavouring by words and actions to irritate me to the utmost of his power, I then walked up to him and said, "What do you mean by saying I should deny my own name?" "Only because you have done it before and have a short memory, that is all." I asked what he meant. He said, "Ah! I need not tell you. Others know as well as I." I replied if he alluded to what others might have said of me I could not help that, some of the people of Camerton would for a pot of porter not only say what was false but even swear to it. I should insist upon his telling me what he meant by his insinuation face to face. He said he should not. I then said he was a scoundrel to say what he could not prove. He said I was a rascal. I immediately struck him two blows on the face, one with my right hand, the other with my left. He did not return them, but said, "This is what I have been wishing for." He then called out to the carter and said, "he has given me a bloody nose," and held down his head which was bleeding. I said he richly deserved what he had got, even had it been more, and added: I supposed he meant to take the law, but I should shew I had been provoked beyond bearing. I am convinced the fellow wished to irritate me to strike him in order to have a setoff against the Exchequer Suit he perceives I am determined to commence, and which he knows will go against him. However, I cannot help it. Such to the best of my knowledge and belief are the circumstances which occurred, and I must abide the consequences.

Sunday, September 19

I was engaged last night and part of this morning in writing a sermon, the text from the 2nd Chapter of St. John's Gospel, the 15th and 16th verses, "And when He had made a scourge of small cords, He drove them all out of the temple." By preaching this it was not my object to defend what I had done in striking Day, but to shew that some provocation had even called forth the personal chastisement of the Great Author of our religion, the Pattern of all meekness and forbearance. I well know this will be a handle of railing accusation against me and my order, and in this light if it does harm or offends one of my weak brethren I am heartily sorry for it; but with respect to myself I cannot say but what I feel satisfied that this personal chastisement was given, and can in no respect accuse myself of having done wrong.

N.B. Day indicted me for an assault at the Assizes, and I suffered it to go by default, and the damages to be assessed at York House, Bath, Wednesday, the 6th of April, at eleven o'clock.

Extracts from Defendant's Case.

"It is evident that the Plaintiff's object throughout had been to irritate the Defendant so as to throw him off his guard and to induce him to strike him—Day called the Defendant a *Rascal* which irritated the Defendant to such a degree as to induce him to strike the Plaintiff twice on the face which made his nose bleed upon which Day exclaimed "That's what I wanted, I have been told you'd strike me."

"It is more than suspected that in all these proceedings the Plaintiff who is a *Catholic* is supported and encouraged by the Heads of a Catholic College in the immediate neighbourhood of Camerton and that he refused compounding as another Catholic of the name of Coombes a Priest residing in the same Parish had formerly done through dislike to the Defendant as a Protestant Ecclesiastic. If this was not the case, why did both these persons refuse to enter into Composition when they might have done so on moderate terms and which terms the other Parishioners were glad to accept."

1825

I DROVE Boodle into Bath to attend a Turnpike Meeting, where I qualified myself to vote on the question whether the Radstock Hill was not a proper object to employ the attention of the Trust as being on the great public road, in preference to a hill near Twerton. Sir J. Hippisley in the chair, and such a chairman never before did I witness. Instead of hearing calmly and impartially what each side of the question had to say, he got up and advocated the cause he had espoused. Indeed, that the said Baronet did not possess the same upper stowage as Solomon it would have been clearly ascertained at this one exhibition, where the worthy gentleman gave us all to understand that he was Asinus Maximus. Old Thomas, the Quaker, spoke good sense. "Let us first," said he, "consider the state of our funds, whether we are able to spend any money whatever in improvements; if not, let us wait till we have the power, and then see the best means for employing it." I left the meeting fully resolved not to visit such a motley assembly again, where men seem openly advocating their private interests, under the specious name of consulting for the public good.

I performed service in the morning, and preached a sermon on the Commencement of the New Year, exhorting my hearers to form and persevere in good resolutions.

Owen has a cough which I do not like, and have requested he will continue within doors of an evening, and not accompany his brother bat fowling. He has grown so fast I dread anything like a lasting cough on the lungs.

I have discovered a new means of exercise, that is, by running up and down stairs a dozen times at a stretch, and then walking along the passage, which measures exactly 30 feet in length; there are 14 stairs, so that pacing backwards and forwards will give 168 stairs in

12 descents and ascents, and walking 24 times along the passage at 10 yards each time will give 240 yards. This, repeated alternately for an hour, will afford as strong an exercise as can be required, indeed much stronger than horse exercise or common walking. The further I advance in life the more requisite does exercise become; I can well afford two or three hours in the day for this medicine, the best of all others, and I must resolve to take it.

Friday, January 21

My housekeeper, Mrs. Williams, was so very impertinent after dinner, I was obliged to say I should part with her this day month.

Saturday, January 22

In my study I am at least tranquil and comfortable, and find my reading turns to good account. I feel my intellectual powers now ripe; I hope they will produce some fruit before I depart hence, and shew I have not lived in vain, but the Great Disposer of all events will direct me and my studies to assist the new era which is about to break upon the world. He will permit me to live to accomplish my object, which is simply the investigation of Truth. Oh! my God! I am the work of Thy hands; dispose of me and mine as most fitting to Thee.

Sunday, January 23

I read prayers in the morning, and preached in the evening on the subject of Private Prayer. I strongly recommended a constant attendance on the public worship of God, and declared to my hearers that it was their duty to repeat the Lord's Prayer at least morning and evening, with attention to the meaning it conveyed, and instruct their children to do the same and hear them repeat it under their roof; that, if they wished to enlarge their stock of prayers, there were Collects appointed for every week in the year; some of these were excellent prayers for daily use, and the collection of Psalms some of the most beautiful models of prayer, praise, and thanksgiving: that if they were not able through want of education to read them, I should recommend their getting some person to repeat them till they had learnt them by heart. I should recommend them to commune with their own hearts in their chambers, and be still; that this internal devotion might be carried on during the labours of the field and at the coal pit, even when they had no opportunity of kneeling on their knees, and I could answer for it the Almighty would be better pleased with such secret communications of devotion than with any of the more ostentatious pretences to the operations of the spirit. This was the skeleton of the sermon I delivered. I have planted, but God will give the increase.

Friday, January 28

This being a very fine day I walked with my sons as far as Falkland Knoll, beyond Wellow, taking the line of the hills across Brês Down beyond Woodborough. The sun being bright and warm, and my companions in high spirits, I do not know when I so much enjoyed a walk.

Saturday, February 5

As Captain Scobel had written to me requesting I would go to Bath to-day to attend a meeting of the Commissioners of the Turnpike Trust, I induced Boodle to accompany me, and a very large number we found collected. Sir John Hippisley, as usual, was pushing for the chair, but as there was an almost universal call to Mr. Gore Langton to fill it he accordingly did. A great deal was said, but to no purpose; as the Trust was considerably in debt, nothing could be done towards new alterations and improvements till the debt was liquidated. I do not feel satisfied in giving up my time to such nonsense; a whole morning is lost in hearing a pack of interested attorneys, I fear to very little purpose as far as regards the benefit to the community; and that great orator, Sir John Hippisley, treated us with two or three long speeches about himself and his inn at Old Down, disclaiming all interested motives for what he did, at the same time shewing everyone present that this was his principal object. The fabulous account of the ostrich may apply to this worthy baronet, as he is always denominated. I wonder really that he can procure a hearing at these public meetings. A fall of snow took place during the time we were in the Guildhall. Boodle persuaded me to dine and spend the evening at Radstock.

Monday, February 7

The day was wet and unpleasant. I was occupied in my study, the boys in packing up their things previously to going to Winchester. I gave Owen the tool chest I received from General Gore, and to Joseph my case of colours. I wish to afford them every facility in taking those simple amusements within their own power. I went downstairs to spend the last evening with them.

Sunday, February 20

During dinner a girl came for some wine for Biven's wife, whom she said had been put to bed (she was only married a fortnight ago), and was very ill. I sent word I should give no wine unless it was ordered by the doctor, as I was sure it was very bad, for a lying-in woman especially. Having to call, I did so in the evening, and found her disposed to speak and, what is better, to think seriously on the state she is in. The poor creature has much to adduce in extenuation of her offences from the bad example continually before her eyes in the conduct of her profligate mother.

Tuesday, February 22

I met with a singular circumstance, which would puzzle the learned Conclave of Cardinals and the Pope himself. The mother of the dumb girl, named Clark, was present while I was speaking to old Rodgers, and I enquired as to the report of her daughter's being with child by the dumb man. She said it was very true, and that the Overseer was about to take steps for sending her to Kilmersdon, which was her parish, but she feared it would cost them much to be separated, they were so attached to each other. Now the fact is they wished to be married two or three years ago, but I dissuaded the mother—who indeed was herself very averse from the match—from giving her consent. They continued the attachment, and the consequence is now become very visible. As they are now both of age, and the young man is able to procure his livelihood, on her removal to Kilmersdon, and *swearing* (if this can be done) to him as the father, I suppose the marriage will be concluded; but *how*, is to me a mystery. I am very glad I shall not have to officiate in the business. The Pope, in the plenitude of his power, would no doubt grant a dispensation with the usual forms, but I do not know how we are authorised to do so.

Tuesday, March 1

In the evening I began to arrange my ideas on the Catholic claims, as I conceive it my duty, at the Meeting of the Clergy of the Deanery on the 7th, of which I have received notice from the Rural Dean, to express my sentiments on this head. I fear few will stand at the breach to oppose the dreaded attack with which we are menaced. What has been the Roman Catholic disposition in past times? In every respect intolerant against those who differed from them in sentiment; they have publicly declared by word as well as by deed a thorough dislike, nay more, an inveterate hatred, against the Protestants. That their disposition is the same as ever may be derived from the proceedings in Ireland at the present day. If the Almighty designs to punish this country in the midst of her apparent prosperity, He need only open the door to——. I will not supply the blank.

Monday, March 21

I was occupied in visiting the sick in Colliers Row. Mrs. Biven seems going very fast. This woman, now at the point of death, is the eldest daughter of Sarah Somer of Red Hill, and has been a prostitute from her earliest years; her mother brought her up in the vocation, as she has done all her daughters. I could not get anything satisfactory from the woman this morning respecting her thoughts of an hereafter; indeed, she complained of not being able to talk much, and did not join in the prayers as usual. Old Rodgers is much the same, very miserable, poor man; indeed, one can hardly wonder at it, his legs are now swollen as large as a child's body, he can put no covering over them but a petticoat. His daughter is so terrified at his menaces and violent exclamations that I fear she is of little service.

Sunday, March 27

Mrs. Biven died yesterday.

Tuesday, March 29

Some practical joker sent me yesterday an old rusty nail wrapped up in cotton and silver paper, with as many envelopes as a mummy, in order, I presume, to laugh at the Antiquary!

Thursday, March 31

As Mrs. Jarrett had engaged me to dine at six o'clock, I went, and met Mr. Barter there. It was treacherous ground I stood upon. We had cards after tea; Barter played with me, and we lost. The Lady was too civil by half: she overdid the part. When I got home I thought how much happier I should have spent the evening in my quiet study, and lamented the sacrifice I had made and the crime I had fallen into of *suspicion*, when I am shortly to kneel down with those whom I think so severely of at the altar.

This being Good Friday, I prepared a sermon on the Crucifixion.
Poor little Goold, the girl I have been so much pleased with as to
her constant attendance at Church and desire to improve herself, is
laid up with the smallpox. She has been vaccinated by Mr. Crang,
but it could not have taken properly, as she is fuller with pustules
than any person I ever saw, but so very patient. I promised to send
her some children's books for her amusement, which I did on my
return home.

Monday, April 4

I called upon Bacon, Junior, at Meadyates, after breakfast, the
man who has been so long ill with the liver complaint, in order to
give him some of the Sacrament money, and in course of conversation asked him respecting old Mr. Coombes, of Meadyates, for
whom both his father and himself have constantly worked as long as
he dwelt there. I learnt some very interesting particulars about the
rise of the Catholics in this immediate neighbourhood. It seems that
the father of Coombes, the priest,[1] who lived at Meadyates and had
there a chapel in his house, was a blacksmith of Camerton, who went
by the name of "Doctor" Coombes, because he added tooth-
drawing and inoculation to his manual exercises on the anvil; that at
the latter part of his life Dr. Coombes kept a gallon house and sold
beer. This personage, who was of great consequence in the Parish on
account of his various and important vocations so much connected
with the welfare of society, having a good stentorian voice for
psalmody, was one of the principal singers in his day in Camerton
Church; but, taking rather too much the lead, there was a violent
schism among the singers, and as they were obstinate and Dr.
Coombes was obstinate, the latter withdrew from their society, and
declared with imprecations that he never would enter the Church
again. In order to keep his vow, he became a Catholic. Had there
been Methodists in his days he need not have gone quite so far to
seek for a vehicle through which to convey his hostility to the
Church; but, having taken this step, he persevered in it with all the
ardour of heated iron, not suffering his zeal to cool till he had
worked it into a more durable and efficient instrument to harm *poor
Mother Church*, and that he did by sending his eldest son to be

[1] William Coombes, 1744–1822, of Meadgate, near Bath, Grand Vicar of the
Western District.

educated at the college at Douay. A nephew also, of the name of Hart, the son of a butcher, was not long after fitted out for the same destination. Coombes continued his education and took priest's orders, when he returned to his native country. Hart having conceived a dislike to that profession, being rather of a gay turn, ran away from Douay, and went to an apothecary, where he learnt the mysteries of the pestle and mortar, and set up afterwards for himself at Marksbury. When old Dr. Coombes, that is the blacksmith, tooth-drawer, inoculator, beer-seller, and Catholic priest-maker, died his son reigned in his stead at the house he had occupied at Meadyates, which was held upon lives, and became, on his father's death, his own. Coombes, the priest at Meadyates, had a chapel in his house where he used to officiate, and made two or three proselytes. Bacon and his son occasionally attended on a Sunday, but never became Catholics; but a woman of the name of Hannah Heal, now living, also the family of Mr. Day of Angelsbatch, father of Samuel Day who now rents the Camerton Home Farm, were constant in their attendance, Samuel officiating as a kind of clerk, that is, making all the responses for the Priest, in Latin.

Having spent the greater part of the morning at Bacon's who slowly walked backwards and forwards in the field near his house while he was relating this history of the rise and progress of Catholicism, I returned from Meadyates by Red Hill, where I saw Hannah Heal, who had been a convert from the Church and used to attend at Meadyates. She is a woman between 60 and 70, perfectly well remembers old Coombes, the blacksmith, when he sold beer, and lived as a servant with his son. She used to attend the chapel regularly. She says she never got much good from their doctrines, but they were kind to the poor—in fact, it was through self-interest she had joined them. She has for some years past returned to the Church. Thus the sons of the blacksmith and the butcher, educated at Douay, formed the germ or nucleus from whence have sprung, first, a chapel in the priest's house at Camerton; secondly, a chapel and nunnery at Shepton; thirdly, a chapel at Shortwood; fourthly, a monastery at Downside, where a number of young men are now educating for the priesthood.

Thursday, April 7

Anxious to hear the determination of the jury, I sent John in early with a letter to Maule. On his return he gave me as answer that the damages were assessed at £50, that the long consultation of the jury was occasioned by some proposing it should be £100. The Catholics had expected more. He gave me particulars of the pleadings, etc., None of my witnesses were examined, and Mr. Smith, the counsel employed by Mr. Maule on my part, had made but a weak reply. My name went forth to the world with all these malicious stigmas hanging to it.

I cannot help remarking in this place, that the Country is now ruled by Lawyers; originally the Clergy had an undue influence, and will again, should the Catholic Religion obtain; but now they are utterly unable to defend themselves. If they are injured in their property or in their reputation, they may have recourse to the Law, and lose their time, temper, and money, and get laughed at in the bargain.

I am tied hands and feet, and placed in a pillory to be pelted at by Methodists, Catholics, Colliers; and have moreover a combination of worthless Farmers, and an overbearing Woman with an unprincipled Steward to contend with; who wishes to drive me by ill usage from the situation I occupy, that her Son-in-Law may step into it.

I hope I shall have strength and *patience* to keep firm to my post, and perform the part promised by my Sponsors at my Baptism, namely to fight manfully under the Christian banner, against Sin, the World and the Devil, and to continue Christ's faithful Soldier and Servant unto my Life's end.

Who will undertake the office of a Clergyman if he is exposed to the miseries I have sustained during the twenty-five years I have been RECTOR OF CAMERTON.

*　　　*　　　*

Friday, May 6

I understand Sir John Hippisley, the Somersetshire orator, is dead. Well, de mortuis nil nisi bonum; if I were asked to write his epitaph it should be as follows:

> *Hic saltem quiescit Sir John,*
> *Dominus de Ston Easton.*

Thursday, May 12

I employed the interval till dinner time in reading Southey's "Book of the Church," which in my humble opinion might have been better handled. The more I read on the subject, the more I am convinced of the duplicity of the Catholics. Indeed, how can it be otherwise? They are educated in deceit from their childhood, and can have no open, manly sincerity about them, otherwise they would cease to be what they are. Let the Catholics only be emancipated in Ireland, the death blow is struck to the Constitution of England as it was established subsequently to the Revolution. Whoever peruses these remarks when the evil has taken place will perceive I am no false prophet.

Friday, July 1

I got an affectionate letter from Owen at Winchester; he seems delighted in the prospect of being relieved from the impediment he has so long laboured under. I only hope our expectations will not be disappointed.

Sunday, July 3

I examined some of the young people who were candidates for Confirmation before Church, and gave them tickets. There were twenty-two going from Camerton, and two of the colliers I sent back, not only on account of their ill behaviour, but gross ignorance, for, notwithstanding both have been educated in my Sunday School, they have entirely forgotten their Catechism and absolutely could not say the Lord's Prayer. When I expostulated with them, both laughed in my face, and I was obliged to beg them to leave the room, as I found it impossible to bring them to a state of their duty.

Tuesday, July 5

My Mother and my daughter, Anna, arrived in the evening to tea. I was glad to find Anna looking better and stronger.

Wednesday, July 6

Anna took a ride this morning on her sleek palfrey, and was delighted with it on account of its docility as well as beauty. I walked by her side, as it was the first time a lady had been on its back; but it did not seem the least frightened at the habit or difference of the saddle. The Boodles dined with us and walked about the premises in the evening after tea.

I have been excessively idle for some time past. However, I finished a few of my sketches this morning for Anna to set, the two volumes of my Journals being complete, and I wish to get them bound out of hand.

We had breakfasted before eight, when Owen and myself read the chapter for the day in the Greek Testament; he afterwards construed what he had prepared the evening before from the first Play of Sophocles, the Ajax. I was glad to find he had made such proficiency in the Greek at Winchester, so that, instead of thirty, I perceive he may get a hundred lines in Sophocles prepared every day, besides his Latin exercises.

Poor Barter was summoned from the midst of us early this morning. The inflammation became so violent it could not be kept under, yet he suffered no great pain. Peace be with him! For five and twenty years I have found him at his post; now I shall look around, and he will be no more. He had hoped to live to witness the completion of the new Church at Timsbury, to which he has been so great a benefactor, but this was not permitted, and the succeeding Rector will have reason to be grateful for what he has done during his incumbency. It is some consolation to reflect he came in due time to the grave, having completed his seventy-seventh year, forty-two of which he was Rector of Timsbury.

I read the same portion of Greek as usual with Owen, who really seems to understand what he reads, and makes pertinent observations.

I preached in the morning and administered the Sacrament at Camerton. In the evening I preached at Timsbury in the schoolroom, which was crowded to excess so that I was obliged to get one of the windows open near me, as I was so oppressed by the heat. The people were very attentive, and many of them shed abundance of tears on calling to mind the kind Rector they had lost.

Monday, November 7

I yearn for quiet, but there are duties I have to perform. I have not, however, neglected Owen, and we make such progress I have little doubt we shall finish the six Plays of Sophocles and all the Evangelists before he goes to *Oxford*.

Wednesday, November 10

A most rainy day. After having read with Owen the 2nd St. John, I came upstairs to my accounts. I find I have spent since August on my journey to Edinburgh £136 5s. 0d., and the entrance of Joseph at Sandhurst £96, with what I paid Dr. Williams for the last half-year (at Winchester) £113, and Owen's entrance at Trinity £39 9s. 0d., and Anna's masters, upwards of £500. I have the consolation of knowing it was not on my own account, but for the benefit of my children. I will endeavour to live as economically as possible to meet future expenses, for I must reckon on this sum, £500 at least, for the education of my two sons and my daughter. How grateful ought I to be that I have it in my power to give them the best instruction the country can afford, and I only hope they will profit by it.

1826

I PREACHED the concluding sermon of my series on the Evidences of Christianity. After tea I continued in my study till prayer time, where I carefully revolved the principal occurrences of the year past, and literally communed with my own heart in my chamber and was still.

Being engaged to spend the week at Southfield, I sent my sons to Bath. At two o'clock I left home in my car; just as I passed Newbury the horse came down, but without injury either to him or myself. I arrived at four o'clock, and walked for an hour with Mr. Peter Hoare before dinner.

At one o'clock I left Southfield with Mr. Hoare for Stourhead; we preferred walking, and took the road beyond Nunney. We found Sir Richard remarkably well, and partook of a fine haunch of venison and some snipes; afterwards played two rubbers of whist.

Mr. Cassan[1] was in the house, but no other company. I did not get to bed till nearly twelve o'clock.

Sir Richard took me into his study to shew me some Roman pavements, painted by a schoolmaster self-taught. As the snow fell fast, and Mr. Peter Hoare had a large party to dinner, we left Stourhead after breakfast and arrived at Southfield a little after one. We found there Captain Seymour, grandson to Lord Francis, late Dean of Wells, who was uncle to the present Duke of Somerset. It is somewhat surprising that this gentleman retains a strong likeness to the Protector Somerset, whose portrait is accurately given in Sir Richard Hoare's "Wiltshire." I compared the print with his countenance and can testify to the fact, although ten generations have intervened. The three Mr. Knatchbulls, Mr. Paget, Mr. and Mrs. Hoblyn, and Mrs. Barrett were at dinner. The evening was very raw and uncomfortable for their return.

[1] The Rev. Stephen Hyde Cassan, A.M., F.S.A., Vicar of Mere, Wilts, author of "Lives of the Bishops of Bath and Wells," Rivington, 1829.

All idea of study is dissipated; the boys took their gun and their skaites immediately after our breakfast and went to the basin at Bengrove, but as the snow had fallen in the night were obliged to employ sweepers. I went to see whether it was hard enough to bear them with safety. They did not arrive at Camerton till nearly dinner time, having spent the morning in shooting. I regret the gun was purchased, as it has been a sad obstacle to reading; indeed, it seems now considered that nothing more is to be done in the way of study this vacation. When once the bow is unloosed it is difficult to new string it again.

Thursday, January 12

Our guests, Mr. and Mrs. Hoare, arrived before five o'clock; Charles, the youngest son, accompanied them. Mr. Hoare walked the greater part of the way from Southfield, as the roads are quite hard with the frost.

Friday, January 13

It was resolved after breakfast by Mr. Peter Hoare and myself to walk to Newton; in our route we visited Priston, where I pointed out the British Settlement on the side of Pentre Hill, also the stone coffin in Edgell's farm yard, part of which is converted into a trough for pigs. At Newton we procured admission to Mr. Gore Langton's gardens, in order to examine the tower of the old castle standing in a picturesque situation above the water.

We returned to Camerton—being directed by Mr. Hoare's watch, I thought we had plenty of time, but on our arrival at the Parsonage found we were ten minutes after five; the Knatchbulls, Hammond, and Boodles, with Mr. Gooch, had been there before the appointed hour, so that we had to dress in a hurry, and, being warm with my walk, I had reason to repent changing my linen without airing, as in the course of the evening I felt a headache coming on, and a pain in my side. However, I took but little wine, indeed within my usual allowance, and was in hopes I should have slept off the approaching attack, but in this I was disappointed.

Saturday, January 14

My guests left me after breakfast. The boys made me feel very uncomfortable after the company was gone, and this added to the complaint which was rapidly approaching, namely, a violent inflammation at the side and chest; my head also suffered such acute pain, I was under the necessity of putting my feet in warm water and a blister on my side. I went to bed before dinner, and was in a violent fever the whole night.

Sunday, January 15

I sent early to ask Mr. Gooch to assist me in the duty, as I was unable to leave my bed.

Monday, January 16

The blister in part relieved my head, but I was unable to set up above three hours, when I made a list of the bills to be paid by Owen in Bath, and gave him drafts for them, also £50 to take to Oxford with a letter I wrote to Dr. Ingram.[1] I had intended accompanying my son to Oxford, and from thence going to Town, but am prevented. However, in one respect it is for the best, as I could not have performed the journey and been absent a fortnight under £20. The children returned to my Mother's [Upland House] in the car before dinner, and I felt very low at their departure, as they have not been all that I could have wished of late; but it proceeds from thoughtlessness, I trust, not from any desire to make me uncomfortable.

Old Mrs. Jarrett, who seemed so well on Thursday when Anna and myself called, dropped down dead suddenly this morning as she was about to set down on her chair. Mr. Gooch called upon me towards the middle of the day to inform me of the event. I had no appetite for my meals; indeed I have taken nothing but tea since Friday.

Thursday, January 19

I understand from my housekeeper, Mrs. Williams, there is to be a grand funeral for the old lady who died on Monday; if there be any satire on poor human nature it is this. Mrs. Jarrett of the Manor, who openly complained of the trouble occasioned by the good old woman after her first attack, and in her heart feels satisfied at the release, now is about to make this parade of sorrow; but so is the world. I am heartily sick of its deceptions; it is like the treacherous ice, glib and smooth on the surface. I cannot say but I feel more displeased with this unfortunate neighbour of mine. She has been sending me game and kind messages, but I cannot receive them as I

---

[1] James Ingram, F.S.A., President of Trinity College, 1824–50.

would one kind word coming from a sincere heart. There is something in view, and time will unravel it.

A letter came from the undertaker appointing eleven o'clock tomorrow for the internment of old Mrs. Jarrett in the vault in which Mrs. Stephens was buried; the pulpit, reading desk, and the Jarretts' pew are lined with black cloth, and the labourers working on Mrs. Jarrett's estate are to be put in mourning; all the farmers are also desired to attend—and all this to mourn for a perfect stranger to them, whose face perhaps they never saw. What a farce is all this! However, I determined if possible to persevere in my intention of attending the funeral.

A message came from Mrs. Jarrett saying it might possibly be twelve o'clock before the funeral would be ready. I waited till twelve, and then walked to the Manor House. Mr. John Jarrett was arrived from Hampshire; all the farmers were present, without even the exception of Day, who, being a Catholic, would not have accepted, I should have supposed, the invitation. I cannot get farmers to attend their Church, but it seems a more powerful interest than I possess can bring them there. Well, I can only lament the cause and deplore the effect.

There were six mutes; all the bearers, as well as the clerk, had mourning. It seems that the Carew vault is closed up, and that a small one was made when Mrs. Stephens's body was brought from Italy, near the door of the Carew chapel; the passage was so narrow that it was with great difficulty the coffin was lowered. Indeed, I was heartily glad when the ceremony was concluded, for all the masquerading farces this is the worst. The undertaker came afterwards with Mrs. Jarrett's compliments to know what was my charge for the funeral. I said there was none on this account; if any was to be paid for opening the vault I would leave it to Mrs. Jarrett and should make no charge. However, after tea a note was brought, with her compliments and that of the family, enclosing a draft for ten guineas. So ended this exhibition. I hope I am not proud, but I feel it much more painful to receive from Mrs. Jarrett than to pay away much larger sums. The black cloth, I understand, is to be my perquisite in the Church, but I will appropriate it to clothing the children of the more tidy of my parishioners when they need it. I am not pleased with my feelings altogether just now. I fear indeed they are not what they ought to be; I will endeavour to correct them.

I preached in the morning on the text, "The hoary head is a crown of glory, if it be found in the way of the Lord." All the Jarrett family attended.

To-day's post brought me a letter from Owen, who has had an unpleasant *entrée* into Trinity, as his tutor did not properly introduce him. Poor Kett was much more attentive to Warren and myself when we entered, and invited some young men to meet us at dinner in his room, who introduced us properly to the society. Mr. Short, Owen's tutor, has rather played Bob Short on the present occasion.

Another letter came from Cassan, who is engaged in compiling the history of the Bishops of Winchester, to ask the etymology of the name of Wolvesey.

I wrote to poor Owen yesterday, who seems to be uncomfortable at Oxford, and to Joseph, and also to Anna. Joseph has apologised for his behaviour, and I have forgiven him, and promised to see him at Bath before his return to Sandhurst.

I read prayers in the morning, and afterwards walked to call upon old Treble, who is much weaker than I have yet seen him. I promised to administer the Sacrament to him to-morrow. My old servant, Hester, followed me out of Church, and all the way to Radford, to entreat me to let her come again to work, and promised if I would she never would enter the house, but continue an outdoor servant. She says she has been so miserable since she went away that she is sure she shall die with grief if I do not let her come back again. I said I would consider about it before I gave an answer. I preached in the evening on the Gospel of the day, the Parable of the Sower. Mr. Gooch was the only person from the mansion house at Church, his lady being confined in child bed, and Mrs. Jarrett, he told me, was ill.

I had intended going into Bath to see Joseph before his return to Sandhurst, but the day was so unpromising I had no heart to undertake the journey.

Wednesday, February 1

By a letter from my Mother I find that Joseph left the York House (Bath) for Sandhurst by one of the stages, on which and in the interior were nine cadets. I hope he will arrive safe at his destination.

The same occupations as usual till bedtime. I do not know when I shall be able to settle to reading; my mind is quite unhinged; indeed, the misconduct of my housekeeper, Mrs. Williams, continues to add to the irritation of my nerves. She was so excessively insolent because Hester is permitted to return to work in the gardens that I was obliged to dismiss her, and give her a month's wages in order to get rid of her. The servants had one and all complained of her abusive language, but she had been careful not to employ it against myself till this evening, when she used the coarsest expressions, and even oaths, so that there is no choice left me. I gave her a draft on my banker before I went to bed, and took her receipt for the same, to which Betty was witness, and desired her to leave the premises early the next day, before I went to Bath. I am convinced my servants are in part influenced by the malignant neighbourhood against their master, and induced to forget the respect they ought to shew him. These are indeed evils. I could bear all outside my roof, that is, in the Parish and in the world, when my books are my companions and my friends within doors; but if I am unsettled and distorted in my own family and at my own fireside, it is indeed then a trial.

Friday, February 3

There are better accounts from Owen, who is settled in his rooms.

Sunday, February 5

I slept but badly, waking at intervals in sudden starts, shewing that my nerves are greatly shaken. I am determined, however, not to give way to it. The Church was pretty well attended. I told the children I should hear their Catechism this ensuing Lent in Church. I felt so exhausted after dinner, I fell asleep for upwards of an hour— an unusual thing for me.

Monday, February 6

I wrote my Journal up to the present time.

1827

I READ the official letter from Sandhurst respecting Joseph, which was by no means what I wished, and worried me much. I spoke to him after dinner on the subject, and, I am sorry to say, with less coolness than I ought to have done; reproof loses much of its effect when delivered hastily, but I fear no reproof will be of service. I found myself so unwell and so much affected. I went to bed before nine o'clock.

I walked to Priston in order to christen a child and church the mother. Mr. Hammond, I think, is wrong in admitting this innovation. The Rubric mentions Sundays and Holydays for these ceremonies. We cannot be too exact now in keeping to the old regulations. After tea I was occupied till bedtime in settling my accounts. I find my sons and daughter have cost me this year nearly £500, and as much last year, which is more than my housekeeping and establishment amounts to. I have spent nothing extra on myself, if I except my journey to Town, which cost me £30, and was partly on business.

I visited Charles Heal's widow, and found her rather better; but the Overseer, Hicks, will not allow her above eighteen pence a week, so that she is in absolute want of necessaries, whereas he allows that bad woman, Garratt's widow, who is married again, fourteen shillings a month. It is thus the parish pay is made an engine of mischief; the worthy and religious being set aside, and the bad are rewarded.

About the middle of the day my sons set off in the car for Southfield, and I on foot, as I preferred walking: we were to rendezvous at Boodle's. I thence proceeded to Kilmersdon, and across the fields to Mells. My sons overtook me in the car just beyond Babington, and on my asking them why they had been so tardy in their route from Radstock, I am sorry to say, replied in a manner very unbecoming them to utter or myself to hear. It was indeed a severe pang, but I have experienced so many of late it did not entirely overcome me.

I got to Mr. Hoare's at least two hours before dinner, and experienced a friendly reception; but my heart was very heavy. Well might I say with Shakespeare, "notwithstanding the wind was keen, it was not so keen as ingratitude." To be kicked and buffeted by my own offspring is indeed a trial, but God's will be done. I must be lowered every way, and I doubt not there is good reason for so doing.

Friday, January 5

I went to bed before eleven, but not to sleep. I am sorely wounded in the tenderest point— my mind. It is a bad beginning for the New Year. I spoke to Mr. Hoare about Joseph, mentioning the unsatisfactory accounts I had received from Sandhurst, but not the insults I have so recently received. He advises me by all means to withdraw him from there.

Saturday, January 6

The servant called me a little after six this morning. I had slept but little, and was perfectly prepared to leave my bed as soon as the candle came into my apartment. Having packed up my things, I went into the breakfast parlour and waited till my sons came downstairs, and one of the young men, to make breakfast. We left Southfield a little after eight.

Sunday, January 7

I could not sleep as my head was racking with pain and very throbbing, insomuch that I felt it lift from the bolster at every pulsation. I left my room as soon as I heard the servants were up, and procured a light. On going into my study, I finished my sermon on the shipwreck of St. Paul, which was the Second Lesson for last Sunday.

My sons still are very far from contributing to my comfort. I had a long and calm conversation after tea, and advised them to go for a few days to Bath to their Grandmother's, as I derive no satisfaction from their society just now. I hope they will think better ere it be too late.

Monday, January 8

My sons went to Bath in the middle of the day. I made up my Journals to the present time.

A boy came to hire himself, but I did not approve of his appearance, and gave him a shilling to take his departure.

I opened, by mistake, a note which came with my letters from Bath, thinking it was a bill. I found it was addressed to my son Joseph, and giving the amount of the cost attending a gig broke, amounting to £12 10*s.* I must enquire into this. My own expenditure I am sure is sufficient, without these additional demands.

I walked along the banks of the canal, and on my return met a man of the name of Bird, who belongs to Timsbury Parish. While I was talking to him, Day's brother, the farmer who lives at Anglesbatch, and to whom I believe I have never spoken, passed me, and looked so extremely impudent that the man Bird remarked he had never seen anyone look so insulting in his life; but he said, "Now don't ye, Sir, say anything to him!" I replied it was not my intention so to do. I said I could partly account for his looks—it was merely because I was a Protestant, and he was a Catholic; but it clearly shewed there was bad blood among them, and I sincerely hoped they would never have the power openly of shewing what they would do in my days. If it is thus one Catholic can act in setting the parishioners against their lawful clergyman, what are our legislators doing when they give them greater power?

My sons came home to dinner. All well at Bath, which is comfortable.

No very inviting weather for a walk; however, I took one for the sake of exercise, with Joseph, and made a circuit along the canal to Dunkerton. I saw a large party skaiting and supposed they were some of Mr. Bampfylde's[1] acquaintances or connections. I am rather surprised that this unprincipled fellow can have anyone of the grade of gentleman at his table; but this is among the fearful tokens of the times. The fearful end of the despicable and disreputable father of this man, Sir Charles Bampfylde, would have acted as a warning, one might have imagined, against a repetition of such things. To see the bastard son of such a father, having the same

[1] The Rev. C. F. Bampfylde, Rector of Dunkerton, 1820–1855 ("the Devil of Dunkerton").

inclination and the same principles, setting as a magistrate to determine on the actions of his fellow creatures, and as a clergyman to preach against immorality and irreligion; this is indeed a melancholy token of the decadence of the times. Were I called upon for my opinion of the said Mr. Bampfylde, I should say I do not believe there is a more worthless fellow in the West of England. I record these things not out of enmity to Mr. Bampfylde, but as a record of the times, and records that may be depended on; for I never would defile my pages with these observations unless I could substantiate the truth of them. When there is such undue influence exercised that the bastard of a worthless, unprincipled man, who himself laughed at all things serious, and lost his life for his iniquity, should be provided for in the Church, notwithstanding he has openly participated in the libertinism of the father, what can be more inauspicious? Indeed, these are bad omens. The dissenters from the Church will blend the character of a Bampfylde with that of a Benson, and say if one churchman does such things, ergo, all must do so. These are fearful considerations: eheu ruit mole sua.

Thursday, January 18

Mr. Gunning, of Farmborough, called. He seems an open-hearted man, but I do not think exactly calculated for a clergyman, as he keeps his hounds, and, having no other pursuit, thinks more of a hare than he does of hunting out what may benefit his parishioners. I cannot suppose that a man who is engaged the whole of the morning in the field, and the evening at the table, can employ the talents he is obliged to employ if he undertakes the instruction of others.

Monday, January 22

There was another marriage this morning. Indeed, the bride behaved so bad by laughing and other misconduct, I was obliged to say I would stop the ceremony; and the man who gave her away put on his hat in the midst of the Church. The clerk, White, asked whether they might ring. I said, Yes, a peal or two, as was customary at marriage; but not make the Church a drinking place, as they had done last Thursday.

Tuesday, January 23

This day I have done nothing but read the newspaper. I went down from my study at nine, and took supper with my sons—a meal I never make when alone, and I believe by no means a wholesome one; but as Owen is to return to Oxford on Friday, I wish to spend part of my evening with him.

Wednesday, January 24

I have sent some coal fossils to Mrs. Ingram, wife of the President of Trinity College, Oxford, as she has the power of shewing civilities to Owen if she chuses. Indeed, these little attentions are requisite in one's commerce with the world, since the quid pro quo is the order of the day.

Thursday, January 25

I was up as soon as it was light, and we had breakfast a little after eight. The snow had fallen in the night; my sons, however, said they would walk into Bath to their Grandmother's, while Owen's luggage went by the cart. The Oxford coach, I believe, leaves the York House at eight to-morrow. I have told Joseph either to come back to-morrow or stay with his Grandmother, as he or she best approves of. I cannot describe how very low in spirits I feel to-day, after taking leave of Owen. I have done everything for him; besides his £50 for the quarter, I have given him some wine to take with him, as I did last term, from my own cellar; also I have sent some fossils to Mrs. Ingram, and a letter to the Dr. speaking in his favour. But I do not feel satisfied, there is a weight hanging over me that I cannot account for. I pray God that what I feel to-day may not be an anticipation of evil.

Thursday, February 1

I find that my worthless tenant, Lewis, is determined to do all he can, under the influence of Day, to annoy me.

I left my study after breakfast, with the intention of calling upon Hicks, the Overseer. In my way, within two hundred yards of my own house, I met Keel, my churchwarden, who immediately said, "Hello! I was going to call upon you, Mr. Skinner, for I insist upon knowing who told you what you told my wife yesterday, and frightened her out of her wits, namely, that I had said you had been at Camerton long enough, and that we would strip your gown from your shoulders?" I said I should not tell him who told me, but I firmly believed it was true since his subsequent conduct was so insolent. He replied, he would be d——d, but he would know! I said that his swearing to his clergyman did not give me a better opinion of his veracity, neither did the menacing attitude in which he put himself; if the farmers chose to insult me in the manner they did of late, that I could not stir from my house without experiencing some fresh aggravations, I could let the whole of my tythe and have nothing further to say to them. "Aye," said he, "you may take mine to-morrow." I said, very well. I would after Lady Day; but in the discharge of my duty at Church and when I was called upon to visit the sick I would ever do my duty, so that there should be no fault to find with me. "Aye," said he, "but we won't come to Church."

I did not find Hicks at home, but had some conversation with his wife, and said that I wished she would tell her husband to bring his books on Sunday to Church. As I returned home I begged Joseph to accompany me to Keel's, for I was determined, unless he made an apology for his behaviour, I would get a summons for his having sworn at me. The man was in a different temper, and very sorry for all he had said; he declared he would take his oath he never spoke a word against Mr. Skinner in his life, but always when people found fault with him took his part. I said I needed no such defenders; that if he acknowledged he was sorry for his insolence I would proceed no further at present, but warned him not to repeat it.

I had not returned home ten minutes before a paper was put into my hand from Lewis; it contained a bill amounting to upwards of seven pounds for the hire of a horse. The fact is, when he came to the farm I made him the offer of old Bess on the same terms that Nicholls had it, namely, that he was to use it for any little purposes about the farm, but not to hard work it, and if I wanted it occasionally to assist my horse I was to have it. I took no notice accordingly of the bill.

Sunday, February 4

The Church was well attended, and I preached on the gospel. The people were attentive, but neither of the churchwardens was there. Hicks brought the Poor Book for my inspection, it being month Sunday. Afterwards, when passing by Keel's house on my way to Red Hill, I asked why he had not attended Church. He said first of all he had been feeding his beasts. I said that was no very proper apology for a Churchwarden to make, who was fineable for non-attendance. He said he knew his duty and what ought to be done, but he had not been well, and so staid away from Church. If he was well enough to feed his beasts he was well enough to come to Church, methinks.

John Rossiter, who was standing before his door, I also spoke to, asking why he had not been in his place; he began making an oration, but, not wishing to be insulted, I walked on, and called upon Sarah Somer at Red Hill, near the Poor House. She has an inflammation on the chest, and seems in great fear of dying. I made some strong exhortations, and told her I could give no hopes that a mere faith could save her, in case she were called from this world to another; she must sincerely repent of her past sins, which had been many and grievous to my knowledge. This woman has been as bad as anyone in the Parish, and has brought up all her family in the same licentious course; but now she is in a most frightful state. The end will be the Methodists will immediately get round her, and if she says she has firm faith, they will give her a viaticum, and make this worst of sinners, for the edification of the parish, die a saint.

Monday, February 5

I got a letter from Hammond, who says the book-sellers in Town whom I commissioned him to speak to respecting the Etymologies will not do anything respecting the printing unless I indemnify them, in other words, pay the whole expense, as I did for the Wellow Pavement, and then give them twenty-five per cent for the sale. I must therefore relinquish the idea of becoming a publisher of my works.

Monday, February 12

I was an early riser, but found it required some difficulty to awaken Joseph. However, as we were to begin our studies this week I was obliged to get him up in good time, to prepare his lesson in the Greek Testament for the day, which we read after breakfast.

I got a letter from Samuel Skinner saying he had not yet been successful in procuring a cadetcy for Joseph, but would be un-remitting in his endeavours; a second, from Owen, saying Dr. Ingram had invited him to dinner, and he had spent a pleasant day; and a third from Mr. Williams, our Rural Dean, saying that Friday was appointed for signing the petition against the Catholic claims, at Kilmersdon.

Tuesday, February 13

I sent my son, Joseph, immediately after breakfast, with especial orders to find the keys I had left last week at one of the places, either

Clifton or Bishops Stoke, as I was distressed beyond measures at their loss.

Joseph was so fatigued with his thirty-mile ride yesterday, he did not come downstairs till nine o'clock. We then read our Greek Testament. I afterwards walked into the village, and called upon several people, Sarah Somer and David West among the invalids. The latter received several severe wounds from the bursting of a small cannon he fired shortly after the fifth of November, which entirely deprived him of an eye, and wounded one of his legs so severely I fear he never will recover the use of it. He was in the hospital for eleven weeks, and is lately returned. I persuaded him to learn netting, in case he should become a cripple, and have agreed to pay a man who lives near him to teach him how to set about a cabbage net, which must be his first essay.

As Joseph was to begin building a boat I sent for the old carpenter and drew out the proportions, and the keel was laid before dinner.

After having read some verses in the Greek Testament I went to overlook the boat-building concern; the keel at first was made too heavy, and obliged to be planed thinner; I also ordered some hoops to be purchased to form the ribs, which are to be covered with oil cloth after the model of a former boat I built at Camerton several years ago. I then walked with Joseph to Radstock, having engaged to accompany Boodle to sign the Anti-Catholic Petition at Kilmersdon. There were only seven clergymen assembled; I signed the name of Mr. Cookson, according to his request. I liked the tenor of the Petition, but it was hastily penned. At Boodles we met Mr. Batchelor, a young clergyman who has taken the curacy of Babington. We sat down to cards after tea, and played three rubbers, all of which I won, which has never before I believe occurred to me; but whether I win or lose I hate card-playing most decidedly; it is a great loss of time, not to say worse of it.

There is scarcely a day at Camerton that does not bring with it some annoyance. I had finished my reading with Joseph and gone to my study, wishing to set to reading, when Mrs. Williams [still here!] came in a violent hurry into my room bringing a letter which she said a man had left and said it required no answer. On opening the cover I found it was a summons to attend the Court of Requests on Wednesday next to answer to the charge of Lewis for the hire of my own mare, which was given him with the express condition that when I wanted her for a little job at the Parsonage she was to be at my service; he moreover conditioned never to take her from the premises, but merely to consider her as liable to do his work on the farm for her keep. Two days I lost the week before last, and now I am to lose a third, and probably a fourth, to answer to this frivolous charge, which has not the least foundation to rest on.

Wednesday, February 21

Having heard Joseph his Greek reading, we drove into Bath and went to the Court of Requests, my servant Heal, and Thomas the blacksmith having preceded us. When arrived at the sublime seat of judicature, the barrister who presides, Mr. Goodden, called out in a stentorian voice, "Mr. Skinner, you are come too late, we have settled the business as you did not appear to answer the charge." I replied that as I came several miles out of the country, I conceived a little licence ought to have been granted me, and other causes connected with Bath might have been entered into before mine came on; that I could not be very long after my time I was well assured. "Yes, Sir, the man has been gone a quarter of an hour," was the reply, "his charge for horse hire appeared to be very just and fair, and I see no reason why you should not settle it." I said there was the greatest reason in the world why I should not do so, since the man had not the slightest grounds to make any charge whatever, since I had given him the mare with the implied condition that, whenever I needed, I might have the use of her on my premises. This I could prove by the most undeniable testimony, and therefore requested I might be heard. Mr. Maule, to whom I had written to attend, then told me he had seen Lewis in the Court. He was accordingly called, and as soon as the cause which was then hearing was finished the man made his appearance, and was placed close to my side. He had behaved in so rascally a manner I could not really bear to look at him; but the Chairman, Mr. Goodden, desired him to shew the bill, and asked me to state my reasons for not settling it. I recapitulated what I had before stated, having taken the oath to speak the truth and nothing but the truth, etc. Maule and Thomas having given their testimony, the complaint was dismissed, Lewis having to pay the costs. But what most hurt me was the manner in which it was done. Mr. Goodden threw the bill to him, without any comment on the iniquity of his conduct and, indeed, his perjury, in swearing to a bill he knew to be false. I went from Maule's to my tailor's in Orange Grove to get a great coat I had ordered, and to chuse the cloth for some pantaloons.

Tuesday, February 27

I read as usual with Joseph in the Greek Testament, and in Homer, after breakfast. We then worked at the boat and got all the ribs finished; it measures ten feet in length, and five in width at the broadest part, and now the framework is completed does not weigh above 50 lbs. I hope that when the whole is fitted for the water, it will not weigh above 200 lbs., as my intention is to keep it in the cart-house, as the colliers would destroy it in one week if it were left in the canal. My principal object in my present undertaking is, I wish to make my sons satisfied with the resources and amusements within their own power, that they may not feel the time hang heavy on their hands while they are with me, and be inclined to seek for society from home.

Thursday, March 1

I was worried by the account I received of the death of one of the colliers of the name of Robert Payne. His candle went out in the pit last night, and in stepping forwards, thinking he was on solid ground, he fell down and was dashed to pieces. What renders his sudden summons more dreadful is the knowledge that he was very unfit to go hence; indeed, I well remember, when his first wife died there were some very awkward rumours afloat; she went well to bed, was heard to scream out in the night, and next morning was a corpse. The man has been a very bad fellow, and it is horrid to think of his exit.

There was a Vestry, and I attended it in order to speak to the Overseer about allowing West (the man who was so much injured by the bursting of a little cannon he fired before Christmas) a little money, as his wife had been with me to say they had none from the Parish, and only were supported by the Club. Hicks and the other farmers seemed to be more civilly inclined than heretofore, but they change like the weather, and there is no dependence to be placed in them.

Old Walters will relate stories of the Camertonians, none of them to their honour. He says he believes God Almighty will send down His judgments upon them, they are so wicked, and nothing has power to check them; indeed, he told me it was worse at Radstock than it was at Camerton, since if a man purchases a piece of meat on Saturday at a kind of Market held there, he cannot put it out of his hand but it was immediately stolen. Well may we exclaim, "O tempora, O mores!" I said that I felt most severely being placed among such a set of people where I could be of no good: that my eyes were now opened respecting many of their machinations against myself; I would forgive what was past, but if ever they attempted to play the same tricks, and I discovered them, I would most certainly make an exemplary punishment.

I walked to call on old Rossiter and his wife, but I do not think they are in any danger; indeed, the old man's pulse is quite tranquil. I read the prayers to him for the sick, and spoke on the situation he was in, as, independently of his illness, a man of his advanced years could not, in the course of things, expect to live much longer. During the time I was waiting downstairs, as the girl told me I could not go into the bedroom just then, I examined her in the Catechism, but found her very imperfect, and told her if she could say it next Sunday I would give her a shilling.

The corpse of the poor man Payne was brought into the Church in the middle of the Evening Service, and it was accompanied by such a crowd of Methodists the Church was absolutely not able to contain them, and they stood up in the aisles and at the door. There was a Churching and a Christening. Having observed that one of the Godmothers did not know how to make the responses as she ought to have done, I asked her, after the service was concluded, whether she was ever accustomed to come to Church. She replied, "No," with all the insolence she could assume. I then said, "How is it possible you can perform the vow and promise you have now made of seeing that your Godchild learns its duty, according to the appointment of the Church, if you never come to it yourself?" The woman turned upon me with a sneer, as much as to say there was no use in coming to Church, when she could procure instruction better suited to her taste elsewhere.

I am free to confess that Sunday, which used to be to me the most interesting day of the week, is now become the most irksome. I feel perfectly assured I am not of the least service to the people among whom I am placed, and I cannot wholly divest myself of my responsibility.

Monday, March 5

While I was occupied with the boat builders in my barn after dinner, engaged in putting a sail to the boat, Harris passed by, with Mr. Dilly, the Butler of Mrs. Jarrett. Dilly and this underling seemed to have been drinking together, or I am much mistaken. Dilly said that the new farmer was come, having at length settled with Day; of one thing I am pretty certain, I cannot have a worse to deal with; some say the man (Day) is to reside with his brother at Anglesbatch, others that he is to be employed at Downside College as a bailiff.

Saturday, March 17

I heard from Owen, who purposes returning in about ten days. A friend of his will be accompanying him to Camerton; I am glad, therefore the boat will be completed for their amusement.

Monday, March 19

I had engaged to dine with Mr. Fenwick at Elm, and to call on Mr. Doveton at Mells Rectory by the way. I therefore proceeded from thence to Elm, a little more than a mile distant and I found that Mr. Fenwick did not dine till six o'clock. I was induced to join him, and a young gentleman staying with him in archery. After tea we had music, Mr. Fenwick being a good performer on the flute, his lady on the piano. Mrs. Fenwick sang two or three of Moore's melodies very beautifully, and seems to have naturally a fine voice. Mr. Fenwick accompanied her on the flute while she played on the piano.

Sunday, March 25

There was no ringing for Church in the morning, and but few people attended prayers; I heard the girls their Catechism, and spoke to the Clerk about collecting a party of boys next Sunday; now there is no Sunday school, I suppose they have forgotten all they learnt. After Church I walked with Joseph into the village to call upon a woman in Whitebrooks Lane, who is not worse than when I last saw her, and I am inclined to think it is actual laziness which keeps her in bed. The house smelt so bad that Joseph was obliged to leave it, and I soon followed his example. I find that a kind of lodging-house for trampers is kept here.

After dinner we walked to Writhlington, and drank tea with Sir Charles Waller, as I had promised to lend him Isaac Barrow's works respecting the Pope's supremacy and the unity of the Church, when I met him on Monday at Mells, as he, being an Irishman, is inclined to favour the Catholics. It was dark ere we got home.

Monday, December 24

Christmas Eve.

The Founder and Finisher of our Faith, Who suffered more than we can suffer, supported His trials without murmuring. Shall we, then, murmur, especially when the good things of life have been enjoyed so long by us? Whatever God has given, God has a right to take away. Thy will be done, O my God, in all things. These are my reflections preparatory to the Sacrament I am to administer and to receive. I can forgive, as I hope to be forgiven. The ringers came for the key of the Church to ring for Christmas evening, which I let them have. I was occupied in my study till prayer-time; I have not stirred out the whole day.

Tuesday, December 25

Christmas Day.

I was awakened early by the ringing of the bells, and could not help thinking how much sound overpowers common sense in all we have to do in the present day. I lay awake last night thinking of these things, and soon after I had closed my eyes they were again opened by the loud peals these thoughtless people among whom I dwell chose to ring, as they suppose, in honour of the day. They had better retire within themselves, and commune with their hearts, and be still.

I walked to Church before service, and I understood from Mrs. Coombes that the large inn, York House (Bath), was burnt to the ground last night.

There was a wedding before Church. The service was well attended, indeed better than it usually is at Christmas. Mrs. Jarrett and the Miss Frys staid the Sacrament, as did my daughter, Anna, and about a dozen more women; but only two men, Smallcombe and Mrs.

Jarrett's footman. After Church I spoke to the clerk, White, and said I had remarked he had not for three times staid the Sacrament, and wished to know why he had not done so. He replied he was not fit, for he could not get out of his mind the ideas he entertained of those who had had him turned out of his situation of bailiff. I said I had experienced far greater evils than those he complains of from the people around me, and yet I could forgive them—that I left them in the hands of God, and He would bring to pass His purposes in good time. And I further said if he, therefore, left the disposition of all his future prospects to the Almighty he could not feel malice and hatred and revenge, although some persons might have injured him in his worldly concerns. If he *did* he was very bad, and I should require that he overcame these evil feelings, and prepare himself to receive the Sacrament next time. I did not wish to force people to participate in this solemn ceremony of our religion, but still it was my duty to say, if they were not prepared to do so, they were not fit to participate in the hopes of eternal life: if they were not prepared to receive the Sacrament, they could not be prepared *to die*!

I walked from Church to call upon Balne, the constable, who excused himself from not having attended Church for these last five Sundays because he had so much to do about taking up bad people, and searching for stolen goods. The man was civil, but I know him perfectly well; he had his daughters and their husbands to dine with him. He promised faithfully I should have no more to complain of respecting the house kept by Mrs. Moon in his lane, as he would have an eye to it, and *present it*, if she continued to harbour improper persons.

I then went to old Widcombe's to ask why he did not attend his Church. On my arrival there I found young Goold, the brother of the lad who lived with me, and on my taxing him with his insolence when last we met, when he declared he would never come to Camerton Church because the Gospel was not preached there, he said it was because I found fault with him. I replied, with great justice, because he not only misbehaved by not standing up in the Church when the Psalms were read, but laughed loudly and in a manner to disturb the congregation. He said if he did laugh he was not the only one, but others set him on; that it was all spite, because his brother had left my service. The youth was excessively insolent, and of course I dropped the conversation since he told me he did not belong to my parish, that he never meant to come to my Church, and what business had I to talk to him. Old Widcombe strove to palliate what he said. How hard it is that I cannot go round my parish without being exposed to such insolence; but these are signs of the times!

Old Parfitt, his wife and daughter, with Hester, dined with the servants.

I went into my study to write my Journal after tea, but returned to spend the evening with my son and daughter.

Wednesday, December 26

Owen and Anna returned from their drive about four o'clock, having gone to call upon Captain Scobel, who asked Owen with Anna and myself to dine and go with his party to the ball at Old Down on Monday, he being one of the stewards. As I have promised my children to accompany them thither, it is arranged that we shall do it in this manner, and a carriage will be sent from the inn to take us to Captain Scobel's, and from thence to the ball.

As Charles Hoare was with us, I played at cards with the young people after tea.

Thursday, December 27

I attended the Vestry, as notice had been given by Farmer Hicks the preceding Sunday. He only was present, and signed the books for a Rate and for the weekly parish expenditure. On leaving the Church I walked to Mrs. Jarrett's. She was gone out, but I saw Mr. Stephen and asked him to dine with us to meet Charles Hoare and young Newnham, whom my son, Owen, had asked to be of the party, which he promised to do. We dined at half-past five, and had music and singing afterwards, and the young people seemed much to enjoy themselves. Study seems to be out of the question just now.

Sunday, December 30

I preached this morning on the text, "Whosoever shall do the will of God, the same is my brother, my sister, and my mother." I began by saying the selection from the Gospel expressed very fully the good fellowship which ought to subsist among all the followers of Christ, Who came into the world as at this time to recommend peace and goodwill. I asked their own consciences, how could man be entitled to the benefits of His coming for the express purpose of reconciling mankind to their Maker, if they would not be reconciled to each other, and united as it were in one family? I should esteem myself most happy to be able to hail among my parishioners a union of sentiment such as became members of Christ's family; the next step would be to exemplify their obedience to do the will of God by partaking of the Holy Communion, which was administered at stated times. I was much concerned to remark how much the receiving the sacred Communion of Christ's body and blood had been neglected. Those who called themselves Christians wilfully refused to obey one of the most solemn injunctions of their Master, Who, when He was betrayed, brake bread and gave it to His disciples, saying, "Take, eat; this is my body which is broken for you."

As I returned from Church I met Goold's sister, who came to Church with Mrs. Keel. On my speaking to her she answered in a very pert and flippant manner, alluding to my having lectured her brother George for his impertinence, and respecting my bad opinion of her brother John. The girl seemed inclined to be full as pert as her brothers; therefore I left her. Surely they ought to have esteemed me as their benefactor, since I had done so much with their grandfather in order to induce him to assist them. The lads he has left £100 each, and to the girl, I hear, £300. I advised her to make a good use of the advantages she had received.

Monday, December 31

As we are to dine at Captain Scobel's, and go to the Old Down ball to-night, I made up my Journals to the present time, and shall begin my next volume with the New Year, 1828.

1828—First Quarter

THE Ball at Old Down was much crowded, the number of persons assembled amounting to upwards of 150. It is somewhat singular that I should date the beginning of the New Year from a ballroom; but such vagaries will happen in this changeful scene. We did not get home till four o'clock in the morning. That these things occur but seldom, it is well for us who have now attained a more advanced period of life, and though we mix with young people we do not feel the interests they do.

Notwithstanding we were so late to bed, we met at breakfast before ten. After tea I read for a couple of hours in my study, but felt so completely tired before nine o'clock I went to bed. It has rained incessantly the whole of the day.

I left my bedroom at the usual hour, feeling perfectly refreshed by a good night's rest. There was the funeral of an infant a little after eleven. After the service was over, I called at Mrs. Jarrett's to enquire how her cold is, but learnt from the servant she had driven out. I met her afterwards in the village, and she joked me about the gaieties of the ball, and asked me whether I would dance with her the next time, merely because I had danced part of a country dance with Miss Newnham.

I might have said that I was glad my going to the ball afforded topic of amusing conversation respecting me, and diverted the vox populi into a more harmless direction. Heaven knows how little I am disposed to gaiety, and what a task it is to go into public. Perhaps it is sound policy now and then to go to a play or ball; if people will talk, the more harmless you can render their conversation the better.

I read the prayers as usual. Afterwards there was the christening of a child of Charles Cottle's; his brother stood Godfather, but the whole of the party came so late, and misbehaved themselves so much,

I had a great mind to put down the book. After I had read the Belief, when none of the sponsors returned an answer, I addressed myself to Cottle and said, "Why did you not reply to what I just read? What do you say?" He hesitated some time, and at last said, "*I renounce them all.*" I said, "Why? Do you not believe the Articles of the Creed?" I then told him what to answer. Indeed, indeed, these things ought not to be. One of the Godmothers seemed inclined to be very pert. I cannot speak to the people now without being exposed to their insolence.

In the evening there was a full congregation, but Mrs. Jarrett did not grace it by her presence. Her son, Mr. Stephen, was there in the morning.

I hope I shall soon settle again to business, as my Christmas holidays have been too extended. I am never so well as when in peace and quietness, with plain fare and regular hours.

I found on balancing my accounts that my expenditure exceeds my income nearly £300. This must be sunk in my capital. Had Joseph continued at Sandhurst, the outgoings would have been more considerable; Owen had to settle bills at Oxford, etc., etc., on leaving it. I cannot think my personal expenses can be retrenched, neither those of the household. I might lay down my carriage and horses, which would be a saving of £30 per annum, but I could not then move from place to place without post chaises.

Tuesday, January 8

I awoke with a bad cough and hoarseness, and was engaged in my study after breakfast in reading and writing. My son and daughter were at Mr. Newnham's, at Chilcompton. About two o'clock a person brought me a note from Mr. Feare, the Bailiff of the Coal Works, saying his wife wished particularly to see me. She had been ill for some time, and I had heard she was better, but fearing the contrary I immediately went to the house. Mr. Feare seemed to be in great distress, and told me that his wife had been in strong convulsions, and had had a paralytic seizure, but was then perfectly sensible, but could not speak.

On going into her bedroom I found Mrs. Jarrett and several women assembled. I asked Mrs. Feare whether she knew me. She answered something which indicated she did. I asked whether she would wish me to read to her. She made the same kind of affirmative. I then read the Prayers appointed for the Visitation of the Sick. On taking leave of her I shook her hands, and said, "God bless you." She pressed mine in token that she knew me, and was thankful for my attention. Feare shewed me his son, a little lad of eight or nine years of age, who seems to be going fast into a decline. He told me he had now hopes of the boy's recovery, from a singular circumstance, which was, he had ruptured a blood-vessel while coughing, which had stopped the inflammation on the lungs. I fear this is but a fallacious hope, however; poor man! I did not hint it. Mrs. Jarrett has been most constant in her attention; she certainly has great merit in bestowing assistance, and I never see her in so amiable point of view as when thus engaged.

It is a dreadful day; the wind is cold and piercing from the east; the snow lies deep; Owen and Anna will have a bad journey from Chilcompton. I spent the evening in my study.

Thursday, January 10

A child was brought to the Parsonage from Redhill to be named. The woman said it was likely to die, but I never saw a more healthy-looking babe. I desired her to tell the mother she must bring it the Sunday after next, when it would be upwards of a month old, to be christened in the Church. I know the people are now getting into the way of getting their children named, and in order to avoid bringing godfathers and godmothers to Church. In fact we, *the Rectors*, are sine regimine, or authority; if a fellow is ignorant of the first principles of his religion, we must take him for a godfather or have none. I continued reading till ten o'clock, when I went to bed, leaving Owen to officiate for me downstairs, as I am still very hoarse, and my cough so troublesome.

Friday, January 11

I slept badly, the frost was very severe, I did not get up to breakfast. Stephen Jarrett called and shewed me a list of coins which the University of Oxford wished him to procure for them. They are all of the scarcest kind. I gave him a silver Honorius, which was on the list.

Monday, January 14

I sent a letter to go by the mail to Wells, containing a draft for £5 to be paid to Mr. H. P. Hope, the banker, for my subscription towards the Friendly Society Committee. I can ill afford it just now, but as it appears to be a general thing I must nolens volens do it. The Bishop gives £50, the two members £50 each, Mr. Gore Langton £25, Mr. Doveton £10,[1] etc.

It was so rapid a thaw that the whole of the valley was flooded, and the waters in places covered the road going to Radford. It gave me a very complete idea of what Camalodunum must have been in British times, when all the valleys were flooded by stopping back the brooks, and leaving only sufficient width to pass over the causeways. I walked to Cridlingcot to see after a child they pretended was so ill that they could not bring it to be named at the Parsonage, and I observed that it was merely a trick to avoid having godfathers and godmothers; that they pretend the infants are ill and like to die. This one indeed, a poor base-born child, I did not think would live, because the mother did not pay it proper attention. The mother said that her reason for not sending the child was because none of her neighbours would bring it to my Parsonage, and she was too weak to do so herself.

I therefore named the child, on the express condition of her having it baptised in the Church on Sunday.

A disagreeable, rainy day. Owen complained of a swelling of the glands, so that I sent for Mr. Crang. My own cold and cough continues to be very troublesome, but I shall not have it doctored. Mr. Crang was engaged to attend a lying-in woman, and could not come. In case of sudden and serious illness it would be an inconvenience to have the medical man living at a distance.

Still an unpleasant day. I visited old Rossiter and his wife. They are much the same, and as Curtis says they may take anything to eat or drink they can fancy, as they had no fever, I sent them some oranges as the old man finds them so beneficial, and a bottle of white wine in the evening.

Still very unsettled weather; I never remember so much wet. My worthy parishioners begin to amuse themselves again; twice this

[1] J. F. Doveton, Rector of Mells, 1824–36 and later of Burnett.

week they have tied a tin pot to the tail of my little dog, merely to annoy and exasperate me. However, I must think as little as possible about them, since I have things of more consequence to attend to. Mr. Crang came to Owen, and ordered leeches to be applied to the part. I sent my servant, Heal, to Bath for the leeches, which were applied as ordered. I fear poor Owen will have a serious business of it, if the glands suppurate.

Tuesday, January 22

This being a finer day, I was determined to try whether exercise might not be of service, and make me sleep better at night.

Wednesday, January 23

I slept the better for my exercise of yesterday, and am therefore determined to persevere in it. Owen, I think, is in a very precarious state. He has not strength of constitution to support these violent remedies, nor a discharge, should this glandular swelling break. Anna's cough is better, and I hope she will soon be off the sick list. There was a wedding at eleven; and I walked towards the middle of the day to call on Heal's wife, and I read to her. She seems fast sinking. From thence I walked to Radford. In my way thither I saw old Sarah Purnell, and sat ten minutes in her cottage, which she tells me has been flooded this winter no less than thirteen times; that the water came once so high as the top of the grate, so as to extinguish the fire. I wonder she has been able to exist so long in such a place so near to the water, yet she tells me she is upward of eighty-one years of age—a few months older than Mrs. Anne Stephens, with whom she lived as a servant upwards of fifty years

Saturday, January 26

I had but little sleep last night, my mind is so worried with Owen's illness, tythe business, and other things. The post brought me a note from my Mother, wishing me to bring Owen and Anna to her house that he may be placed under Mr. Norman. I wrote to say that Anna and Owen should come, if my Mother would send over a chaise on Monday, but I could not. Owen afterwards told me he had much rather continue at Camerton, and wrote a note to my Mother to this effect, which my servant, Heal, is to take to-morrow when he goes for some more leeches. Mr. Crang, I find, strives to prevent its coming to a head. I walked for an hour in the upper garden before dinner. I am by no means well, but medicine can do me no good. I went to bed before nine; but I heard all the clocks strike till five, when I dropped asleep.

Sunday, January 27

I read prayers in the morning, and preached in the evening on the Ninth Commandment. The Church was more crowded than ever I have seen it since the summer, indeed, so much so, there was no room for some of the people, and I desired the clerk to shew them to my pew. When I returned home I took half a glass of wine, as I felt quite exhausted, but thankful I had been able to perform the service at all.

I am pretty well assured, from the signs of the times, and the indications of my δαίμων, that the miners are about to *spring the powder* the Guy Fauxes among them have laid, with what effect we shall see: finis coronat opus.

Owen has put on the leeches which were brought from Bath.

The post brought me a letter from Mrs. Campbell. Captain Campbell said he had the promise of a cadetcy from Sir Robert Farquhar, and that my son, Joseph, was the ninth on the list. He begged I would keep quiet, and be assured that his promise would be fulfilled.

Tuesday, January 29

I called on old Rossiter and his aged spouse. They both still keep their bed.

Wednesday, January 30

Owen and his brother went to Bath, as I wished to have Mr. Norman's opinion on his case.

Thursday, January 31

I called with my daughter, Anna, on Mrs. Heal, who is declining rapidly, and I was surprised she was in want of the common necessaries, respecting linen, sheets, etc., which we sent down to her from the Parsonage. Owen and Joseph returned to dinner. Norman, I find, has but a bad opinion of the general state of Owen's health.

The post brought me a letter from my cousin, Samuel Skinner, saying that his friend's application for a cadetcy for Joseph has failed, and that he has heard nothing from Sir Robert Farquhar. Mr. Skinner further said he had met the Bishop of Bath and Wells in

Town, who spoke most kindly of me, and said he wished it were in his power to make interest for Joseph.

I preached in the morning on the Tenth Commandment. Mrs. Jarrett was at Church part of the service, but left it before the sermon. I called on old Harris, who talks of going to Bath next Wednesday. I told him I thought, if he went such a distance, he might contrive to come to Church. He replied, Aye, he must go, then, to get a surcharge off from a dog! I then called on Balne, the constable, to tell him to do his duty, as there are some bad people harboured at Mrs. Moon's. The people were ringing so badly when I returned through the churchyard, and White was lounging about without attending to them, that I spoke to him; the man seemed disposed to be impudent, but did not proceed to extremities. I must get rid of him as soon as I can, but whom to procure in his place is the question, and I may take a worse.

Mr. Crang says that he sees no material difference in Owen, and seems surprised that the rash continues still so troublesome.

I called on Mrs. Jarrett at the Manor House to thank her for the books she had lent Owen, and the rabbits she has sent. The lady was very gracious.

I have had to investigate a business respecting the girl who keeps the school for young children, and to whom I paid for twelve per week. Old Rossiter, when I called on him on Wednesday, told me that this girl, the daughter of Jeremiah Perfett, who had care of the children, was a very different person from what I conceived her to be; in fact, that she had been running after a fellow who came from Bristol, who was a married man; and he further said that, as soon as her Father was gone to the coal pits, she left her school and went after this fellow; that once she got up behind him on his horse and rode through the village, for which her Father had beaten her severely, and given her a black eye, which was the reason she had stayed away two Sundays from Church; that the daughter had told him, if he did that again she would go to Bath and get her living there as others do, upon the town. I asked Rossiter if he had received this intelligence from persons who could be depended on: that I knew the Parish was very prone to calumny.

I had myself a good opinion of the girl, as I always saw her attentive to her Church, and and that she had borrowed some religious books to read with her Father.

Rossiter said that, unless he had been certain of the facts, he would not have mentioned them to me; that the girl went four or five times a day to the house where this man was lodging; that he had left his wife and child in Bristol, and had come to Camerton; that the girl did not know at first he was a married man, but, after she had been told of it, she continued her visits as usual.

I asked him who was the person she went after. His answer was, a shoemaker from Bristol; that he kept a disorderly house. And further that on Friday last there were four or five girls there, Biven's daughter, Tucker's, Hill's, Harding's, and this girl Perfett; that they made every kind of fun, pretending to preach a sermon in a tub, saying they would take a text, and that the words they uttered were beyond belief nasty and improper.

I felt very uncomfortable on hearing this, and, for my own satisfaction, was under the necessity of investigating it.

I found that the girl had been very faulty, and in consequence I determined to put an end to the school. I told my daughter to send for her account since Christmas, and I will allow the parents of the children, twelve in number, to send them elsewhere—I paying for their schooling till we have a proper place established in the village.

My servant Moses Heal's wife is very ill indeed, now having been brought to bed.

John Rossiter borrowed £15.

Saturday, February 9

I expected John Rossiter to call, as he borrowed £15 of me yesterday. He has not brought the acknowledgment as he promised. After tea I had a summons from Heal to attend his wife, who they thought was dying. I read prayers to her, and asked whether she had any wish to receive the Sacrament to-morrow. She told her husband in a whisper she wished it very much, and I promised to visit her after Church.

Sunday, February 10

I read prayers in the morning to a thin congregation. Afterwards I called on Mrs. Heal, and administered the Sacrament.

As John Rossiter did not bring a note of hand for the £15 I lent him on the 8th, I sent for him this morning. On coming, he said he had not been able to procure a stamp. I said he must get one immediately, as I could not let him have the money without a proper acknowledgment, having been so often deceived and defrauded. Accordingly he brought it, but I was much displeased to find that, instead of having the loan for six weeks, he had inserted three months in the promissory note.

If this fellow plays me false I shall draw my purse-strings close, and only give small sums to those who immediately need, and *never lend* to any of them.

I told my servant, Heal, as his wife was so ill, that he might continue with her, and I would not deduct his wages. Owen I hope is getting better.

Mr. Boodle called about two o'clock to ask whether I meant to attend the meeting at Kilmersdon to-morrow in order to sign a petition against any further concessions to the Catholics. I have received a letter from the Rural Dean, Mr. Williams, on the matter, and meant to attend.

Heal's wife is dead.

It snowed so fast during the whole of the morning that I did not go to Kilmersdon. Indeed, it was impossible to ride. I sent Joseph to Radstock Rectory to tell Mr. Boodle, if he went, to affix my signature.

The Church was as much crowded during the prayers in the evening as it had been in the morning. I buried Heal's wife after the service of the Church was concluded, and baptised the child.

A man came after breakfast to request I would go to attend a poor woman residing in the new houses lately built in the hamlet of Cridlingcot. He told me the woman had been churched on Sunday last, and since her return had been quite raving, saying that, unless

Mr. Skinner came to pray with her, she was sure her soul would be lost; that she was so violent several women were obliged to be in the house to hold her, and that she whooped and made such a noise you could hear her all over the place.

I went there about two o'clock. The poor creature seemed very well to know me, and listened attentively to what I said to her and declared she felt much more comfortable, and begged I would pray for her in Church, as she was sure I could keep the Evil One from destroying her poor soul.

On making further enquiries I am inclined to think the whole of this poor creature's malady proceeds from having caught cold after her confinement, as the house she lives in is newly built and is very damp. Finding that she required some medicine, and was fearful of employing an apothecary for fear of the expense, I promised to let her have some Scott's pills. The poor woman then asked me to name her child. I told her, if she said her prayers with sincerity to God, she would find herself quite well by the Sunday after next, when she might bring her child to the Church to be christened.

Joseph returned in good time for dinner, and has appointed Monday for Owen to go into Bath to see Mr. Norman at his house.

As I ordered some fish to be brought for Owen, and my Mother, not knowing this order, had sent some, my children had a pair of soles dressed for supper, which I partook of, and paid the forfeiture of my temerity by passing a sleepless night.

Sunday, February 24

It was a fine, bright morning, which I am always happy to see on a Sunday. Mrs. Jarrett and the Miss Frys attended prayers in the morning, Mrs. Jarrett afterwards coming to pay a visit to Owen.

I then called on the old Rossiters. They both still keep their bed; but they seem able to eat and drink as usual, and indeed fare sumptuously every day, as Mrs. Jarrett supplies them with soup, rabbits, etc., and they generally have a bottle of Cape Madeira from me per week. But this I said nothing about to Mrs. Jarrett.

I preached in the evening upon the third clause I have divided the Lord's Prayer into, namely, "Give us this day our daily bread." The Church was quite full, and the people seemed attentive. There was a churching and christening after, of Farmer Kimberry's wife and child. As Mrs. Kimberry looked quite chilled as she drove in a covered cart from Lemansfield, and the evening was turned off quite cold, I offered her a glass of wine at the Parsonage, which she seemed thankful for.

Monday, February 25

As the chaise from Bath to take Owen was ordered at eleven, and I thought it was a good opportunity for Anna to visit her Grand-mother for a few days, they were all busily occupied in packing their things. I have promised to join the party the latter end of the week, but having young servants I do not like they should be left to their own machinations more than we can help.

Anna agreed with a person to take the washing for four pounds a quarter, instead of having it done at home, which will cut off one channel of village gossip—the main cause of unsettling one's house-hold.

Tuesday, February 26

Hiscox came to make the hedge round the Glebe Field. He began a history about Harris; he is a gossiping old fellow. I suppose Hiscox has had some quarrel with Harris, and therefore mentions all these circumstances to me, I told Hiscox I had been with the people of Camerton upwards of twenty-seven years, and could bear testimony, if I were called upon to do so, that they were as bad as the people of Sodom and Gomorrah, about whom I had read in the lesson of last Sunday. If he only reflected upon what had occurred within this little place: what was become of all the farmers who had lived at Camerton when first I came there? All were come to a wretched end, or were reduced to poverty. I not only seemed as one who mocked to the people around me, but, as they could not bear reproof, or to have their conduct called in question, they leagued themselves together against me; but they never would succeed in driving me from my post; my eyes were opened, and one of these days they would find they were.

Mr. Williams, the Rural Dean, called to visit the Church.

Friday, February 29

I drove into Bath to visit my Mother. I had forgotten it was Owen's twentieth birthday. My mother had prepared a set-out on the occasion. After tea, we played at cards till bedtime.

Monday, March 3

After I had finished my Journals I went to attend Mrs. Feare, having received a summons from her husband to administer the

Sacrament to her. I found her perfectly sensible, but unable to speak; indeed she could scarcely swallow the small bit of bread I gave her. It was most distressing to see her.

I hear that John Rossiter is at his old tricks, and I may have some difficulty in receiving the £15 I lent him. I find in his note of hand, although on a stamp, he has omitted "value received," which I believe in a legal point of view will invalidate the note. It is very hard one cannot find one honest man. I drove to Mells to attend a clerical meeting, and arrived a little after two. We sat down fourteen to dinner, which was an uncomfortable one owing to there being only one waiter. After some rather desultory conversation one of the party, of the name of Bumstead, asked me what was the etymon of his name. I did not perceive it at the time, but have every reason to believe, on account of what afterwards occurred, that it was done purposely to put me on the subject of Etymology for the amusement of the company. The expense of the dinner was eight shillings, my horse and ostler one-and-sixpence. It was nearly ten o'clock when I arrived at my quiet parsonage. Anna did not much expect my return on account of the rain, which indeed wet me through. Having taken some warm tea, I went to bed a little after ten, not altogether pleased with myself or with my associates. If it were not for the sake of my family I would now follow the bent of my own inclinations, and devote the remainder of my life to a proper regulation of my thoughts, words, and actions, which can best be done in solitude; when I enter into society I can do neither.

I had a comfortable note from Owen, stating moreover he had received a letter from one of his Oxford friends who would visit him at Camerton if I had no objection. I will put no obstacle in the way, but the repairs we are about to commence at the Parsonage will throw the house into disorder. I did not go down to prayers exactly at ten, neither have I done so lately, as Anna is engaged in teaching the servants to write and cypher, from nine o'clock till they come to prayers. I hope it will be of service, but I begin to have my doubts about teaching the lower orders beyond reading. I know much may be said on both sides of the question.

Sunday, March 9

I read prayers in the morning, and afterwards visited the village as I am accustomed to do. I saw an ill-looking fellow begging at old Widcombe's door, and I told him he had no business to do so, or to be prowling about for no good purpose. I went to Balne, the constable, who lived only a little beyond: as I came into his house, he pretended to turn over his Bible. I said, "Mr. Balne, you told me once before, when I applied to you to apprehend a vagrant in the Parish, that I must see him begging myself, otherwise you could do nothing. I have just seen a man begging at old Widcombe's, and a bad-looking fellow he is; will you apprehend him?" He said it was not his business; why did I come bothering him, when he was setting down to read his Bible. I said, "Nonsense!" that I had frequently told him to do his duty in the office he held, and I must once for all tell him, unless he did so I would present him at the Sessions. "What do I care for that?" he replied; "you tried to do so once before, but who would listen to you? You are mad half your time, and do not know what you say or do." I then left this worthless fellow, and will make a complaint against him the first opportunity.

I preached in the evening on the concluding clause of the Lord's Prayer. The evening being fair, after dinner I walked with Anna as far as Radford, and met young Cottle on the way, who had been to Church, but never does so unless for some purpose not exactly connected with religion. He generally sits himself just in front of the pulpit, and makes some noises, either by coughing or hawking, in order to interrupt my discourse or withdraw my attention from it. When I spoke to him concerning the great impropriety, he seemed to be insolent, but afterwards apologised.

Saturday, March 15

I prepared my sermon in the evening, having previously dismissed the mason and his boy, who have finished the walls for the flooring in the best parlour. I am inclined to think the mason's boy, son of Harris, late clerk, wrote some vile obscenity on my gates, which would have been a disgrace to the worst part of St. Giles's. I desired my servant to wash it out before the people are about to-morrow.

Sunday, March 16

A shop was broken into in the village, and money and goods to the amount of £20 taken away. I am convinced some of our own people were engaged. I was much worried by this evil race, and felt far otherwise than I should wish to do on this day, more especially appropriated to peace and tranquillity.

Tuesday, March 18

The six larches I purchased of Mrs. Jarrett were brought by the timber waggon in the evening to my saw-pit. I cut down two fir trees in the upper walk, as I have not wood enough to go on. The six larches have not yet been valued. I am so fully occupied, I have scarcely time to eat my meals.

Thursday, March 20

Owen writes that he is getting quite well and means to return home soon. I hope I shall get the upper room in a state to be useful before his friend pays his expected visit from Oxford.

Feare's wife is, poor creature, become quite blind, and it is impossible she can last long. Old Rossiter and his wife are as well as ever, but chuse to keep their bed for some reason I cannot divine.

Saturday, March 22

It snowed hard this morning. Bacon, my tenant, has not gotten the security he promised for the payment of the Rent of the Glebe Fields he occupies; I had heard that Hicks would be his surety, and called upon him to know if it were true, and found it was not. After dinner I called upon Bacon, but as he was in bed and fast asleep, I told his wife that as I had heard of no security her husband could give me, I must look about for another tenant. The woman seemed inclined to be impudent: I believe she is a very hard-mouthed woman, as they term it, so I got out of the way.

Tuesday, March 25

This being Quarter Day, I was obliged to go and regain possession of my Glebe. Immediately my servant, Heal, had finished his breakfast I took him into the nearer Glebe Fields, lately occupied by Lewis, and with the spade he carried I cut up a portion of the turf, and said: "I take possession of this my ground."

MEMORANDUM.—March 25, 1828

This being Lady Day, 1828, I, John Skinner, went into the Glebe Fields lately occupied by John Lewis, who had left the same before his term expired, and took possession of the premises, by turning up some of the Pasture Ground with a spade, in the presence of my Servant, Moses Heal.

JOHN SKINNER.

Witness: MOSES HEAL.

They told me one witness was sufficient; but perhaps there may be some quibble on this head, it being land.

I returned home a little after eleven, and went to the Vestry, and found that the accounts had been looked over by Feare. There were some poor people, two girls, orphans, and a boy nearly blind. I spoke in favour of their allowance continuing, and met with no opposition from the farmers.

Mr. Purnell came to the Vestry, and said he wanted to speak to me for a few minutes, and I walked with him to my house. He had something which he carried in a parcel, which I found to be two large *mince pies*! which he begged my daughter's acceptance of, saying they were the last remaining of his Christmas store; he also brought the £15, the half-year's composition for Woodborough, due this day.

Wednesday, March 26

Mrs. Jarrett called at the Parsonage, and she said, respecting the larches I had gotten, that it was not worth while to talk about a few sticks.

Thursday, March 27

I walked to Cridlingcot to call upon Adam Nash's wife, who is in a very precarious state of health. She met with a great alarm last night, as the outhouse caught fire and the roof was entirely consumed, and they were fearful of its catching the thatch of the dwelling. She was carried out of her bed to another house. I promised to administer the Sacrament to her to-morrow at eleven, and to send her up some port wine this evening.

On my return to the Parsonage I found old Walters had made another mistake, and I must not now leave the workmen even for an hour without setting them their portion to perform. We sent the wine and some of the Bouillon, etc., for Mrs. Nash's dinner. I got a note from Owen saying he meant to come home to-morrow by the mail. Mrs. Feare died in the morning. I paid for the schooling of one of the children at Cridlingcot, twenty-one weeks, and I promised to pay for another till my school is established, and its subordinate branches.

Moses Heal had the day off to move his goods into my Glebe House. I shall let him stay there rent free, on condition that Hester continues in the house; and I have promised to give him five pounds a year for attending to the Sunday School, and my daughter has promised to assist.

Squire Purnell sent for old Walters, the carpenter, to come to him at Woodborough to-morrow. It is very strange the said Justice knows neither Law nor Justice. At any rate he is ignorant of the golden rule to doing to others what he would wish to have done to himself.

Friday, March 28

I went to administer the Sacrament to Mrs. Nash, at a little after eleven. During our conversation I said I perceived that a new Meeting House was about to be erected at the back of the premises, the foundations of which I had seen when I went to see the damage the fire had done. Mr. Nash pretended to be ignorant that such a work was going on. Her aunt, Mrs. Lancashire, before she knelt down to receive the Sacrament with myself and Nash's wife, on my asking after her husband, said he was gone to Bath to speak to the Insurance Company respecting the fire, whereas I heard him talk and cough in the adjoining room when I was leaving the house. Does *Faith* account for such palpable lies? Adam Nash has for years been a preacher in the Methodist Society, and it is not improbable the Chapel now building will be partly under his direction. There is one Meeting House already licensed at Camerton: perhaps the Magistrates would not licence two in the same parish.

Owen arrived, and seems better in health. Mrs. Jarrett brought me the "Quarterly Review," and said she would leave directions for it to be sent to my house during the time she was abroad.

Sunday, March 30

I walked to Mr. Feare's after breakfast to speak respecting the funeral of his wife, who is to be buried to-morrow. He wished me to be at the house at eleven to attend the corpse to the Church; although I have never done so since I have been at Camerton, and am not fond of masquerading, yet, as he seemed to wish me to do so, I promised I would.

Monday, March 31

I have now finished the first quarter's Journal, and will, if possible, spare a few hours to tint the sketches I have taken, and then get the book bound.

1828—Second Quarter

THE same occupation as heretofore. Skuse, the farmer, is disposed to give trouble. Hicks, as I suspected, and Day are his supporters; but I have given the business up to my son, and will keep myself aloof and not expose myself to his insolence. Richard and Charles Hoare rode over from Southfield with an invitation for me to spend the ensuing week there, but I of course could not leave home.

This being Good Friday, I preached in the morning, on the text, "He was oppressed, and He was afflicted, yet He opened not His mouth." Very few were in Church, as the usual occupations of the week are carried on this day in the country; all the colliers work as usual, and so do the farmers. I found my carpenters and sawyers came to Church. As I do not make any deduction from my outdoor servants, I suppose they expect to be treated the same, but this I shall know to-morrow. I walked with my son and daughter and Mr. Flower to Priston after Church, to visit the Hammonds: he has been building, and was then indeed engaged with his workmen, which I was rather surprised at. As to the keeping of this solemn Feast, doctors differ. I may have my opinions on the subject, and my neighbour his; but really I think if we of the Church do not scruple to employ workmen, we cannot expect that our Churches will be attended. We returned to a five o'clock dinner.

I preached in the morning on the Resurrection, and administered the Sacrament to sixteen Communicants, among which number was Feare the Bailiff, whom I have not seen receive it before; White, also the clerk, did so, as I had spoken to him on the subject before three times, and said I should entertain a very bad opinion of him if he did not attend this necessary duty. There were eight children christened in the evening. I do not like this custom of attending in crowds a ceremony which ought to be considered of more consequence than it generally is. One of the children they had named Ama; I suppose it was intended for Amy, but the woman who presented it twice repeated Ama. I learnt afterwards it was an illegitimate child, so its name has, I suppose, some reference to the cause of its birth—according to Pope, the Poet's definition of Love.

Monday, April 7

There was a Vestry for the election of Churchwardens; as only Collins attended, besides Hicks and Skuse, it was determined they should continue in the office the ensuing year. Skuse told me he never meant to give me more trouble than he could help in setting out his tythe. I said if he continued in the office of Churchwarden I expected him to attend the Church constantly, in order to see that the people behaved themselves properly, and that the boys did not leave the Church in service time, and go into the churchyard to play. The man was civil, and said he would attend constantly. I believe John Rossiter expected I would have nominated him again; but, after the specimen he gave, I am afraid to trust him. I went to the Camerton Inn a little after eleven, and was engaged till half-past three in receiving the tythe. Most of the people attended. Twelve, besides my son, his friend, and myself, dined in the parlour. Every payer, however small his sum, had a piece of cold beef and a pint of beer in the kitchen. After the farmers began to smoke we left them, apparently well pleased with their fare. We got back about six, but all the workmen were gone. On looking over what had been done during my absence, I found but little to be pleased with: so true is the old adage, "When the cat's away, the mice go to play"; but they shall make up for lost time.

Old Walters was ill yesterday; I found the boy had let a piece of wood fall on his head, I hope not on purpose; this might have shaken the old man. The carpenter, Gay, who did not make his appearance yesterday, said he was ill and could not come. The workmen are plaguing and, if spoken to, insolent. I am almost weary of overlooking; if an Episcopus has to deal with such workmen as I have I do not envy him his office. By the way, I think the Test Act,[1] when introduced into the House of Lords, will try what some of them are made of: in this liberal age a martyr's doublet is now reckoned very coarse clothing not fit for a gentleman.

I am sick of workmen, and sick of myself for letting them work upon me. My mind is quite unhinged. We have a continuation of

[1] Repeal of the Test Act, 1828, an Act originally levelled against dissenters from the Established Church.

heavy wet weather; this, together with the tormenting workmen, may make me see things in a gloomy point of view. I endeavoured to rouse myself, but cannot.

I visited Mrs. Heal's boy; he is no better, and takes so much laudanum to lull pain he cannot attend to what I say.

Tuesday, April 8

I called the servants up after six. On going to the workmen, Walters told me that Mr. Purnell has sent to desire him to come to Woodborough, and that he had promised to do so. I felt very hurt at the old man's conduct, for he had told me he would not go anywhere till my work was finished. He is a double-faced old man, as I have proved; but Purnell shall not carry his point without difficulty.

I read to Walters what "Burn's Justice" says on a workman leaving his work without leave after he had undertaken it!

He said he did not wish to leave it; he had much rather stay with me.

I balanced my accounts. I find that according to the arrangement I have made, I shall have a clear income of £500 from the Living. At the high times it used to be £620; but I am satisfied, if Skuse does not plague me as his predecessor, Day, did.

Wednesday, April 9

My son and his friend went into Bath to deposit the money in the bank, and pay some bills. They purpose driving to-morrow to Clifton, and do not return till Saturday—at least so I hear from Anna. I paid Owen his half-year's allowance. I hope he will not be too lavish, as he will have to pinch for it afterwards. I foresee that my expenses in the house will be beyond my calculation, which is always the case in building. I called on Mrs. Jarrett after breakfast in order to settle for the larch trees I have had, but the lady would not hear of my paying for them, as she said what I was doing would be such an improvement to the Parsonage, and hoped I should live many years to enjoy my present labours and expenses.

Kimberry, who has just taken Sheephouse Farm, came in the evening to say he wished to be married to-morrow at nine, or a little after: he had procured a licence.

Thursday, April 10

I married the happy pair a little after ten, and said I hoped to see them at Church; they complained there were no seats; I said my pew would be large enough to hold them, and they might use it if they chose. But this was an excuse, as both Kimberry and his brother are Methodists. Well, be it so, the clergy at least may perform their mechanical part of the procession, that is, marry, baptise, and bury, but few will require of them the more important services which their residence in the Parish might enable them to perform to so much advantage. I went to see Hannah Heal's boy, who I fear is in a very bad way through some scrofulous humour which is fixed in his leg, and the discharge is so great I fear it will exhaust him: the poor woman will have a heavy loss, as he is a well disposed boy. We have done a good deal of work to-day; indeed, I have kept the people well to it, not having left them but when the wedding took place, and when I visited the sick. Mrs. Anne Stephens called on my daughter; she is a very extraordinary woman for 80 years of age and upwards, having little or no ailments, and walking as upright as when I first knew her nearly thirty years ago. I got a little time in my study before prayers.

Tuesday, April 15

Between ten and eleven Mr. Purnell called to me as I was standing in my garden, where he saw me as he passed by the rails. I went to him in the walk, and he said he had just been paying a visit to Mrs. Jarrett, and thought he would call upon me. He then began saying that he had looked in his lease and found it was worded as I said, that he was to pay £30 a year clear of all rates and taxes, etc., either parochial or parliamentary; this clause, he said was merely introduced to save me from the Property Tax, in case such should have been laid by Parliament. I asked what the term Rate meant; whether it did not apply to the Parochial Rate, or Poor Rate, which was to be paid by him for the grounds he and his tenants held at Woodborough, as it used to be paid. That I had recently agreed with all the farmers, excepting Skuse, for their present composition, on condition that they paid my Poor Rates for the term of 14 years; that I should expect him in future to pay the Rates for Woodborough, as he used to do when our agreement was made. . . . He then began quibbling according to his usual custom. . . . I said in my dealings with him he was a shuffling fellow, and that he would not pay even his dues without he was compelled to do so. He said if I called him a shuffling fellow I was a rascal for doing so. I replied that if he gave himself a little consideration he would be convinced that he was a rascal for endeavouring to cheat me, instead of myself who was cheated by him, but I was determined I would oblige him to pay me the Rates in future. He then muttered something as he was walking away which I did not distinctly hear, but I called out aloud that I should not alter the opinion I had ever entertained of him, that he was a shuffling fellow. So much for this mock Magistrate, made out of a petty-fogging Attorney: how can we complain of our workmen's cheating us, when their superiors, as they are taught to think them, would do it tenfold? If ever there was a muck-worm, this is the creature; he was born, will die, and will rot without the solitary satisfaction of having done good to anyone who will lament his departure from the face of the earth.

Sunday, April 20

I preached in the morning on the subject of Balaam and Balak: very few at Church on account of the rain; this prevented my walking between the services. There was a churching in the evening, and two burials. Some of the boys behaved very badly at the funerals by talking and laughing out loud, so I desired the clerk to take a stick and chastise them. This is a most untoward race, and it is impossible to deal with them.

Sunday, April 27

I slept but little last night; my nerves are in a high state of irritability, which I endeavour to counteract by every means in my power. I rose a little after six and looked over my sermon on the first Article of the Creed, respecting the belief in a God. The day is much brighter, and the gloom of yesterday is in a measure dissipated. What poor creatures we are: in what does the boasted philosophy of man consist? the east wind or the heavy clouds collecting from the west may make a stoic shrink like a sensitive plant.

I walked to see the widow Heal's boy before morning prayers, and gave him something to buy oranges. The poor lad has the Evil dreadfully. Is not this the sin of the fathers descending upon the children? He has no less than four open wounds in his leg and thigh. I fear he will be a cripple, if he survives the great discharge. Old Rossiter and his wife will, I hear, be soon about again. I cannot guess what was their fancy to keep their bed so long, unless—but I will not surmise. I have not been there for several weeks, for I did not wish to encourage idleness.

Owen rode after to dine with the Freres. I thought he had better not have done so, having made a good dinner and taken a sufficient quantity of wine at home; but he chose to go. Alas! what authority has a Father now?

Tuesday, April 29

The Camerton Parsonage will be improved by my exertions, and I hope will not need further repairs as long as I occupy it, therefore my time is not entirely thrown away; but if my mind is not able to support the daily annoyances I am exposed to, and sinks under them, what will the improvement of my residence avail me? . . . I procured three or four hours' reading in my study this morning. The carpenter, Gay, not here; the rest all in attendance; the slating of the roof is nearly finished. I hear Balne, the constable, is put out of his office, and it was high time that this should have been done. There is a pitched battle, I hear, on Clan Down, and people have been passing the Parsonage in carriages to be present at the brutal exhibition. If Purnell, the magistrate, were anything but an old woman, they would not have dared to come in this neighbourhood. I have heard them shouting several times; the whole collieries are put into excitement, and the pockets of their families picked, because we have no proper person to control the turbulence of the people.

Wednesday, April 30

I got but little sleep, my nerves are so completely shaken; the screaming of Mrs. Jarrett's peacock, who roosts close to my garden, wakes me twenty times in the night. I went to the gardener and told him I would give him half-a-crown if he could contrive to make it change its place of abode, but not to mention anything to Mrs. Jarrett on the subject, as she would think it very strange that a bird like this should prevent my sleeping. If he be not removed, I mean the bird and its horrid notes, I shall remove to another dormitory; indeed, I have given instructions to Heal to finish the front bedroom as soon as possible, and I will occupy it when dry, without waiting for the painting. For this week I have not slept two hours together.

Saturday, May 3

After I had read prayers to the servants I went to bed. I slept badly, and called the servants a little after six, as I waited to see whether they would get up without calling. All the old school of housewives is gone by; instead of punctuality and regularity, we have pertness and rascality. The plumber from Temple Cloud came to put the lead on the new slated roof, which is now complete. I was worried by one of my servants, who refused to go and take the milk tythe: there is not a day without something unpleasant.

Mrs. Jarrett called "pour prendre congé"; she says she leaves Camerton on Monday, and spends a week with her son in Hampshire before she sets off for the Continent. We may tell our English travellers, and this good lady in particular:

> Coelum non animum mutant
> qui trans mare currunt.
> Domum Domum dulce domum.

Sunday, May 4

I called upon Jacob Balne, who I understood had been very ill. He told me he had been obliged to relinquish his office of constable, but he did not value it a farthing; indeed, he had rather, he said, be without it. I am sure the public are much better circumstanced, be his successor whatever he may be.

Sunday, May 11

When I awoke this morning, having passed a better night than I have done for some time past, I reflected that it was my birthday, and that 56 years of my mortal career were finished.

I walked in the village after morning service, and I preached in the evening; the Church quite crowded. There was a christening and two funerals after my dinner. After tea I walked with my children nearly as far as Splot, calling on Widow Heal's boy. We are to keep my birthday to-morrow at my Mother's; this is a family custom.

Monday, May 12

I rose early as usual, but my early rising is of no avail, for the people did not come to work, neither was there anything done in consequence, till I drove Anna into Bath to my Mother's at one o'clock. We dined at four, and had a sumptuous entertainment in honour of my birthday and Joseph's. What is the meaning of eating enough to bring on a surfeit on a day when many happy and of course healthy returns are wished you? . . . After tea we drove home in time to save the light: Owen rode.

I slept but badly in consequence of the feast I had had. I never could expect to live long if I were to eat a variety of viands, as I am sure to suffer from bile. Indeed one dish is quite sufficient, and that as plain as possible; but fish, flesh, fowl, and fripperies are enough to finish my days full trot.

I slept but little on account of the old nuisance, the screaming of the peacock. I rose a little after six. The mason told me he had been working all night in Radford coal-pit after he left me yesterday, and had not taken off his clothes or closed his eyes. This is rather different to the evil I complain of. He told me that his brother, who attends the engine, for one whole week only slept four hours, as he was engaged night and day for that period in the engine house. I hardly think this is true, and indeed, if it be, it argues great want of foresight and humanity in the masters of the works.

To-day's post brought me the following letter from Mr. Brougham:[1]

"HILL STREET, LONDON.
"*April* 14, 1828.

"REVD. SIR,—

"I trust you will have the goodness to excuse the liberty which I take in requesting you to favour me with answers to the queries contained in the table subjoined, as I am desirous of knowing what change has taken place in the state of education in your parish within the last ten years. . . .

What is the number of Day Schools taught by men and not Endowed?

What number of Children attend them?

What number of Sunday Schools taught by women, and not Endowed?

What number of Children attend them?

Are the means of Education of the Poor sufficient?"

[1] Henry Peter Brougham, Baron Brougham & Vaux, 1778–1868, Lord Chancellor.

I got but little sleep.

Respecting the Schools in my parish, that is as to the number of scholars: [there are]

At Mrs. Jarrett's School	61
Girls at Mrs. Seller's	20
Mrs. Moon	16
Mrs. Maggs (30 Boys, 20 Girls) . . .	50
The Woman in Edgill's Building, Cridlingcot . .	7
Job Edwards	12
	166

I wrote the following letter to Mr. Brougham:

"SIR,—

"There are six day schools in this parish, not endowed; about 150 or 160 children attend them. Out of this number 61 girls are, free of expense, taught to read, write, and work by a Schoolmistress appointed by Mrs. Jarrett, Lady of the Manor, for the purpose. About 50 boys and girls are taught by a woman of the name of Maggs; 20 children by a woman of the name of Seller; 12 or 14 by another female named Moon; 8 or 10 by another person, and nearly the same number by another female.

"N.B.—These four last schools are merely for small children, sent by their parents to learn their letters, at 2*d.* a week each. The means for the education of the poor are not sufficient, there being great need for a regularly-established school for boys at this place; the population, owing to the collieries, amounting to upwards of a thousand. I have in consequence endeavoured—though without success—to raise sufficient funds for the building a school and residence for the master, and will readily pledge myself to pay £10 a year towards his salary, and will give the ground if the building can be effected.

"Having thus endeavoured, Sir, to satisfy your queries in these particulars, may I be permitted to propose some to yourself which I cannot perhaps expect you will answer, knowing how much your valuable time is occupied.

"Is not the education of the Lower Classes intended to increase their comforts, and render them better members of Society?

"Can this object be obtained unless they are instructed in their duties towards God, and their duties towards Man?

"Should not all Schools therefore which are established under the sanction of Government, be obliged to instruct children in the principal obligations of the divine and moral law, as contained in the Ten Commandments? Indeed, the Sponsors for an Infant at the Font promise it shall learn the Creed and Ten Commandments, and whatever else is necessary for it to learn. But how seldom this is done. Should not all Schoolmasters, if licensed, whether (or not) a Churchman, be obliged to perform what the Sponsors have promised at Baptism?

"With every apology for having trespassed on your time,

"I am, Sir,

"Your very obedient and humble servant,

"JOHN SKINNER.

"CAMERTON PARSONAGE,
"*May* 16, 1828."

Sunday, May 18

I preached in the morning my third sermon on the Creed; the people sufficiently numerous considering the rain. I called after Church on Mrs. Clark, a poor woman who is bedridden. She has been one of the Society of Ranters, but wished to see me: and on old Harris, who I think is not yet in a dying state, but he thinks he is, and is as much frightened as he was in the winter; but when the fear of death was passed he devoted himself to the world with the same anxiety as he was accustomed to do. I read the Prayers for the Visitation of the Sick to him. The world has been this man's idol, and it now vanishes like an evil genius, leaving the wretch desolate and almost despairing. He now says he has given up all thoughts of this world—according to the old rhyme—"When the Devil was sick," etc., etc.

I had a notice read in the Church, morning and evening, stating that my Sunday School would be re-established at the Glebe House, and requesting that parents would send their children in the course of the week to the Parsonage to have their names enrolled. I am anxious, now the measles are subsiding in the Parish, to get my number complete. Mr. Brougham, I suppose, will not reply to my queries; but if education of the lower orders without religion forms the basis of it, I shall not be disposed to patronise.

After Evening Service I visited Widow Heal's boy, who is getting about again. It rained incessantly the whole morning, and in the evening we had some severe thunder; my hall was flooded.

Two children lie dead in the Parish.

Thursday, May 22

While writing in my study about nine o'clock this evening I heard the neighing of one of the horses in the grounds, and wished to send our boy, George, to take him to the stable. Knocking, as I am accustomed to do, over the kitchen for Betty to come up, but having knocked till I was tired, I went into the kitchen to enquire what was become of the two female servants. George said they had been gone to the orchard about three minutes. Distrusting this account, I waited a little downstairs, and then walked along the Church walk going to the village, where I met them coming from thence. On asking what induced them to act so directly contrary to my orders, which were positive not to leave the premises, or have any communication with the village, Betty replied that she had only been to Mrs. Dilly's, and those other houses on the hill, and had not been absent ten minutes: that the village was down where the Coal Pits were! I said that she knew I had given strict orders not to leave the house at all, that this was not the only time she had been in the village, and the last time she did so I told both her and Goold I would not keep them if they did so again: that it was disgraceful to see girls like street-walkers stealing out by twilight; one could have but a bad opinion of their modesty; indeed what I had overheard by chance the other day, when they were seen at full romp with the post-boy who drove my Mother over, was no good specimen of their behaviour, and as I could not depend upon them I begged they would take it as a warning that on that day month I would dismiss them my service. I said they had acted so very badly that I would not read prayers as I had purposed doing, and hoped they would endeavour to regain the favour of a greater Master than any on earth, namely, God.

N.B.—I went to bed before ten o'clock, very much worried by the bad conduct of this girl.

Tuesday, May 27

Still tied to the stake! I find there is not sufficient flooring board, although I saw it with my own eyes cover the space of the whole room, and six of the boards over. There has been some thieving carried on, as I missed all the shelves of my bookcases from the best parlour, also some of the panels. I expostulated, but one and all denied any knowledge of it.

Thursday, May 29

The masons, and my servant Heal, deserted to attend the Camerton Club. Mrs. William Skinner and Anna went to Bath in my phaeton. In their way through the plantations they dropped Owen's military cloak, and a poor man brought it me. As he was a stranger to the place and, I believe, much distressed, I rewarded him, so that it was altogether a lucky occurrence to him, and he was well repaid for his honesty. I had occasion to speak again to my servants, who I fear have improper acquaintance in the village, which has ever been the ruin of my domestics. Old Harris died last night.

Sunday, June 1

This being Trinity Sunday I preached in the morning on the ordinary operations of the Holy Spirit, shewing that as miracles had ceased no one could pretend to the extraordinary powers bestowed on the primitive Apostles without subjecting himself to be considered as an imposter by all reasonable men. I was rather induced to enlarge upon this subject just now, as I understand from the Bath papers that a number of my parishioners attended the Ranter's Camp Meeting on Coombe Down last Sunday: there were three waggons and their female preachers. The director of the Meeting thus addressed the motley mob: "You Camerton friends go to the left; you Frome friends you go to the right; you Coleford friends continue by the waggons." A most barbarous scene was then exhibited, men and women ranting and roaring and bellowing till they were black in the face, calling upon the Spirit to come down upon them—I presume in allusion to the descent of the Holy Spirit on the Apostles, as recorded in the service of the day. Old Smallcombe, who staid to receive the Sacrament, on my asking whether he had been there answered in the affirmative. On my expressing myself surprised that anyone who had the least sense should go such a distance to witness the exposure of folly, he replied, if I had heard them myself I should not have called it folly, since the Lord was indeed among them!

Monday, June 2

Miss James, the daughter of the late Rector of Radstock, and her Aunt, with a gentleman named Briscoe, and two children came from

Bath in a carriage. Miss James said she wished to see the house and premises, which she had not seen for many years. I was rather surprised at this visit, as I have kept up no kind of acquaintance with the family.

Thursday, June 5

Old Harris was buried after dinner: several attended his inanimate corpse who never pay any attention to the soul which animates their own.

Sunday, July 8

I told George, the servant boy, if he would assist at the Sunday School at the Glebe Farm I would give him sixpence a time extra. I have no confidence in this boy, yet it may teach him to employ his Sunday leisure better than he now does: he cannot employ it worse than in making acquaintance in the village.

I read prayers in the morning, and took my usual round with my son and daughter after the service, and saw Harris, the quondam Clerk, carrying a bottle of comfort to his Mother. I find there is a great feud between him and White, the latter having complained to me that the former would only let him have seven shillings for digging his father's grave, whereas he had paid him eight shillings when he, Harris, was Clerk, for one of his relatives. I said I thought he might require eight shillings, but I did not think he had a right to demand nine; that it would be much better to get a table of fees set up in the Church, according to the usual custom in the country, then everyone would know what he had to pay. I believe that these two worthies are fitly matched. I preached in the evening on the Resurrection, in continuation of my course of sermons on the Creed, which has been interrupted by Whit Sunday and Trinity Sunday. One of the people, a half-grown lad, laughed out loud frequently during my sermon. After it was concluded I spoke to him, and lamented that neither of the churchwardens was present to take a more serious notice of his great misconduct. The lad looked very insolent, and I have reason to think that it was he who destroyed one of my favourite flowers in the Church walk as he left the Church.

Monday, June 9

I mentioned to my son, Owen, that I wished him to be very particular in the accounts he kept of Farmer Skuse's agistment stock, as I had seen some oxen which I thought he was fatting and not using as working beasts. He said, if I knew better than he did he would have nothing to do with the concern of taking my tythe for me, and I might do it myself. On my asking him this morning for the list which Skuse had sent in of his stock, he gave it me, and brought me all the papers he had in keeping respecting Skuse's tythe; he also gave me back again the map of the Parish, saying that he would have nothing further to do with the tythe concern, since he could not give satisfaction. I said, although his conduct formerly had been very reprehensible, I never could have expected such cool, premeditated ingratitude as this. If he would not assist me I must look about for some person as a bailiff, and if it cost me £50 a year there would be this less for my children.

Sunday, June 15

I prepared my sermon by making a new introduction to an old discourse, on a text taken from the Epistle for the day.

I endeavoured to point out that a true Faith and Belief in Christ consisted in practice, not in words: that it was to be shewn by active duties towards our fellow creatures, not by mere expression of feeling: that Christ had said over and over again that this was the sum and scope of His religion. In these days those who separated from the Church had run into strange fancies, imagining they were to be heard for their much speaking and substituting sound for sense: it was my duty to shew what was the meaning of the Sacred Writings, and I would do so in a rational manner: that as I had been appointed their pastor, it was my bounden duty to endeavour to retain my flock in their pastures, and not suffer them, unless they were determined to break bounds, to wander into other grounds.

The people were attentive, and there was no misbehaviour such as I had occasion to notice last Sunday. Hicks the Churchwarden attended, Jacob Balne the ex-constable also was in his place. I read notices both morning and evening respecting the Confirmation, which is to take place on Monday the 14th of next month, desiring that all candidates of above the age of fourteen years will send in their names the ensuing week, and attend at the Parsonage next Sunday at 10 o'clock, that I may converse with them on the subject.

Monday, Jnne 16

It rained hard almost all night. To my state of mind it seemed fitting: I expect moreover the storm which has been so long collecting will burst over my head, but I do not think it will beat me to the earth! My greatest affliction is what springs from my own household. I could better support all the storms which spring from without than that which agitates me from within. I am completely weaned from the world and all its attractions, for now I confess it has none for me, and if it be the will of God to call me hence I can depart without a murmur or a sigh. . . . I feel an unusual depression of spirits this day; the violent thunder we have had, and heavy atmosphere may in part account for it. We dined at one o'clock, and Owen, I understand, went out to fish afterwards. He consults only his own amusements, and will not stir a finger to assist his Father. I feel his ingratitude more deeply than any wound the world has ever inflicted. . . . All the clover now cut must be spoilt, as the rain falls incessantly. How fortunate may I esteem myself in having had such fine weather last week. . . . I just perceive my son coming home from his fishing—I suppose completely wet; we have for some time done tea. I feel so unwell and unhinged in every respect that I shall desire Anna to read prayers to the servants, and go to bed, as my pillow now is my best comforter.

Tuesday, June 17

After a restless and feverish night I rose at seven, and was occupied in my study for a couple of hours after breakfast. . . . I spoke to Owen, whose conduct to me since my return home has been very insulting, as far as speaking and rude behaviour will go, and I had determined not to say anything to him; but, as my peace of mind is at stake, and it must be to me a source of continual disquiet to see my son discontented, sulky, and sullen under my roof, I went to him and asked what was the cause of his behaviour, and why he chose to insult his Father day after day by his misconduct? I had done everything for him, and when I expected he would be of some service in assisting me in taking the tythe he had refused. I had reason, therefore, to be displeased, not he; that if he felt uncomfortable at home he had better tell me so at once, and what he designed to do with himself, as he did not appear to study for the law with any energy—it was but idling away his time to pretend to that profession. He said he had given up all thoughts of following it, and had other plans. I asked what. He said he should not tell me. I replied that I did not merit this conduct; I had ever assisted him heretofore, and was prepared to mention now I would assist him still if the plans were rational; but I would give up no money to be idled away. He said that he would not tell me his plans, and if I did not let him have some money to forward them, he would take up some on his reversion of what Mrs. Manningham had left him: he knew he could do this. Seeing that it was useless to speak to him any longer, I left him. On quitting his room he followed me, and banged and bolted the door against me.

I drove to Bath, taking young Frere with me as far as my Mother's, where I put him down. I mentioned to my Mother the great uneasiness I had experienced on account of Owen's behaviour, and she wrote him a letter on the subject.

Saturday, June 21

I received a note from Owen by the post, wherein he said he was sorry for his behaviour, but declared he did not mean to study for the law, wishing to get into the army, and, if he could not procure a commission, should like to go out to India as an adventurer. This is entirely out of the question. If he can point out any line in which I can assist him, with a prospect of benefit to himself, I will do it, but not throw away money, and have him return a pauper on my hands.

Sunday, June 22

I heard some of the candidates for confirmation before Church, in number fourteen. After the service I walked to Meadyeates with my son and daughter to speak to the schoolmaster, Maggs, and the teacher of the Methodist school, to ask whether there were any young people under their care who would wish to be confirmed. . . .

Monday, June 23

Owen and his sister went to call on Mr. Stephen Jarrett and Mrs. Anne Stephens before dinner; the former made an engagement to take a drive with Stephen Jarrett after our dinner. I thought he might have rather assisted me in the tything business, but he has made up his mind to consider solely himself. On my speaking to him I had a repetition of the same unfeeling insults I have of late so much been accustomed to, and, when he was gone with Stephen Jarrett, I went into my study and wrote the following note to him, meaning to leave it, as I had ordered my carriage to drive to my Mother's, finding it impossible to live longer in the same house with so undutiful and ungrateful a son.

Copy of a note to Owen Skinner, dated June 23, 1828:

After the insults which you have this day coolly and premeditatedly offered to your Father—a Father who has overlooked and forgiven similar insults several times, it is incumbent on that Father to tell his son that his own peace of mind requires that his feelings should not again be put to the trial of fresh insults. He is therefore come to the determination of again quitting his own house; but as he cannot do so for any long period without great loss—there being no one who will superintend the tything and farming concerns in his absence—he has to request, *nay more, to command his son to leave him.* This Father, however outraged, will still consider the interests of his son as far as the purchase of a commission will go; he moreover will request his Grandmother to receive him for a time till steps can be taken to accomplish this end, and however repugnant it may be to his Father's better judgment. But it is decided by his Father never again to be exposed to similar insults from a son who eats of his bread and drinks of his cup, and yet abuses the benefactor who has sustained him from his youth up until now, and was his best and only true friend.

On going down I found Owen had returned from his drive, and gave him the note. I said it was the last time we should meet, as I could not live longer with him; his behaviour was so contrary to everything that it ought to be that I was going to my Mother's to request she would receive him for a time till something could be done, and asked whether he had any objection to go to her house for a time. He said, "Certainly not." I then proceeded to Bath, taking my servant with me to return with the carriage to Camerton. I wrote by him to Anna, saying a chaise would be at Camerton at ten o'clock the following morning to convey Owen and his things to Bath, but that I should not see Owen any more. A little after eight I went to bed, completely worried.

Wednesday, June 25

After dinner I went into Longlands field, where the remainder of the hay is tything, having been summoned thither by the misconduct of the farmer, who will not suffer my men to remove my tythe cocks till his own is carried. He was very insolent because I happened to make use of the word "fellow" when speaking of him, which word he could not comprehend. But I think it cannot be law to prevent my tythe being carried from his field till his own is disposed of, since directly the bough is placed on the tenth cock with the assent of the farmer it becomes mine, and if I cannot remove it without his permission there is no great use in calling it mine.

Thursday, June 26

I was busily occupied the whole day in my tything concerns, and went round the farm with Joseph to estimate the several crops on the ground. There are 75 acres of clover, the same number of natural grass to be mowed, 60 of wheat, 45 of barley, 14 of beans, and 6½ of oats. Skuse has taken the tything into his own hands, and has positively refused to let my man tythe, or to take away the cocks when tythed for me unless his own portion be first removed. I wrote requesting an appointment with Mr. Pratt, the Bishop's tythe lawyer at Wells, whom I must see in order to get a citation for Skuse to the Court, as we cannot go on as we are now doing. He has sheared his sheep without giving me notice, and retains the wool; he has not given me any tythe of pigs or calves, and will not come to any settlement for his agistment.

Saturday, June 28

On walking into the field after dinner I found my men at a stop, there being six rows fit for tything, and Skuse would not tythe it because his men were unloading, and there were only a few cocks— not a quarter of a load— for them to carry. As I had received notice for tything in the morning, I desired Heal to take some boughs and tythe the six rows in order that he might take another load to the mow. Skuse came running like a wild bull, and bellowing as such, snatched the boughs out of my servant's hands, and said no one should tythe but himself. I desired Heal to persevere, and get some other boughs; I also told George to leave the cart, and witness what was going forwards. Skuse collared Heal and pushed him beyond the first row of cocks, and his son took George by force in his arms and, notwithstanding his struggling, threw him also beyond this barrier, which he said he had a right to keep, and neither my people nor myself had a right to be there. Seeing the party ripe for an assault, I desired my men to leave the field with the cart, and told my son, loud enough for Skuse to hear, I would not take tythe so put out, and have my men assaulted for doing their duty.

I would not let my cart go into the field to take up the tythe, but drew out the Memorial for the perusal of Mr. Pratt on Monday, or one of the Proctors of the Wells Court, against William Skuse, Farmer, for improper setting out of, and subtraction of Tythe; June 28, 1828.

The cart-horse I bought this morning, for which I gave £18, promises to turn out well.

Sunday, June 29

I preached in the morning on the subject of Baptism, as connected with Confirmation, having previously given tickets to nineteen young people whose examination I approved.

Monday, June 30

I drove to Wells, and immediately called on the Bishop,[1] who was very kind and polite, as is his usual custom, and asked me to dine with him, but said he must leave the table soon as he was engaged in writing his Charge, having to go to Bath to-morrow.

Not finding Mr. Pratt at Wells, I drove to Glastonbury, where I dined with him at his brother's house, and gave him all the necessary documents respecting Farmer Skuse.

He says there can be no doubt but he has done very wrong in adopting the mode of tything he had done, and that the Court would decree double damages for the clover.

[1] The Right Rev. George Henry Law, D.D., F.R.S., F.S.A., Lord Bishop of Bath and Wells, 1824-45.

1828—Third Quarter

ON going to the Glebe I found nine haymakers, including Moses Heal, White, and George, in the four-acre field which was cut, part of it on Saturday, and five mowers in the twelve-acre field. There ought to have been the whole of that ground down, as it is only about ten acres, although computed at twelve, and nearly three-quarters of an acre is in barley. I spoke to the haymakers about being idle; they said they only stopped to take a lunch at eleven, and had not been idle. White, who was the spokesman and had brought a clan of his relations into the field, said that they had been working very hard. I said I could not perceive it by what had been done in the field.

I went up into the Glebe field after tea. The haymakers had complained of the beer which was brewed by Feare, and some of which I drank at dinner and thought it very good. The mowers said they thought it excellent. I told them if they were dissatisfied I would not employ them. I went to White, who is a sly fellow and the secret instigator of this mutiny, and paid him off.

A little after all the women went, and were paid by my daughter at the Parsonage. As it seemed to threaten rain, and the grass was left about in the four-acre field, I desired the mowers to put it up in great cock. Moses Heal was inclined to be insolent when I spoke to him about permitting the haymakers to leave the field till the hay was put in cock, and said, instead of the beer being bad, it is actually too strong to be drunk in great quantities.

On my return home I spoke to Betty and her fellow servant, whom I had seen standing before the door to gape at everyone passing by, saying it was a discredit to any modest woman to do so. Betty then said that the month's warning I had given them was more than up, and that she and Goold wished to leave me to-morrow. I told them they certainly should do so.

I see that White and his people have been with them, and absolutely made common cause; and they think to distress me by leaving my work just now. I will not, however, let them feel they are of any consequence, and shall send in Joseph early to get some of the tradesmen I deal with in Bath only to recommend a couple of servants for a time: indeed this *bellum servile* is what I am not fit for.

I was obliged to go to Feare, the bailiff, late in the evening to get a promise of some more haymakers in the room of those I have dismissed.

Wednesday, July 2

I rose before six, and wrote before breakfast. Joseph and young Upham, who dined yesterday with us and slept at the Parsonage, drove into Bath immediately after breakfast. I sent a note to Captain Scobel, excusing myself from dining with him, stating I had to change my servants, and could not leave the house. My mind is in a constant state of irritation, and that is what my bad tormentors wish it to be.

I got six more haymakers into the field, who worked very well. On returning home I found the two female servants, notwithstanding my daughter Anna told them to stay till six o'clock, went at four, leaving us without a person to answer the bell. As the parents of both girls live in the Parish, they might have deferred going an hour or two later. The gross ingratitude of the elder girl, Betty, is beyond all parallel. I took her absolutely a pauper, because I thought she had shewn a kindness of disposition in attending to a sick family. I clothed her, and gave her wages, beginning at £5 and ending at £10 per annum, so that she has saved £14 and has a large stock of clothes; but she chose to leave me at a time when she thought I should be distressed just in the midst of my haymaking.

But, alas! It is not this ingratitude which affects me. No; it is that of my children! Joseph, I hope, will not follow his brother Owen's example. Again I have forgiven what has passed.

Old Walters came in the evening for his tools, as he left my work some time since to go to Squire Purnell's, and I told him I could not again employ him. Mr. Purnell, as a magistrate, ought to know better than to send for workmen when engaged in the employment of another.

Thursday, July 3

A woman Joseph had engaged at Bath came after breakfast by the coach; but a second is not arrived. After I had left the hayfield the men, I understand, grumbled for not having as much beer as they chose to drink. I therefore made these regulations: That the men who mow are to have a gallon an acre besides money and their victuals.

The women, three pints and a shilling apiece. I desired the beer to be taken up to the Glebe Farm House, and Heal to see that the people have this allowance. It is most painful to have dealings with the brutified vulgar.

Now I have laid down the allowance, those who do not chuse to abide by it have orders to leave the ground.

Friday, July 4

Still the same unpleasant, unprofitable occupations! I was the whole of the morning overlooking the people. Joseph was despatched after breakfast to Bath, in order to enquire after the servant who had promised to come over to officiate as cook. Young Frere came to dine.

I much wish young people could possibly feel when their company is considered as intrusive! But that never enters into the catalogue of modern cogitations. I spent the whole of the evening in the hayfield. Joseph returned before tea, and he and his friend, young Frere, went out shooting swallows.

I was so much hurt with this want of all propriety, in following amusement when actual assistance was requisite, that I retired to my room before the tray was brought in for supper, in order to shew what I felt.

Saturday, July 5

I understood at breakfast that the servants made heavy complaints of their beds and accommodations, telling Anna it was like a farmhouse more than a gentleman's, or words to this effect, and after breakfast they said they should not stay beyond the day. I am inclined to think that my workboy, George, for reasons best known to himself, wishes to increase the difficulties we are in; but time will shew.

This is the march of intellect with a vengeance. I wish Mr. Brougham had only a tythe of what I am obliged to submit to from the lower orders. He would not then shew himself so strenuous an advocate for the liberty of their doing what they please, which in fact is anarchy and insubordination.

Mr. Brougham has his steward, his butler, his footman, his housekeeper; but I have none of these, so the whole weight of the contest falls upon me. I do not think Mr. Brougham has even been put in a similar situation to feel at all in these matters. A man in his Chambers, or a Fellow of a College, has no idea what a master of a household in a parish has to sustain, especially if he ventures to oppose iniquity and error.

Our two soi-disant servants have struck, and are determined to return this evening. Therefore Joseph and Anna drove to Bath in order to get some person we might depend on for giving us food. After I had finished my dinner I continued at home in order to pay the women, who had told my daughter they meant to quit in the evening, and had in consequence packed up their clothes. They went away about three o'clock.

Just after, the newsman from Meyler's library arrived and sent in his paper, which I had been reading ten minutes when a knock at the door of my parlour disturbed me. On going to the door I saw the newsman quite drunk. I handed him through the kitchen, back kitchen, and garden to the entrance door. He was so drunk that he knew not what to say in apology for his intrusion into my parsonage house, but said he had a right to do so, and that his mistress, Mrs. Meyler, the proprietress of the "Bath Herald," would support him.

This drunken fellow was doubtless sent by some one or other of my bad parishioners, knowing I had no one at home at present, and thinking to provoke me to a breach of the peace by his insolence. I only took him by the shoulder and shewed him the back door.

Returning to my parlour, I see by the papers that O'Connell has succeeded in stirring up the rabble through the agency of the priests against their superiors. The same thing is going forward in this country and in this neighbourhood as in Ireland, and Day, their agent of Downside, trying what may not be done by the same arts on a smaller scale.

I wrote the following letter to Mrs. Meyler, the proprietress of the "Bath Herald," respecting the conduct of her newsman. Surely I have worries and insults enough to sustain from my domestics and the people around me, but need not have them augmented by strangers:

"MADAM,

"The person who brought your newspaper this evening came much intoxicated, and walked through my back kitchen and kitchen to the parlour: what his object was I know not, neither did he himself know. On my leading him off the premises he was very insolent.

Henceforward I wish my paper to be forwarded by another conveyance; if this cannot be done, I shall prefer dropping it altogether rather than be exposed to such intrusion.

"I am, Madam,

"Your obedient Servant,

"J. SKINNER."

Sunday, July 6

I had so violent a headache, owing to fullness of blood occasioned by worry, that I could get very little sleep; indeed, physically I cannot support these constant agitations. A philosopher may support the occasional paroxysms of the stone, but the hourly biting of bugs and fleas, which destroys one's rest, who can support?

I prepared my sermon for Confirmation as soon as I left my bedroom to go into my study, and I examined five more candidates for Confirmation, to whom I gave tickets.

We dined with Mr. Stephen Jarrett and his aunt at five, as they had invited us yesterday when there seemed little prospect of our having servants to dress our dinner. We returned before ten, in time for prayers; the two fresh servants imported yesterday attended. The housemaid, recommended by the Warners, may become a fixture, but the appearance of the other I do not approve of.

Monday, July 7

I wrote to Mrs. Richard Warner after breakfast, thanking her for the interest she had taken in my domestic arrangements, and saying I hoped we should be able now to boil an egg, and to have the old hen's feathers shaked up in a bed!

I could not help hinting that her spouse had withdrawn himself from all difficulties, although he had at his baptism promised to fight under the banners of the Church Militant, and acquit himself strenuously. That when I wedded my Parish at Camerton I did so for better and for worse, notwithstanding she was a cross jade and sometimes gave me untoward kicks and scratches; still, as a matter of duty, I was determined to cherish her as she had cherished me. I begged she would tell my friend Richard [Warner] he had been a sad fellow, having married one, two, three, four, and five wives of this description, all of whom he had deserted, excepting one poor old dame whom he left lying desolate in a field—Chatfield—and seldom visited her to administer consolation.

And I further said that the Church now required the active and personal exertions of all the children she had brought up; that I would as a matter of conscience, even if left alone, continue to sing out lustily the Lay of the Last Rector, and even if it did no more service to survivors than the death-song of the expiring Indian. I said the supine and time-serving behaviour of the negligent clergy will be their ruin, they having climbed over the walls of the sheepfold to profit by the warm fleeces within.

Just as I had finished my letter to Mrs. Warner, Farmer Hicks called to know how many children were to go to Visitation, in order that he might provide them with a vehicle.

He then said he wished that Skuse would compound, as the others did. I said I wished so too, but he was so stubborn he would not listen to reason, and was determined to give no more than £90 for the farm; and I further said if he did not pay me for the clover I would put him in the Exchequer!

I now hear Skuse's people are become very civil, and have put out the tythe of the wool fairly. There were thirty-nine fleeces and I had four, as Joseph *threw up* whether I was to have the ninth or they! and so gained it. I refused taking the young calf, because the other nine have been sold to the butcher, and it has ever been customary here to receive the tenth of the *value* of each calf sold.

Friday, July 11

Mr. and Mrs. Hammond called. I learn from him that a society is forming to uphold Church and State among some of the principal noblemen in Town. God be praised! My paper to-morrow will probably give me an account of it.

Saturday, July 12

The day has been threatening, but I hope that the hay of the two fields now about will be on the rick, as two waggons and a number of hands from the coal pits are gone to assist. I do not go into the hayfield to witness the saturnalia of the colliers, they have drunken three hogsheads of beer already, and there are seven more acres to mow and make. I may truly say the business of farming has been forced upon me, but I cannot recede a step now whatever be the consequences. The hay harvest will soon now be over! I cannot agree with the poet Virgil: "O fortunatos nimium, sua si bona norint,

Agricolas!" nor with the orator Cicero: "Nihil est agricultura melius nihil uberius, nihil libero homine dignius."

I am heartily sick of it, and the bleating of sheep and lowing of oxen is as unpleasant to my ears as it was to Samuel when he heard these audible testimonies of the spoil of the Amalakites. How I long for the study and the calm pursuits I so much prefer to any amusements that company can give.

After having written my Journals, I went to bed, the most tranquil place I can now command, at nine o'clock.

Monday, July 14

I rose before six, and having finished breakfast before seven I proceeded with Joseph in my phaeton to Frome, my servant, who was to be confirmed, being on horseback; the rain accompanied us nearly the whole way, where we arrived before nine. There were multitudes to be confirmed, so that the Bishop was occupied upwards of two hours. Two of my foolish flock lost their tickets, so that I had to certify respecting their having been examined.

Mr. Algar, the minister of the New Church, Frome, preached an appropriate sermon on the text, 21st S. Matthew, 28th verse: "Go work to-day in my vineyard." The Bishop afterwards read a very impressive charge to the clergy, confining himself more particularly to the enforcing the parochial duties of the resident minister, in performing which with propriety, he said, much of the evil we had to complain of might be obviated, as the resident minister would thereby conciliate the affections of his flock and prevent their straying after new pastors. He lamented that the sacraments of Baptism and the Supper of the Lord were so much neglected; that the former was by some considered as a mere ceremony which must be complied with in order to admit a new member into the Church, of which Confirmation was the seal. That the Sacrament was indeed still more neglected—that few but females now were communicants, and not so many of them as ought to attend. He also alluded to the ceremony of Marriage, which had of late been considered rather as a civil rite than connected with the offices of the Church. The visiting of the sick, and the solemn service of the Burial of the Dead, he touched upon with great pathos and feeling. With respect to the Poor Laws as now administered, he declared his disapprobation, since the moral obligations which existed between children and their parents became much weakened. He also spoke in decided and very appropriate terms of reprobation against the increase of licensed Ale Houses which, although they might increase the revenues of the State, must also increase the immorality of the people. It was a very good Charge; the delivery was excellent, and had double effect, as the sentiments thus conveyed evidently came from the heart.

The singing during service was excellent, as was the reading of the prayers by the Vicar of the Parish, and I heard both to advantage, being in the chancel where some benches were set out for those who had not gotten seats in the body of the Church.

This gave me an opportunity of witnessing also the benevolence of a brother clergyman (Glossop, of Wolverton), which rose him highly in my estimation. A poor blind man, who had been led in by the chancel door during the service, felt his way up to the seat before which Glossop was kneeling and placed himself in it. Glossop immediately rose from his knees, went to the back of a pew beyond, where he stood till the sermon was concluded, leaving his seat to be enjoyed by the poor blind man.

At dinner I endeavoured to imitate this truly clerical conduct of the worthy Rector of Wolverton: "sed eheu non passibus aequis." Mr. Mead, of Marston, whom I have not seen since our Guernsey tour last year, and wished to have some conversation with, had secured a seat for me at the dinner table, just above himself and next to the chair of the Archdeacon, Mr. Law. While I was standing at the back of my chair Mr. Spencer, of Hinton, a gentleman lately come into the diocese, who was, I believe, at St. John's, Cambridge, with the Archdeacon, came and placed himself into the chair which had been reserved for me. Mead immediately said, "Skinner, you have lost your place." I took no further notice, and walked to the bottom of the table, where I had the pleasure of sitting next to Glossop, of whom, of course, I thought more highly than of Mr. Spencer, who thus superseded me. When the Bishop and his son had left the table I had some conversation with Mead, who came to say there was then a place vacant; but I did not sit long, [having] already finished my feast, which cost me eleven shillings. I am very glad I have not to attend public meetings very often, as I derive no kind of satisfaction from them; indeed, I feel particularly uncomfortable when forming one of a party at a dinner comprising thirty or forty guests; neither do I think it is merry in the hall, when chins all wag, the being obliged to take wine with those who think they confer a compliment by asking; the drinking of toasts and listening to speechifying, without which no public dinner can now pass, wherein each speaker tickles the vanity of the person to whom he replies, and returns flattery for flattery like two horses nibbling each other's necks under a hedge. All these things are my aversion. I had rather eat my beans and bacon at the Parsonage solus than be particeps, I will not say criminis, of such indiscriminate conversation, for after all it is time thrown away, and usually ends in "vox et praeterea nihil." Proceeding to Southfield, I did not get to bed till nearly eleven o'clock, completely tired.

Tuesday, July 15

I rose before seven, and walked with Richard Hoare to the Iron Works at Nunney to purchase a scythe for mowing the garden, as the best in the county, perhaps in the kingdom, are made by the Fussells, who have mills at Mells, Nunney, and Little Elm, and have realised an immense property among the fraternity by their superior skill in hardening edged tools. We saw two men grinding scythes, with their noses literally at the grindstone; if any of our West Indian slaves had been seen by any of our modern philanthropists in such a situation, the tocsin of anti-servial malediction would have resounded from John of Groat's house to the Land's End. Oh! ye Liberals and ye soi-disant Philanthropists! ye strain at a gnat and swallow a camel; ye confine the people in bonds more heavy to be borne than any the most cruel of Indian planters ever imposed on their property.

I continued at Mr. Hoare's till one o'clock, and then drove home to Camerton—the rain accompanying me nearly the whole way. I never remember such a continuation of thunder weather. The water from the hills around Bath accumulated so suddenly on Tuesday evening last, and rose to so great a height, that two people were drowned at Widcombe in their beds. Mr. Baker, of Telisford, informed me that a man was also drowned in his parish.

I went to bed before prayers, very much tired. Anna continues to officiate when I do not read myself, which I hope will be equally efficacious to the servants, that is, if they feel inclined to profit by the service.

Thursday, July 17

The old man and woman, Rossiter, whom I attended so long when they kept their beds, I verily believe had nothing really the matter with them, but made this finesse in order to be well fed. Mrs. Jarrett, of the Manor House, sent them things from her table constantly, as we also did, and no less than seven bottles of Cape wine, as they had one a week. At length I began to perceive the imposition, and both withdrew my attendance and donations. I have observed among the lower orders that this kind of cunning is frequently considered the acme of wisdom.

Friday, July 18

Mr. Stephen Jarrett and Mrs. Anne Stephens dined with us. Mr. S. Jarrett introduced the subject of the Church Walk, which I never like to have started, as his idea is I ought to have given up every document, that the right to the road may never be contested by the parish after my decease. I could not help speaking warmly on the subject, and requested it might not be again introduced on the tapis.

I begin to hate mixed society, and had much rather live alone than be exposed to irritation and uneasiness; indeed, even a preparation for an entertainment and the participation of it is painful.

Sunday, July 20

The servants were very late this morning, and the cook told Anna she could not possibly prepare for Church. Anna said I always insisted on the servants going. She then said she could not stay beyond the month. She engaged to come on trial. There is now no comfort in society, either domestic or public: we are, indeed, come to the dregs!

It rained incessantly till about eight o'clock, when the weather cleared. I spent a couple of hours in my study; at prayer time the cook made her appearance, although she had declined going to Church both morning and evening. I asked her if she was a Protestant; if so, why did she not attend the service of the Church. She said she was *not* a Protestant. I asked her whether she was a Catholic. She said she was not one of the *Irish*, and therefore no Catholic. She then hurried out of the room. I have only spoken to her this once since she has been in my service about a fortnight. I will part with her at the end of the month at all events, since my servants must attend their Church constantly, whatever my parishioners may chuse to do.

Monday, July 21

I passed an uncomfortable night, and rose little refreshed by the sleep I procured.

Tuesday, July 22

The affairs in Ireland to all appearance must soon come to a crisis. Indeed, we cannot temporise if we consider the safety of our fellow Protestants in that country, who may experience a second edition of the massacre of St. Bartholomew if our Government be not vigilant, firm, and prompt. I have every reliance in Mr. Peele[1] and the Duke of Wellington; but still their hands are fettered by designing men. There is an excellent petition drawn out and circulated as a bond of union against the machinations of the Papists in this country. I hope it will be seriously attended to, and subscribed to by every staunch supporter of the Constitution. Alas! how can our senators know what will be the result of their absurd concessions! Should my papers survive, it will be manifest what was the state of society in the time I wrote, and the determination of one person at least among the millions of Britain to oppose the torrent of iniquity which in all probability will bear him away with it.

Friday, July 25

I walked with Richardson as far as Squire Purnell's, but we were driven back by the rain. After dinner we tried again to walk as far as Writhlington to visit Mr. Cookson, as we had done in the morning, but could not get to his house on account of the floods, which covered Writhlington Bridge. The thunder and rain were very violent during the morning, and the lightning vivid.

Saturday, July 26

I was much worried by the behaviour of my children, and, what was worse, could not help shewing what I felt before Richardson. I am now writing in my study—not being able to sleep—and the clock has struck one! I feel very uncomfortable, and must go somewhere next week for a change of scene, as I perceive I cannot continue as I have done of late, and dread the consequence of continual excitement.

Monday, July 28

The morning commenced by fresh irritation given on the part of my son Joseph. His visit to Bath and his conversation with his brother I was well aware would be of no service to him; indeed, he has shewn himself as insolent as ever his brother did since his return,

[1] Sir Robert Peel, (1788–1850) 2nd Bt.

and will not now bear to be spoken to without using the most insulting gestures and expressions towards his parent; and indeed I was obliged to come to the determination of separating myself from him, as I had done from his brother Owen, and I accordingly wrote the following letter:

"My Dear Mother,

"It is with the most heartfelt regret that I again request your assistance in receiving Anna and Joseph. I was fearful the visit last week would have been productive of no good, that is, if both were to return to Camerton, and I have found it so. I will not worry you or myself about reverting to particulars: thank God I am now calm, and shall continue so when the cause which has made me otherwise is removed. I am ready to make any arrangement I am empowered to do for the purchase of a commission for Joseph by the sale of part of my marriage settlement; I am ready to allow Owen the interest of the third part, but I will not consent to the sale of the capital on any wild scheme he may wish to embark. My own mind tells me I have done everything I ought to do for my *ungrateful children*.

"Now with respect to yourself, my dear Mother, with my heartfelt thanks for the asylum you have afforded them, I enclose a draft for £10 for the present, and I will send another the end of next month, and continue to do so, if you please, monthly as long as they continue with you. Owen's allowance of £30, which is to pay for his clothes and pocket-money, I will continue as long as he remains with you. I am ready to make the same allowance to Joseph, but had rather you should have the direction of it, and have not mentioned it, therefore, to him. Anna's £30 per annum I will continue. I assure you, my dear Mother, I have struggled hard against the evil with all my resolution, and I may add a much stronger term, with *all my religion*; but it is now become too weighty, it presses me down by day, and by night, my sleep flies from me, and if I do not return again to my studies and to the tranquility which has been interrupted by my idle, ungrateful, and insulting children, I know not what may be the consequence.

"Anna will, I make no doubt, be more comfortable with you and her cousin. She has been unfortunately circumstanced, and when her brothers have left you and, I hope, embarked in some line of life which may be profitable to them, she may return hither if she prefers it. I can send her piano as soon as I am able to spare the cart, and the weather is settled. You may be perfectly easy on my account, as I know, as soon as I resume my studies and am freed from the constant irritation I have been exposed to in my own house, I shall be *myself again*.

> "Yours very truly,
> "JOHN SKINNER.

"P.S.—The origin of all the evil I complain of in my sons is *Idleness*, and a want of proper principles. Idleness and insolence end in ruin. All my other trials are nothing in comparison. I am here wounded in the tenderest, nay, even the most vital part, and when I think what I have sown and how I have reaped, I feel a sensation of great disappointment—and the prospect is dark and dreary in the extreme.

> "J.S."

My son and daughter left my house about two o'clock. I desired Joseph to tell his brother (whom I regard as far more culpable than he is—being the person who has stirred him to this fresh rebellion on his return to me) that I never would see him again under my roof, unless he came as the Prodigal Son did to his Father, and confessed he had sinned before heaven and before me, and was no more worthy to be called my son. I learnt from Joseph in the course of his conversation that Owen had said he had been putting his own conduct in its proper light to the Freres and others who might have thought he was to blame. Alas! and thus one's family concerns are to become a topic of conversation at the tea-table of triflers, who will have a pleasure in abusing me—merely because I am a clergyman. I have ever acted most delicately respecting my family, and never mentioned at length, or, indeed, without much extenuation, the conduct of my sons; and I wrote to-day expressly to Richardson to beg he would not mention what he had seen on Saturday.

I was occupied the whole of the evening in my study looking over my accounts. I find I have expended since January £583, far beyond what my income will allow, so that I must again resume my own household episcopacy, even when Anna returns. It will not do to trust to young people; with the allowance I have promised my Mother I shall be ruined if I expend as I have done. I did not go to bed until a very late hour, as I returned to my study after prayers, and did not conclude till I had balanced my accounts.

I lay awake the great part of the night meditating what was best to be done respecting my sons. They must be launched into life, and quit the nest; they then may be brought to their senses.

I drove to the Hammonds, having engaged to visit them when they called on me the day before.

I rose at seven, having slept better on the whole than I have done for several nights. Change of scene and ideas is absolutely necessary sometimes, to me indeed just now it is peculiarly so.

I was occupied in Mr. Hammond's reading-room before breakfast. He has an excellent collection of the classics, and some other useful and valuable books. Mr. Hammond read in the newspapers, while I was drawing, a strange account of the disinterment of Hampden, which states that the flesh still remained on the arms and face, which must be in the nature of things untrue, as the body was not embalmed. I rather think it is a hoax upon the folly of antiquaries—not to call it by a worse name—who ransack the tombs within our Churches, which can be productive of no service whatever to science: but curiosity is the hunger of the day, and must be fed. Could it be supposed that in a civilised country and among thinking people, that crowds should collect day after day, merely to see the barn where a prostitute was murdered and interred, and, more, that the barn floor has absolutely been destroyed by persons who wish to take away a piece of wood as a relic of the place where this vile transaction[1] occurred, thus making a martyr of a meretrix? Yet this is a fact, and a dilapidation of the premises is still going on to such an extent that a person is paid to watch them! When Gilham, of Bath, murdered his fellow servant, a cast was taken in plaister of Paris of the murdered woman's face, and doubtless the artist met with many purchasers of his horrible busts. Is not this one of the infallible tokens of the decadence of the country? It was the same in Greece and Rome, and in Judea when they declined from the strong and masculine character.

Receiving a letter from the Bishop of Bath and Wells, inviting me to meet Sir Richard Hoare at the Palace on Tuesday, this letter I answered saying I would do myself the pleasure of going.

[1] The Red Barn Murder.

We had an early breakfast, and mounted our horses immediately after in order to take Chilcompton on our way to Midsomer Norton, having engaged to dine with Captain and Mrs. Savage at Norton House, which gave me an opportunity of calling on the new Vicar, Mr. Colville.

On our return I learnt that the woman who was sent from my service on Tuesday continued at the Red Post till she went off in the evening, and that the bad creature took this opportunity of saying everything to my disadvantage; since, Hammond told me that a gentleman in Bath said to him the other day: "So there are strange doings at Camerton Parsonage; Mr. Skinner has turned his children out of doors," or words to that effect, and that he replied that he knew that was not the case, since they were then on a visit to their Grandmother.

My wound is so painful of itself that I shall not heed this additional smart; besides, after all, it is only self-love which is wounded by the opinions of others. All I have to lament in this respect is that what has occurred may afford a handle to the lower orders to condemn their teacher, to accuse him of being hard-hearted towards his own children, and a variety of other malicious perversions from the reality which they derive from discarded servants. I well know what advantage may be taken in this respect, but I cannot help it.

I visited Hammond's reading-room, as usual, as soon as I left my bedchamber, and as it rained incessantly I agreed to spend the morning in it. After dinner I returned to Camerton, highly gratified by my visit, which gave me a change of scene and tranquility to my ideas.

I had no sermon to prepare, as what I wrote some years ago on the Parable of the Unjust Steward I adapted to the occasion, as it formed the Gospel for the day. It rained so heavily that few attended the service, either morning or evening. However, I contrived to walk to Meadyates to administer the Sacrament to Sperring's mother as I promised. She is a very respectable old woman, and such as I wish there were many more of among my parishioners. I called also on Old Green, who is better. (I had observed he was very late last Sunday in coming to Church, which he is not accustomed to be, notwithstanding he is so weak from a bowel complaint that he can scarcely shuffle along with his crutches, and it takes him an hour and a half in general to walk from Redhill thither.) I had sent him some rhubarb dissolved in brandy, with directions to take a spoonful at a time. Mr. Flower has taken no further notice of him, neither Hicks, the Overseer. I desired him to send his girl for some money to aid him during his illness, and to say I recommended his doing so. Mr. Stephen Jarrett pressed me much to dine with him, but I declined, saying I had been so much from home during the week I wished to have a little rest and quiet employment in my study, that I might commune with my own heart and in my chamber, and be still. He then made me fix to dine with him the following day.

Again this sound of abundance of rain!

Monday, August 4

I received a very kind letter from George Burrard in reply to mine requesting he would exert his influence with his brother, Sir Harry Neale, to procure a commission in the Marines for my son Owen. He says he will do what he can; but as Sir Harry has to make two applications to the Duke of Clarence for his nephews, the Rooks, he fears he cannot ask it just now. Burrard mentions that his son George is returned for Lymington by the aid of his brother, Sir Harry, who has the borough.

Tuesday, August 5

As the carpenters were to remove my book cases and place them in my new study during my absence, I consigned all my MSS. to their old stations in my iron chests. Whatever the world may say to my disadvantage, these at least will remain to shew I have not misspent my time during my pilgrimage through life: had my sphere been more enlarged I might have done more; and this I know, not more will be required of me than the use of the talents bestowed. Doubtless there are many duties I have neglected and errors I have committed, but I hope that notwithstanding I may be exposed to difficulties in my way to my last home, I may arrive safe at my journey's end.

I left Camerton about twelve, and drove through Paulton to Chelwood to take up Warner and convey him to the Palace at Wells, as I had promised to do—both of us being engaged to spend the week-end with the kind-hearted Bishop.

The day was altogether more promising than it has been for this fortnight or three weeks past, and we arrived without rain to our journey's end. I met with a pleasing welcome, which I anticipated, notwithstanding I doubt not many things have been said to my disadvantage that I shall never have the power or opportunity to contradict. Mr. Bowles,[1] of Bremhill, and Mr. Cassan, from Mere, were of the party; Sir Richard Hoare was expected, but did not arrive. Mr. Bowen, in his way to Bath from his Living at Bawdrip, also dined with us, as did the Archdeacon, son to the Bishop, who is in residence.

There was a rubber of whist in the evening, and I took the opportunity of going to my room to write till prayer time.

Wednesday, August 6

I slept but little. It was mentioned before I went to bed that we were to visit Banwell Cave, and spend the day there. As it blew hard during the night I received no very pleasing anticipation respecting the weather, and when I looked out of my window I perceived the rain falling fast; and the dingy colour of the moat which surrounds the Palace indicated that it had done so during the greater part of the night. However, as it cleared a little after breakfast, we proceeded in the Bishop's coach and four, his Lordship, Bowles, Messrs. Cassan, Broaderip, and myself being inside, and Warner with the footman on the box. The rain soon recommenced, and continued the whole way to the end of our stage, which was 16 miles. It was melancholy to observe the devastation occasioned by the floods, the marsh beyond Axbridge, the whole way from Wells being flooded and the hay wholly ruined. We stopped at Cheddar to visit the Church, and Bowles employed my pencil to sketch two of the monastic crosses, as he thinks (on what grounds I know not) that they will contribute to establish a singular system he has set up respecting the Pillar of Thout, Teut, or Hermes.

We drove to a cottage the Bishop has erected on the hill contiguous to the cave, but the rain fell without intermission. Bowles was to be in requisition to write a poem on the occasion, myself composing some lines on the subject and contenting myself with [sketching] a view or two of the cottage and of the interior of the cave.

We returned to Wells just in time to save our light, stopping by the way at Axbridge to enquire after a gold coin, which long ago I heard

[1] Reverend William Lisle Bowles, (1762–1850), Poet and Antiquary.

had been dug up on Brent Knoll and given to Mr. Symonds, who is lord of the soil; but his wife (he being from home) assured us she knew nothing about it. The good lady's testimony and judgment I cannot entirely rely on, as she mistook me for the Bishop, near whom I was sitting, and continually addressed me by the title of *my Lord*. The sight of a gay equipage and four horses stopping at her door doubtless drove all minor concerns out of her head. On our return we found Sir Richard Hoare, who seems quite well.

Thursday, August 7

The weather was so stormy I did not leave the Palace, excepting in the evening after tea, when I went into the town to purchase some Indian ink at the stationer's in order to renew my drawings.

I suffered a severe attack during our symposium from all the party (excepting the Bishop and Sir Richard Hoare), who, from not understanding, endeavoured to ridicule my system of etymology by asking me the derivation of several strange abstract words in order to perplex and puzzle me.

I told them a story, which had the effect of putting a stop at least to the malicious criticism of Mr. Cassan.

Friday, August 8

During the storm of last night, which seemed to threaten the chimneys and the roof in order to make a second tragical edition of the history of Bishop Kidder[1] and his wife, not being able to sleep, I composed some lines as a private not a public memoranda of my personal feelings:

> *Ah me! what frowns terrific now deform*
> *Bland Nature's face—incessant drives the storm;*
> *Tho' earth's disjointed frame to shreds be riven,*
> *Yet will we fix our steadfast eye on heaven.*
>
> *Etc., etc.*

I get but little sleep now, and to prevent a recurrence to subjects which have such power to pain me whilst I lie awake, I have recourse to this kind of occupation. I find my memory sufficiently retains the lines I compose when waking, so that on leaving my bed in the

[1] Richard Kidder, Bishop of Bath and Wells, 1691–1703. (Killed by the fall of a chimney at the Palace, Wells, during the night of the Great Storm, November 26, 1703.)

morning I am able to commit them to paper. Such occupations are at least innocent, if they are not instructive; they are at least sedatives, even if they do not remove the complaint.

I finished my drawing of Banwell Cottage before breakfast and gave it to the Bishop.

Bowles says he has written 500 lines already on the subject, and purposes leaving them with Crutwell, so that they will soon be before the public. He is the most absent man I ever knew when engaged in his versification; no company prevents his writing, when he ought to be engaged in conversation; this morning we had done breakfast ere he came to the table, dripping with rain, having been walking backwards and forwards in the garden during the heavy storm. I was obliged actually to rub him down with a silk handkerchief, fearing he might take cold. Yesterday evening, while Sir Richard Hoare, the Bishop and two others of the party were playing at cards, he threw himself on the sofa, close to them, and snored loudly. Such eccentricities may be the companion of genius, but they certainly are not pleasing in society, especially where real distinctions ought to be made. When Bowles is in residence as Canon of Salisbury he will, I think, cut a queer figure, and read a ridiculous chapter of accidents to the people. He left after breakfast for Bath in his close carriage, as did Sir Richard for Devonshire, and Mr. Cassan for his residence at Mere. I drove Warner to Glastonbury, during a cessation of the rain, in order that he might see the progress made by Mr. Reeves in his mansion: indeed, it will be a beautiful building and very much in character, as it is constructed in the style of the reign of Henry VIII, and this may be supposed to have been coeval with the destruction of the Monastery.

A Mr. Lunn, who has just been presented to the Living of Butleigh, and his pupil, Lord Alexander, grandson to Lord Hardwicke, dined with us. Mr. Lunn, I think, is a well bred and intelligent man. The subject of etymology was again brought on the tapis, but not by myself, and it was treated by him in a very different manner from what it had been by the former party. I understand he was considered at Cambridge as a first-rate mathematician, and his opinion, which is evidently in favour of the analytical process which I have adopted, has more weight with me.

The Bishop, I am assured, thinks entirely with me, and is very anxious to have me complete the work; indeed, he was kind enough to offer me his cottage at Banwell, if I chose to retire there for a few months in order to proceed in my studies without interruption; but this I declined, as I must have my books with me; besides, the interruption of strangers coming to see the cave would be almost as bad as that of the farmers at Camerton.

As my assistance was needed to play a rubber in the evening, I did so, and as a rare occurrence I note it: I was the winner of three shillings.

Saturday, August 9

The wind blew and the storm raged nearly as violently as ever during the night. On looking out of my window I perceived the rain driving fast, and the elms beyond the moat waving like willow trees. My carriage was ordered at half-past ten; I promised to convey Warner home, and to take an early dinner with him at Chelwood. Therefore we determined to weather the storm; but, ere we left the Palace, a violent gust split in twain one of the largest and most beautiful tulip trees, perhaps, in the country, while it fell with a loud crash, much to the regret of the worthy Bishop: but his serenity of temper is, I firmly believe, not easily discomposed. Oh! that I could attain to this composure; but I fear I never shall, and I much doubt will ever be calmed excepting *in the grave.* Nothing could exceed the real benevolence and kindness of the worthy Bishop; he has quite won my heart and attached me to him. Surely I have no reason to complain of my fellow creatures when I meet with such men as Sir Richard Hoare and this kind-hearted man, and many affectionate relations besides. It is thus Providence ordains our trials, and gives the means of supporting them. I have ever found it so, and in that confidence I commit myself and all that I have into His all-merciful disposal, and shall under every dispensation rest assured that whatever is is right.

> Hope humbly, then, on trembling pinions soar;
> Wait the great teacher, Death, and God adore.

Monday, August 11

I settled the accounts after breakfast: the haymakers have cost me more than the value of the hay which has been cut since the rain has commenced.

The season is most awful, and will, as a dispensation of Providence I apprehend, be productive of the most serious consequences to the country at large. "Thy will be done on earth as it is in heaven" is our daily prayer, and we must not change in our hearts the sentiment the tongue expresses. Unless some benefit was to result from this fearful state of things, we are assured it would not take place.

After dinner I took up Plutarch, with whom I have always a feast, and dipped upon the life of Pericles.

Tuesday, August 12

I was occupied in my study and in overlooking the workmen till one o'clock, when I drove to Mr. Hammond's. The rain recommenced with such violence that I thought it folly to pursue my drive to Stowey, where I was engaged to dine with Mr. Hartress, and wrote an apology for my non-appearance. I therefore dined with the Hammonds, and spent the evening there. Hammond's coachman, rode my horse to Stowey with my note, on his return threw the poor, old, and faithful creature down, and broke his knees. I would rather have given ten guineas, poor as I am, but as it was an accident I had nothing to say on the subject. But I had rather have incurred the risque of many drenchings than it should have happened.

Wednesday, August 13

I slept but little last night, and left my bedroom more languid than when I entered it. I walked to the stable the first thing to examine the poor horse's wounds. One knee is badly cut, the other only slightly scratched. I will never again suffer any servant to ride it, not even my own. I took leave of my kind host after breakfast. I then resumed my vehicle and proceeded to Radstock and to Midsomer Norton, having engaged to dine with Captain and Mrs. Savage. It rained so violently I could not attempt to draw the Church, as I had purposed doing previous to its being pulled down.

The new Vicar, Mr. Colville, dined with us, as did Mrs. Stukeley and her niece, Miss Palmer, who are staying with the Savages at Norton House. After tea I was occupied in making two drawings for Mrs. Savage. I did not get to bed till past eleven.

NORTON HOUSE, MIDSOMER NORTON,
Thursday, August 14

Still the same dreadful weather. I read before breakfast in the newspapers an ample and particular account of the execution of the horrible murderer, Corder.[1] It occupied nearly two sides of the paper,

[1] William Corder (The Red Barn Murder).

that is, including his trial and remarks upon it. There needs not any other proof of the deplorable state of depraved feelings to which this country has gradually arrived through the instruction of novelists and fatalists, than this document.

I have before remarked (in my Journal) the eager curiosity with which people of all kinds and classes flocked to the barn in which the corpse of the unhappy woman[1] had been interred, and that these pilgrims to the shrine and novelty took away portions of the barn floor as reliques! but the acme of depraved feelings was exemplified on the day of the execution, when the detestable wretch was launched into eternity. No less than 10,000 persons assembled on the plain surrounding the gallows: there well-dressed and delicate females exposed themselves to the rude jostling of the mob, and all the horrid language which generally is uttered by base and unfeeling men on the occasion, in order to witness the death of a fellow creature. These females pressed even to the foot of the gallows to witness his mental pangs and his bodily torments, which in all probability were very violent, for the executioner held by and pulled down the legs of the wretched sufferer for two minutes in order that his convulsive pangs might be shortened. Yet, notwithstanding this, even when *ten* minutes had elapsed the limbs were still convulsed.

The worst part of the recital is yet to come. So eager were the populace to retain some memorial of the transaction, and of the executed murderer, whose end ought to have excited the utmost horror and detestation, that they vied with each other in purchasing the cord with which he was hanged at a guinea an inch, and even the Sheriff took home in his carriage the pistols and sword (with which the murder was supposed to have been perpetrated), and declared he would not part with them for 100 guineas: there had been a quarrel as to the right of possession between the keeper of the prison and one of the constables—doubtless occasioned by the expectation of gain. Surely all these are indications of a dereliction of all sober sense and feeling, and an overruling folly which depraves the understanding. taking the sole possession of the vulgar mind.

I have read nothing nor heard of nothing of late which has so completely disgusted me as this horrid narrative.

We did not breakfast till ten o'clock. The rain still continued without intermission. Towards the middle of the day I walked to the Church under the escort of Captain Savage's gardener, who held an

[1] Maria Marten (The Red Barn Murder).

umbrella over my head while I sketched the devoted edifice, a memorial of which I was anxious to preserve before it be *levelled to the dust*! According to appearances I think it might have stood a century longer, had repairs to the amount of £200 been bestowed; but architects are not the persons to advise repairs, especially if they may be afterwards employed to draw the plan and superintend the building of a *new* Church. The beautiful stone cornice of quatrefeuilles on the outside of the edifice, which I believe is unique, will be destroyed, also the doorway, which I have before noticed in my Journals as very curious, retaining the Anglo-Norman and Saxon zig-zag over a Grecian scroll. I made a sketch also of the wooden effigy of a Knight, probably one of the Gournays, who possessed the Manor of Norton, I believe, in the reign of Henry I, from grants by the Norman Conqueror. On my return I planned a plain altar, like those in use seven centuries ago, and requested Captain Savage to use his interest to have the said effigy laid upon it under a plain canopy near the Altar. The doorway betokens the antiquity of this Church which is about to be demolished! The tower was built during the reign of Charles II, and chiefly at his expense.

It is somewhat singular the man who attended me from Captain Savage's with an umbrella was servant to Archdeacon Coxe when he made the tour of Monmouthshire, of which he afterwards published the account, in which iter Sir Richard Hoare was the Archdeacon's assistant. I was engaged in drawing till bed-time. It rained almost without intermission the whole of the day; the consequences will be most awful.

Friday, August 15

I rose early, meaning to finish my drawings of the Church before breakfast, but while shaving in a hurry I cut my chin, which detained me in my bedroom endeavouring to staunch the blood till half-past seven o'clock.

I left Norton after breakfast, and called on the Boodles (at Radstock) on my return. Mrs. Richard Boodle and her husband returned home yesterday, and are as well as can be expected; but I dare say the kind-hearted daughter has felt, and will feel her Father's death severely, although the good old man came to the garner in due time, like a ripe sheaf of corn, at the age of 78. Although he was a lawyer, yet I firmly believe that he was *an honest man*.

I found on my return home that the parlour was nearly painted,

Emery himself being occupied in finishing the last coat of red. It appears more gaudy at present than suits my taste, but I hope it will be rendered more sombre by the pictures.

Mr. Stephen Jarrett called in the evening to return some papers I lent him last week. He is possessed of all the curiosity of his Mother, without her tact; he made several enquiries respecting the dimensions of my orchard, and two bedrooms abovestairs, which he says he never before had seen. He is not, I hope, anticipating the produce of Naboth's Vineyard, like his Mother, who resembles the wife of Ahab in more particulars than one: Eheu satis! my spleen need not be shewn on paper, nor shall it be if I can help it. I therefore shall proceed to employ my mind on more profitable subjects. How time passes! and day succeeds to-day, and nothing is done but trifles. If I live till next month I shall have been twenty-eight years Rector of this place, and I fear I have done no good whatever as to the real benefit of the Society of which I am an instructor. Still, I have not slumbered on my post.

I paid young Feare £3 15s. 0d. for the colliers his Father kindly, as a neighbour, permitted to come and mow the grass. This is nearly 3s. an acre, besides all their food, and more than a gallon of beer an acre. I never therefore shall require their assistance again: what with their food, money, etc., etc., I have already expended nearly £30, and the harvest is not yet begun.

Saturday, August 16

Notwithstanding I strove to employ myself and prevent the intrusion of unpleasant retrospection before I went to bed, I lay awake thinking upon the situation in which I have been placed by the malice of my fellow creatures, and the base ingratitude of my children.

This morning dawned brightly; there was not a cloud on the horizon: again it is overcast! My mind has of late been as gloomy as the atmosphere. Lighten this darkness, O Lord!

I went to Meadyeates after having written thus far, and called upon old Green, who is very ailing, and the Parish Doctor has neither been to him nor sent anything for him since his first visit; the Overseer, Hicks, has only given him half-a-crown at one time, and two shillings at another during his illness, and he has no pay from the Parish. He worked as long as he could work, breaking stones on the roads, and received sixpence a day: this has been stopped. Hicks it was that let the old man, *Evans*, die in the Poor House, actually eaten up with maggots which bred in his flesh through nastiness. He is the most hard-hearted fellow I ever knew—a truly brutified English farmer of the modern school. I called afterwards on old Mrs. Taylor, and read to her parts of the Psalms, and conversed for nearly an hour. She is getting weaker, but I do not think is in any immediate danger. I am much pleased with her manners and really religious remarks, and will endeavour to see her at least once a week. Mr. Trelawney Collins, the new Rector of Timsbury, is expected to-day.

The errand woman brought my newspapers and a letter from my Mother, also another dunning epistle from Joseph's tailor at Sandhurst, for which money had been left when this idle boy quitted the College, to which I wish in the agony of my soul he had never gone. It was the most unfortunate thing that could have happened to one of his disposition; but it is useless to repine at what is past. I did all for the best, although it has turned out so badly.

I went to bed immediately after prayers.

Sunday, August 17

I slept but indifferently and rose about seven, when I went into my study before breakfast. Afterwards I wrote to my Mother, [but] when I wished to seal my letter, no seals were to be found. My servant lad, George, says he told the maidservant when I was from home to lock them up, as workmen were in the house, but she did not do so. I make no doubt they have been stolen. One of the seals I much value, as it was my father's, and bore the family arms. Nothing can make up the loss to me, but I must bear it. When Bush and his wife were with me I lost two gold rings. The son, who was employed by the painters last week, I hope has not been the guilty person. If he were, I hope I may never know it, as I should not like to prosecute him for a capital offence, as he was born in this house, and is my godson. The smaller one's possessions are the less chance there is of being annoyed by losing them; if I had not a gold set of seals, the person who stole them might not have been tempted to the theft.

Monday, August 18

I was a very late riser. On going into my study after breakfast I made [some extracts] from the inimitable Barrow, on the visible and distinctive marks and characters of an overruling Providence directing human concerns. Strange that the greater part of mankind prefer the trash of modern bookmakers to this genuine gold; but this is another symptom, and perhaps one of the principal causes of the rapid decadence both in mind and morals of the English nation.

I returned home after breakfast, and, it being a fine day, went into the hayfield. The crop is not spoilt, although it has been soaked by the rain upwards of a fortnight.

I found two letters when I got back to the Parsonage, one from Samuel Skinner, the other from Henry Hoare saying there was a vacancy in a regiment going to the West Indies he thought I might procure for Owen, and that the impediment he had would not be of much consequence. Samuel Skinner mentioned the several applications he had made through his friends for a cadetship for Joseph, but without success. I am sure I know not what these youths are to do. If they had employed their time and talents as they ought to have done, and prepared themselves for the university and, by steadiness, have gotten scholarships, as I expected they would have done according to the plan I had chalked out for them, all would have been well; but they *were idle*, and, what is worse, *insubordinate to their superiors*. Therefore they marred their own prospects in their first set out in life, as well as disappointed the expectations of their Father, who had made such sacrifices for them by bestowing on them the very best education that could be procured. They will not see the matter in this light; but they will do it ere long, as they will enter into a different grade of society to which they have been accustomed to move in, if the situations I am requiring for them cannot be procured.

I wrote a long letter to my Mother before breakfast stating the necessity there was for the boys occupying their time while continuing with her, as idle habits were not easily overcome. I had recommended to her their reading Plutarch's "Lives," and something more solid than newspapers and novels; but this is the *mental* food of the rising, or rather, falling generation.

The bell tolled after breakfast for old Ruth James, sister to Stephen Rossiter; she was nearly eighty. I had for several years paid her £2 13*s*. 0*d*. as schoolmistress to six children. I sent to her, but she preferred committing herself to the direction of the Methodists at the last. I am more and more convinced that the regular clergy are now of little or no use to the people: whether they who purpose thrusting us from our seats will do better is another consideration. If the Government were to support the Catholics, and make that the *sole* religion, I cannot but acknowledge the people would be kept in better order.

Thursday, August 21

The people in the hayfield, who had had a double potation of cider, were not, however, contented; but just as I was stepping into bed, the servant knocked at my door to say they were come for more. I desired her to tell them to go home, that I was sure they had had too much already, and that my parsonage was not a pothouse. My life is indeed become a burden. In order to supply employment for my wounded spirit I occupied the whole morning in tinting the sketches I have lately taken. This employed me till dinner-time, after which I took up one of the volumes of Montfauçon, and had just applied myself to reading when my servant, George, came to the parlour door giving a violent knock and saying that the people had no drink in the hayfield. George also said he had been working all day without beer, and could do so no longer. I asked why he had not gotten any. "Because," he said, " the barrel is out!" I asked what he wanted me to do; they were such a set of gormandising gluttons, they never were content: that they had sent for cider last night, when I was just going to bed: that I had granted them cider as well as beer because I thought they would get in my hay before dark; on going to the field I found they had not done so. I said that if they had drunk up all the beer I could not help it; how can I get beer at a moment's notice? But he should have his wish—that he might take the horse and cart and go to White's at Red Hill, and get an 18-gallon cask of small beer, such as was drunk in my family: and if he did not like that, he might leave me; if he imagined that I thought him of any value he was mistaken; I had done much for him, and had met with the same ingratitude I had done from others.

Saturday, August 23

Sarah brought the seals I had lost, saying she had found them in the drawer of the little cabinet in the best parlour, where she had placed them herself. This is somewhat strange that she should so strenuously deny all knowledge of them, even when the boy said he told her to put them away. Warner assured me that she was a woman of the strictest probity. I have, however, had all the silver things locked up which are not in immediate use. I am doomed daily to witness the growth of iniquity in this wretched place, and may almost exclaim with the Psalmist, "There is none who doeth good, *no not one.*"

Sunday, August 24

On going into my study I endeavoured to shake from my thoughts the occurrences of the preceding day, and strove to be calm and composed, in order to perform the sacred functions of the day. The subject I selected for my discourse was *Death*. I am quite ashamed of having suffered myself to be hurried away by my feelings so frequently of late. It has been well remarked that an angry man is one of the most weak and absurd of all people; indeed, it is with humility I turn into myself when I have thus offended. If I had not walked to the churchyard (yesterday) I should not have met Stephen Jarrett. I had written to him, and in this letter had given sufficient check to his undue interference in the matter of his trying to prevent the cutting of the ivy from off the Church, which was much needed, and putting the lock on the Church gate; why, then, put myself in the way of personal irritation? I was put to the test during the morning service. Mr. Stephen Jarrett came into the pew with his aunt (Mrs. Anne Stephens), and banged the door as he entered it with great violence— the children were singing the morning hymn; he, although unaccustomed even to join the singers, when they came to that verse:

> *Let all thy converse be sincere,*
> *Thy conscience as the noonday clear,*
> *For God's all-seeing eye surveys*
> *Thy secret thoughts, thy works, and ways.*

sang it out loudly, fixing his eyes on me with the greatest imaginable insolence. Mrs. Stephens, his aunt, looked at him with surprise, and, as I thought, with reprehension. He did not sing beyond these words. Hicks was in the pew next him, and, I observed, noted what he did, as indeed everyone must have done in that part of the Church. I kept my eyes to my book during the whole service, and never took them off, fearing that I might have seen something to draw away my attention from what I ought to be engaged in. I found some difficulty in getting through the service.

The post brought me a letter from my son Owen, written in a style which indicates he is returning to a sense of duty, which, indeed, affords me sincere satisfaction. I could not help thinking it was sent to reward me for the endeavours to overcome my own perverse feelings. We must not be too severe in reproving the failings of others, if we have a sense of our own imperfections.

The Church was crowded in the evening with attendants on the funeral of Ruth James. The corpse was brought into the Church, and I read the portion of Scripture appointed for the Burial Service instead of the Second Lesson for the day. The people were very attentive, a pin might have been heard to drop.

Monday, August 25

I did not sleep well, [but] felt during the time I lay awake more satisfaction in the idea of my son's turning again to his right way of thinking than anything I have felt for some time, and was eager to get into my study to write to him in reply to his letter, the purport of which was that he was not anxious to go into the army or to embark in any profession without my consent, and wished me to point out what I thought might be most eligible under present circumstances. I accordingly stated I was glad to find [he had] discovered that the army would not suit him; also found how difficult it was now for a young man to procure any situation in a respectable line of life, especially with the little interest and money I had to push him with. He seemed now to wish to return to the law as a profession; but if he undertook the study, he must at least devote eight hours a day, and not suffer any amusements or interruptions to divert him from his purpose.

With respect to the Church, if he had ever turned his thoughts that way (which I understood he had done, but thought the impediment in his speech an insurmountable obstacle), I had to say I did not think his impediment would be a bar which might not be surmounted. I had lately seen a Mr. Parfett, the present Incumbent of Glastonbury, whose stammering was infinitely worse than what he had laboured under, and he had been in the Church twenty years; and I have heard of others. If he thought from his heart that he should feel more comfortable in this profession, I would not oppose it: he might not be an idler, but might prepare himself for taking pupils, which would increase his income and perhaps extend his interest for procuring a Living. I begged he would weigh carefully what I had written on this subject, and rest assured if he put his own shoulder to the wheel I would endeavour to assist him, and I only prayed he might make a choice not subject to change.

In the evening came a note from the undertaker, inviting me to attend Mr. Deeke Smith's funeral at Timsbury, on the 28th.

I continued reading till prayer time. It seemed to me that my servant, George, had taken too much of the beer that he was so anxious to combat for.

I also wrote a note to Long, the tailor at Priston, to make me a new coat against the funeral on Thursday, for my present garb is so shabby I shall be ashamed to appear in it. The carpenter's man has been painting in the new room abovestairs the whole of the morning, but the smell is so powerful in my study I can scarcely bear it. In the evening there came an invitation from the Hammonds to dine with them on Saturday, which I declined. What a strange custom the English have gotten into of giving dinners, not merely for eating and drinking, but to keep up such and such sets and societies. If you are not found at the dinners of such and such people you are nothing! Even political parties are principally decided and known by the dinners people give, and the greater matters of business are discussed over the bottle. For my part, I think the morning the best time for business. I am never able to do anything which requires attention after I have eaten a hearty dinner and taken more than three glasses of wine.

Tuesday, August 26

On my road to Timsbury this day I had half an hour's conversation with Mr. Trelawney Collins,[1] who is a well educated and well disposed man; but he little knows what he will have to undergo in this detestable neighbourhood, governed by attornies, apothecaries, and coal heavers. The people have been civil to him, and I hope they will continue to be so; and so they will till interests clash, and then he will find what I have done—if he sails with the stream, he will give up the best interests of the Church and be at the beck *of all the seceders*, and if he acts as I have done, with firmness, he will have to withstand a host of foes; and, poor man, I perceive by his weak state he cannot have the physical strength to withstand them. From my heart I compassionate him on his coming to reside here. I spoke in

[1] The Rev. Charles Trelawney Collins, A.M., Rector of Timsbury, 1825–1841.

general terms that it behoved us to assist each other, and said whatever assistance I could give on his coming amongst us he might depend on as being sincere: that I had smarted myself, and if I could save him any pain or unpleasantness he might be assured I should not be found wanting.

I saw old Bacon, who broke his thigh some time ago and was so very insolent to me when lying on his bed—it might have been his bed of death. I went up to him and said that his quarrel with me about money matters some time ago should not make him quarrel with his Maker: why did he not come to Church? I asked him whether he had forgotten the way to Camerton Church. He said he was so lame he could not walk so far. I said I was going to preach on the Resurrection from the Dead, and our hopes and prospects in another life; it was a subject we were all alike interested in.

The man was civil, but did not come.

Wednesday, August 27

I slept but little last night. On leaving my bedroom I heard a voice saying to my servant: "Yes; but has he had his breakfast?"

On going downstairs I saw young George Burrard, who told me his father was on the road to visit me: that they were passing through Bath to Cheltenham. Burrard soon arrived, and, as is his manner, in a most friendly and feeling tone said, "I am come expressly to require you to do what I am come to ask, and I will take no refusal." I said that no one in the world, perhaps, could so fully command my exertions as himself; I only asked what it was he wished me to do, and if I could do it he might be assured I would. He said, "We are going to France, and you must come with us!" I began to hesitate, and to point out the unsettled state of the parish, and the workmen in the house. But he would hear nothing on this head, and said that I must accommodate these matters: that change of ideas would do me much service, and I must at all events promise to accompany him: that he did not mean to go for a fortnight, and that I might arrange accordingly: that, as he went for the education of his children, he meant to take a house at Versailles; but that George and myself might make our excursions ad libitum, but that George must return the beginning of January in order to attend to his duties in Parliament! (of which *he, George, aged* 22, is lately become a member). I said I liked the arrangement, and would return with him. Burrard and his son left me soon after breakfast.

I rode from Timsbury to Priston Rectory. Hammond requested I would stay to dinner. The day being fine, and a moon, I thought I might do so, and get back to Camerton in the evening. I accordingly put up my horse. As their dinner was so late, I gave sixpence to a man working at the house to go to my parsonage and tell the servants not to set up for me, as I should sleep at Priston.

Thursday, August 28

I counted every hour-strike of the deep-toned bell of the Church tower from eleven till four, and then dropped off to sleep. The servant came in early for my clothes, and roused me, so that I may safely say I only closed my eyes for two hours. I went into the reading-room for an hour before breakfast, and occupied myself with some of the Letters of Junius. I left Hammond's at nine.

On getting home I found the tailor, of Priston, had made me a frock coat, instead of a dressed one, which I ordered to attend the funeral of the Rev. Mr. Deeke Smith at Timsbury this day. I found I had written to him to make me the same kind of coat as the former— thinking that he had made me a dress suit, so that I had nothing to say, only to request he would not continue gossiping in the kitchen, which he is accustomed to do, I hear, in *this* neighbourhood longer than ordinary.

I was in good time at Mr. Smith's (at Greenhill). He died of an ossification of the heart. A large party with myself attended the corpse to the grave. Mr. Collins read the service in an impressive manner. Poor man! When I looked at him I thought he might soon be called to occupy his own narrow house, near him he now committed to the ground. He is to all appearances in a consumption. After the service was concluded we went to Mr. James's, who spread out a hospitable luncheon, which I took as my dinner, and left my finery, that is, a hat and scarf of satin, in Miss James's custody, for my daughter Anna.

The want of sleep unhinges me entirely. The smell of paint also incommoded me during the night.

Friday, August 29

Still the smell of paint!

Saturday, August 30

The smell of the paint is very offensive.

I walked after morning Church to the old woman at Meadyeates. I found that the dropsy had increased, and her hands as well as her feet are much swollen. I read the Visitation for the Sick, a Psalm, and afterwards the sermon I had preached on the Resurrection, with which she seemed much pleased. Her husband, she tells me, died of the dropsy ten years ago, and that she has no hopes of getting over it; that Curtis told her he could scarrify her legs, but it would afford only temporary relief, and therefore she would not submit to the operation, and will, in all probability, depart hence ere I leave my home, which will be a weight off my mind. Hammond will take charge of the Church, and, being so near, I hope the Parish will not be much further troubled; but the visitation of the sick I hold an indispensable duty. I shall leave monies in his hand to distribute, and I hope to do so without appearing ostentatious. If there was any staid, trustworthy woman in the parish I would prefer her having this fund, but where am I to find such?

The Church was well filled in the evening; there were two baptisms and two churchings. One of the godmothers quite disturbed the ceremony by grunts and groans. I looked hard at her, but it had no effect.

As I walked back from Church I saw my poor old horse so lame that he could not put one of his feet to the ground. I accordingly sent my servant, after dinner, to Radstock to speak to the farrier, who came before dark and said it was merely a corn. I hope it may prove to be as he says, for the old horse is such a favourite I cannot bear to have him suffer any unnecessary pain. I was occupied after tea in the dining parlour, which I now use as my study, for the upper room is painting and preparing as a setting room for my daughter. I had intended it for Owen on his occasional visits to my house; but, alas! these will never now perhaps take place, as he has written to say he has given up all thoughts of the law, and sees nothing but the army likely to suit him. I am sure I know not what is to be done, unless the long-expected explosion takes place in Ireland; then there will be sufficient call for our youth to be laid quiet. Alas! this is a sad alternative. I hope I have preserved my mind this day. I noted down the occurrences before I went to bed—in fact, these pages are sketches of my own mind, but I fear self-love draws too flattering a picture.

In reply to my Mother's letter respecting my permitting Anna to come with her brother Joseph to Camerton till I move from thence, I sent a messenger expressly to her house, desiring that my son and daughter might come out by a chaise, to be here in time for dinner. Joseph had written me a very feeling and penitential letter the beginning of the week, and promised most faithfully not to do again what made him so miserable on reflection.

Stephens brought me two [letters] and the newspaper; one from the Bishop, very kindly written, saying he was at Weston-super-Mare, and should be most happy if I would come to him there on a visit, in order to view the country in the vicinity. The other was from Sir Richard Hoare, saying he was very glad to hear I meant to visit Brittany and Normandy, and that he had sent a book to Ford's Library he thought would be of service to me in pointing out what was best worth seeing.

When such upstarts as Stephen Jarrett endeavour to lower one in the eyes of the people, it is some consolation that the most sensible still continue to esteem one.

My son and daughter arrived about one o'clock, and seemed delighted to return. I felt happy in seeing them happy, and I sincerely hope they will not make me uncomfortable again.

Friday, September 5

Whether it was owing to the paint or over-fatigue I know not, but I awoke about one o'clock with so great a giddiness in my head I was obliged to light my candle and walk about my room. I also bathed my head and temples with opodeldoc and took some medicine, but could not fall again to sleep; and there was all the time a kind of buzzing in my ears, which rendered it very uncomfortable. I left my bed, however, at seven, and continued my employment.

Saturday, September 6

We have done a great deal since Thursday, the new room, the passages, and the best bedroom being stencilled, and the new bookcase put up. I am obliged to write my Journals when I can catch a minute or two, being completely turned out of all the rooms. How glad I shall be when this my last enterprise in housemaking be finished with. It will certainly be a most comfortable habitation, if the people permit me only to enjoy it for the few years I have, and do not hunger after my empty chair before my hour be ripe. I certainly am far from well—heavy and stupid I feel, and collect my ideas with difficulty. It may be that bleeding may relieve me, but I do not like to begin this remedy.

Wednesday, September 10

I am happy to say the harvest is nearly gotten in, and the crops much better than I expected. I have agreed to have the dining-room painted for two guineas.

Thursday, September 11

I assisted in getting my books up in the study. The bookcases will be more than sufficient to contain them. As the time approaches for my departure I feel a kind of indescribable qualm, but I must get over it, as I know a change of scene is absolutely necessary, my mind having been so unhinged of late. I purpose being at the Star Inn, Southampton, on Friday next, when the steamer starts for Havre.

Friday, September 12

This being a fine morning, I made several drawings of the Parsonage, Hermitage, and tomb of my dear wife and daughter, in order to complete the 84th volume of Journals before I leave home. After tea I retired to my new study—the first time I have occupied it as such. The fire draws very well.

I gave directions to Owen about receiving my tythe, and also wrote to Hammond, who has the care of my Church, respecting his visiting the sick, etc., etc., during my absence.

I hope now there will be no obstacle to my setting off, as I purpose to-morrow evening. The weather has changed, but the clouds will, I hope, blow away.

I wrote my Will on one sheet of writing-paper, which I shall leave with my Mother, in case anything happens to me. In this Will I have given all my MSS. Volumes, now eighty-four in number, to the British Museum, in case they will accept them on the terms of making no extracts for fifty years after the time of my decease, and to preserve them in the *three iron chests*!

1829

As I lay awake last night I reflected on the extraordinary custom of ringing in the New Year; the bells at Bath were very audibly heard while employed in this service last night and this morning. How many are there who have heard those bells will cease to hear them next year? Some employed in ringing them will perhaps have them rung as knells at their decease. So passes the world; we know not how long our journey may be; but this we know, that when the Great Author and Provider for our existence calls us hence, it is the most fitting time for our departure. We must neither delay nor hesitate, nor busy ourselves therefore like foolish children in playing with trifles on shore when our attention should be on board; we should be prepared to obey the voice of the Master of the Vessel which is to convey us to the ocean of eternity the moment He calls us. . . . Still, my place would be *soon filled at Camerton*; but there are some things in respect to literature which could not well be completed by another hand when mine is cold in the grave. "God's will be done on earth as it is in heaven!"

Friday, January 2

I wrote to Sir Richard Hoare, who has ever been most truly my friend.

Sunday, February 8

On looking over the Prophecies of Isaiah this morning I met with the following pathetic exclamation, which may be well applied to the recent loss we have sustained in the fairest Church in Britain by the hand of an incendiary, vide chapter 64, verse 11: "Our holy and beautiful house where our fathers praised Thee is burnt with fire, and all our pleasant things are laid waste." If the visible signs and prefigurations of the Almighty obtained now, as they did in the time of the Jews, I should denominate the burning of York Cathedral[1] a token and omen of the destruction of a great part of the Protestant

[1] February 1, 1829.

379

Church—the purest and most enlightened, and I may add too the most adorned establishment of any in Christendom. Alas! who were the incendiaries?[2]

Friday, February 13

Burrard, who returned from Town last night (12th), tells me that he heard some very able speeches in the House of Commons, and thinks the Ministers will carry their Bill by a great majority there, but it is by no means certain that they will do so in the Upper House. I cannot think how men can be so blind as to surrender one of the vital principles of our Constitution, and be induced to believe it is absolutely necessary so to do to preserve harmony in the country, without which Mr. Peele pretends that the whole machine of government must stop.

Monday, February 16

This is a very mild day; I shall endeavour to go down into the parlour to-morrow. I have now been a prisoner to my bedroom nearly two months, which in addition to the month I was ill in France makes a period of three months; now, with returning strength returns the wish to prolong existence. Perhaps I might have been spared much misery if my career had been shortened, for perilous times are at hand.

Owen is making his arrangement to go to Cambridge, to Sidney College; he will procure a bene decessit from Trinity College, Oxford, which will enable him to count the terms he has kept. I have told him his future prospects must depend entirely upon his own exertions—he must determine to study hard in order to obtain a good degree, when he may procure a fellowship. He has promised me to do so, as the college he is going to is a small society, and I hope very different in all respects to what *Trinity College, Oxford, now is*. I hope he will really do something.

Tuesday, February 17

The papers to-day are alarming as to their contents; the Ministers have taken an awful responsibility on themselves; how far the King has been persuaded, we know not.

[2] Jonathan Martin, a religious fanatic; proved insane.

1829

Saturday, February 21

Owen goes to-morrow to Cheltenham in his way to Oxford, and from thence to Cambridge, where he must be in college by twelve o'clock Wednesday. He has my best wishes and prayers for success; if he has resolution to pursue mathematical studies, I think he will be able to accomplish his wishes; he will have a private tutor, and not return home before the long vacation, at least so is the arrangement now.

Sunday, February 22

Owen went in the middle of the day by one of the Cheltenham coaches, as the places in the Oxford were all engaged on account of the contest about the re-election of Mr. Peele. I hope to my heart he will be thrown out as a turncoat.

Monday, February 23 *to* 26

We have been in much trouble since Monday, but I hope things will mend. My brother Russell, Anna, and Joseph being engaged to drink tea with a lady who lives at the bottom of the hill, Anna asked whether I had any objection to Joseph's driving them thither. I must confess I did not much like it; the idea of getting a post chaise was banished, and they accordingly went about six o'clock. I drank tea with my Mother downstairs—the first time I have done so for two months. Nearly an hour after they were gone I heard someone calling out on the lawn before the house; a few minutes after, Mrs. Treherne, the upper servant, came into the parlour saying she wished to speak to my Mother, who accordingly went out. I did not remark my Mother's absence till it had exceeded an hour, and I heard the front door open and a great bustle, as if there were several people coming in. I immediately went from the parlour, and saw the little hall full of people, who were bearing Anna without sense or motion. They said she had been thrown from the carriage, but had no bones broken. Soon after my brother Russell was brought home and carried upstairs to his room, and Joseph at last arrived, having hurt his knee and suffered several bruises. From him I learnt the particulars: not having a drag-chain, as soon as they came to a steeper descent the horse, finding the carriage press upon her, set off at full speed, when the breeching broke; not being longer manageable, she ran the carriage against a post, broke the axle, and with the shock they were thrown out. Joseph and his sister were so stunned, they were taken insensible

381

into a gentleman's house close by; Russell was able to walk thither. I got to bed about twelve, but could not sleep. I went several times during the night to Anna's room door; she got no sleep, and complained much of her head. Still I trust, as there is no local injury, she may recover the shock.

I heard to-day from Owen; he has settled all his business, and is admitted at Sidney. I am glad he has been spared what we have suffered.

Saturday, March 7

As all the invalids are so much better, I purpose going home on Monday.

Sunday, March 8

I begin to long to return to my duties at Camerton, and find myself so much better I shall certainly go home to-morrow.

CAMERTON PARSONAGE,
Wednesday, March 11

I have been so uncomfortable for some time past in not having balanced my accounts for the last year, which I knew well would greatly exceed my income, that I was determined to set about the unpleasant but necessary task to-day. Indeed, half the world is ruined from this kind of cowardice. I find that my outgoings have been upwards of £1,200. The later addition to the house, and repair and painting, amount to £152 8*s.* 0*d.* exclusive of the new furniture, which I expect will be £50 more; Anna's piano, with attendant expenses, £60; wine bought of Mr. Hoare, half a pipe and bottles, £43, which are all extras which will not occur again.

	£	s	d.
	152	8	0
	60	0	0
	43	0	0
	£255	8	0
Spent in France	130	0	0
	£385	8	0

I have told Owen he must live within £200 a year at Cambridge. I am determined to lessen my scale of living, and accordingly I shall send notice I do not mean to have any carriage or livery servant in the house; and with respect to my household expenses, I must look to them myself, as Anna is not able to speak to the servants when things are going on wrong. I am determined to settle all bills weekly, which will soon shew the scale I am living upon.

Saturday, March 14

My daughter, who is quite recovered, being anxious to return to Camerton, I desired, by letter, she would order a post chaise, and her brother Joseph attend her. They arrived in time for a five o'clock dinner. It is very singular, the carriage had nearly been overturned within 300 yards of my house, and if Joseph, who was on horseback, had not jumped off and held the horses' heads it certainly would.

We must have done with carriages for two reasons, economy and safety; one's own legs are the best carriers after all. The more we can do for ourselves in these times, and indeed at all times, the better; we shall not then feel the change of circumstances so much. I am perfectly indifferent what I eat, and what I drink, and wherewithal I am clothed, so that what I use be only neat and clean. I have left off wine for my health's sake; the more we depend upon the things of this world, the more we become enslaved. The great secret of life, if we look for comfort (happiness I will put out of the question), is to be constantly occupied, *indefessus agendo*.

Tuesday, April 14

Owen came a little after breakfast time, with his brother Joseph. I was glad to find him looking much better than I expected, and he seems better reconciled with his College.

Friday, April 17

This being Good Friday, I preached in the morning on the text, St. John, ch. 19, v. 5, "Then came Jesus forth, wearing the crown of thorns, and the purple robe." There were only a very few persons present. I wish I could get a good Clerk, but my little state of Camerton is somewhat like the state of the country; I am obliged to work with bad tools or get none at all to work with. Neither of the Churchwardens now attend. What is to be done? I am like the captain of a king's ship sent to sea with a bad crew, and no officer I can depend on.

There were two persons in Church who behaved improperly, but no Churchwarden now attends to preserve order. I administered the Sacrament; only twelve attended, among them only two men —Smallcombe and White—the others were women.

The same unpleasant weather. Owen and Joseph, however, continue to get rid of the heavy time by fishing. Books are out of the question. How singular it is that my children seem to dislike every kind of pursuit which has contributed to my comfort. When I gave them a good education I expected they would have taken a turn for literature, but alas! a book seems to be a bugbear with both. Idleness is the order of the day. Owen assured me he meant to study hard in order to take a good degree and entitle himself to a Fellowship, but I am convinced he will not do so. Joseph will, I suppose, eventually go into the Army at home, if he cannot get a Commission in the India Service; but I shall not have the means of purchasing on to a captaincy, and then he will be discontented, and more displeased with me than ever. The system of education at our public schools now seems to be to throw off all restraint; they rebel first against their teachers, and then insult their parents if they presume to admonish them for their good; because young men of fortune do such and such things, they will imitate them, and without the means are equally ambitious of distinguishing themselves *in mischief*.

I find the Bill respecting the Catholic Emancipation has a much larger majority in the House of Lords than I expected, so the King will be powerfully upheld; but, alas! before he dies he will rue the deal which will lose him the affection of his subjects, and afford them a plea hereafter for tampering with their oaths of allegiance with him or his successors, in the same manner as he has tampered with his Coronation Oath.

Mr. Crang, the apothecary, sent a message this evening to say Mrs. Hammond died as he expected in the course of the day. She had been so blooded there appeared to be little chance of her rallying. What a system do the gentlemen of the lancet now pursue in cases of inflammation! there appears to be little chance if the disorder be violent, and can alone be remedied by copious drafts of the vital stream. The only difference seems to be, the patient may die quiet through exhaustion, instead of quitting the world in a raging fever. Poor Hammond is left with a family of seven children; religion alone can support him under his afflictions.

Tuesday, April 21

I learnt that Hammond was become quite tranquil, and derived consolation from having his children round him. This is a most happy frame of mind. I was fearful from what I heard, [on sending] to ascertain if possible whether I could be of any service, that he could not have borne the society of his little ones.

Wednesday, April 22

I have nearly finished the drawings, etc., etc., of the six first volumes of my French Tour. Anna is of great assistance to me in setting the sketches on cartridge paper, but her brothers take no part in what they know would be giving me pleasure; when it rains so hard that they cannot pursue the amusement of fishing, they might amuse themselves by doing something useful, instead of smoking segars. Joseph, when I spoke to him about something very trifling, was very insolent, and grossly insulted me; when I said I would not put up with such treatment from anyone in my own house, and begged he would behave properly as long as he continued with me, he said he would not remain a moment longer, so he took his hat and returned to my Mother's. It is a great misfortune that my Mother is so near, and that she moreover listens to his improper representations of his conversation and conduct towards his Father. Owen also misbehaved himself exceedingly; in the course of conversation he told me he meant to go into the Church. I said that, with his present disposition, he was not fit for such a profession, and if he went into the Church merely for the sake of passing an idle life I could prophesy he would be mistaken, since a storm was rising against the Church which would prove all its members, as it were by fire. I will not attempt to recapitulate what passed, and what insolence I experienced. It seems I am destined to have these heartrending interruptions to my quiet. I had fondly imagined when I built me a comfortable study I might have enjoyed peace and tranquility in my own mental resources, but alas! I am wounded in the tenderest part; I have been a most indulgent Father, as every act of my past life must testify. I fear what I complain of is too general; all discipline is gone; the rising race are self-willed and ferocious, but due retribution will be made. I spent a miserable night. How can I expect to get well if my mind is thus kept in a state of anxiety and irritation?

Friday, April 24

Mr. Hammond's brother came to ask whether I would perform the service at Mrs. Hammond's funeral. This I told him I could not do, I felt so nervous and low, and should not like to expose my feelings; indeed, I could not help bursting into tears while he spoke to me, I am so much shaken by late occurrences. Owen went in the mail to Bath after dinner. I hope he will think better. I told him he must begin at the root, unless God were with him he would derive no lasting benefit from man; that as he was going to devote himself to the service of religion he must begin by the reformation of his own heart. I gave him the "Works of Thomas à Kempis" in a small pocket volume, which has been my companion in all my travels many years; it was given me by my uncle Page when I was at Oxford, and has frequently administered consolation when nothing else had the power of doing it. I made him promise to read a section every day. I felt very low when he left the Parsonage, but must still endeavour to bear up. The weather still continues stormy and uncongenial for the time of year; but what are external tempests to disquietude of mind? "Blow, blow, thou winter wind. Thou art not so unkind as man's ingratitude."

Tuesday, April 28

It has blown a heavy storm from twelve to three o'clock; when I am now writing in my study, my room shakes under me.

Mrs. Hammond was buried to-day.

Thursday, April 30

I received a letter from the Bishop, who is on his way to Town; he signs himself my friend, and I hope he will prove so when it comes to the push. I only ask for justice, and a patient investigation of the documents I have in my possession in order to prove there has been a regular conspiracy of the bad people in this parish under the authority of those who ought to know better. The time will soon arrive when I shall speak out, and not in hints.

During the Prayers at Morning Service Cottle's son was hawking so loud when I commenced the service I was obliged to look at him in order to check him from interrupting the service. The pew which Burfitt built without any authority from me or the Ordinary, has been more than once the scene of great impropriety of behaviour during Church time, for the sides being higher than the seatings, so that the congregation are not able to see the people who are sitting down, they talk and laugh and misbehave themselves greatly. This evening the pew was filled by two sons and a daughter of farmer Skuse, a son of Hicks, John Rossiter, and a female in mourning; the elder Skuse I saw talking and laughing with the person in black, and I said aloud that, as there had been great impropriety of behaviour in that pew, I requested there might be no repetition of it this evening. John Rossiter stood up in the pew and looked very insolently at me, but I took no notice.

Thursday, May 14

I put up the following notice on the Church door:

NOTICE

"Since I have had occasion to notice misbehaviour for several times in the pew built by Joseph Goold and Burfitt, who had no authority to erect it without my consent and the consent of the Ordinary, this is to give notice, if the misbehaviour is repeated I will present the pew to the Court at Wells in order to its being restored to its original form of separate sittings."

Saturday, May 16

The weather is now quite summer; we seem to have overstepped spring this year. The apple and pear trees, as well as the plums and cherries, have abundant blossom, which will in all probability bear much fruit unless a cruel blight assails them. The post brought me a note from Joseph saying how sorry he felt for his past behaviour, and promising not to offend in future; but he has so often made the same declaration that I cannot confide in it. However, I am very glad to find he does not continue obstinate, and shall write to him soon. After tea I composed part of my sermon before I went to bed.

Thursday, June 11

The Camerton Club marched to-day, in number about 1,400. They played "God Save the King" as they passed the Parsonage.

Friday, June 12

I learnt a piece of intelligence which did not surprise me, and I may truly say did not distress me, namely, that Mrs. Jarrett had offered Camerton for sale, and that the Advowson of the Living was to go with it. The latter part of the intelligence I did not expect, as I had understood from Mrs. Jarrett herself that Mr. Gooch was to be my successor in the Living. Perhaps the whole may be a ruse de guerre. The plot this Medea has been so long hatching is now nearly ripe.

Sunday, June 14

After tea I took a walk with Anna to Writhlington by Woodborough, where Purnell's dogs were like to have proved obstacles in our way. This worthy Justice keeps curs in order to deter people from passing his house, which is situate on one of the oldest British roads in the kingdom. This hot weather I should feel very uncomfortable to have blood drawn by one of them. Luckily I had a stick when a lop-earned creature rushed close by me. I desired the servant who was on the premises to deliver a message from me to Squire Purnell, saying, if his dogs came near me while passing along the public road, I should do what I could to prevent any further attack.

Monday, June 15

John Rossiter, my quondam Churchwarden, who has entirely deserted his Church, behaved himself very insolently, merely because I mentioned the particulars of his having induced Harris the Clerk to find out the wrong lesson, to lay a trap for me. This is a bad fellow; he told White that there was no use of clerk or parson at Camerton, and that they had better wall up the Church door.

Tuesday, June 16

The post brought me a letter from Sir Richard Hoare to make enquiries after my health. I determined to commence my sixth letter to him on the subject of Camulodunum, giving him a comment on the text of Tacitus as far as regards that celebrated colony.

As Mrs. Jarrett sent me some hothouse grapes yesterday, I went with my daughter to thank her. She seems out of spirits. She says nothing about selling the place.

It rained the whole day, which will be of infinite service to the whole country. I finished my letter and notes for Sir Richard Hoare; it occupies thirty-four pages, closely written, and I hope will carry conviction with it.

The post brought me a letter from Bowles, but he holds out no hopes of doing anything for Joseph; as he says it is as difficult now to procure a cadetcy as an office under Government. I felt low. Indeed, not all the powers of my mind are able to bear up against the depression of spirits I now feel. I pray for tranquillity. I am sure it was in the Bishop's power to have done what he promised for Joseph. What am I to do under present circumstances but remain patient? If the Bishop has forgotten Joseph, he may have an opportunity hereafter of befriending Owen.

I passed a bad night, and had a return of spitting of blood, so that I did not leave my bedroom till past eight. My conscience is not my tormentor, otherwise there would be reason enough for my not sleeping. After breakfast I wrote thus far of my Journals. The weather still seems unpromising. I am quite surprised that I have heard nothing from Sir Richard Hoare. Butterfly friends seek their hiding-places as soon as they perceive the storm approach, but I thought he would not have deserted; perhaps he has not. At any rate, there is One who never will desert me, if I only cleave fast to Him. What is man! No, rather let me make friends and consolers of my books; I find them the same to-day, to-morrow, and the next day. Still I note down the workings of my own mind; these memoranda are in fact records of humanity. I shall take care that they are not read till this generation be passed away; it will matter little who were the actors in the drama, and what part they played, either good or bad; they are but sketches of human life. I cannot but notice on looking back upon the pages I have written several years ago the same querulous complaints against my associates. I ought to have exerted more energy, and risen above such considerations; so much self-love in all we do that there is ample room for humiliation. Indeed, indeed, I do humble myself; the world with all its malevolence cannot make me so low as I actually feel in my own opinion at times. Let me correct my own failings first. With truth does St. Paul exclaim, "Wretched man that I am, who will deliver me from the burthen of this death?" Oh, that I could before I die bring my mind to that perfect state of reliance in the Superior Director of all events, that I might look upon passing occurrences as I do on the clouds which now move *dark and threatening before my window.*

> *Exaudi genitor sancte meas preces*
> *Clamorisque sonum percipe lugubris*
> *Nec vultum misero subtrahe hostibus*
> *Omni ex parte prementibus.*

.   .   .   .   .

1830

ALTHOUGH the ringers were so noisy at the commencement of the last year, they were very quiet at this; not a clapper was moved. I hail this as a happy omen, and hope my parishioners will restrain their nonsensical tongues the ensuing year—I mean in those matters which do not concern them; but I have strong anticipations that they will not be taught to understand, but will proceed in the career of their iniquity. Such are my reflections at the commencement of a New Year.

Tuesday, January 5

Joseph went into Bath immediately after breakfast to bring back his brother. I walked to the Manor House to call on Mrs. Jarrett, who is going into Bath for further advice, but Mr. Crang says he cannot think she has any actual malady beyond that of being extremely nervous, which is indeed the worst of all maladies. On my return I found Owen arrived. He seems in good health and spirits, and proposes accompanying his brother and sister to the ball. After dinner I continued with my family, and played two rubbers of whist before supper, which I partook of for the sake of sociability, although it never agrees with me. I went to bed immediately after prayers.

Wednesday, January 6

I read with Joseph the 6th chapter of St. Matthew's Gospel, and one hundred lines of the "Odyssey of Homer," beginning Book 4th.

Thursday, January 7

When my sons and my daughter returned from Chilcompton they expressed themselves highly pleased with the ball, which was well attended. I told Owen if he felt an inclination to accompany me to the musical meeting at the Bishop's I would introduce him. Accordingly we drove to Wells, and arrived at the inn before five. We dined en famille at the palace, and at seven the company began to assemble in the two large drawing-rooms, which communicate with each other, the organ being in that farthest removed from the gallery, in which an elegant supper was set out, extending nearly the whole length of the noble apartment. The music was chiefly from Handel: "Comfort ye my people"; "Oh had I Jubal's Lyre," the pathetic piece from Jeptha; Haydn's "Creation" afterwards. These were sung by performers from Bath. Afterwards some amateurs played and sang some voluntaries, among whom Miss Maria Powell, the Bishop's grand-daughter, seemed most to excel in the sweetness of her voice and the execution of her playing. They compute there were upwards of 120 at this concert, besides the Bishop's own family. It was nearly midnight when I retired to rest.

Friday, January 8

We assembled to breakfast in the gallery at nine, having first attended prayers in the chapel. Afterwards the performers took their stations near the organ, and we were again gratified by harmonious strains. Some of the songs we heard even exceeded in my opinion the former selection.

As the Bishop had invited Owen and myself to continue over the day, we occupied the interval till dinner-time in visiting the cathedral, St. Cuthbert's Church, and the environs of the city. We dined at five. After dinner I was attacked and was obliged to defend my position of Camalodunum. Tacitus was produced, and some unfounded assertions respecting that author negatived on my part, I have reason to believe to the satisfaction of the company. I cannot help remarking from certain oblique hints that the Bishop begins to waver in opinion respecting me in more important circumstances than that of Camalodunum. The Bishop little knows me, but when he does so he will severely blame himself for entertaining suspicions which are injurious to me; like Caesar's wife, I require to be placed above suspicion. But enough; so much for egotism. After tea my good host and some of his guests sat down to cards. I got to bed before ten. During the evening I had an opportunity of telling the Bishop that I conceived it behoved us all to be firm and collected, and not corrupted by empty reports. I know not whether he perceived what I alluded to in my own case. He promised to call at Camerton in his way to Bath, and gave me an invitation to his house when there. I am convinced of his regard, but he should not be warped by others.

Sunday, January 10

I felt uncomfortably irritated to-day by the behaviour of the people.

During the Evening Service I had to notice the bad behaviour of the schoolgirls, and also of my foot-boy, George, who was laughing; when I spoke to him on the subject he denied it: he is a bad boy. I have often said if the patient Job had been Rector of Camerton he might not have had much celebrity on account of that virtue.

I know my infirmity, which is too great irritability, yet I endeavour to correct it; of one thing I am certain, I never retain the unwelcome guest beyond the impulse of the moment, and every hour of my existence at this place is so exposed to insult that one must be a stock or a stone not to feel it.

I continued in my study after tea till bed-time.

Saturday, January 16

Mr. Wynne, from Nostal Priory, Yorkshire, sent me three pheasants and a hare, which arrived to-day. Sir Richard Hoare never used to omit sending me some game at Christmas. I fear, though a kindhearted man, he is not without the little weakness of being hurt because I differ from him in a mere matter of opinion, and am about to publish what I have written on the subject of Camalodunum. I have observed a difference in his manner towards me, but this may be only imagination; time will shew. Thank God I never solicit nor care for the worldly countenance of any man: I am too proud to solicit patronage.

Sunday, January 17

I read prayers in the morning, and preached in the evening to a very thin congregation. If I who take some pains to instruct my hearers, and have their interest at heart, cannot succeed, how can the ignorant and time-serving Clergy do anything for their benefit? but I will bear yet further. I feel very uncomfortable, on a day, indeed, when no unpleasant feelings ought to ruffle and discompose the mind, and one ought to be solely resigned to the will of God. Do I not teach this, and ought I not to be influenced by the consolations I hold out to others? Why do I say with my mouth, "I commit myself and all that I have unto Thy keeping, O Lord," and still look to second causes? Is not this folly, nay worse, hypocrisy? Ought I not to esteem myself favoured, If I am employed as an instrument to bring about in any way that which is fitting to Him?

After dinner came a note from Mr. Strachey, inviting myself, my sons, and my daughter to Ashwick to dine on Wednesday, and offering beds.

Wednesday, January 20

It had snowed so much during the night that I considered it as sufficient apology for my putting off our visit to Mr. Strachey, which I did in a lively letter to laugh off, if possible, the dreariness of the season. Heal, who delivered the letter, told us that some of the lanes were impossible for a horse or carriage to pass, especially that going from the Parsonage towards the public road; so that even had we wished to have fulfilled the engagement we could not.

I was able to complete some writing, but suffer much from the cold, and from some circumstances among my children, worse than the cold. King Lear suffered, and others have suffered like King Lear, but this is more burning than a cancer to one's flesh: surely they will reflect when I am no more, of the pain they have caused me: are my children worse than those of other parents, or is it the fashion of the times to do exactly as they like?

Friday, January 22

A man named Rogers called after breakfast with a certificate signed by the Apothecary and Churchwarden, and stating that his wife wanted assistance from her parish. I said I could not set my hand to the certificate without I knew it to be a fact: I should see her if she was really as ill as he had represented. The man said, "You will come soon then, Sir?" I went accordingly with him.

That the poor are much distressed, and will be more so if this weather continues, I have no doubt. I told my daughter on my return to order some coarse beef, and tell the cook always to have a quantity of soup in the boiler, that we may be able to assist those who are really in absolute want; but as our Collieries are in full work we shall not be so much pinched here as at other places.

Saturday, January 30

Just as I went into the breakfast parlour this morning my daughter told me she had seen a carriage pass in front of the house; who could be our visitor at so early an hour? My surprise was not of long duration, as I heard the Bishop's voice in the hall. He took his breakfast with us, in his way from Wells, and I have promised to dine with him at No. 1, Royal Crescent, on Monday, having previously engaged to spend a week with my Mother in Bath.

It froze harder last night than it has done the whole winter. Joseph had ordered a chariot to come from Bath to take us in: the road was in parts very slippery owing to the snow, but we arrived without accident at my Mother's. Joseph preferred walking to going with us in the chariot. At half-past four I walked to the Royal Crescent, where the Bishop has taken a house belonging to Sir Thomas Strange for as long a period as he continues in Bath.

I found a pleasant party: the two Duncans, Warner, Mr. Shew, and Mr. Montgomery; also Mr. Meade[1] of Chatley [?] I returned to my Mother's at ten. I was not a little astonished, as I walked through Bath, to observe the streets so crowded with prostitutes, some of them apparently not above fourteen or fifteen years of age.

As the Bishop had overnight invited me to breakfast, I walked to his house by nine o'clock; Mr. Meade and Warner were there and I took Joseph with me, who was rather in fortune's way, as our kindhearted entertainer gave him three tickets for concerts to which he subscribed without being able to attend them himself.

I afterwards walked with Warner into the town, and made several calls; among them we stopped a quarter of an hour at Reeves the sculptor's, which gave me an opportunity of seeing the tomb about to be erected in Camerton Church to the memory of my predecessor, Mr. Prowse, or rather to the memory of the whole family, since it embraces the pedigrees of his Father, his wife, etc., etc. . . . . What nonsense!

In order that Pride should have a hint, if not a punishment, I told Mr. Reeves, and begged he would mention it to the family, that although I readily gave permission for a tomb to be erected in the Chancel to the memory of my predecessor free of all expense, I did not suppose it would have contained the genealogy of his whole family: that for the inscriptions not connected with the Rev. Mr. Prowse as Rector of the Parish something should be paid.

It is now nearly thirty years since this gentleman died, and no memorial of him having existed has hitherto been here, till one of his daughters left £200 for a monument to her family.

---

[1] Probably Richard John Meade, rector of Marston Bigot, (1821–34) and later of Christ Church, Frome, and Canon of Wells.

When I came to the Living of Camerton the house and premises were in such bad repair that I might fairly have required £200; whereas on the plea that the family were distressed, I only took £20, and paid £35 for fixtures, so in fact I was £15 out of pocket. I only mention this as a forcible example of vanity and family pride.

Wednesday, February 3

I again took my breakfast with the Bishop, and afterwards walked to visit Hammond, who I understand is about to forget his late loss in another connection. This is another proof that violent emotions are less lasting than those which are not expressed: the shallow stream makes the most noise. I must confess I did not think he would so soon have forgotten his late wife, but that is his concern, not mine. The present age is an age of insensibility; indeed, all feeling of men of the world is of a selfish kind.

Thursday, February 4

The easterly wind of yesterday has made my throat and chest quite sore, and on rising this morning I felt no inclination to leave the house; the Bishop sent down his servant with a note to ask me to dinner, but I felt so ill and uncomfortable I was obliged to decline it. I am very sensible of his great kindness, and his wish to shew himself my friend, when others hang back.

Friday, February 5

My son and my daughter, accompanied by their Uncle Russell and their Cousin Elinor Page, went to the concert at the Rooms. I continued within doors reading Sir Walter Scott's novel of "Rob Roy." We dined at half-past four, and stayed to drink tea with my Mother; at seven we returned home in a close carriage, as I do not like to expose myself to the open air. The ground was so slippery the horses could not keep their legs descending the hill to Camerton, but absolutely slid down on their haunches. The servants were gone to bed, and I had much ado to awaken them; it was not nine o'clock, and methinks they might have been found watching.

Saturday, February 6

Joseph, who had not accompanied us last night, skaited home this morning, and just as we were settling down to dinner Mr. Dennis arrived from Bath, and spent the evening; he is a man of great information, and I enjoyed his conversation much.

As I knew from report that my guest, Prebendary Dennis, was a celebrated extempore preacher, I requested he would officiate in the pulpit. He took his text from the Epistle for the day, "Know ye not that they which run in a race run all, but one receiveth the prize?"

Without hesitation he entered upon the subject, which was well arranged, as though it had been written, which is saying a great deal. His discourse was well delivered, and seemed to make such impression on the people that I asked him to give another discourse in the evening.

He was not so happy in this, since he got into a very diffuse explanation of the Jewish religion, and a comparison between it and the Christian, which I am sure scarcely one of the congregation could comprehend. I could not compliment the Preacher as I had done in the morning on his discourse, which was as remote from practical divinity as the former had been applicable to it. I do not mean to detract one iota from Mr. Dennis as to his abilities, but I am afraid that extempore preachers are not perhaps themselves aware how opposite such pleadings would be, with regard to consistency, were they recorded by pen and ink.

We spent the evening in conversations. Although Mr. Dennis is a man of decided abilities, I should be tired with the treat of his conversation too often repeated: it is like a rich-made dish which one may taste of now and then, but would not suit for one's daily food.

Joseph drove Prebendary Dennis after breakfast to his house in the upper part of Bath; with half a dozen of elder wine which he admired so much when warmed after supper, that I thought I could give him this satisfaction at a small expense. I hope he was satisfied with his visit, but I had rather another time that he should come to Camerton on a week-day rather than on a Sunday.

I sent my Journals from January to my brother Russell by Joseph, who is gone into Bath to have his hair curled for the Ball in the evening. No letter from Owen, who has now left me a fortnight. I was given to understand that he was to go immediately from Bath to Cambridge, but now I hear that he took Oxford in his way. I fear much that he is spending beyond his allowance, and keeping up expensive and improper acquaintance. I see no chance of getting any appointment for Joseph; I wish to my heart he could get some employment, as it is a sad state to be unemployed. Alas! I have but a gloomy prospect before me.

Joseph returned about the middle of the day, and brought with him the four volumes of my Journals which have just been bound, making ninety-seven, and one which my brother has in blank paper to insert my letters on antiquities will be numbered ninety-eight, so that the hundred will soon be completed. After all it is much ado about nothing, for what interest will my transactions be to anyone after I am gone hence?

I continued in my study after tea till prayer time reading one of Sir Walter Scott's works, for I could not settle my mind to anything serious.

My son and my daughter attended the Old Down Ball.

Sunday, February 14

I saw Wilcox, before Church, respecting whose child I had received a letter from Dr. Barlow of the Bath Hospital, and remitted three pounds for caution money, for the child's admission, who has the leprosy. After Church I walked to Tunley to call on Hicks, the Churchwarden, and get him to come in the evening to sign the certificate for the poor man Wilcox; it would, I knew, be of no use to send him a note, as he says he cannot read my writing; how decidedly reversed are all our clerical institutions: the Clergyman is now obliged to wait upon the Churchwarden to request he will condescend to attend the Church to do his duty.

The service in the evening was numerously attended, the congregation attracted by the Singers, who now muster a large band of various instruments. I do not like their mode of performing this part of the service near so well as that of the schoolgirls; but if it induces the people to come to Church, I will bear with them patiently. I am wedded to my charge for better and for worse, and I must be content.

I fear if we occasionally analyse our feelings, there is more of vanity in our regrets than we are inclined to allow: thinking we have abilities to shine in a higher sphere, and instruct a more enlightened assembly, pleased with the soft incense of flattery stealing in our ears: then perhaps all the daily disgusts we are in the habit of receiving would be no longer complained of, and we should be pleased with the people because they would be pleased with us.

After tea I composed the following lines in my study on the subject:

> How chilly howls the sullen blast,
>   How ceaseless falls the snow,
> Ah! see how Winter binds all fast
>   Nor suffers streams to flow.
>
> Vain selfish Mortal, why repine
>   Because a narrow sphere
> Thy arduous energies confine
>   Frost-bound and torpid here.
>
> If the Great Giver does not chuse
>   Thy talent to employ,
> 'Tis thine to keep it from abuse
>   Nor mix it with alloy.
>
> In storms, in sunshine, and in shower,
>   Thy will, it must be best;
> Great God! I own Thy Sovereign Power
>   Deep on my Soul impressed.

I write down my thoughts, in order to shew that I do feel as a Christian, but I trust not as a coward: time will shew all things: if I am to be called into action shortly, I must feed on strong food figuratively, after the manner of the pugilists, or in other words, buckle on the whole panoply of Religion: of one thing I am certain, I will keep my post till absolutely driven from thence, which is more than probable will be the case.

Wednesday, February 17

I feel very unwell, and think it is the bile which hangs about me. I strive to amuse myself by reading novels and have finished that of the "Black Dwarf" by Sir Walter Scott. I must be reduced to a sad state when I feel obliged to such nonsense for a pastime.

Sunday, February 21

There was no ringing for Church; when I spoke to White he was impudent, and when I told him I had given the ringers a Christmas-box on condition that they would ring the bells for Church regularly, and attend themselves, he said, if I minded so much about the money, they would give it me back again. White told me afterwards that the reason he had not rung for the last two Sundays was because he had gotten drunk Saturday night, and had too bad a headache in the morning to bear the sound of the bells.

These are sad reflections to occupy my mind on a Sunday; they quite destroy all the serenity which I at least ought to enjoy one day in seven.

Wednesday, February 24

I have felt so unwell lately I am resolved to see what horse exercise will do, and accordingly purchased a little pony for my own riding this morning, for twelve pounds. My son on old Jack, and my daughter on her mare, accompanied me for two hours on Clan Down, and whenever the weather is tolerably fair I mean to continue the exercise.

I forgot to say, notwithstanding my various occupations this week, I was enabled to read a novel called "The Young Reformers," shewing the tendency of the doctrines of the New School to demoralise Society. I am so much pleased with the plan of the work, and indeed with its execution, that I propose buying the book, as a standard addition to my Library, the only novel I believe I ever purchased or wished to.

Sunday, February 28

It rained so hard last night that the water streamed through the roof of the Chancel. I read Prayers in the morning, and preached in the evening on the Seventh Commandment, "Thou shalt not commit adultery," and having discoursed on the heinousness of the now too prevalent crime, as destructive to all social comfort, I enlarged on the government of the thoughts.

We walked to Meadyates to call on Frapnell; he seems going rapidly. A woman of the name of Barr was sitting with him, who also had been ill, that is, in a low nervous way for some time.

On my entering into conversation with the poor man, he began to say that he had been brought to that state by the enemy; that, in short, Witchcraft had been practised upon him and that the woman who was sitting with him had been also a fellow sufferer. He told me a man had called upon them and shewn them a paper which said that others had been bewitched like them, and that they would not get well again unless they could undo the charm. I said I had read that paper, and it was a pack of the greatest nonsense I had ever seen, and that the person who gave it him, and received money for thus deceiving him, might be very severely punished by the Magistrate.

I wished to make the poor man smile, and I succeeded by saying I had heard of a man who believed he was made of glass, and begged his friends not to come near him for fear of breaking him; another had fancied himself a tea-pot: that his own mind might be so weakened by illness, and his nerves so relaxed that he might not be able to shake off such absurd fancies: that nothing could harm him if he believed only in God, and if he said "Get thee behind me, Satan," when any evil ideas came into his mind he would sneak away like a coward.

Tuesday, March 16

There was a wedding by license this morning, the Miller of Cridlingcot and a woman from Wellow. This was to be kept very secret, and I perceived the reason, for the bride was already far advanced in the way which women sometimes are who love their lords.

This frequently occurs amongst the lower class of society, but I did not think those who moved a step higher adopted the fashion.

I had a letter from Owen by the post, thanking me for the £50 draft I sent to Cambridge to him, and promising to do everything he can to contribute to my comfort by attending to his studies. It has given me more satisfaction than any letter I have had from him for a long time, and I answered it with great pleasure.

Wednesday, March 17

I walked with Anna to visit Frapnell, and endeavoured as much as possible to do away with those unfortunate fancies he labours under about being bewitched, but I fear I shall not succeed. I explained to him the nature and full meaning of the Sacrament, which he never yet has received. He says he means to come to Church on Good Friday.

Tuesday, March 30

We walked to Paulton after dinner, and attended the funerals of five of the colliers who were killed by the breaking of the rope last week: two more are expected to die. There could not have been less than 1,000 people collected. Mr. Rees-Mogg, the Clergyman, shewed us to a seat in the gallery, where we were out of the crowd: not only the churchyard, but the street itself was thronged. Cabel, the engineer to the Old Pit, said he believed fifteen persons had lost their lives in that pit.

I was made very uncomfortable by Joseph's behaviour before I went to bed: it seems I cannot have any long cessation: if this excitement continues, I shall not be able to do anything for myself, but I hope I shall get rid of the weight on my heart, and I will get blooded to-morrow if it be not better.

Monday, April 5

It was a beautiful morning. I went to receive my composition for tythe of the farmers, this being the day appointed for their payment. Joseph had previously written out the memoranda of the payment of each individual, so that there was no difficulty or delay. There were sixteen sat down to dinner, and everything went off very well, as all the farmers were very civil, excepting John Rossiter, who has taken Keel's farm. Ever since I dismissed him from the office of church-warden for his very gross behaviour in conspiring with the clerk to lay a trap for me he has carefully avoided touching his hat to me when we meet, which is certainly of no consequence whatever to me; but when he has the meanness to eat at my expense and behave in that manner it is rather going too far. Poor Keel came to the Parsonage before I went to the meeting of the farmers to say he could not then pay his tythe, but was going to have a sale, and would then pay it. He could not help crying. I really feel for his situation; he has contrived to keep his head above water for ten or twelve years. The farmers paid in general pretty well.

The post brought me a letter from Owen from Cambridge; he says he shall return in June. I hope he will be inclined to make me more comfortable, but I always dread it when he and his brother are together.

Easter Sunday, April 11

I awoke early, and on opening my window-shutters was happy to perceive it was a fine morning. I felt very anxious about getting through the duty, as I heard there was to be a wedding, baptism, and churching, in addition to the services of the day. However, I never performed the service with greater ease to myself. The wedding was much of the same cast as the Camerton weddings in general are. I took the opportunity, after the ceremony was concluded and the parties were detained in the Church owing to a heavy shower of rain, of giving a word of advice to the young people. I asked them in the first place whether they had a house to live in. The girl answered, No; that they were for the present to live with her father (a wretched profligate fellow). I said they ought at least to have been as wise as the birds of the air, who made themselves nests before they brought up their young. The man, or rather the cad, said they could not wait for that. I said I was certain it never would answer for any newly-married couple to live with their parents; however, it was my advice that they should make their parents as comfortable as they could for the house-room they afforded, and get a place of their own as soon as they possibly could. I then asked them whether they ever came to Church, and I advised them for their own good as they were beginning life to attend to the duties of religion: that nothing would prosper unless they made God their friend. They must not think I advised them to attend their Church for my benefit, it was no such thing; as an individual it was no benefit to me whether my Church was properly attended or quite empty. I must and should perform the services, even if there were no other than my own family and the clerk present. Now, as the rain fell fast I could not better employ the interval than in endeavouring to say something which they might remember; of course, they would always recollect the day of their marriage, and I wished they would connect it with the advice I gave them: if they did not think of it in the springtime of life I knew they would do so on their deathbed. I therefore begged they would attend their Church, and listen to the instructions I gave.

It had not ceased raining when I returned to my parsonage, and it continued with but little intermission till Church-time, so that there was but a thin congregation. Mrs. Jarrett, however, was there with the two Misses Fry, and staid the Sacrament. There were only thirteen communicants. I spoke to Joseph after Church about his neglect of this important duty, and the necessity there was of preparing his mind. Just before Church in the evening I called at Dilly's to ask whether he wished to have the prayers of the congregation offered for his better state of health. I heard from his wife he was better. Mrs. Jarrett drives him out constantly in her four-wheeled chair, which may be of service to him more than any medicine. I was delivering the message at the door, as I feared there was not sufficient time for me to converse with him before Church. While thus speaking Mrs. Jarrett came out from the room where Dilly (her Butler) was, and begged me to walk in. I then mentioned the object of my coming, and thought it would be a good opportunity to explain my reasons, namely, that it was a benefit to those who were well to pray for the sick, as well as proper for the invalid himself; that in country parishes this ancient custom of praying for the sick was much neglected, but I felt anxious that it should be restored. Mrs. Jarrett said when she was ill she should have had it done herself, but thought the people would have said the rich may be prayed for, but the poor have nothing done for them. I did not exactly see the force of her ladyship's meaning, since it was as much open to the poor as to the rich. I said, if a few of the more respectable people in the parish requested the prayers of the congregation it would become general. Mrs. Jarrett then said she was sorry to see so few communicants; the greater part of them, she remarked, were her own servants—only three men, Smallcombe, her footman, and the clerk. I said she could not possibly regret it more than I did, and had mentioned it over and over again, and lent books and explained the subject to the people. She then began to ask me how I was, as she had heard I had not been well. I said that I had suffered with an oppression on my lungs, and cough, but it was better; indeed, that I felt very grateful that I was able to go through the service in the manner I had done. The lady then began to compliment me on my voice, saying it was as *clear as a bell*, and wondered that I had not been a *good singer*. Without exception this is the most extraordinary personage I have ever met with. On my wishing her a good morning, she held out her hand as if we had been the most cordial friends in existence. I promised Dilly's wife I would spend a quiet half-hour with her husband before I went to Bath on Tuesday.

During the evening service there was a christening; neither of the godfathers had any idea of the responses they were to make. The clerk put a book in the hands of one of the men, but he would not find the place, so I was obliged to answer for them, or rather put into their mouths what they were to say. During the christening the girl Somer, whose mother I had given a caution to about dressing in so improper a manner for one in her station, was close to me with two or three girls dressed in the same flashy manner, who looked everything but what they ought to be.

One of them began laughing when I read the service, and I reproved her; no churchwarden attends. I will speak to my servant Heal; I can insist on his attending Church at least once a day. Things are come to a sad state, and it proceeds from the total unconcern of the superior orders to religion; but this cement, once taken away from the building of the Constitution, it will soon sink under its own weight. This sentiment I wonder how often I have had occasion to repeat during my Journals, but indeed it is uppermost in my mind. After dinner I had some conversation with Joseph about the nature and full meaning of the Sacrament, and the danger those were in who lived unprepared.

Monday, April 12

When I rose this morning I felt quite overcome and exhausted through my exertions of yesterday. I may say that Sunday is to me a day of painful irritation; I strive to prevent feeling on the occasion but find it impossible.

I visited Dilly, and read prayers to him. I do not think, poor man, there is any possibility of his recovery. Curtis, the apothecary, says it is a liver complaint, and that he has been a hard drinker. I never knew this, and perhaps it is not true.

I was occupied in my study the whole evening. I had rather at any time have a good book for my companion than a titled fool, and I can far better please myself in my study than in a drawing-room of a Duke—if the company were so frivolous and uninformed as they generally are.

Tuesday, April 13

About the middle of the day I mounted my horse; Joseph accompanied me. We arrived at my Mother's a little before three. We did not dine at Burrard's till nearly six. On going there I met Warner, whose manner I thought constrained and, if I am any Lavaterist, deceitful. This man I never depended on; but that I should find my friend Burrard altered, which indeed he was, gave me a pang. I have known him ever since he was a child, and have always looked upon him as a steady friend.

I spent an uncomfortable evening, and what was worse walked to my Mother's in the night air, for Burrard's servants seemed so much engaged that I did not like to ask one of them to call me a hackney coach, or, as they term it in Bath, a fly!

Wednesday, April 14

I was much worried by these things when I returned to my Mother's, and to-day, after dinner, entered more warmly into a conversation which began in trifles than I ought to have done, and the irritation continued, for Joseph continued the conversation as we rode homewards, and told me that I had taken a pack of fancies into

my head without any foundation; although people did say queer
things of me it was true, and not without reason. When I asked him
to explain what he meant, and that it was the duty of a son to
acquaint his Father of whatever was said to his disadvantage, in
order to give him an opportunity of meeting his adversaries, he then
said I had no adversaries but in my own imagination: that I treated
my children like servants and not sons: that Mrs. Jarrett he thought
a very civil, good sort of woman, and that I was to blame in not
behaving in a more neighbourly manner to her. As I found that this
kind of conversation only contributed to excite the irritation I wished
to get rid of, I rode on, leaving Joseph behind!

Sunday, April 18

As I heard during the morning that the colliers had it in contemplation to strike work on account of their wages being about to be
lowered, I spoke to one of the colliers, and said if they had any just
ground for complaint how much better it would be to send two or
three whom they might depend on to state their grievances, and if
there was any foundation for them I had no doubt but they would
be attended to; but if they struck work it would only be taking
bread out of their own mouths and the mouths of their families.
The man said he thought with me on the subject, and that they
would get no good by opposition. It is now six or seven years ago
that there was a combination among the colliers, and the Camerton
people struck with the rest and did not work for several days. I then
went to them and gave them the same advice, which they would not
listen to then, but afterwards told me they wished they had done so,
as they were influenced by other people, having nothing really to
complain of themselves.

I called at the Manor House. Mrs. Jarrett entered into a long
account of the intended opposition of the colliers to their employers.
She said it was only for the matter of about £80 that they made all
this fuss, for it would not be more if the person who rose the steam
was continued instead of dispensed with, and that this was the reason
they felt dissatisfied; that the Proprietors of the Works knew nothing
about the management of them themselves; that she had desired that
things might go on as heretofore till the meeting of the Coal Proprietors, and would pay out of her own pocket the wages of the
steam man. I had never understood that there had been any dispute
about the steam man, but only heard they objected to a diminution

of their wages. What authority Mrs. Jarrett had to interfere with the management of the works is another question. She has only a free share; but this politic lady has one thing which gives her the fullest power over the men, and which, if the Proprietors ever come to open contest with her, they find to their cost, renders her power absolute. She has authority over the residences of all the colliers, who are only weekly tenants, and may be dismissed ad libitum.

Monday, April 19

I walked towards the middle of the day into the village, as I understood that the colliers had struck work, not on account of the steam man being taken away, but because some of them were lowered 3*s.* a week in their pay, which they said they could not afford, as most of them had to pay £5 or guineas for the hire of their houses, and sometimes they did not work above four days in the week. I said I was sure if this was properly represented to the Proprietors by two or three of the men, and if on examination they found it true, they would not persevere in the measure; that it was not their interest to have the men work for sums on which they could not live; that I should recommend their deputing three of the most intelligent men to see the Proprietors before they came on Wednesday to Camerton. It would not do to meet them, as I heard them say, in a full body, for that would have a mutinous appearance, and nothing was ever got by that. The men were very civil, for I spoke to no less than three sets of them to this effect, but they said that it would be difficult to find any to go on the mission, as the masters had determined, they said, to turn the people out who should venture to speak to them on anything of the kind, and would first be dismissed from their works. I know there are some artful, ill-disposed fellows among the colliers, but there are also others who will suffer beyond bearing if the three shillings a week are taken from their scanty pay.

I was occupied in my study the whole evening in writing some lines on the state of the times. Should they be read fifty years hence, they will shew at least that I was fully aware of the storm which was coming. The King's health, if it should terminate fatally, will perhaps accelerate the ruin. God's will be done.

Tuesday, May 11

My Mother arrived at the Parsonage a little after ten, and I was engaged with her nearly the whole morning. We walked before dinner to the Church. I have not seen my Mother looking better, or apparently so well able to walk and exert herself for years. She is now 77, and may perhaps *outlive me*, who this day number 58 years. I feel certain indications which warn me not to expect a long life, and I am sure I do not desire it. We passed a pleasant day, and my family left me after tea to return to Bath, when I went into my study and wrote up by Journal till the present time. If I live till September I shall have held this Rectory 30 years. Servus indignus servorum; but perhaps when I am gone some of my parishioners may wish I had stayed a little longer with them.

Saturday, June 5

Having a few days before seen Mrs. Jarrett's Butler looking wretchedly [ill], I went immediately to Dilly's as I heard the poor fellow was dying! Mrs. Jarrett and Miss Fry were with him, fanning his face and giving him salts to smell to. Mrs. Jarrett said she had been with him nearly the whole day. I read to him the more important prayers appointed for the Visitation of the Sick, and wished to converse with him a little, but he complained so much of exhaustion that I desisted.

Monday, June 7

I rose soon after six. I then went to enquire after Mrs. Dilly, having heard that her husband quitted this world, I hope for a better, early this morning. The poor woman is quite stupefied by the shock, and will not quit the body for an instant. I perceived that I could be of no assistance.

Tuesday, June 15

The post brought me a letter from the kind-hearted Bishop, saying as he had heard nothing from Lord Hill,[1] he had called again upon Greenwood, and he thought something might be done for Joseph through Lord Fitzroy Somerset.[2]

The funeral of poor Dilly took place about the middle of the day. Mrs. Jarrett sent to say she should be glad to see me at her house previous to the commencement of the service. I walked thither. Stephen Jarrett came to meet me in the hall, and extended his hand with a shew of great cordiality; I never retain hostile feelings beyond

[1] Commander-in-Chief.
[2] Afterwards Lord Raglan.

the excitement of the moment, and immediately gave him mine, and was also received in the same way by Mr. John Jarrett. There is a pleasing consciousness in having acted rightly which is gratified by such a tribute, though it comes late. How much more comfortable would Mrs. Jarrett have been at Camerton had she not suffered herself to be deceived, and instead of increasing her darling authority and adding to her power by opposing the clergyman she would have done far better to ensure it by making him her friend.

Some conversation was entered into respecting the building of a new mansion. I ventured to repeat an opinion I before gave, that at the expense of £6,000 and the old material the same might be done, and there would not be any occasion to employ a London architect. Notwithstanding all this talk about it, I still have my doubts whether any such thing is in actual contemplation. Mrs. Jarrett said it was impossible to live in the old house; I say with Burchell, "Fudge."

Saturday, June 19

After dinner we walked to the canal, my sons wishing to sail in the boat, as the wind blew fresh; they amused themselves awhile. As Anna and myself were returning home by Colliers Row, a stone was thrown at me from the end house, where Goold lives; it could have been no other, as the stone came from that direction. There is really not a day passes over my head but I meet with some fresh insult.

Sunday, June 27

I had to marry a couple at half-past eight; the bride was as round as a barrel, and according to custom, I suppose there will be a christening in the course of the honeymoon. On my return from the wedding, Mrs. Jarrett's footman brought me her paper, mentioning the death of the King; it seems he departed on Saturday morning; if the storm was so violent at the time of his death as it was here in the evening, the oppression of the atmosphere might have accelerated his transition.

Sunday, July 4

A letter came from the Bishop, and enclosing a letter from Lord Hill in reply to his, wherein he says he has established as a rule not to admit any youths more than can be helped into the Army above the age of nineteen, so all hope from that quarter fails: still under present circumstances *it may be for the best*: for if Joseph were to abuse his superior officers in the manner he has done his Father, he would be called to a court martial, and turned out with disgrace! Time, I hope, will work a change in his conduct; indeed, it is my most anxious wish that he should get some employment from home, but I know not how to procure any for him; and unless he thoroughly establishes his principles ere he launches into life, he cannot succeed in any profession.

Thursday, July 15

Mrs. Jarrett sent me twenty-four volumes of books of light reading, but they are sad, mawkish stuff.

We had scarcely finished dinner when I heard a peal from the Church strike out. This rather surprised me, as no one had asked for the key of the Church, and I had told the ringers they should not have it without my leave, since a pack of collier lads got together to ring only for the sake of drinking afterwards. On going to the Church, they said they rang for the King and had no occasion to ask my leave: that other Churches were ringing and they did not see why they should not do as the rest did. I said that if they had asked me properly for the key to toll for the King, who was to be buried this evening, I should have let them have it; but they had got it without my leave. They said it was false, they had not gotten the key; they found the Church open and had gone in.

My sons came from Bath after tea, and say that the shops were shut up, and the bells tolling: I also heard some bells tolling, I believe Farmborough or Priston, but I heard no such peal ringing as the worthies of Camerton chose to exhibit in honour of our deceased Sovereign who was, they said, a very good sort of man and did all he could for poor people, and it became poor men to shew all honour to him: that notwithstanding I had said I did not care for the King, *they did care!* Thus was the memory of the late King attempted to be honoured and his worth recorded by the Camerton Colliers.

These memoranda will shew what was the situation of a Clergyman in the midst of his parishioners in the year 1830. I often think, notwithstanding my bodily ailments, etc., that I shall not die on a bed of sickness, but taken off by some act of violence!

Saturday, July 17

I wrote the following lines in the evening on the death of George IV. Comparisons are odious, but he never was nor will be regretted by reasonable men, as was his father, whom all adored, whom all agreed in esteeming him an honest man.

> *In obitum altissimi*
> *Olim principis,*
> *Sed nunc humillimi.*

GEORGII QUARTI

When George the Third was on his bier
Britannia shed a filial tear;
When George the Fourth lay lately dead
We did not see one tear she shed;
Perhaps she wip't it ere it fell.
And if she did it was as well.
But she might weep for common weal,
And for that wound no time can heal,
That festering wound which feeds her pain,
And sings his dirge this doleful strain.

I see by the papers that all the world were interested, not only in the funeral but in the particular description of it. As people decline in manly sentiment and in simplicity, an insatiable curiosity is increased and encouraged, and it must be fed by offal. The papers are filled even to nausea with minute particulars of rapes, adulteries, intrigues of actresses, the dialogues between hardened culprits and would-be witty magistrates. Ideas are communicated through the medium of our nasty newspapers throughout the kingdom, with which the purer minds of their grandmothers were wholly unacquainted, but according to the *march of intellect* they were but ill-acquainted with, or in other words had no knowledge of, the world. This is the picture of the English people; alas! if they needed no other witness against their manners and conversation their own newspapers would condemn them. If such nastiness was not grateful to the palate of my countrymen, it would cease to be administered in such copious doses.

Sunday, July 18

I prepared a sermon on the Gospel for the day, "Except your righteousness exceed the righteousness of the Scribes and Pharisees." There were very few at Church in the morning, as it rained hard. Mrs. Dilly told me yesterday she had received a summons to go immediately to Mrs. Jarrett, who is staying at her son's near Salisbury, in order to attend her, as she is *dangerously ill*, and that Mrs. Gooch was gone to her mother. If she is really ill I am really sorry for her, and I sincerely hope her illness will conduce to her amendment, and that she will, if she be permitted to live longer on earth, take a new course, for artful and deceitful ways cannot be pleasing in the sight of that Being Who knoweth everything.

How little do we know what an instant may bring forth? I had written thus far in my study after tea, and felt that I did wrong to indulge such a strain of ideas, for God brings about His purposes. The person I thought, and perhaps unjustly suspected, to do me disservice was at that time *dead*! A note from Mr. John Jarrett who is just arrived at Camerton informed me that his Mother died this morning at 9 o'clock at his house near Salisbury, and he was come on business—I suppose respecting the funeral, etc., etc. Why do we feel anxious about second causes? God is all in all; the agency of secondary persons ought never to have had any weight on my mind. Great God forgive me; I will strive to be more resigned, and wait what is intended for me; if I am surrounded with difficulties and dangers, yet Thou canst in an instant deliver me. I wrote to Mr. Jarrett saying if he thought my being with him could be of the least comfort I would either come this evening or to-morrow morning. Mrs. Dilly, who came back with Mr. Jarrett, says her mistress died without any pain, from exhaustion.

Monday, July 19

I called on Mr. Jarrett after breakfast, and tendered my services. He said he was well aware of my sincerity, and knew how to appreciate it; that he did not know whether his Mother was to be buried at Camerton till he had seen the Will; that although differences had occurred between others and myself it should be his just wish and endeavour to guard against them. I said that I never had any object in view but the welfare of my parishioners, therefore I could with confidence look forward to his co-operation with me. He seemed really to speak from the heart, and if he comes to reside among us, as I hope he will, he may both see and act for himself, and he will ever find me ready to render every assistance in my power.

I had a visit from the poor dumb Collier, Clarke. The poor fellow lost his wife in childbed this morning, and I fear she was not properly

taken care of. The man seems the picture of misery; indeed, to him
it is a wreck. He was induced, however, to make a meal, and seemed
recruited by it.

I got a letter from John Jarrett saying he had fixed Tuesday, half-
past two, for the interment of his Mother, who is to be brought out
of Wiltshire. The poor dumb woman will be buried in the evening
of the same day. Via una cogimur.

How have all my unpleasant feelings against this once despotic
Lady of the Manor subsided! I forget all that gave me pain, and now
only think of her good qualities and charitable deeds; may they be
her advocates and plead for her before the throne of mercy. Charity
covereth a multitude of sins.

We walked after prayers to the house of the dumb woman who
died in childbed. Mrs. Bush, her neighbour, says no one was with
her at the time of her delivery, and that the child was born, and not
being properly taken care of she bled to death. Poor Mrs. Jarrett!
nearly the last conversation I had with her was endeavouring to make
an arrangement by subscription to have a medical person instead of
an ignorant female to attend them in difficult cases.

This being the day for Mrs. Jarrett's funeral, I went to the Manor
House at two o'clock and was shewn into the parlour where Mr.
Fry, her lawyer, was sitting. He began to lament the loss he had
sustained, in common with the rest of the dependants on the deceased,
and I doubt not he spoke with sincerity, for she was a very steady
friend to himself in particular. The corpse was brought to the Manor
House from Warminster, and placed in the hall, where all the servants
assembled round it, and while they were thus engaged in lamenting
their mistress poor old Mrs. Anne Stephens, the aunt of the deceased,
arrived from Bath. She is upwards of 85 and, I understand, was much
affected. About three Mr. Gooch and Mr. Stephen Jarrett coming
into the parlour, I shook hands very cordially; Stephen was in
tears, and I really felt for them all as though they had been my
relations. How trifling are all our little heartburnings and differences when we see the cause which excited them humbled in the dust,
and are well assured we shall shortly ourselves be tenants of the

grave. I felt much during the service, but was able to read it with composure. All the farmers attended, as did Mrs. Gooch, Mrs. John Jarrett, Mrs. Anne Stephens, and all the female servants. The body was interred in the vault, or rather at the bottom of the stone steps leading to it, as there was no room beyond, and the Carew vault had been walled up. I suppose there could not have been less than 300 people assembled in the churchyard, and the Church was crowded to excess. I did not go to the Manor House after the ceremony, but took leave of the family before they left the pew. I strolled about the premises in the evening, and was not sorry to retire to rest immediately after the prayers.

The poor dumb woman, I forgot to say, was interred between eight and nine o'clock, and the child of which she was delivered named, as they thought it would die.

Sunday, August 1

I rose before six to finish my sermon, or rather correct what I have written on the death of Mrs. Jarrett. The Church, as I expected, was crowded to excess and the people were very attentive, so that not a whisper was heard among them. I hope what I said, which was meant for the best, will produce some good effect on the living; the *dead*, whom the large congregation was designed to honour, cannot be profited.

Monday, August 2

I forgot to mention that the day after the funeral Mr. John Jarrett sent me enclosed in a polite note £15 as a remuneration for my services. I wrote in reply saying that it was far beyond what I had any expectation of, neither had I wished for any such. This unexpectedly procured money I gave to my children, £10 to Owen to pay for his illness to Norman, etc., etc., and £5 between Joseph and Anna.

Joseph has good natural talents for drawing, which he might cultivate with success if he chose; I would readily pay for his learning to paint in oils hereafter of Benjamin Barker, but this profession of an artist is infra dig., and our gaily dressed ensigns and lieutenants look down on all as beneath their notice who have not the permission to be shot through the head as they have, which permission is to be purchased at an extravagant rate by their unfortunate fathers and relatives.

1830

About the middle of the day, a footman of the late Mrs. Jarrett's called at the Parsonage and said he had ill news to tell me; that some people had broken into the Church and had stolen all the black cloth with which the pews and the pulpit were hung on account of Mrs. Jarrett's funeral; every article of black cloth is stripped from the three pews, the reading desk, and the pulpit to the value of thirty or forty pounds. I said I was sorry to hear anyone could be so wicked as to commit sacrilege of this kind. I would give half-a-guinea to anyone who would trace the fact to the offender.

The papers retail the Insurrection in France, and the impunity which attends it, and may excite much disturbance in Spain, Germany, Prussia, and perhaps Russia. Kings are out of fashion, and all authority is now kicked against, unless it proceeds from the People. What I have seen of the People does not impress me with high ideas either of their principles or their practice. I shall not change; I am too old to bend, so if they strain me I must break.

As we purposed to reach Bristol, being under the escort of Mr. Richardson who had business there in the evening, and is acquainted with every part of this vast and dirty city, I did not wish to interfere as to our station for the night, but only requested we should take up with cleanly quarters if possible. The first inn we asked to be accommodated at was without success, as we had the mortification to find the morrow was the first day of Bristol Fair. At the second inn we stopped, they agreed to give us beds, but alas! I had reason to regret that which fell to my share, as it was so abundant in vermin I could not close my eyes till their supper was concluded; and as soon as it was properly light I was glad to leave my bed and wash off as much as possible the pollutions to which I had been subject during the night.

I was occupied in the evening preparing my sermons. I purpose preaching on the duty of returning thanks to God after any deliverance from danger, and I hope this will become more general; indeed, I shall have a good opportunity, as the child I sent to the hospital of the name of Willcox is returned in a good state of health, having been cleansed of the leprosy, and a notice is sent of thanksgiving.

Monday, September 6

We had nearly done breakfast when a servant of the Bishop's arrived at the Parsonage, saying his Master would soon be with us to breakfast and with a party of ladies; and by nine he arrived with the three Miss Laws and their brother, the family of the late Lord Ellenborough. The two elder ladies seem to be well-informed women and have made proper observations during their travels abroad. The youngest is very handsome; and so I think Mr. Law would generally be considered, as is his brother the present Lord Ellenborough.

I have engaged to visit the Bishop at Weston-super-Mare.

Tuesday, September 7

I received by the post to-day a letter from the Bishop which ought to have arrived yesterday, but that would have been too late to announce his intended visit; he is indeed a kind-hearted man, and if he had only been a brother Clergyman residing in the neighbourhood, it would have given me pleasure always to have received him; but as a superior from whom I have received so many proofs of kindness and hospitality, it is a delight to me to make any returns in my power.

I feel every kind attention from my superiors in rank: I accept their attentions with gratitude. I ask no pre-eminence, I seek no honours: ambition and pride, if ever I entertained such guests, they have long since deserted me. I am more and more inclined to anchor my frail and more than half-decayed bark in this its anchoring place, and lay its timbers where it is in port. How my log-book of life lengthens as I approach nearer the termination of my Voyage; I get more and more weary of common topics, yet I am only high-minded in one particular, which is to court the converse of purer spirits, and to endeavour to avoid everything which will estrange my mind from such communion when I hold converse with my own heart as I do now in my chamber and am still.

Wednesday, September 8

There was a wedding in the morning, and as it appeared to be one comme il faut I gave the bride the fees to buy her some tea-things.

Soon after it was concluded I left the Parsonage with my son and daughter on a visit to Mr. Richardson at Farleigh Hungerford. In our way we stopped at a nursery garden, and I ordered some apple and peach trees for my garden, and a particular kind of pea called the Tamarind Pea, which is so productive that the crop continues to return its produce the whole summer.

Monday, September 20

After dinner some conversation took place about a trifle, between my daughter and myself; her brother Owen took her part and it ended in just such a scene as has been before acted: everything that could be said or done to irritate me my son employed, and unfortunately succeeded; but I told him as I had been obliged to separate from his brother on that account, so I should from him. He said he would readily leave me if I would give him the money to take his degree, but if I did not he would continue in my house, as he had a right to do, and if I used any force to expel him he would use force to force, and he broke one of the parlour chairs as a foretaste of what I was to expect! I said that his conduct had shewn him so complete and so callous a villain that when he left my roof I should feel relieved of a heavy load. "You are a damned liar to call me a villain," he replied. "Who cares for such a Father? I despise you from my heart."

Doubtful of my ability to restrain tears if this scene continued, I told my son I would let him have £300, but I should expect an acknowledgment for this as well as for the other I had advanced on this condition. He said he would do so and should be glad to quit my house, and never see my face again. He and his sister chose to go to bed before Prayers. I read to the servants, and with a heavy heart retired to bed but not to rest.

No one, excepting my brother who transcribes this, will read the sad recital. When I am dead and fifty years have passed over my grave, and when this base and ungrateful son has finished his career, someone who peruses my Journals will read this as they would a novel, and think the recital has been heightened through feelings wounded almost to a pitch of madness, but this is not the case. The feeling I experience is not revenge, it is sorrow: let me not bear it long, O God: forgive him, change his mind, punish him by those chastisements which may conduce to his reformation. Oh! my God! support my mind on this trying occasion. . . .

I am astonished to see how much I have written, but I know not what I write. . . . Oh, let me be tranquil. . . . I am not angry, I feel too much. I can bear all the malignant world can say or do, but my sons and my daughter, those I have fostered and loved: let my sufferings tend to my future patience, let me submit and kiss the rod! I can do no more.

Tuesday, September 21

I left Owen and his sister to breakfast in the parlour, and had some tea sent up into my study: I could not eat anything the whole day and went to bed early.

Wednesday, September 22

When I was in the greatest distress imaginable yesterday, Owen was amusing himself with his lathe, and my daughter in her usual occupations. I attribute a great deal of the misery I experience to sending my sons to Winchester College, where they were educated. During the time of their abode there the boys were two or three times in a state of rebellion against their masters, and brought the same feelings home with them against their parent whenever he ventured to say anything or do anything which seemed to trench on their natural liberty. Joseph when at Sandhurst, after leaving Winchester, was put into the black hole, the severest punishment they have for insolence and disobedience, and Colonel Butler afterwards wrote in such strong terms I perceived there was no chance of his getting a Commission from thence, and so after the expenditure of £400 for two years, I took him away; and now he is an idler with little chance of getting employment. Owen is equally idle. And what is my daughter bringing upon herself by her ungrateful conduct? She has identified herself in the rebellion of her brothers against their Father: I never saw so great an obstinacy in anyone as in this deluded girl. She was perfectly mistress of my house, and all the money went through her hands; she had a horse to ride, and a carriage to drive in: she was everywhere received as the mistress of my house and was as independent as if she had been so. She is now going to my Mother, where she will in fact be little better than what is called a companion to an old lady. Alas! these are indeed sad times: the domestic fireside will be no longer known, or its comforts experienced: I shall be left alone through the dreary winter without a single person whom I can speak to: and why? because after all I have done for my children they have no affection for me: but I shall not be alone; I shall have books to occupy my time: God will be with me.

My daughter came before dinner and said she was very sorry for the uneasiness she had given me, and hoped I would pass it over; and that with respect to Owen, as the dispute began with her she hoped I would not think of it any more.

I said I knew my infirmity, and all I could do was to keep out of the way of those who would purposely provoke me; and was it not their duty to put up with a few angry words spoken in the heat of the moment: that when I spoke to my children about anything, let the fault be ever so trivial, they always answered me in such a manner as to make me angry. If Owen had anything to say in extenuation of such conduct, or to promise that it should not be repeated, I was ready to listen to him, and to forgive him as I had done her.

I desired Anna that she would tell her brother I wished to see him for a few minutes in my study.

On his coming into the room I perceived no very promising omen from his countenance that there would be an accommodation.

I said, "I have received a note from Mr. Hoare saying the £300 is paid into their hands, therefore there is no obstacle to your leaving this house according to the conditions: that the money be applied for the purpose of taking your degree: it will be the last sum you will receive during my life. When I am dead you will be entitled to an equal share with your brother and sister. I do not, cannot look unmoved at your present situation; you have risen in open rebellion against your Father. Had you, instead of irritating, endeavoured to conciliate, would these epithets, with which you are so grievously offended, have been applied to you?"

He said he never would condescend to soothe anyone, or to bend to any; that this was not his disposition, and he could not help that more than I could help being angry. I said did he reckon Duty nothing, Religion nothing: that a mild answer turneth away wrath: had this ever been tried? Ought he not, as my son, to bear with me for a few minutes and to endeavour by a little conciliation to prevent my saying what my own mind could not approve of; words hastily employed, although his own conscience must tell him not without some foundation for the application. When I was angry I knew I was in fault; if I could overcome this feeling, no exertion should be spared.

These were the principal arguments I used in my conversation, which lasted nearly an hour. My son was melted and promised that he would use his utmost endeavour to make me comfortable.

I went down to dinner in the parlour with Owen and Anna, and to bed before the evening shut in.

Friday, September 24

Mrs. Trew, the schoolmistress whom I called upon, complained to me of the conduct of the children, saying they behaved so badly she did not know what to do with them, and begged I would give them a public reproof. I hear sad accounts of some of the girls who were educated at the school, who are become common prostitutes: as soon as they go to Bath they are spoiled.

Saturday, September 25

As Owen wishes to have a place for his lathe which is now in the greenhouse, I have promised to fit him up a place, and it shall be done directly; any pursuit which will occupy his attention and divert his mind I will make a point of encouraging. His sister has many pursuits: drawing, music, gardening, and rearing poultry, besides working and attending to the concerns of the family. I have gotten some more geranium plants so that her greenhouse may be filled this winter.

Sunday, September 26

I spoke to the school children according to the request of the Schoolmistress, and after Church I repeated my admonition. Young Harris, who is now a mason, behaved so badly in Church I was obliged to speak to him, and on leaving the Church, I saw written upon the wall of the Church porch the same obscenity that this boy once wrote on the door of my orchard, so I am inclined to think the hardened wretch did it because I reproved him for his misbehaviour. It were better far that the lower orders knew nothing about writing if they produce such fruits as these.

I got a very kind and affectionate letter from my Mother in reply to that I sent her when my children had thoughts of leaving my house. Poor woman! she has a most feeling heart. What a state is Society arrived at: had I known what was about to take place I would have sent my sons as apprentices to some honest occupation wherein they might have procured their bread, instead of squandering hundreds to enable them to associate at college with unprincipled rakes, free thinkers, and gamesters, and return home to abuse their Father, and pine in secret because the hour of his dissolution is protracted.

Tuesday, September 28

I was engaged to visit the Bishop at Weston-super-Mare this day; Owen refused to accompany me. I left home at ten o'clock and drove through Cheddar Cliffs, as I needed some change of scene to change my ideas. I wrote to Owen from thence, as I found I had brought the key of the wine cellar with me, and knew he would be displeased at the privation, and construe it into a premeditated neglect. I desired he would procure some wine from Bath or the vicinity. My horse I baited at the little inn at Cheddar. Having quitted Cheddar in a heavy storm of rain, and driven through Axbridge Cross, I fell in with a troop of gypsies who had a train of donkies carrying their baggage before them; in an instant the wheels of a carriage sounded in my rear, and having the umbrella over my head held by the right hand, and the reins in the left, I was not so active in getting out of the way as I might have been: indeed, the postillion who drove the horses had himself taken the middle of the road to avoid the donkies, and was close behind me ere I perceived him, and not being able to hold them in, ran against the hind wheel of my light phaeton and overset it with a crash! sending me headlong into the middle of the road, where I lay for an instant on my back, quite stunned.

On recovering my legs the first feeling was that of anger against the awkward fellow who had occasioned my degradation, but lo and behold! on looking into the carriage I found it was the Bishop of Bath and Wells.

After congratulations and explanations he took me into his carriage to Weston-super-Mare; my own having been refitted by an active gypsy man, his servant drove it to the end of the journey, so out of evil came good. On arriving at his lodgings, Claremont Lodge, close to the sea, I had some refreshing tea and was not sorry to go early to bed.

Wednesday, September 29

Mr. Barlow, the Rector of Weston, dined with us, and we had some interesting conversation in the evening. As the moon was in

her full glory, we accompanied him along the beach part of the way
to his parsonage.

As the morning was everything which could be desired in respect
to clearness for the prospect we determined to ascend to the Camp
on the summit of Brent Knoll.

I cannot omit a circumstance which occurred when I was walking
through the village of South Brent which was gratifying to my feelings. The Bishop had been enquiring of a couple of old men respecting
the present Curate of the Parish, and whether the Church was well
attended, etc., etc. After he had done, I asked whether they remembered a curate of the name of Skinner some thirty years ago. They
both replied in the affirmative, and said they never had one they liked
so well when with them, and felt so much for when he went away:
that they had talked of him and his kindness to the poor. When I
made myself known to them, they both shook me by the hand, and
one of them said he hoped I should preach to them next Sunday as
he wished to hear me again before he died.

This was not acting in the men, for they did not know me or the
Bishop in the first instance, but entered into conversation with us as
strangers passing through the parish, for the Bishop had left his
carriage at the Vicarage.

After all the bitter almonds I am constrained to swallow, a sweet
nut now and then is grateful.

We drove without stopping back to Weston-super-Mare.

I understand that Mr. Jarrett has Mr. and Lady Elizabeth Repton
staying with him; the latter is daughter to the worthy Earl of Eldon;
her husband is, I believe, the celebrated layer-out of grounds whose
taste is so much consulted by the great. Perhaps Mr. Jarrett means
to consult him respecting the alterations he is about to make at
Camerton.

I paid my respect to Mr. Jarrett and Mr. Repton, and invited the
party to dine with us on Monday; the Parishes are to meet them, as
are Mr. Hammond and his lady, and Mr. Trelawney Collins.

Mr. Jarrett introduced Mr. Repton to me; he seems a gentlemanly personage. I suppose it will soon be known whether Mr. Jarrett is to build a new house.

Friday, October 29

We drove to Timsbury to dine with the Parishes and met a large party: we had music after Tea. Mrs. Parish read Prayers to her household before we retired to rest. I am very glad to see this adopted by the laity.

Monday, November 1

I spent a restless night, the bile affected my bowels and kept me awake: it is unfortunate that we have company to dinner. I have just given directions for some toast and water to be made and put in a small decanter near me to take it at dinner instead of white wine. I think I can carry off this harmless ruse.

Mr. and Mrs. Hammond, Captain and Mrs. Parish, Mr. and Lady Elizabeth Repton, Mrs. Brooks, Mr. and Mrs. Jarrett, Mr. Trelawney Collins, and Mr. Wickham formed our dinner party.

To prepare an entertainment for so many with our small accommodations, we were obliged to enlarge our table by another flap, which occasioned for our sending for the Carpenter. Poor Anna was destined to feel many mortifications, for the pastry and good things she had prepared were burnt by the inattention of the cook, for she, I hear, did everything to shew her malevolence at a time when it might be most felt. We were obliged to have servants from the Jarretts' to wait (three men), to borrow some of their silver forks and spoons; we were moreover indebted to them for a hare and pheasant and grapes for the dessert, and also to their housekeeper supplying the deficiency in the pastry. How much better is it to keep a moderate scale instead of aping those other than our set. The Clergy, I think, ought to agree among themselves to break through this sad thraldom; but they will not do this, for Hammond and Collins, I daresay, when we dine with them, will give a greater set-out than we gave. We certainly lose our consequence instead of increasing it by the imitation of the more wealthy in these respects.

After all this, however, we found our Company very pleasant, and disposed themselves to be pleased with our efforts; still they would perhaps have been equally pleased to have taken according to our usual scale of entertainment. O imitatores, servum pecus is a good old adage: those who have something of their own need not stoop to become imitators; but such is now the fashion of the times: hence it is that so little originality is to be seen in Society. We are all become imitators, not only in clothes but in manners and conversation; there is a sameness throughout, that one dinner party is only the counterpart of another.

The evening was spent in looking over the coal fossils, and Shakespere prints by Boydell. Lady Elizabeth Repton seems to inherit her Father's strong sense, if one may judge from casual remarks. Mr. Repton, her husband, is a pleasing, gentlemanly man. I could not eat anything at dinner, and as soon as the party were gone went immediately to bed.

Monday, December 13

While writing in my study I saw numbers of men, at least fifty, cross the Park in front of my study window to go down to the pits at Camerton. I had learnt that the colliers meant to make a rise. Soon after, I saw this mob proceeding to our pits. I then walked to Clan Down, having heard that there had been a mob of the colliers assembled there yesterday, and that the Riot Act was read by Mr. James, accompanied by other magistrates; indeed, they told me that some of the Camerton people had joined them, and meant to be there again to-day.

I saw all was quiet on the Down, and the Steam Engine working, as I approach the pit. I walked thither, and found that the Radstock Rioters, for I can call them by no other name, had gone on to Paulton. The people at the pit said they were well satisfied with their wages, but that these fellows from Radstock had ordered them to stop work. I counselled them against cutting the ropes of the pits and the damaging of machinery, etc., and advised them to return to their duty: that there were barges then waiting for their loads. The men said they would load the barges, and should not stop work: that they had nothing to complain of, only that they thought the small coal landed ought to be paid for as well as the large coal, since they procured one as well as the other. I said that this ought to be a consideration with their masters: if they considered the demand just, I made no doubt they would allow it: it were far better not to be moved by the multitude to do evil, but if they had any just complaints to petition their employers to remove them, but never attempt to drive them by force to comply with their demands, for whatever was extorted by compulsion would never be lasting: that there was no distress among them was sufficiently proved by the increased number of public houses: if the men were in want of food, they could not support the trade of *eleven* public houses, instead of *three*: if they could find money to spend in the numerous Ale Houses, and to buy of all the pedlars and hucksters who were daily coming into the Parish, they could not complain of distress.

Friday, December 31

N.B.—I have looked over the memoranda of some of the last years of my life, but I have never seen the prospect so gloomy as it is at present. I only pray for strength to perform the last concluding scene of my life with decency, and prove at least I have not myself been affected by the degenerate practice of the times.

I am strongly assailed both at home and abroad, for my children will not listen to reproof, and where it fails to produce a good effect it hardens the heart, and makes it worse rather than better. . . . Everything seems tottering around me!

1831

THE beginning of a New Year makes a pause between measured and
numbered strides we each of us take towards the grave; nearly 59
of these strides have I been permitted to take from my cradle; how
many more remain to be taken to the end of my pilgrimage that Being
alone can determine Who gave me existence. There is nothing in this
world which can induce me to ask for a protracted course; as soon
as the period of my probation be complete, and my warfare be
accomplished, I am prepared to go hence, and shall not for a moment
regret what I leave behind me.

I was occupied in arranging the drawings for my Journals. It gives
me some pleasure to perceive the energies of my mind do not decay,
and that I am able to perform as much, nay even more, than I could
do in the prime of life.

I am ready to continue on my station as long as my Great Com-
mander orders me to do so. At the commencement of a New Year,
I make this introduction to my Journal under a kind of presentiment
I shall not live to complete another annual register.

I read prayers in the morning to a thin congregation: the cold
weather seems to make devotion cold; I cannot increase the warmth,
although I feel it myself and it consumes me.

I walked with Anna to Braysdown, and heard a sad account of old
Swift and his wife. On visiting their cottage a most distressing scene
presented itself; never have I seen a greater picture of misery. Our
Overseer has not been near them. The woman is the granddaughter
of a clergyman, is upwards of 80; the husband I believe is older; they
have no one to assist them, both being so infirm they cannot assist
themselves. They lived as servants to that wretched miser and magistrate, Purnell of Woodborough, who had the villainy last Easter to
blame the parish officers for allowing these old people 2s. 6d. each,

and desired them to take off 1s. from their allowance, when he himself had, by advancing sums for their support, bought the house they dwell in, and which through his permission they had erected on the waste adjoining his estate.

If there is any crime which calls upon the Almighty for His vengeance it is surely this of oppressing the poor. I left half-a-crown with the poor man in order that a proper person should be paid to attend upon his wife, who is at times delirious, and I procured a prayer-book from a neighbouring house and read to the old woman, and afterwards returned home with my daughter. These are sad scenes for young people just entering life to witness, but it is necessary they should witness the sufferings of others, for God alone knows what they will be exposed to themselves.

Tuesday, January 25

I wrote the annexed letter to Mr. Purnell, the magistrate. I thought it my duty to speak to him in strong terms. Here is a copy of the letter as taken by my daughter:

> "CAMERTON PARSONAGE,
> "*January* 25, 1831.

"SIR,—

"As the Minister of this Parish I have a right to ask whether you can reconcile it to your conscience that your old servant, Swift, and his wife, who have served you and your relatives at Woodborough for nearly 50 years, should die destitute of every comfort, being in more absolute want than any paupers in the place? I could scarcely believe my ears last Easter Vestry, when you desired the parish pay of 5s. a week (for two people each more than 80 years of age) should be lowered. For your own sake before you die, Sir, I hope you will think and act differently.

"JOHN SKINNER."

Wednesday, February 23

There was a wedding this morning after the Camerton mode, I find, as the woman has already produced. Hicks the Overseer says she is worse than any of them, having before sworn a child to another man to extort money when she was not with child at all. White, the clerk, after the wedding mentioned another case quite as bad as what

Hicks had told me of the girl I had just married, who by the way, had for a *bridemaid* a common prostitute, who was not long since tried for her life for stealing out of a shop in Bath, but her punishment was commuted to imprisonment.

Saturday, February 26

It was a stormy night. I spent half an hour before breakfast in my study. The papers of to-day speak of an insurrection in Ireland. I am weary of reading the nonsense of the newspapers; the sovereign people are to be pacified with pots and pipes, so the taxes on beer and tobacco are to be lowered; and that they may derive every kind of instruction from the newspapers, part of the tax is to be taken off, which will make them a penny cheaper. Pipes, pots, and papers, and the permission to debate ad libitum the advantages of a republic; what the deuce would they have more! But, joking apart, for indeed it is too serious a matter to joke about, I see no hope of averting the storm which threatens the country, unless by one patriotic effort. If it is calculated that a twentieth part of all the property, landed, funded, and personal, in the kingdom would entirely and completely liquidate the National Debt, let that loss be voluntarily sustained by all who have property, as taxes would for the most part be taken off. Were this done, the income of every individual would be nearly the same as at present; and would any patriot hesitate to part with the twentieth part of his possessions to insure years of comfort and prosperity to his country? I answer, real patriots would not; but shew me the real patriot, and I will call him Phoenix! rara avis in terris indeed. But (alas!), touch my property, touch my life.

Good Friday, April 1

This being Good Friday, I read the prayers and preached on the text, "He was oppressed and afflicted, yet He opened not His mouth." Very few were in attendance at Church, as the colliers and agriculturists now work on Good Friday, but I never suffer any of my servants to do so; the times are ripe for punishment.

Easter Sunday, April 3

I preached in the morning a sermon on the Resurrection, and afterwards administered the Sacrament. Very few attended: only 15, including my own family and servants. That is their fault, not mine. I have done everything to persuade them for their good, itaque liberavi animam meam.

Monday, April 18

I rose early, then walked into the village before breakfast. Some of the colliers, as I passed the coal pit afterwards, indicated a marked insolence towards myself. I walked after breakfast to attend the sick.

Wednesday, April 20

Combes mentioned that the brewer, Collins, wanted to have the house he has lately built at Meadgates licensed as an Ale House, should the licence of the beer houses be repealed, and that he had been soliciting the farmers for their votes. I said he would never get mine, I could assure him, as I attributed a great deal of the mischief in the parish to these houses; and I further said that as his (the Camerton Inn) had been established for many years, and I had reason to believe kept good order, that I should not myself consent to another's being opened so near to him.

Friday, April 29

I buried Clarke, who died suddenly on Sunday at four o'clock. They have it in circulation round the parish that he was struck dead for profaning the sabbath in measuring out the ground for a house he was about to build. If my worthy parishioners never did a worse crime they would at any rate be more pleasant people to live with; but, like the Jews of old, they are ready to accuse even their Divine Teacher of sabbath breaking as the most heinous of all offences. These are the people among whom I dwell.

Saturday, April 30

After dinner this evening there were lying on the rug before the fire my three dogs and a pet lamb of my daughter's, also a large tom cat, and at the window presented itself a tame jackdaw; all these different creatures were perfectly quiet, and to all appearances good friends. If my son and daughter and myself, perhaps, had left the room for any time the discordant dispositions of these inmates would have produced mischief, since all these creatures are as happy as creatures can be under our protection, and I may ask, were not my fellow creatures far more happy under the protection of their more powerful superiors years ago when the laws were duly executed than they are now amidst that great diversity of parties in religion and politics?

I take no merit to myself for inheriting a little of the old English spirit, as an immediate progenitor of mine, my great, great, and I believe I must add another great, grandfather, Robert Skinner, was a staunch adherent to Charles in his troubles, and did his duty manfully; he that followed his son into exile, returned with him at the Restoration, and died Bishop of Worcester.

Why should I not act upon the same principles as he did when Bishop of Oxford and Worcester, being Rector of Camerton, and be as ready to maintain my principles by my voice and by my writings, and even to die in defence of them if it be required of me? It is easy enough to determine on a stoical behaviour, but it is very difficult to practice it, for I continually meet with insults; nay, the Master I serve is insulted through me, and I long to be removed from this continued state of irritation.

Thursday, June 9

I rose early, and wrote some of the arrears of my Journals before breakfast: "Nulla dies sine linea" was the motto I assumed when first I began journalising, and I hope I shall adhere to it.

Monday, June 20

I rose early to write to the Magistrates of the Bath Forum Division respecting the public house Collins wishes to have licensed in the parish, and to express my disapprobation of the increase of these excitements to evil, for I can call them by no other name. I am well aware of the unpopularity I incur, but I am willing to incur it, nay, even insults, rather than sacrifice my principles by calling evil good and good evil for the sake of expediency. The magistrates of Bath are more subservient to the opinions of any Jack-in-Office—their clerk, for example—than it becomes a person to be who has so responsible a duty on themselves to perform. I am convinced that these clerks even direct and lead by the nose their superiors who ought to direct them. There has been a respectable public house established in this parish for upwards of thirty years in the centre of the collieries, now occupied by Combes; a second, called the "Red Post," is on the outskirts of the parish, if not immediately in it; a third was not long since opened in a hamlet in the Parish of Camerton, and is within a short distance of that now proposed to be opened. Indeed, the three houses already licensed are within a mile or a mile and a half of each other, and two of them not further distant from the public house in Timsbury parish. Besides these houses we have eight or ten *beer houses*, which I am sorry to say are conducted on a very different plan to what we were given to understand would have been the case in the first instance: being in fact *Ale Houses* in everything but the name. I well know they will attend to their clerk, Mr. Page, rather than to me on the occasion, for now the rabble must be pleased, and the name of Rector in a parish is become an empty and offensive title.

Friday, June 24

At breakfast time I had some serious conversation with Joseph, and asked whether he was already tired of farming, as he seemed to prefer fishing and swallow shooting to overlooking his men and attending to his business; if he was he might give up the concern altogether, and I would attend to it myself. He said he much wished to continue, and would attend to business; that he was sorry he had been so insolent to me, and begged my pardon.

* * * * *

Thursday, September 14

I rode with Anna, and called on old Swift and his wife; they are much the same, that is, approaching their long home, but I fear without a proper feeling respecting a future state, but God will never require of them more than the talent He has bestowed.

Some persons are naturally ignorant, and unfeeling even with respect to bodily suffering; the poor woman whose leg is mortifying seems to feel but little.

Friday, October 7

I spent the morning in my study. At dinner I met with the same kind of improper behaviour from my son Joseph I have been of late so much accustomed to, merely because I hinted he was taking more cider at dinner than would do him good, as he always has his wine after, and, I believe too, something else when he walks up to his farm. Alas! the young men of the present day, instead of exerting themselves to produce fruits for what has been bestowed on their culture, imagine they are to be supported in idleness and extravagance, and to do nothing but eat, drink, sleep, shoot, fish, and ride about the country—being as lordly in their ideas as if they were men of £2,000 a year, instead of having yet their independence to boot.

My death! even this will not put that sum in the pockets of each of my sons. When this is gone—I cannot bear to dwell on the unpleasant anticipation.

I went to bed much agitated and spent a sleepless night; the pang of ingratitude in one's children more especially bites much deeper than any other venomous tooth.

I did not go down to breakfast. About ten o'clock, however, I left my bedroom. On going into the parlour, Joseph began by saying he was not to blame that I had been in a great passion with him because he had drunk a few glasses of cider; that he had a right to drink as much as he chose as long as he continued in my house, and that it was not behaving like a gentleman to take notice of it. I said if he were in the army, and was taking more wine than would do him good at the mess, the Colonel, or Major, or Superior Officer would be doing a young man a kindness to remark it. He said that if a major or colonel did so to him he would throw a bottle at his head. I said, in my house and to my own son I had a right to make such remarks, and if he would not submit to hear them he should not stay in my house. His brother Owen then took his part, and said there was a great fuss made about drinking a few glasses of cider; that Joseph had a right to feel offended, since I spoke before the servant. He was then still more abusive than his brother had been, saying that I wanted to get rid of the expense of having Joseph in my house; I also wanted an excuse to stop his allowance after he took his degree, which he is going to Cambridge now to do, and has received £50 from me for the purpose, and therefore had laid the plan of quarrelling with them; that he owed me no obligation whatever for anything he had received at my hands, therefore there was no occasion for gratitude. He said, if I did not continue him an allowance after he had taken his degree he would compel me; he knew enough of the law to be assured that he had the power to make me pay £60 a year to him out of my marriage settlement, and he would make me do it; he hoped God would strike him dead if ever he came into my house again, and he quitted about twelve o'clock. Among the taunts my ungrateful son threw out was this: "I suppose you will put in your Journals what has taken place, and of course make it all your own way; but I don't care, I shall never read it, and whatever you may think of your great collection of MSS. books, everyone, as well as myself, only laughs at your folly in thinking the occurrences of your parish and family events worth reading; and with regard to your poetry, it is merely sing-song! I have written some poetry," he continued, "which is much better than anything you have ever produced." In the course of conversation he said that there never was a good classic who came from a private school—alluding to Cheam, where I was educated under Mr. Gilpin—but that the Winchester men had carried away all the Latin verse prizes.

After Owen was gone I knocked at Anna's door, as she had retired to her room and locked it, and asked her whether she meant to give directions about the rooms being put in order for the reception of our company (the Hoares, from Southfield, who were expected to dinner, and were to spend a few days). She said she had given orders to the servants, and they must do what she ordered; she should not go to look after them, that was not her business. I said, as she did not seem inclined to do as my housekeeper I must resume the office myself, and see the house was put in order for the reception of my friends. I then told her that her conduct was as reprehensible as that of her brothers; that they had insulted me most grossly, and that she had given every countenance to it. She said that I had been put into a great passion for a trifle; if I was angry with them, they had a right to be angry with me. I replied I was ready to acknowledge this weakness: if my children by their insolence endeavoured to move me to anger they were more than half partakers of the transgression. She said it was her duty to love her brothers, and she should do so. I replied I had often forgiven them, but it had only led to a repetition of their ill-behaviour. I should not now forgive them till I found their repentance sincere; that neither of them should again enter my house. She said if they had not permission to come here, she would not herself stay.

Finding that this unfortunate girl had been entirely warped and influenced by her brothers, and knowing I could not command my feelings sufficiently if she misbehaved herself before the company I expected, and feeling also too unwell myself to entertain them properly, I determined to put them off, and therefore wrote to Mr. Hoare saying, as the weather was so unpromising, and owing to something which had occurred to distress me greatly, I hoped he would not be offended if I again put off the day of our meeting at Camerton.

I felt in reality so unwell with the pressure of blood at my temples

I was resolved to take some laudanum, and took three times fifteen drops at a time without producing any effect, so that I passed a miserable time in bed.

Sunday, October 9

As soon as the morning was sufficiently light I dressed myself and went into my study and got some tea, which refreshed me greatly, so that I was able to look over my sermon, which had been prepared before on the text, "God gave them over to a reprobate mind, to do those things which are not convenient." There were but few attended the Church; among the absentees was my son Joseph. Whether he returned from Bath yesterday I know not, neither have I enquired. Anna attended, but I did not think with a countenance which betokened contrition for having acted so ungratefully towards her Father. On returning home I wrote thus far in my Journal. I have written eighteen pages since the morning, my mind quite calm, for which feeling I am indeed most grateful, and may the minds of my children become so sensible of their error that they may return with humility to the improvement of their minds in religious knowledge. Oh God! into Thy good keeping I commit them, as I do myself this night. May I be preserved from future excitements to anger; I will strive to avoid it—indeed, I have striven from my youth up until now: Fas est et ab hoste doceri. Owen said I was a madman, and ought to have a commission of lunacy to investigate my conduct. How could such an idea enter into the head of a son? Although I have sometimes been hurried away by the excitement of anger, never has anger been permitted to engender malice, hatred, or revenge, and as soon as my sons return to themselves again I will forgive them again; but I know it is better to let them feel what it is to lose even for a little affection and assistance of their best friend. "Father, forgive them, for they know not what they do."

Monday, October 10

I have written the account of what took place between my sons and myself. What I have written will do no harm to themselves should they improve and hereafter become useful members of society.

By Will I have bequeathed my Journals to a public institution, that they are not read till fifty years after my death, when most of the characters here drawn, as well as myself, will have retired from this troublesome scene to render up an account of their thoughts, words, and actions, and the use they have made of the talent committed to their charge.

Several of the farmers paid tythe this morning at the Parsonage to my daughter, as I was obliged to keep upstairs on account of the medicine. Anna seems determined to give me no further cause of uneasiness, and I trust she will continue to enjoy herself under my roof (where she has as many real comforts as though she were an earl's daughter).

I felt my mind relieved by listening to my daughter's music and singing for an hour before I retired to my study, where I brought up my Journals to this point, and am now going to bed—I hope in peace and harmony with all mankind, since I forgive all as I hope myself to be forgiven.

I felt considerably relieved, and got up about ten, having taken my tea in bed. Joseph wrote the following letter:

"MY DEAR FATHER,

"I am very sorry to hear that you have been so unwell as to prevent you receiving your tythe. I shall be most happy to receive it, at Combes's or elsewhere. If I had known it before I should have been most happy to have attended, if you would have allowed me. Of course I am sorry for all that has passed. Be assured that it will be my endeavour to please you for the future. I hope to hear that you are getting better, and can only say how sorry I am at being the cause of such mental and bodily pain to one whom I have always found in essentials a kind friend and affectionate father.

"I remain,

"Your affectionate Son,

"J. H. SKINNER.

"THE GLEBE FARM,
"*Wednesday evening.*"

to which I gave the annexed answer:

"DEAR JOSEPH,

"As I said in my letter yesterday, I forgave as I hope to be forgiven; as you are sensible of your past dereliction of duty towards me, your Father, and on condition of your avoiding the like in future, I will strive to wipe all recollections of the past from my mind.

"I feel much better for the quiet and the mental and medicinal discipline of yesterday, and shall be glad to see you at any time: and hope you will preserve in future the same sentiments you profess to entertain respecting your Father in your letter of to-day, namely, that you have always found him your best friend; and this sentiment of sincere regard towards you I again repeat by signing myself your affectionate Father and sincere well-wisher through life.

"JOHN SKINNER."

Joseph came soon afterwards and repeated what he had before said, namely, that he would endeavour to give me no cause for uneasiness in future.

Tuesday, December 20

Having to attend a Clerical Meeting at Mells, I drank tea and slept at Mr. Doveton's. Before breakfast I walked round his beautiful domain, nearly half a mile in extent, of shrubberies and plantation. There is not such a rectory in the county; it used to be called a bishoprick when the late incumbent, Dr. Bishop, resided there. It rained the whole way till I reached Camerton.

Saturday, December 31

> *Another year has wing'd its airy flight,*
> *Still wrapt the future in mysterious night;*
> *What may the next reveal?*

Oh, my God! I will commit myself and all I have into Thy good keeping this night. Let the words of my mouth and the meditations of my heart be now, and always, acceptable in Thy sight, O Lord, my strength and my Redeemer.

1832

I ALTERED a sermon I had written and preached when I was ordained priest, on this text: "Seeing we have this ministry, as we have received mercy, we faint not." After shewing the necessity there was for those who had engaged in the important office of instructors to declare boldly the doctrines of Christianity and to oppose the iniquity and licentiousness of evil men, even though affliction and persecution might await them for the word's sake, I was well aware that men of little minds and little knowledge not only envied, but misrepresented and calumniated, the instruction bestowed by the regular clergy, and there was no story too gross but what they would receive, no slander too iniquitous but what they would propagate underhand to vilify the regular clergy and lower them in the eyes of the people. This was, I felt assured, one of the principal reasons why the inhabitants of this parish had been alienated from their Church; that I should continue to preach the doctrines of the Gospel in the face of opposition and insult. I don't remember ever to have seen so small a congregation when the weather is fair; among the farmers, only John Rossiter, and scarcely any of the colliers.

I walked to Wick Lane to enquire after our old cook; she is speechless and hastening fast to her end. I also went to the schoolmistress and heard two of the children repeat what they had learned from the Psalms and Testament, and gave them a penny apiece, also half-a-crown to the schoolmistress. I visited old Mrs. Moon, and gave her daughter, who is a dwarf, something because she only receives sixpence a week from the Parish; and I said if she could only weed in the garden I would employ her during the time my man was so busily occupied. I also gave a shilling to the woman who looks after the old cook, because she has been kind and attentive to her.

As Joseph's cough still continues unabated, and he complained this morning of a sharp pain on his chest, I did not feel comfortable in his delaying his visit to Norman, which has been put off from day

437

to day on the plea of his being better. I sent to order a post chaise to
convey him to Bath, entreating he would mention everything he
complains of to Norman, since nothing could be more absurd than
attempting to deceive his doctor. I am apprehensive, as he says when
he coughs he feels a sharp pain like a knife running into him. I have
had too much experience in these matters not to feel alarmed.
Hitherto he has attributed the pains in his chest to rheumatism, and
to a blow he received some time ago from a ladder: I am of a different
opinion.

Wednesday, July 11

Joseph is not so well; his cough hard, and the expectoration
considerable.

Thursday, July 12

I walked in the morning to make some visits among the poor
people. Crow's wife had been to say her husband was out of work,
and had scarcely enough to support himself. I promised to employ
him occasionally.

Sunday, July 15

I determined, while lying awake, to write to Norman and ask his
candid opinion on Joseph's case, and put it to him whether change
of air might not be serviceable just now; if so, I will contrive next
week to leave home with him in a steamer and take a trip to Ireland
and back again, or to Liverpool. Anna will, I know, like to accompany us. I am decidedly of opinion that change of air would be
serviceable if the complaint is not yet established; if it be, nothing
can, I fear, be done. I felt very low and went to bed before ten o'clock.

Monday, July 16

Poor Joseph was blooded on Saturday, and continues in Bath till
to-morrow to come out with his brother Owen, and his friend Mr.
Stewart.

Thursday, July 19

Having promised my godson Alfred Boodle a kite, I was determined to let nothing interfere until that important business was
accomplished. On leaving my bedroom at six I walked to the cooper's
at Cridlingcot to procure a hoop for the bender of the kite and an

upright to attach it to, so that before breakfast time the skeleton was complete, as was in the course of a couple of hours afterwards the whole of the manufactory. Joseph drew and painted the stars, and his companions made the tail. When it was perfectly dry after dinner we essayed to fly it, but there being scarcely a breath of air we gave up our undertaking.

Saturday, July 21

Anna put into my hands a letter just arrived from my Mother, mentioning that my brother Russell had a very alarming inflammation in his leg which threatened mortification, and that he was attended by a physician as well as a surgeon. I resolved to see my Mother and brother to-morrow.

Sunday, July 22

Mr. Boodle officiated for me to-day, as I was obliged to go into Bath, my brother Russell being dangerously ill. I got to my mother's house a little after eleven; Russell was then asleep, and I read the Morning Service to my Mother before I went up to see him. After an early dinner with my Mother I walked to the White Hart Inn to order a carriage from thence to take us to Weston-super-Mare on the morrow.

Monday, July 23

I was in my study before six, and wrote a letter to Sir Richard Hoare, now at Bath, to inform him of my going to Weston, which would preclude my seeing him. Soon after breakfast we left home. We got to the hotel at Weston a little after three. The place was quite in a bustle, it being the Club Day. Joseph bore his journey better than I expected, as he complained much on the road of a pain all round his chest, and his cough seemed hard and the expectoration difficult. However, after dinner he seemed better. Anna and myself walked before tea to the baths, and round the village of Weston, that has nothing at all to recommend it as to external appearance, and the noise and rioting of the Club by no means adds to its agreeableness just now. We had tea a little after seven, and enjoyed a calm sunset over the water from the inn window. At ten we went to bed. Joseph seems certainly better as to his cough, but complains of fatigue.

We were disturbed by various noises, ringing of the door bell at three o'clock in the morning, etc., and I got up more fatigued than I went to bed. However, having procured a jug of salt water, I sponged myself all over, being afraid to venture into the swimming bath with a tendency to fullness of blood. I accompanied Anna to the bath during the middle of the day, and while she was bathing I made a sketch of the place where the lodging houses and baths are lately purchased by Dr. Fox, of Brislington, who seems to be doing a good deal on the spot. We dined at four, and Joseph and Anna afterwards took a ride on the sand, but the poney and donkey they hired were not of the most delightful description!

I accompanied my daughter to the bath before breakfast; afterwards I walked from the hotel to Kew Stoke. I returned across the fields to the hotel, from whence I accompanied my daughter and Joseph to the pier, where I engaged a boat to take a sail in the bay at high water. We dined at four, and a little after five were seated in the sailing boat, but had so little wind we could scarcely move along. Had there been a little more we should have enjoyed our two hours' excursion much. We had sufficient water to land on the pier under the baths and lodging houses belonging to Dr. Fox. I well remember the rock which was called Knightstone before a single wall was erected; now there are two capacious houses besides the baths.

After tea I was obliged to speak about another sleeping-room, as that I had occupied the preceding night was by no means tenantable. My daughter had been put there on our arrival at the hotel on Monday, with a promise that no one was to sleep on the other side of the partition; for in fact it was a small bedroom divided into two by a thin deal partition, so that everything that was said and done was as audible as though the chamber had not been thus subdivided. The chambermaid put two young men into the apartment, which my daughter mentioned to me next morning; and, as no other alternative then presented itself, I gave up my room to her, and a miserable night I passed.

Owen and his friend joined us at dinner; they had taken Wells and Cheddar in their way from Camerton to Weston. The little lecture I had previously given the master of the house respecting our want of accommodation had a good effect, since they were promised comfortable beds.

Friday, July 27

I walked in the evening with Anna, Owen, and Mr. Stewart along the sands to Uphill, and returned so completely tired I was not sorry to go to bed as soon as I had penned my sketches. Joseph evidently is the better for the air and amusement he has found at Weston; but we all agree it is a wretched place to continue in for any length of time.

Saturday, July 28

After breakfast, having paid the bill which, with servants, etc., amounted to upwards of thirteen pounds, we got into the carriage which came from Bath overnight to convey us to Camerton. I first took an opportunity of speaking to Mr. Reeves, the proprietor of the hotel, respecting the great impropriety of putting young men in the room contiguous to that my daughter slept in, and put it to himself whether he, as the father of a family, would have felt well pleased had a daughter of his own been so circumstanced, where two young men, after having taken too much wine, might have said and done things very improper for a modest girl to hear or be privy to. He said he was very sorry, but it was the chambermaid's fault. I said I gave the hint which I hoped would prove serviceable in the future.

We drove to Banwell Cave; Owen and Mr. Stewart continued to be our outriders through Banwell, Churchill, and the beautiful vale called Wrington. At Blagdon we stopped to bait the horses, and procure a mutton chop for ourselves. While this was dressing I walked with Owen to the Church, whose beautiful tower has been degraded by a modern nave—the most ugly and ill-proportioned of any I have yet seen in these times of Church disfigurement. Resuming our vehicle about four o'clock, proceeded on with fresh vigour, and thence to Camerton and found all well; and, what is of more consequence, Joseph is certainly much better for his excursion, so that our time, trouble, and £20 expenditure will not be regretted.

Wednesday, August 1

I found on going down to breakfast that some of Mr. James's family had been to see Anna yesterday evening to invite us to join the party this day at Timsbury, where a sermon is to be preached, and much prating to take place about the propagation of the Gospel in foreign parts. Methinks they had better strive to mend matters at home, instead of going abroad to unsettle the minds of their fellows. I suppose the miraculous operations of the Spirit, which of late converted such numbers of *dark* colliers at Timsbury, will be brought on the tapis. I am no friend to such exhibitions. It is our business to check the extravagancies of enthusiasm and superstition, not to countenance them, and I am therefore concerned to hear that the Bishop has been induced to sanction this meeting by his presence.

Thursday, August 2

Although I had declined attending the omnium gatherum at Timsbury yesterday, I walked after breakfast with Anna, Owen, and Mr. Stewart, to be present at the opening of Radstock Church, which has undergone repairs and additions, and to contribute somewhat towards defraying the debt incurred by the expenditure exceeding the estimate, as it does in most other cases, as Boodle had sent round circular letters to his friends and neighbours. We found a considerable number assembled in the Church, and the collection amounted to upwards of £38. Mr. Trelawney Collins, of Timsbury, preached on the text: "And Jacob awaked out of his sleep, and he said, Surely the Lord is in this place, and I knew it not. And he was afraid, and said, How dreadful is this place!" Mr. Collins adapted the expression of "How dreadful is this place," etc., to the occasion for which we were assembled. The sermon more than an hour in length. The first part of the discourse, which lasted nearly half an hour, was a well-finished treatise which had been written with care and, I should imagine, by a different hand than his own, and the sermon would have made more impression has it ended with this; but, wishing to excite attention to a stretch beyond what it was capable of attaining, the discourse lost much of its effect. Mr. Collins ought certainly to have defined the precise meaning of *dreadful* when applied to the *House of God*, which he neglected to do, and I fear the ignorant were left to their imaginations.

We returned to Camerton in good time to dinner, as we were unwilling to leave Joseph longer alone, and strolled about the premises after dinner.

Sunday, August 5

I preached in the morning on the miracle of the seven loaves, being part of the Gospel for the day. The people were attentive, but I am sorry to say I do not think there were one hundred in the Church. If I were to commence a new system as an evangelical teacher, the Methodists would attend; but I cannot prevail upon myself to do evil to work no good, unless it be good to gratify one's vanity by procuring full benches at the expense of one's principles.

Monday, August 6

Owen and his friend Stewart left us for Bath on their return to London. They dine with my Mother, and go by one of the night coaches. Joseph seemed low and out of spirits at their departure.

Wednesday, August 8

Anna and myself walked to Radstock at five to dine with the Boodles. After tea they got me to play at cards, which I hate and have not touched one since I was with Boodle at Christmas. We played three rubbers which lasted till nearly eleven o'clock, and I got a bad headache for my pains, as well as three shillings loss. I would readily have paid thrice the sum to be excused. We did not get home till twelve, as I declined sleeping on account of Joseph's being left alone. The servants were gone to bed, and it was with difficulty we awoke them.

Thursday, August 9

Joseph over-exerted himself, I fear, yesterday, as he went into the Court of Requests to complain of a man who has cheated him in the purchase of some hay; and he also walked instead of drove to see Norman, who lives in the Circus. He tells me he has accepted an invitation from Mr. Upham, who has a house on Combe Down, to go there for a few days. He seems so bent on the plan I shall not oppose it further; but I fear close rooms and over-exertion to keep up conversation with strangers will not be so conducive to his amendment as the quiet of his own home.

Friday, August 10

Having engaged to shew my godson (young Frederick Warren) Cheddar Cliffs and Wells Cathedral, in conjunction with Boodle and his family, I drove there in time to breakfast at seven, and in the course of an hour we were on our way to Cheddar. The young people much enjoyed the drive through the cliffs, which appeared to the greatest advantage of light and shade, the sun being in full splendour.

Having put up our horses, we entered the cavern under the direction of some of the old women with candles, and we afterwards made a comfortable luncheon in the open air. I shewed the young people the paper mills, each being permitted to make his own sheet by way of memorial of his visit to the spot. It rained nearly the whole of the way to Wells, but held up, fortunately, to enable us to visit the Cathedral and Bishop's Palace, where we arrived about five o'clock. I meant to have made my visit to the crypt incog., but it happened unfortunately that the Bishop had seen us approaching, and Mr. Strachey came down to say he wished to see me. I found the gallery filled with company, and his Lordship in pontificalibus, as he was about to perform the ceremony of Baptism on his great grandson, Strachey's infant. Being myself stained with the variation of each soil from Cheddar to Wells, I was not sorry to retreat as speedily as possible.

We arrived at Radstock by eight o'clock. I was wet through and accepted the offer of sleeping there, and sent back my carriage and horses by Boodle's man, who on his return brought me a note from Anna saying that Joseph during a fit of coughing had ruptured a small vessel, and in consequence she had ordered a chaise to take him to Bath, and had gone with him. This intelligence, although I have long prepared my mind for the worst, gave me much uneasiness, and I passed a sleepless night.

Saturday, August 11

The Boodles had an early breakfast, and I walked back to Camerton before ten o'clock, and got to Bath before one. I found Joseph much better for his bleeding, which Norman advised immediately on his arrival at my mother's. Norman told him he had taken too much nourishment since his return from Weston, and that it was absolutely necessary he should lose blood even if this had not occurred. I saw Norman, and had a plain, straight forward conversation with him with respect to Joseph, saying I wished him to be under his care till he gave him full permission to move back again to Camerton: that I had made arrangements to move to the South of Devonshire or to the extremity of Cornwall before the cold weather set in. He said that he had known patients recover under far worse circumstances than what he observed in Joseph; that there was no occasion for accelerating our movements westward till the cold weather began; the winter would be most trying to him, but he was in hopes he might rally. He says he may take ices, which I know my poor wife was so fond of. I have accordingly given directions he should be supplied with them; he may also have fruit. I have promised to go in to see him on Monday, and shall do so every other day as long as he continues in Bath. I drove Anna back to Camerton, where we arrived about seven o'clock.

Sunday, August 12

The four lads from the Boodles' came to enquire after us, and drank tea. I put off their coming here to dinner to-morrow, as we go to Bath; indeed, I shall make no engagements anywhere now, knowing how much Joseph will have claims on our attention. Indeed, I felt rather uncomfortable that this accident happened when I was from home, but Anna managed very well in taking him at once to Bath.

Monday, August 13

Quitting home at twelve o'clock, we took up a note from my Mother at the Red Post saying Joseph was going on well; but on our arrival we were greeted with the sad intelligence that during a fit of coughing the bleeding had returned from his lungs, and that in consequence Norman had been obliged to take more blood. On seeing him, poor fellow, he seemed very low, saying if this continued it must soon be over with him. We dined at my Mother's, or rather made a show of doing so, for neither poor Anna nor myself made half a meal. We got home to tea in order to avoid the damps and night air; indeed, I find I have a bad cold coming on, and I was glad to be in bed soon after.

Wednesday, August 15

I drove Anne to my Mother's soon after breakfast. On our road to Bath we saw several people, and among them some of my own parish, going in to the Political Union,[1] which was to take place at Sidney Gardens.

The rabble brawl about their rights; we who are not of the rabble have a right to enquire, nay demand, of the Servants of the King and Ministers of State why they did not immediately enforce the Proclamation issued at the express command of the King respecting the putting down of these disorderly, nay, these rebellious meetings.

[1] Formed in 1831 to promote the Reform Bill.

I read on several of the banners, "Grey and Reform"—"Althorpe and Reform"—"We will maintain our Rights"—"We will be free." Free, indeed! What am I saying? The Great Disposer of all events, if He wills our destruction cannot better effect His purpose than by leaving everything in the direction of such fools and knaves as are now placed at the helm of government, thus verifying the truth of the old adage, "Quem perdere vult prius dementat."

Before I went to bed I wrote a note to Mrs. Boodle asking her permission to let Georgiana come and spend some days with Anna at the Parsonage, as I know her spirits will flag if left too much to her own feelings during her brother's illness, and I am so much in my study I contribute but little to change her ideas.

Friday, August 17

I see by the Bath papers that the Reform meeting at Bristol was attended with riot; that at Bath without any overt acts of insubordination. But a silent, sly dog is worse sometimes than one that barks.

Tuesday, September 4

It being a beautiful morning we resolved to pay our long-meditated visit to Southfield, and set off after I had read the paper.

We got to Mr. Hoare's before one o'clock, and found the house full of his relatives. They set down eighteen of a day to dinner, all of the name of Hoare—quite a patriarchal family. Henry Hoare has sold out of his regiment, which was going to the West Indies. If he did so on the score of health, I think this country is in a worse state on account of the cholera than that he was going to. There are now eleven cases in Bath, and at Bristol it rages with great violence.

Thursday, September 6

Pestilence stalks over the earth, but still we all eat and drink, and rise up to play. A beggar woman or, as they call them, mumpers, came to the place. On my asking where she lived, I found she was an inhabitant of that wretched place Avon Street, in Bath, and that she was come into the country to sell matches, etc., etc. On questioning her about the cholera, she said it was not so bad as they had reported it to be. This woman will probably go to sleep at Mrs. Moon's in Wick Lane, who still receives persons of this description in spite of the admonition I gave her not long since, so that we have good reason to expect it will reach our collieries: God's will be done.

I made a point of going to the shop, the public-house, and several of the colliers' residences to caution them against receiving mumpers or beggars coming from other parts, especially from Avon Street, Bath, into their houses, since by this means the cholera might be brought into the parish, and rage in our collieries here as it is still doing in Staffordshire. I told them it was absurd to imagine it was not infectious, for I had heard from my son who is residing in London that the sexton of the parish where he resides had caught the infection from digging a grave and assisting at the funeral of a person who died of the complaint, and died himself the next day. The people seemed to be convinced of the prudence and propriety of my advice, and promised to be guided by it. I also recommended cleanliness; and this perambulation of my parish occupied me nearly till dinner time.

Having promised the Bishop to be with him on Thursday I could not disappoint him, and I got to Wells at half-past eleven.

Arrived at the Mitre Inn, Wells, I found myself very unwell; I therefore employed the interval in taking rest. We dined at five, only the Bishop and his daughter, Mrs. Powell, and her daughter, sister to Mrs. Strachey. When the dinner-bell summoned us, I went into the drawing-room, but felt very far from well, since the pains which had accompanied me to Wells had now returned. At dinner it was still worse, and there happened to be a haunch of venison of the haut goût which, though approved of by the generality, I found too powerful for my nerves, in that nothing remained for me but to make my exit, which I did as quietly as possible. My kind host, however, shortly after, supposing I was not well, sent his butler, who brought me some Epsom Salts, of which I took a good dose, and I procured some other medicine, which fortunately relieved me, and I verily believe saved me a serious illness, as the tension of the stomach was such, had I not removed it, inflammation must have ensued. I officiated as Chaplain at Evening prayers in the Chapel, as the Archdeacon was from home; and we got to bed a little after ten.

I had but little sleep during the night, but felt myself so much better that I got up and attended Chapel and the breakfast table.

I rose at six and walked on the terrace for an hour, the morning being beautiful. Afterwards I accompanied the Bishop, who was on horseback, to the Park and the potato grounds he has let to the poor people, nearly sixty acres in extent, and the plan seems to answer even beyond his expectations. The renters of these portions of good ground at twelve shillings a rood amount to upward of two hundred, and I was glad to hear they were not only punctual in their payments, but so industrious in their habits that no one has received parochial relief since he has become a renter. On our return I read the Prayers in the chapel, and after breakfast, having taken leave of my kind host, I hastened forwards to Camerton.

Saturday, September 15

I found the Jarretts had sent three brace of birds, so we were well stocked. We called to thank them after breakfast, and found only Mr. Stephen and his aunt, Mrs. Anne Stephens, at the Manor House. I think his manners are much altered for the better. Adversity is a good tutor, and he has experienced losses in his West India property, which may be of real benefit if it teaches him humility, as well as a determination to employ his own talents, and rely on his own resources more than on uncertain wealth.

We drove round by Priston to see Hammond, and to leave a brace of the birds there.

Monday, September 17

I rose early and finished my answers to the list of enquiries sent by the Commissioners respecting my Living, which I have stated to the utmost farthing, perhaps greatly to my own detriment when an Income Tax is laid on, for the only deductions I have made are on account of repairs on the premises, and the pensions paid out of the Living at the Bruton audit, and the Procurations, etc., paid at Visitation; in all about £21, so that the gross amount is about £478 per annum. I have also laid out £1,100 on the house and premises, and £250 in building the new Glebe Farm House, barns, stables, walls round the garden, etc., etc. The rates and taxes going out of the Living are at least £50 per annum, so that when the purchase-money that was paid by my Uncle Haggard be added to the capital I have sunk, I do not think my present income ought to be lowered, since an annuity might have been purchased for £3,500, which would have given almost an equal return of the clear profit. When we add to this sum £2,000 spent in education to enable a clergyman to take

Orders, it is quite a fortune; and yet there is an outcry against our Order that we are too well paid, and that £200 a year would be ample provision throughout the kingdom for each incumbent.

The Bishop read to me the other morning a well-written pamphlet which he has prepared for the press of the Commutation of Tithe, in which he has proved that the average value of the Livings in his diocese is not above £200 a year.

Wednesday, September 19

After breakfast we drove to Vallis, accompanied by Mr. Stephen Jarrett and his friend. Taking Kilmersdon in our way, we stopped to visit the Church under the escort of Mr. Edwards, the curate, which gave an opportunity of seeing the painted glass, set up by Mr. Thomas Jolliffe, of the Mount of Olives which he visited in his expedition to Jerusalem, and had the glass stained at Bristol after a sketch taken by himself. It is literally as green as an olive—if this be any merit in the artist to make his work accord with the name of the place he described. We passed through Mells, and thence to Nunney; I entered the little Inn for the purpose of procuring some bread and butter, and was not very much pleased at the intelligence afterwards conveyed that the landlord was upstairs ill of the cholera!

Wednesday, September 26

I borrowed a gig at the Manor House to drive Anna into Bath, and bring back Elinor Page to spend a few days with her, as my own carriage is repairing. We found Joseph much the same; he has begged me to give up the farm and sell the stock, which I have consented to, to make his mind easy; but I fear I shall be a considerable loser. There seems to be a fatality about the Glebe Farm, since not one of the four tenants who have occupied it but have left it half a year in my debt, and yet the rent is by no means beyond what it ought to be. If the Farmers this Michaelmas are behindhand in their payments, I am sure I do not know how I am to meet the outgoings of the ensuing year; but ere that perhaps all our property will be involved in one common ruin. If the Conservative Party are sufficiently strong, and can influence the King to have a new Ministry, the evil may yet be arrested; but, alas! I have small hopes this will be so.

I rode "Ellen," and Anna rode "Cam," who had followed the carriage into Bath, back to Camerton to a four o'clock dinner. On our arrival we found Mrs. Boodle, with Marianne and Georgiana.

After tea we had some music, and I went to bed immediately after prayers. Marianne was left with us.

Thursday, September 27

I hear that some cases have occurred at Timsbury which are considered as having much the appearance of cholera, which Mr. Collins has doctored with success by giving laudanum, spirits of wine, and soda.

Tuesday, October 2

I accompanied Elinor Page to Woodborough in order to shew her the beautiful situation of that place, and the great oak contiguous to Waram Mead on the situation between the streams facing Woodborough. While passing Woodborough I saw Mr. Purnell, who is almost blind and upwards of 80 years old, standing on the roof of his house and directing the tilers about the work they were engaged in. This old miser, who can look *to an inch* as to what concerns his temporal interests is as blind as the tiles on the roof as to what concerns his future state, since he neglects to confer happiness, nay, even common comfort on his fellows during his long career through life, and even permits his old servant to be dying by a lingering death, close to his door, and will not give him a shilling to procure even the necessaries of life. But why should I intrude these sad considerations?

The day was beautiful; our walk was beautiful, and I enjoyed it, as did my companion, to the utmost.

Wednesday, October 3

I find the cholera has broken out most violently in Paulton, and nine died of the disorder the day before yesterday, and three or four cases are considered hopeless. It seems one of these vagabond matchsellers from Bath conveyed it to the house where he was taken in for a night's lodging, and immediately conveyed the infection to the household and to others. He was buried in his clothes the following morning, and those who died are buried in a piece of ground without funeral ceremony. Curtis says that he finds bleeding the most efficacious remedy, and says he is pretty confident he can stop it if called in at the first; but it seems that out of nine cases the whole perished under his management and that of Flower and Baynton, of Radstock, so I for one should have little confidence in their skill. If it comes to us, I suppose pro forma we must send for some of these worthies, but perhaps we may as well let it alone. I am happy to hear the common people, now the danger is come to their own doors, begin to take some precaution, such as whitewashing their houses and purchasing camphor, upwards of a pound having been sold in one day at the shop at Camerton; they also burn juniper, which grows in quantities under Falkland Knoll. Curtis says that he takes no precautions to avoid infection. I shall commit myself unto the Great Director of all events, saying, "Thy will be done on earth as it is in heaven." At the best my clay tenement is but a weak domicile for the active spirit which occupies it, and is very easily discomposed; but it cannot well be otherwise, it has stood the changes of the seasons for sixty years, which is a good lease of any house, and no wonder if it be not so strong as at first.

It rained violently during the whole night, which beating against my windows, contributed somewhat to spoil my rest, and as soon as it was light I went downstairs and got Sir Walter Scott's "Lay of the last Minstrel" from the bookcase, with which I was fully occupied till breakfast time.

Saturday, October 6

I drove Anna to my Mother's after breakfast. We had been prepared by a note to expect a considerable change had taken place, but I saw but little alteration in the poor fellow's countenance, and he has been amusing himself with drawing. According to Norman's recommendation he is going to burn tar in his sitting-room, as the fumes arising from thence are considered as being favourable to the cough. My Mother worries herself more than I thought she would have done, for she must know by sad experience that the progress of the complaint is so gradual that there is no immediate cause for alarm.

Monday, October 8

The cholera, I hear, rages at Paulton, and four more cases are dead! This damp weather must, I think, contribute to increase the pestilence, especially within the confined residences of the colliers.

Tuesday, October 9

The clerk, who came for the surplice to have it washed, states that two of Hill's family in Bridge Place have been attacked by the cholera, which they caught at Paulton.

I hear that nearly forty persons have died of the cholera at Paulton, and that they are interred without funeral service.

After breakfast I received a letter from Mr. Lewton, the bailiff of the coal works, announcing the breaking out of the cholera at Camerton. I immediately walked to his house, taking with me some camphor and aromatic vinegar to give him. This being pay day with the colliers it occurred to me that if the infection be among them he must take every precaution to avoid it. The poor fellow seemed much alarmed, for the boy who died was at the Evening School he keeps at his house yesterday, and appeared quite well; but he must have caught the complaint from old Mrs. Raisin, his grandmother. I immediately wrote to Curtis, the apothecary, desiring him to come to Camerton. I also saw Cook, the father of the boy who died and now lies in the same house with his grandmother, and said he must get the bodies put instantly in coffins and interred out of the way. I then spoke to White about digging a deep grave in the churchyard, out of the line where bodies are now interred, but within the consecrated enclosure.

Curtis, accompanied by Flower, the apothecary from Chilcompton, came to me about the middle of the day and said that prompt measures must be taken to prevent the spreading of the infection, and we must accelerate as soon as possible the interment of the bodies. I walked with them to the churchyard, where the clerk and his two lads were digging the grave. They said it was much better that I did not officiate at the funeral: that at other places it was not done. I said I should be guided by the feelings of the people themselves who attended the funeral, for if I shewed myself fearful of catching the complaint while interring the body, it would have the effect of deterring them from bringing it to the grave and of assisting at all at the interment.

I ordered the man at the shop to distribute two ounces of camphor among the people who came to his house, and desired him to say to them, if they kept a little in the mouth now and then it would be beneficial as a preventative.

I also told the clerk to purchase on my account at the public-house a bottle of spirits to give a glass to each of the people who attended the funeral in the evening, or rather those who conveyed the bodies to the grave. I determined to read the Funeral Service, which I did in the presence of five or six persons and the clerk after dinner, and saw the grave filled in. The foolish fellow White had let them have the velvet pall, but I made him bring it back and had it laid upon the ground for two or three hours, and ordered him to let it stay in the open air for some time to prevent infection.

I desired the schoolmistress to dismiss the girls' school till the disorder was abated, and give notice to their parents to keep them clean in their persons, and prevent them going to infected places. I desired Anna to send a bottle of port wine and one of elder wine to the schoolmistress and her daughter, as they seem completely terrified and really may be more liable to infection through apprehension if they have nothing to cheer their spirits. I was occupied in the evening till prayer time in preparing my sermon for the morrow, on the distinction to be made between the adhering to the letter of the law and acting according to the spirit of the law. The text was taken from the Gospel for the day: "It came to pass as Jesus went into the house of one of the chief priests to eat bread, on the Sabbath day, that they watched him." It had pleased the Almighty Disposer of all events to permit the pestilence to visit these parts. "It is now raging," I said, "at our very doors; our companions and associates are dropping off around us, misery of all descriptions must in consequence be the result. It is our duty to prove ourselves, both in our private and public capacities, kindly disposed to the afflicted and distressed, by essential acts of useful service, instead of wordy professions and unavailing lamentations; and implicitly conform to the advice and directions given by the medical persons who attended them, and who, under Providence, were the only instruments of checking the violence of the disorder and preventing its further extension, etc., etc."

Sunday, October 14

Between the services we walked to Colliers Row to enquire whether the house where the infected died had been properly fumigated with the tobacco which I ordered to be taken there for the purpose. I found it had, and the people were also burning tar ropes in the other houses. Three fresh cases are lying: Perfett, who attended the coffin of Cook's boy, and assisted putting it in the grave; another at Redhill; and Raisin's wife, [widow?] who is married to the son of the woman who first died. John Rossiter called at the Parsonage after dinner; he seems completely upset, and cried while speaking of the increase of the complaint and its probable consequences. I desired him to get some quicklime to put in the grave dug yesterday and the other graves which may be dug, also some juniper to burn; and I offered my Glebe House as a receptacle of patients, should the number increase.

Monday, October 15

I walked into the village to enquire after the sick and see if I could be of any service. The boy Perfett, at Bridge Place, is in a fair way of recovery, but I was much hurt at the apathy of his parents, who had not bought anything for him with the money I gave them yesterday, although Curtis said he might take mutton broth; and when I spoke of the nasty dung-heaps, and filthiness of the children before the doors, which I said would prolong their son's illness, if not give contagion to others, the father replied, "They ought to clear it away." I asked who he meant by "They." He replied, "The people of the parish." I was really *angry*, and said, if they were so very careless and lazy as not to work for themselves in making their places clean, I for one would not assist them with one halfpenny of my money.

I spoke afterwards to Green, the under bailiff of the coal works, and told him he should see that the drains were opened, and the dung heaps removed or put into a hole in their gardens. He said, *it was the Lord's will they should die; that he could not prevent it*. I said he was a greater fool than I had supposed him to be, and if he would not see it done I would speak to Lewton, as overlooker of the collieries, who would enforce the performance of what the laws enjoined to be done. This seemed to have its weight, and he said he would see that the nuisances were removed. After dinner a note was put into my hand from Mrs. Boodle, who urges Anna and myself to come to Radstock while the pestilence is raging around us. I wrote as lively a note as I could in reply, saying I should be a poltroon to desert my post when the enemy was about to attack it. I shall get Anna to return to Bath to-morrow to be with her brother, and then I shall be at liberty to perform my duty without distressing her feelings.

Tuesday, October 16

On walking into the village after breakfast I learnt that Cook's girl died last night, and that they had buried her about four o'clock in the morning, but no new case has occurred. I cannot help thinking that the infection continues to be conveyed by the bed-clothes, as they ought to be burned. On my return I found a kind note from Mrs. Boodle, in reply to that I had sent her, in which she begged me to be careful and not put myself in the way jo infection unnecessarily.

Wednesday, October 17

To-day I continued my walk to call on the Boodles. The pestilence has not reached Radstock, but I think it will ere long. I sincerely hope it will not reach the family of my good friends: I love them affectionately. I told them to be under no apprehension about my having brought the infection, as I purposely avoided to visit the sick before I came to see them, but should do so on my return, which I did directly when I got back.

Friday, October 19

The Schoolmistress called and wasted nearly a couple of hours!

Sunday, October 21

I heard on going down to breakfast that the old woman Lockyear and her son-in-law were interred in the night, and that new cases had occurred. The mode of carrying the bodies in a cart to the grave is liable to great objection, as they must be handled to put them into the cart and take them out. We have a bier in the Church, which would be far better. I desired the harness maker to get an order for some straps to enable persons bearing the coffin to put over their shoulders.

Should the mortality increase, a hole ought to be dug in my Glebe Field at Meadyates, as I before proposed, and a couple of men expressly appointed for attending the interments.

Monday, October 29

Anna arrived about nine, and said how anxious Joseph was to come home, and how much more comfortable she should be to have him back and attend upon him here. I thought it most advisable to write to Mr. Norman, which I did in the following words, enclosing a draft for £50 on the Bladud Bank:

"MY DEAR SIR,
        "I cannot sufficiently express the feelings of gratitude I have long entertained for your unremitting attentions to my dear son. I

only wish it were in my power to make a more adequate return: sed non omnia possumus omnes: if the amount of the enclosed sum were to be multiplied ten times it would be inadequate to come up to my ideas of what I conceive to be your due. Let my gratitude make up the balance of the account.

"Believe me, dear Sir,

"Most faithfully yours,

"John Skinner."

"P.S.—I feel very anxious that the poor fellow should return home, that I may be enabled to pay *my attention* also to him while I can so do."

Anna left us a little after five. I feel so low and uncomfortable after her departure that I cannot fix my attention to anything, so shall go to bed. I can write no more: "In manus tuas animam meam commendo Domine Deus,"—Amen.

Wednesday, October 31

The note I received from Anna, intimating that Joseph had indications of another expectoration of blood, hurried me into Bath immediately I received it. I found him better than I expected, and at his desire I administered the Sacrament. My Mother seems very nervous, and my brother Russell, alas! far from well; but still he is able to amuse himself with writing my Journals, etc., etc., which is a great comfort, otherwise his time would hang heavy on his hands. Poor Joseph cannot help being irritable at times, owing to the complaint; fain would I be released from this thraldom, and almost envy the freedom my son will shortly procure when released from this sad life. Staying in Bath the night, they made me up a bed in the parlour—the house being quite full.

Thursday, November 1

I may truly say I spent a sleepless night. What with the noise in the street, the ringing of bells, and the striking of the clock every quarter, together with the bawling of the watchman and the blowing of the wind, and the snoring of the dog, "Vallis," who would not leave my room, having accompanied me from Camerton, I could not close my eyes, and passed the heavy hours in a state of mental and bodily pain till the morning again cheered me for a while. The chaise took myself afterwards to Camerton.

Friday, November 2

It rained incessantly the whole morning. It is most providential I I am not called upon to visit the sick, the parish being again healthy, although someone has inserted in the Bath papers stating that we have had seventy on the sick list.

Monday, November 5

The post brought me a note from Anna saying Joseph had passed an indifferent night. I drove to Widcombe immediately and found him in bed, but he said he felt better. I find my Mother is very averse from his removal home, but what can be more foolish? She has left her own home and lodges on the South Parade, declaring it makes her so nervous that she could never think of seeing Joseph again, and now when I want to relieve her, and Joseph is most anxious to return home, she is doing all she can to prevent it and to agitate his mind by putting obstacles in the way.

Before dinner I had a good deal of conversation about Russell, who should have a skilful surgeon instead of a bungling apothecary to attend him. My Mother seemed also to be convinced of the necessity of having Norman's advice. Poor Russell has a complication of disorders, so, poor fellow, he will be dosed quantum sufficit, I will answer for it. He is really looking very ill, and it grieves me. I did prevail so far with him, I hope, to send for Norman, and I promised to settle all the additional expense. My Mother considers none of these things, in fact she is now so much under the control of a base woman who has gotten into her service and confidence, estranging my Mother from her own family and her other servants who have been with her several years; what will be the end of this unfortunate infatuation I know not. This woman, I learn, has been found out in a number of bad doings, and I hear that she has already prevailed so far that her name is inserted in my Mother's Will for a legacy. Now my poor Mother is left entirely at her disposal, she has succeeded so far as to get my Mother away from her own house and, I hear, is endeavouring to persuade her to give up housekeeping altogether and to live in lodgings attended by her alone.

I did not touch upon the subject of Joseph's removal and my Mother seemed quite composed. I told her I was convinced that she was in the power of ill advisers; but her own son was the best and properest person to advise her, and she would not attend to his advice: that if she did not dismiss Mrs. Lake I should not again visit her. My Mother then got up from her chair, took the candle and went out of the room to her dear adviser, who I doubt not had been listening at the door.

Anna returned to Camerton to give directions about what was requisite to be done for the reception of dear Joseph. I have so arranged that we are to bring back Joseph either on Wednesday or Thursday without acquainting my Mother, as she is very averse from his removal home, and declaring it will break her heart if he leaves Bath.

My Mother forgets that a Father has as much interest in the welfare of his child at least as a grandmother. When she knows he is removed she herself will be more comfortable.

Sleep was far from my eyes. I felt sorely oppressed as the result of my visit to my Mother.

Wednesday, November 7

I removed my writing-desk from my study to the bedroom over the parlour, where I mean to sleep and keep what books I have need of, so that poor Joseph will have no interruption in his asylum, which I am sure he will find quite as comfortable as the two rooms he will quit at Widcombe; and when we have put up the sandbags on the windows and doors we shall keep the rooms quite as warm as those he now occupies. I find as it is we can get the thermometer at 60.

Thursday, November 8

I walked to Shoscombe, visiting Jacob Balne, a poor wretched old man who is brought to the severest misery, and will soon, if I mistake not, be summoned into another world to give an account of his misconduct in this. His wife has left him, and is now in a brothel in Avon Street. I read prayers to him, after a long and serious conversation. I, moreover, promised to lend him the sheets and blankets I had lent to Thomas's wife as soon as they removed from the Red Post, for he says he has nothing to cover him in his bed but his old great-coat. I gave him 2s. 6d.

On my return to Camerton I found that my son Owen, who returned from Town last night, had been to Camerton and brought me the following note saying that Joseph and Anna meant to come back to-morrow:

"MY DEAREST PAPA,

"I have had rather a bad night, so that I am not so well to-day, but was up at ten fully prepared for my journey. I had thought that it was fully fixed that I was to go yesterday, and I was up early and quite strong. Norman called at twelve, thinking we were to go. I hope, my dearest Papa, that nothing will hinder my being again under the roof where I was brought up, and believe me that it imparts a happiness to my mind, which has of late been low and melancholy, that we shall all meet again; and if it be the will of God that my time should be short at home, it will be a source of happiness to be amongst my nearest and dearest relatives.

"Adieu, dearest Papa, and remain

"Your ever affectionate Son,
"J. H. SKINNER."

I was delighted to hear of this determination. A great load has been taken from my mind, as I was much afraid the poor fellow had been induced to continue away from his own home, and that I should have been prevented the melancholy office of attending him and administering to his comforts at the last.

Friday, November 9

At twelve I walked through the plantations, hoping to meet with them, as Owen said they would be here at half-past twelve, and I wished to open the gates for the carriage myself. They did not arrive till past two, and I was most happy to find Joseph bore his journey so well; indeed, the day was beautiful, and nothing occurred during the journey to disturb or distress him. I sat with him till dinner time, and again went to him after tea. We shall be able now, one or the other, to attend him constantly.

I hear the Bishop has given Warner the two Livings vacant by the death of Mr. Quick, Corston and Chelwood: in these times perhaps it had been better if his Lordship had given one of them to some poor Curate, especially as Warner has had before two Livings given him by the Bishop, and two by Bishop Beadon, all of which he relinquished without any ostensible motive for his so doing. I fear he will expose his patron to disagreeable animadversions on the subject.

I must endeavour to arrange it that Anna does not continue the whole day in Joseph's room. She sat up till twelve o'clock last night with him, and as we have so attentive a nurse she need not do so, and I am well assured that the disorder is infectious to those of the same family. I will endeavour to persuade her to take regular exercise on horseback with her brother Owen, and I will take my station in the sick-room meanwhile. I must relinquish all other occupations and attend solely to one, which is to make the poor fellow as comfortable as possible as long as his hour-glass continues to run. I am happy to find the servants seem disposed to give no trouble.

Wednesday, November 14

I offered to come and read with Joseph, but he seems better satisfied with his sister. I took some of the drawings I had finished for him to look at.

Thursday, November 15

I find it is almost too much to bear the pressure on myself. Owen is no comfort to me, and Anna is almost the whole day with her brother. Joseph received the Sacrament in Bath, but since that has not spoken on the subject of religion; and, when I have asked Anna or hinted something whether he wished to see me, I have always heard some objection—either he was going to sleep, or just going to his meal. I observe, poor fellow, his mind is not inclined to his Father: to what am I to attribute his being set against me now?

Saturday, November 17

When I went down to breakfast scarcely one word was spoken by Anna, and Owen was sullen and sulky. On my remonstrating with him, he said that he had nothing to converse with me about, as we had not one idea in common. This led to a renewal of his insolence. I could not help saying he was as conceited as he was ignorant and idle, and I could prophesy he would never be a lawyer. He said, at any rate he knew more than I ever did; and as for my writings, no one would ever read the nonsense I had written. When I mentioned my having gained a prize at Trinity College when I was an under-graduate, and that I had written for the University Prize as soon as I took my degree, his reply was that none but the most stupid fellows ever thought of writing for the college prize, and as for the University it was a clear token my composition was not approved of, otherwise I should have gained that prize, which might have been of some credit to me. I need not recapitulate the conversation that ensued: afterwards I went to my own occupations. Soon after, Mr. Boodle called, and although I heard him speaking with my daughter below stairs I did not go down to him, finding myself quite exhausted and unable to converse. Joseph sent to say he wished to speak to Mr. Boodle, who continued some time in his room. I went thither about a quarter of an hour after, when Boodle was gone. Joseph appeared to be satisfied with the little attentions I shewed him, but when I offered to come with my drawings to his room after tea he said he felt fatigued and should wish to get to sleep. At dinner Owen directed what conversation he had to his sister. After dinner when the wine was placed on the table, and I had passed the bottle to him after I had helped his sister, he shoved it away, saying he should not take any. Seeing he was in no humour to make either me or himself comfortable, I went into my bedroom and shortly after to bed.

Sunday, November 18

I rose with a heavy heart, and with no very pleasant anticipations respecting the performance of the Sunday's duty. There was but a thin congregation. On returning to the Parsonage after Church, the newspapers being brought, Owen took one and I the other; but he made such a rustling and crumpling with his I could scarcely read at all, so I took a walk round the plantations, and came again to the parlour where Owen was sitting. I said on entering, of which he took not the slightest notice, I was sorry to see him in the same humour. He said there was no reason, because he had given me his hand, that he had forgiven what I said to him! by no means: he did not mean to speak to me, and that was enough. I said I thought the service he attended would have put better ideas in his head. He said nothing I could say, either in private or public, would have any weight with him: that I pretended to be religious, but that was a mere farce: he knew I was a Deist or a Socinian if I was anything; but certainly I did not teach the religion of Christ. I was so much hurt by this new and unexpected charge, which I never could have dreamt of, I said to him: "Wretched youth, do not bring upon yourself your own damnation by speaking on such a day as this what you know to be false." He then began swearing, and repeating all he could to provoke me; but he did not succeed at the time, for I left the room and walked on the Church Walk, and shortly after I went into the Church and read the service. On my return I asked Owen where his sister was. He gave me some unpleasant reply, and I went upstairs and found her in her brother's room, for he was got up and sitting in the armchair in the study. On my saying "I am sorry you did not come to Church," her reply was, "You know I never do of an evening." Joseph said something about begging me not to agitate him, although I spoke low, and without the least anger. I told him I had offered to read to him, and on that day would do what I could to compose rather than agitate him. He said he did not like my doctrines, and had rather not hear them, since they were not the doctrines of the Church. I begged he would point out in what respect they were not the doctrines of the Church. He said he was not able to enter into arguments, but he expected to be saved by grace. He then said he would rather have some other person to converse with on the subject of religion than me; that he begged, therefore, I would not trouble myself to read prayers to him or do anything to disturb him; if he had known what he was to experience when he came here, he should not have come: I had been quarrelling with his brother and sister, and if that was to go on he had rather go back to Bath; there he should be quiet: that he had £200 and could pay for a lodging. I replied I should leave him, for I saw I could be of no service to him. Surely I have done nothing to deserve all this. After tea I went up to my bedroom and wrote thus far; all these things are against me, and will bring down my grey hairs in sorrow to the grave. I am now going to bed, I cannot say to sleep. There is surely not one thing now in the world that can excite in my mind a wish to live longer in this toilsome state. But not my will, but Thine be done, O God.

Monday, November 19

I had no sleep, and I kept my bed the whole day, and could not take any kind of nourishment whatever. Anna came into my room in the evening; she still perseveres in the same mind as heretofore, that is, to side with her brothers in their unnatural rebellion against their Father. I told her both she and her brother were incurring a great responsibility in setting Joseph against my religious assistance, and I hope he will be brought to see things in a different light before he dies. I wrote thus far in my chamber when I arose from my bed, and have in part disburthened my mind by so doing.

1832

I got up to breakfast: still the same sulky behaviour in my son Owen he has shewn for some time. I walked up to the Glebe Farm to enquire about the hay which Collins had bought: as Owen told me he would dispose of the stock in spite of me. I thought this precaution necessary! On my return I met a sister of Moon's wife, whose family has . . .

Poor Russell, who finished writing at this place, being too ill to attend further to his accustomed employment, might say "Lassus artemque repono." On the 21st December my Mother wrote to me saying he was so ill there were no hopes of his recovery. I drove into Bath directly and saw him in a most weak and exhausted state, and a few days after he died.

These lines I retain as a votive offering.

_____

These lines are now a blank for ever;
No one will employ them again.
Cold is that hand which once was guided by them
    in its course,
And cold and stiff will soon be mine
Which now, with a fluent pen, records this true
    observation,
That high and low, rich and poor,
Shortly must be with the dust.

Here is indeed a blank: who will fill it up?

   Let us close the door, there is nobody at home.

J S.

Memoranda

respecting my severe trials in 1832, *which may well be called*

AGONIA

THE contents of this volume are Journals from November 13, 1832 to February 24, 1833—covering the death of my brother Russell, when the power I had before enjoyed of transcribing my Journals by another hand ceased, and I was obliged to bind up the daily memoranda I made in the rude manner here exemplified; but still as memoranda to myself they will be equally valuable, and I may hereafter refer to them as the records of melancholy transactions which for the time weighed heavily on my heart; for I was doomed to experience the base ingratitude of my children, who had ate of my board and drank of my cup, and yet . . . [*some pages missing*] . . . then these Journals were sent to my brother Russell to be copied a short time before his death, and he had copied as far as November 21 when he gave up writing. Vide Vol. 110 of my Journals . . . "I met a sister of Moon's wife whose family has . . ."

Wednesday, November 21

. . . been visited by the Cholera. She said she was on the way to his Parish (Holcombe, I believe) to get relief, for they were absolutely starving, not being able to work, either himself or his boy.

I gave her five shillings for them and begged she would not mention to anyone that I had given it, but keep it to themselves, since if it were known that I did anything for them it would prevent the assistance they ought to receive from the Parish.

Towards the middle of the day I walked to administer the Sacrament to old Swift beyond the Red Post.

Moger (the old broken-down Farmer who resides in Wick Lane) attended. He seemed a very sensible old man. I gave Swift a shilling and another to a poor woman who has been ill and derives no assistance from our Parish.

On returning to the Parsonage Anna came into the Parlour and I told her as she did not like to deliver my letter to Joseph on the score of agitating him, and as she said she was sure he would mention the contents to his brother, Owen, I had resolved not to agitate myself

464

further in the business and therefore should put the letter into the fire, which I did, only observing to her that both she and her brother incurred a great responsibility in preventing Joseph from receiving the benefit of my advice at this most important crisis when his eternal welfare might be at stake. That with respect to myself I had just received the Sacrament and had resolved to keep my mind as much as possible and *transgress no more with my lips if I could possibly avoid it*. Yet what *I had done* was not in haste, or through excitement, but according to the sober dictates of my Judgement and Conscience; but it had not succeeded. . . . but I would not revert again to those subjects.

I had declared I was in Peace and Charity with all when I received the Sacrament, and I would continue so, and if Joseph did not wish to see me, it was no more than if I resided at a distance from him instead of in the same house.

Our dinner passed much as usual. When Owen left the Parlour, Anna recommenced the conversation respecting Joseph, saying it was my Duty to go to him and read prayers to him, and lead his mind to Religious considerations; did I not do so with my Parishioners, was I not constantly visiting them and reading prayers to them, had I not been this very day doing that which I refused to do for my son—I said, by no means—my son had told me that he *did not like my doctrines* and that he should decline listening any more to my instructions; he moreover bolted his door against me and it was on that account I had declared I would not again visit him till he sent for me, and I continued fixed in that determination—there was no similarity between the cases—my Parishioners *did wish to see me* when they sent for me; *but* I did not read the prayers to them as a mere form, but always by previous conversation brought their minds to that kind of feeling as to wish themselves to join in this Act of Devotion, otherwise it was of no service to them. That I had wished to bring Joseph's mind to this state that he should feel anxious for prayer and Religious consolation, and that was the principal object I had in view when he was received into my house. Anna said, then why did you not do so when he came here. I replied, because he declined my assistance. I had offered to read to him several times but he always made some excuse for not hearing me. She said that was because he thought I meant to read amusing books not about Religion . . . that it was my duty to have come and talked to him first and thus to have brought him to ask me to pray as I said I had done in other instances with my Parishioners. I asked her whether it was not great presumption in her to tell me what was *my duty* or to pretend to teach me what I ought to do in the exercise of my professional discretion.

I had had every opportunity of being acquainted with the disposition of her brother from his youth up till now. I therefore expected as his illness increased he would be brought to solicit my advice and assistance, and come with a proper frame of mind to profit by what I said. . . . the medicine I had conveyed in the letter I addressed to Joseph might have appeared harsh and unpleasant at first, but if it produced ultimately a salutary effect and aroused him to proper exertions it would have answered the purpose I intended it to produce.

I felt very uncomfortable and yet I know I am doing right.

Thursday, November 22

I walked with Anna to call on poor Mrs. Colbourne and found she had died Tuesday. On our return we found Mrs. Boodle and the two girls but they would not stay for dinner.

Before tea Anna came downstairs to say Joseph wished to see me. I went into his room and was much affected at the meeting. I told him he must be assured that I had his interest at heart and had ever consulted it but felt more interested now in his Eternal welfare. I drank tea with him and it was agreed that I should come every day into his room to read and say prayers. I felt more comfortable on the occasion than I have done for some time. I forgot to mention I sent the Journals to my brother up to the 20th to be copied, also a note requesting he would inform me how he was going on, and that he would not mention the contents of the Journals to anyone and be particularly careful that the vile woman, Mrs. Lake, did not read them but would lock them up after he had done writing.

Friday, November 23

I went into Joseph's room after breakfast and entered into some serious and interesting conversation on the subject of Religion as I wished gradually to lead his mind to that most important duty of repentance. I first read the 53 Chapter of Isaiah proclaiming the Advent of Jesus Christ. Afterwards the first of St. John. Joseph seemed to listen very attentively to what I said, and having already spent more than an hour with him I took my leave.

Anna and her brother rode into Bath on his business, and I walked to Radstock to call on the Boodles feeling much more comfortable than I have done for sometime past.

I found Joseph was so much occupied with his brother on money matters and on the sale they have in contemplation of the things on the Farm that I did not continue my reading as I intended; but should have done so, of course, had he expressed the least wish for my company. I just went into his room to wish him good night.

Saturday, November 24

On going into his (Joseph's) Bedroom to ask whether I should read to him I found him still engaged in talking with Anna on business and I said we would defer our reading but I would come to him when he sent for me as we should not ourselves talk of business.

It rained the whole day and I continued downstairs in the Parlour drawing—expecting I should have been sent for when his mind was in a state for reading, but I had no summons. Just before dinner Anna came into the Parlour and I mentioned to her I had been in expectation of hearing from Joseph. She replied that her brother had said he should not send for me; if I chose to come I might have done it. This introduced some unpleasant conversation and again made me feel very uncomfortable, but the main purport of my argument was—surely it would be better he should send for me than that I should come to him when his mind was occupied with other subjects.

Owen came into the Parlour to dinner and according to the usual manner he has adopted for some days, scarcely spoke, and if he did address me it was in a sullen and sulky manner; he refuses now to take my wine, but I much fear continues his laudanum.

We were going on with every prospect of comfort—that is Joseph and myself—until Owen and his sister went to Bath to call on my mother. She would not wilfully, I am sure, encourage them in their opposition to their father, but perhaps inadvertently dropped something which might have had this effect, since I perceive a visible difference in the behaviour of Anna; and so I told her, and begged her again to reflect on the part she was now playing and her very improper behaviour to her father; for at a time when he needed most consolation she gave him the most pain by her marked neglect for she never comes into the room now where I am sitting but continues upstairs with her brother the whole morning.

Just before dinner to-day I heard her singing as she came down-stairs and on her saying as she came into the room what a dark and gloomy day it was, I said, she did not appear to think so *as she was quite gay.* She said if there was any harm in singing why did I get her to sing and play to me of an evening? I replied, she had done so so unwillingly the last time I should not trouble her again—respecting her not coming into the Parlour sometimes to see me, she said when I had my study I did not come down into the Parlour and we used not then to meet—only at meal times and at prayer time; and she had to be with her brother. In my agony I could not help saying that one of these days she would feel how improperly she was acting, she had received every kindness from her father and returned it with the greatest ingratitude. She came into prayers with her brother and I wished them good-night, but I could not offer them my hand.

I went into my bedroom but could get no sleep, so I put on my dressing gown and went into the Parlour where I finished my Journal up to this hour (four o'clock).

As Joseph was coughing violently I went into his room to enquire if I could assist him with anything, and got him his honey: The new attendant who is in my study I fear sleeps too sound—otherwise she must have heard him. I am now going to bed again to try and get a little sleep having to perform the Service at Church.

My trial now presses heavy but I hope I shall support it, and not verify what my son said when he had almost driven me beyond myself.

Sunday, November 25

I read Prayers to a thin congregation and afterwards walked with Anna to call on Hiscox, who seems declining rapidly; we then continued along the Canal to Colliers' Row—the cholera is now quite out of the Parish and I included our grateful remembrancy for the same in the General Prayer of Thanksgiving during the Evening Service. I preached a sermon I had before written on the Divine Sermon on the Mount to an attentive congregation. After tea I went early to bed being tired with the exertions of the day and the little sleep I had the preceding night.

N.B.—Owen seems returned to a proper sense of his duty which will make me more comfortable than anything else can possibly do under present circumstances.

Monday, November 26

I read a portion of the Gospel of St. John to Joseph after breakfast and explained whatever appeared to be a difficulty to him—Joseph seemed very attentive and I read two chapters; referring to the Greek Testament when there was any doubt about the true meaning of a word.

Tuesday, November 27

I sleep so badly through want of exercise and mental worry that I quit my bed of a morning much more fatigued than when I go to bed. I continued my reading and explanation with Joseph after breakfast and am happy to find he takes such an interest in this exercise which gives an opportunity of inculcating instruction and shewing the groundwork of our future expectations.

Wednesday, November 28

I slept so badly I did not get up to breakfast. After breakfast I read as usual with Joseph who enters very fully into the subject and feels most interested—indeed I had given him the Journals to peruse where I continued the same kind of reading with his Uncle Fitz Owen till his death.

I hope he will be as tranquil at the last as his Uncle was.

As it continued raining the whole day I did not attempt to go out, we have had some very stormy weather accompanied by Thunder and Hail which I fear will do much damage to the shipping, especially off the Dutch coast; but we had no business to join in this unjust war. I read in the Papers last week that one of the French ships had run foul of one in the Channel and both had received considerable damage, we are in hourly expectation of receiving accounts from Antwerp. I cannot say but I wish well to the cause of the Dutch, their king being a just and Religious man and his opponent much the reverse. The Present Ministry I trust will not be permitted to continue their ignorant and iniquitous career much longer unless by their means the great Disposer of all events means to accelerate our ruin.

Thursday, November 29

I received a note from Mr. Mogg of Chewton, who wishes me to attend on the seventh of next month at Paulton when a Thanksgiving Sermon will be preached by him on the subject of the place being relieved from the severe scourge of the Cholera—upwards of 60 persons I hear have perished, and nearly £800 been collected for the families of the sufferers. I excused myself from attending on account of my son's illness.

I walked under a heavy rain to inter old Swift at three o'clock.

Friday, November 30

Much the same weather and same occupations as the preceding days.

Saturday, December 1

I heard from Mr. Phelps who wants to come to Camerton, but I cannot receive him just now—I have been so negligent as to leave letters unanswered till this time but if I live till Monday I will write. I have no goût for writing now, even my Journals become irksome to me. Still I will endeavour to keep this my log book of life going on till the last if I am not prevented by illness or by the last summons. I have felt very low and uncomfortable the whole of the week—sed spero meliora, I am now going to bed.

Sunday, December 2

I read with Joseph after breakfast and finished the Gospel of St. John which I took a general view of at the conclusion and expounded to the best of my abilities—the collection of opinions of our best divines at the conclusion of the Gospel in Mant's Bible was of some assistance to me.

Monday, December 3

The weather still rainy and boisterous, however, I read as usual with Joseph—afterwards I was obliged to take a walk in spite of it, and I proceeded round the Plantations before dinner it being the most sheltered situation I could find.

The Post brought me a letter from Mr. John Jarrett who is staying in Suffolk, enclosing £20 draft on Tufnell's Bank, Bath, and desiring me to lay it out in remunerating the sufferers who burnt their bedding on account of the Cholera. It will be of great service in providing other things besides.

Tuesday, December 4

I walked into the village and visited Hiscox who like poor Joseph is daily getting weaker and weaker and his cough is if anything more violent. I called on different persons who have suffered any losses on account of the Cholera.

This being Joseph's Sale of the Live Stock etc., etc., on the Glebe Farm, Owen was occupied on the premises the whole morning and did not return to dinner. Boodle and Newnham called during the morning. The former told me he was going to visit the Bishop at Wells the next day and I sent my remembrances to him by this opportunity. I continued drawing till bed time.

I understood the things went badly at the sale. . . . I have learned to value all around me at a very small price—let them go, the moth hath eaten them and the soil hath corrupted them—let them pass away and let me pass away too. I have no pleasure in the things which others covet, the only thing I do esteem is the smile of artless innocence which I now and then am cheered with in my walks. How can they pretend to say that children are under original sin till they are Regenerated by Baptism—did not our Saviour himself declare that unless we had the simplicity of children we could not inherit the Kingdom of God. I am cheered by the smile of children: when nothing now has power to cheer me I am comforted by their artless looks: the bleating of the fleecy flock also has more charms for me now than the finest music. I begin to dislike the countenance of my fellows. I like not my own when I see it in the glass!

Wednesday, December 5

I walked with Anna to Radstock, and felt refreshed with that hitherto unsophisticated family. Mrs. Boodle and the girls walked back with us part of the way to Camerton. I felt the weight which daily and hourly oppresses me partly relieved, but it returned again when I descended the hill and came within the atmosphere of the Parsonage.

I forgot to say the Ringers were very impertinent and I turned them out of the Belfry when I found they distressed my sick son.

Thursday, December 6

Day succeeds to day—the fogs of the atmosphere penetrate even my mind, rendering it heavy, and all natural objects seem dull and insipid—will it ever recover its energies? I seem to apprehend it will not, yet I have some hope: the fatigues of my body had so entirely weakened my mind on my return from France four years ago I almost despaired of recovery but I did rally again and may do so hereafter; but I have so thorough a distaste for all things I am become as it were a mere caput mortuum.

I occupied the morning in the Parish. I visited Hiscox [and also] Parfitt at Bridge Place to speak to the parents on the misconduct of their son, a lad of 18 or 19 who was one of the Ringers I turned out of the Belfry the day before yesterday. They had rang after the Wedding and continued doing so till near four o'clock, which must have been a great annoyance to poor Joseph to hear the jingle of the Bells so near the whole of the morning—they were still ringing when Anna and myself returned from our walk from Radstock at four o'clock: they seemed at first to oppose my authority but I succeeded in turning them out of the belfry and locking the door.

Parfitt's mother said he was so wild a youth he [did] them much trouble; indeed not long since he stabbed Harris with a bin knife and was sent to prison, and lately he was attacked with the Cholera and was near dying, but his mother said it made no change in his wild habits. This youth when I hurried him and his companions out of the Belfry said he would go to the Red Post Ale House. I told him if he did so I never would permit him to ring again as he was not of the Parish, neither would I give the Ringers any Christmas box.

It is these half-grown youths who are the instigators to all kinds of mischief: at the Bristol Riots more harm was done by them than by grown up people.

In the course of my walk this morning I visited Harris of Dagland, Edward Luton, Moon, and Cook of Colliers' Row, and old Mrs. Harding of Cridlingcot. Luton, the Bailiff of the Coal Works has been, I find, very kind to the people during their affliction and has distributed money and bed-linen among them. I did not find him at home either time I called, but begged the servant to tell him I wished to see him at the Parsonage to speak on the business as I must in part regulate Mr. John Jarrett's Donation by what he has done.

Boodle and the girls called about three. He tells me the Bishop of Bath and Wells and the Bishop of Exeter breakfast with him at Radstock on Wednesday next. He wishes me to join the party but I cannot enjoy company now; at another time I should have been interested in having an introduction to Philpot as a celebrated man, and more especially as I was his competitor for the [Bachelor's?] prize at Oxford 34 years ago, which he gained and perhaps in a great measure owed his success in life to that circumstance, but I envy not his Episcopal honours for from my heart I may declare—nolo Episcopari—I had rather walk about my premises at Camerton unnoticed and unknown than be exposed to the constant intimidations and interferences incident to the See of Exeter.

Not having my Study, I am obliged to scribble my Journals and prepare or rather look over my Sermons in my bed-chamber.

Sunday, December 9

I spent an hour with Joseph, and read prayers in the morning to a thin Congregation, then walked with Owen and Anna in the Plantations. I felt much exhausted by my exertions and went to bed before 10 o'clock. Joseph has been but poorly to-day and could not eat his dinner.

Monday, December 10

Owen and his sister drove into Bath and after I had read the portion of Scripture as usual to Joseph I had my drawing things brought into his room and continued finishing the sketches I have yet to complete for my Journals. I feel little interest in anything now, it seems as though all my accounts are to be wound up; this year I have already numbered 60 winters and that is perhaps space enough to complete my trials; if so, I hope I may depart in peace since the World retains no ties to bind me to it.

I waited dinner till after five for Owen and Anna. Immediately the cloth was removed Anna quitted the room and went to her brother. On my expostulating on the little regard and attention shewn to myself when I saw her at tea her brother, Owen, defended her conduct, and it ended as our conversations now generally do in a renewal of unpleasantness, and I went to bed quite dissatisfied with myself and all around me. How have I merited this treatment? But it must not be suffered to get ahead, otherwise—adieu to all comfort the remaining weeks, months or years I may be permitted to live.

Tuesday, December 11

Memoranda of monies disbursed on Mr. Jarrett's account to the Colliers' families who have suffered from the Cholera at Camerton. I had supposed that ten pounds would settle the whole of the

Colliers' disbursements on account of the Cholera and so I mentioned in my letter to him, and the other £10 I said I would lay out on clothes for the little boys who are not yet able to work in the Pits, as some of them are nearly naked.

Anna, when yesterday in Bath, bought 12 suits for children of and under seven years of age for less than five pounds, the remainder of the £20 will be laid out in shirts and stockings and shoes—We ourselves shall distribute £10 and Mrs. Anne Stephens of the Manor House, £5 besides this, so there is some little prospect of comfort in store for the Parish this winter. It was nearly dinner time when I finished my Memoranda. On going into the Parlour I sent the servant girl upstairs to Anna to beg she would come to me: she sent down she was dressing and could not come; dinner meanwhile came in, and as she did not return I helped myself to some soup and asked Owen whether I should help him.

He said, certainly not, till his sister came down. He would not be so ill bred as to begin dinner till the Lady of the house were set at table. I said I hoped I knew good breeding as well as he did and should make no scruple of beginning my dinner although his sister were not present—he said it was not gentlemanly at any rate, that he always acted as a gentleman and would do so though I did not. I answered nothing further.

After dinner he and his sister went out of the room, not staying for Wine and Dessert. After I had finished and it was near six I rang for Tea and made it, and helped myself when they came into the Parlour, Owen banging the door as he entered the room. I begged he would not make so much noise as I had a headache. He said he supposed I had been drinking a bottle and a half since he had left the room. I replied I had only taken the usual quantity I was accustomed to—that he might have partook of what I had on the table but he chose to leave the room immediately the cloth was removed. He said he did not like to stay to be abused, that he was no longer a boy and knew his duty much better than I did; that the times were gone when Parents thought they had licence to lecture their children when they were grown up: that he was as much a gentleman and more so than I ever was and had as many gentlemanly friends and acquaintants as ever I had, who knew how to value him if I did not. If I began to lecture him he would not bear it, he never should have come into my house had it not been to see his brother, not me, since he had told me before he had not one single grain of affection for me: that whatever I had done for my children I was obliged to do it, otherwise I could not have held up my head in Society: even as it was, everyone knew my character and despised me: that I was the most selfish of beings and had spent all my disposable Property on myself.

I could contain myself no longer and said although he was my son I had the unhappiness to decláre he was the *most unprincipled ungrateful scoundrel I ever conversed with*.

I then took my bed candle and went upstairs into my Sleeping Room, but not to sleep, for that Balm was far from me.

I passed a miserable night.

Wednesday, December 12

At breakfast Owen looked as though he was about to renew the conversation of the preceding evening, but I said I requested a truce, for I cannot support this kind of warfare, and should leave the house if he would not.

About the middle of the day Anna came in with a long account from Mrs. Moger, the cook, to whom I had given a draft for six guineas for her half-year's wages on the 3rd of this month, saying there was another quarter due and also nearly five pounds for things Mrs. Moger had paid for. I said I thought everything was included in our weekly accounts, but it seems that Anna had let Mrs. M. advance *her* the money. I said it was bad policy to borrow money of a servant to deceive her father. I gave therefore a draft for the additional wages and the bills included—amounting to ten pounds more.

This bad servant who gave [notice] on pretext of not being able to do the work as her legs were so bad, leaves us on Monday and Walford's wife is to come for a time—much against my daughter's inclinations; but I must nevertheless look into these matters myself or I shall be entirely ruined if my expenditure increases thus.

I would support everything from without, but when my domestic comfort is thus broken in upon and I have Thorns & Briars planted on my table and in my bed, then there is no peace left.

I left the Parsonage at two o'clock, determining not to return to dinner. I walked to Radstock, when the Boodles received me with the same friendship as they were wont to do.

There being an hour to spare before dinner I accompanied Boodle to the Church to look at the pews. About £800 has been laid out in enlarging the building, to the best advantage.

On going into the Churchyard I made eight sketches, five of the Church and three of the nearby countryside.

Thursday, December 13

After breakfast I walked home. Owen is gone to Bath and Anna received me in the same ungracious manner which of late has become so familiar to her.

I went into Joseph's room—he tells me he feels no pain whatever. I continued drawing in his room until his brother and sister returned.

At dinner we had little conversation as usual, but I learnt from Owen that there has been a riot at Frome on account of the Election and the Military called in. I had much rather myself be exposed to public insurrection and tumult than wounded by a domestic one. I went early to bed.

Saturday, December 15

I struck a light as soon as I awoke and dressed. On going downstairs Anna wished me good morning and Owen looked as usual and said nothing.

It rained hard and I said to Anna that the servant Mrs. Moger had better not go to Bath in the rain. That Walford was to drive her in and bring [back] his wife; and as I perceived that Owen was dressed to go into Bath I supposed he had made some arrangements to go thither, as he had told me he had taken his place on the Coach to return to Town. I said I hoped that he would not leave the house with a chance of taking cold, but he still preserved his silence and went upstairs to Joseph.

Monday, December 17

I finished writing up my Journal to this time and enclosed it in a parcel to take to my brother when I go into Bath tomorrow.

Collins of the Mill took the after grass of the Glebe for two pounds.

Tuesday, December 18

I drove to Bath a little after one o'clock and went directly to Sydney Gardens where the Poll was held and took Walford with me. There was no crowd, and on entering the room appointed to receive the Rolls of the Parishes in our division I find that Gore Langton is at the head of the Poll—nearly 250.

After quitting Sydney Gardens I drove to the market to purchase some fish for Joseph and sent Walford with the Journals I have finished, to my brother to copy, and I got home a little after four.

When Walford got back he told me he had waited 20 minutes at my Mother's in the South Parade as "two gentlemen were with Mr. Skinner," Afterwards he delivered the papers to him, for I had given him strict orders that he should deliver them himself—fearing they might fall into the hands of others, for whose perusal they were not intended.

Walford said my brother was looking very ill indeed, and that Miss Page, who was in his room, had told him he was too weak to attend to writing.

Wednesday, December 19

Not being able to sleep I left my bed at mid-night and lit my candle, in order to write to Ellen Page to request she would lock up all the papers I had sent to my brother, and also to mention to him respecting the MSS books he transcribed from my Journals, which he promised should revert to me if I survived him.

I also requested that she transcribe my Journals from the point where I left off, which will not cost her any great trouble if she only finishes a sheet a day, to the termination of this sorrowful year.

I have shewn myself a sincere friend to herself, and her mother when she was a widow, until the time of her death at Clifton, where I attended her to the grave.

This letter I sent by the Post after breakfast.

Thursday, December 20

I continued reading with Joseph as usual and then attended to the mason engaged about white-washing the house, and in ordering dinner and arranging the household concerns, for Anna continues to take no share in the management of the house without I let her keep the accounts also; which I never can do, without it runs to ruin—as my expenditure has increased two fold and she has been dealing with no less than three persons for Grocery and I have three bills to pay, amounting to upwards of £16, when I thought everything of the kind had been included in the weekly accounts.

The Butcher's bills, notwithstanding the Pigs and Poultry we have killed, were much greater than they have ever been since I kept house—and everything in proportion.

Of late I know her attention has been greatly taken up by her brother's illness and she permitted Mrs. Moger to do whatever she liked. Now I have got Walford's wife in her place she never orders anything excepting for Joseph, and says she will take no part whatever in the domestic affairs.

In the middle of the day I visited Hiscox & Osborne the Blacksmith. The former is more advanced on the road to the grave than Joseph Osborne [who] has been ill of what they call the "Complacent." That means the Cholera, but I rather think it is the Typhus.

I forgot to mention, John Rossiter called on me yesterday to get me to remit £4 10s. to town for Aaron Heal, by a draft on Hoare's House, which I did. I then mentioned to him that I had seen him the evening before on my return from Bath, exceptionally drunk. He said most of the voters were in the same situation and he seemed to think it rather meritorious than otherwise.

Friday, December 21

When I called to deliver a letter I had written to Mrs. Stephens acknowledging the receipt of £5, for a re-imbursement of the money I have laid out for the poor, I learnt that Mr. Purnell had been attacked and stabbed near his own house the other day.

Surely iniquity has now come home to us—it is at our very door. They seem to suspect Thomas, the Blacksmith, but I do not think there is sufficient grounds.

Having heard from Ellen Page that my brother was very ill I drove to Bath and put up my horse at the Angel Inn and walked to the South Parade.

He did not seem so much fallen away as I had been taught to expect from Walford's description, who told me his face was drawn and the flush of his cheeks gone. Whilst I was there Mr. Marriot the Apothecary called. It is his opinion there is water on the chest and in the region of the heart, which may produce instant death.

I asked my brother whether I could do anything for him—he said no—if he needed my assistance he would send for me. He seemed rather to wish me to curtail my visit than otherwise as he constantly looked at his watch, but I do not think he was in a state to think properly for himself or about his own situation.

I asked what he ate—his reply was "Nothing—I can eat nothing."

I asked what he had taken already to-day. He replied "Only some brandy and water."

I said "Do you take opium," He replied "No—perhaps they give me some in my evening pills, but I have taken no medicine today." For my impression was he was under the influence of opium or that in his weak state the glass of Brandy and water was too much for him and made his mind wander; for when I asked him about the Journals I had sent him to transcribe he seemed not to understand what I meant, but when I explained he pointed to the chest of drawers and said they were all locked up.

As I left, I passed my cousin Ellen on the stairs. She told me that my Mother was upstairs but too agitated to see me. I said I could not have staid as I had to go to the market to purchase some things for Joseph.

I purchased a small piece of Turbot for Joseph as he had long set his heart on it, and some more Turnips, which he seems to fancy. These a Basket Woman took to the Angel Inn where I had left my horse, and I made all speed to get away, as the evening soon closed and it threatened rain.

Descending Dunkerton Hill I heard the bells ringing on account of the victory gained by Mr. Brigstock over Mr. Miles; as I found later, he had above 400 votes.

Just as I came to the Swan Inn my carriage was recognised, on account of the grey horse which drew it, and I was assailed by about 50 Brutes, who stood outside the Ale House, clapping their hands and using the most abusive words.

I stopped my horse and demanded by what authority they insulted me, passing quietly along the road on my return home. I declared that if they continued their insults whatever it might cost me I would shew at Court there was one true Englishman remaining, for I would horse-whip the first person I could lay hold of, whatever the remainder of the mongrels might do to me afterwards.

I laid my hand on my whip and not a voice was heard. A better-dressed man who turned [out] to be the Attorney, came out of the Inn door and said "For shame, for shame. What business have you to insult the gentleman who has said nothing to you."

I then proceeded leisurely up Dunkerton Hill. So much for English liberty and the blessings of what is called "Reform."

I just saved daylight to reach the Parsonage not a little pleased to reach home without further adventures.

I read as usual to Joseph. I found afterwards, when overlooking the mason who has been white-washing the kitchen and offices, that Batten, his master was not sent to prison, but is returned to Camerton. That when my letter was read to the Magistrates one of them cried out "Since Mr. Skinner takes so much interest about your wife, you had better let him have her heart also"!! Whoever this man was, he is very unfit for the situation he holds as a dispenser of Justice. What are we not to expect when such low-minded persons are put on high among us.

I have long expected this acme of iniquity in the Bath Magistrates; but I will not flee from my post, but fight the good fight till the last.

After reading to Joseph I prepared my sermon. I intended preaching in the evening on the Ministry of our Saviour.

There were but few people in the morning who attended, and not many more in the evening. Cottle's child was baptised. It was so dark owing to the rain, I could not see to read the service at the Font and had the water brought into the Chancel.

I received a note from Ellen saying Russell[1] was much the same and had not left his bed.

Still the same kind of weather. I had made up my mind to continue within doors, engaged with my sketches after I had been with Joseph; when I was surprised by a visit from Mr. and Mrs. P. Hoare and their daughter, Isabella, who staid with us nearly a couple of hours and their society gave a pleasing change to the melancholy of my ideas.

Christmas Day

There was a wedding this morning and, it being Christmas Day, they made up for their prohibition against ringing overnight and we had plenty of noise before Church.

I preached on the text 1st S. John 10 & 11 verses. There were but few of the people attended. Only eleven staid the Sacrament and my daughter was not one of the number. I collected 6*s.* 6*d.* including the

---

[1] Russell Skinner died on 30 Dec.

half-crown I gave. During the course of the day I read the Sermon
I had preached at Church to Joseph.

The people continued ringing the greater part of the evening.

Half a dozen of the old people of the Parish dined with my servants
and were thankful for their fare.

I put up the three vols. of Journals and sketches in separate parcels
ticketed for the Book Binder—the fourth I hope will be complete by
the end of next week and in all probability it will be the last I shall
write, since I have no interest now in the occurrences of the day—all
is vapid or stale and toothless. I have hitherto borne up against the
evils which most closely beset me but have now no inducement to
continue the struggle or record heart-breaking transactions. One son
will soon be taken away, his brother is already dead to me—my own
body is hastening to destruction and my Parishioners every day
become more degraded and unprincipled—still I will continue on my
Post and wait the summons to leave it. I will endeavour to bear my
trials with Patience, if possible, if not with hope that the termination
of it be not long delayed.

I am writing this in my bedroom and am according to my personal
feelings as little likely to procure repose this night as I have done for
several preceding ones. I write this in the agony of my heart when
unable to sleep.

I sat the greater part of the morning with Joseph. He is always
very comfortable when I am with him and seems grateful for the
attentions I shew him, but my daughter seems always to prevent as
much as possible my sitting with him when she is there, for reasons
best known to herself. I cannot think her yet so base as to
premeditatedly do this.

I prepared a Sermon before written but altered for the occasion,
on the Text taken from the Epistle for the Day—4 Gal. 4 verse—
"When the fulness of time was come, God sent forth his Son . . . that
they might receive the adoption of sons."

I am weary of recapitulating what is written, as it fails to produce
any good, and how can I expect any good to be worked on the people

when my own family are conducting themselves so basely against me. Mr. and Mrs. Jarrett attended morning service and were very attentive. I believe from my heart he is a well meaning young man, and his wife is a woman of sound judgement and Religious feeling.

Joseph had appointed to receive the Sacrament between Churches. I told Anna I still continued adverse to administer it to her in Private as I had before felt, as I told her, to administer it to her in Public on Christmas Day, since I was convinced that her mind was not in a proper state to receive it from the expressions she used to me, her father.

After Church—on my return to the Parsonage—on going into Joseph's Room expecting to find him ready for the solemn occasion I had the mortification to perceive him *eating a pheasant* which my mother had sent him from Bath, and his sister was apparently enjoying my disappointment. I said nothing other than—"I find you otherwise engaged than I expected"—and left the room.

My daughter made her appearance at dinner and behaved so improperly before the servants—for Walford waited, it being Sunday, as well as the girl—that I could not help speaking in their presence which I am sorry for, but the behaviour of this ungrateful girl was so bad I could not constrain my feelings.

I wrote up my Journals to this time before I went to sleep, or rather, to broken rest—for sleep is gone from me. Soon will my Journals be closed; my son is at the point of death and I shall not wish to record the misbehaviour and misery of my family when he is gone. I am weary of all and fervently pray that God will take me hence that I may not longer behold the progress of the ceaseless stream of inquity which flows so rapidly, which in this my Public Station of Rector of the Parish I am called upon to stop but cannot.

I got up during the night to pray God would strengthen me. My heart is broken.

1833

I generally read for an hour with my son in his bedroom—to-day I read some of the Psalms as he said he could not fix his attention to Thomas-a-Kempis and apologised for turning his face to the wall as I read.

I cannot continue long if I get no sleep for my nerves are so shaken I know not what will be the consequence.

After my usual reading with Joseph I determined to walk for exercise, and went over to Radstock and called on the Boodles.

When left by myself after dinner I was seized with so uncontrollable a depression of spirits I could not forbear weeping, and that the servants should not hear me, went upstairs to my bed chamber.

About two o'clock the Bishop drove to my door, saying he was very anxious to call upon me and should have done so before but was fearful of intruding on my distresses; he enquired in a most friendly manner after my concerns, and I am too good a judge of human nature not to know he felt what he expressed on the occasion. He talks of our long intended tour to the North this summer in order to trace the Vallum of Hadrian as being certain—indeed it will tend much to divert my mind and prevent my wandering abroad which in these unsettled times we are not authorised to do.

I was writing this in my bedroom after having read as usual with Joseph—I heard my eldest son come into the Parlour beneath and conversing with his sister—I went down to dinner and understood that Owen was returned to Bath: this is a new way of shewing off a Father before his servants, pretending he comes to see his brother and not come into the society of his Father or partake of his provision. Of course, the servants in the house consider him as an alien to me and make their remarks on the hardness of my heart as a Minister of the Gospel to entertain a rancorous disposition against one brother now that another is dying, and to be unforgiving to the last.

N.B. The Journal has been mutilated here and several pages are missing. (Editors.)

CONTINUATION OF JOURNAL

I wrote the above in an agony of spirit almost bordering on distraction, but my mind settled in a proper calm before I retired to rest. I offered up the annexed prayer to the Almighty to forgive me my angry expressions and the irritation which occasioned them, and I will endeavour in future to amend.

Sunday, January 27

I was summoned by the servant who waits on Joseph before six to say he was very much worse and wanted to see me. I immediately put on my dressing garment and went into his room.

I found him in a cold perspiration and recommended his taking some wine and water. I then read the Prayers for the Sick and added some of the Psalms, the 23rd especially—he seemed to rally and when I went to his bedside after the servant had left the room he said he was certain he should not live over the day, and continued—"Oh my dear Papa, how sorry I am I ever made you feel uncomfortable by my perverseness. I always loved you most affectionately and was ever assured you loved me for you have always been my kindest and best friend—do forgive me all that I ever did to vex you." I said that was ever done at the time it happened for I never retained unpleasant recollections. I was accustomed to be quick in my expressions and on that account could make every allowance for the quickness of others; that I had always loved my children with the greatest sincerity and had only to lament that there had been any divisions among us, for that wounded my heart more than any afflictions I had been exposed to during the whole course of my life.

He said "I *do* know it dear Papa—do come and kiss me." I did so with the greatest fervour, his cheeks being as cold as stone. He then said that he wished the good and merciful God would receive him, he had been sensible of all his errors and had repented of them!!

I sent in the carriage for *Owen who has continued in Bath ever since his arrival from Town, coming over in the morning to see his brother and returning again to dinner at my Mother's house,* and I wrote to White to say there would be no service in the morning at Church, and to Boodle that he would perform the duty in the Evening and to bring the Sermon he had preached the Sunday before for the National School Fund, since I was fearful he could not read that I had written.

During the whole of the morning I was upstairs with Joseph endeavouring now and then to get his sister out of the room, but she was so unwilling to quit his bed-side at last I gave up the attempt. Towards the evening the difficulty of breathing became much greater and he continued dozing at intervals till nearly eight o'clock, when I heard a considerable alteration in his breathing, and on going to his bed side took his hand; his eyes were closed as in a sleep, his breathing became less audible, the pulse ceased to beat and in a few minutes I found he was gone.

Anna I believed had no idea what had taken place, as his head lay on the pillow and his eyes were closed as in a deep sleep.

I knelt down by the inanimate corpse still retaining the cold hand in mine, and said "I thank Thee O God that Thou hast heard my prayer and the transition has been thus peaceable and tranquil."

In a few minutes I persuaded Anna and Owen to leave the room —and having called the nurse and the other attendant, gave the necessary orders what was to be done—and in the course of an hour we all went to our bed-chambers.

Monday, January 28

I could not sleep for my heart was too full, and I could not divest myself of the idea that I still heard him cough, and his pale countenance still seemed before me, for I went to see that everything had been properly done before I went to bed. Anna had the servant girl who waits on her to sleep in her room.

Whilst lying awake I composed the following inscription for my tomb in lieu of that I first placed there, which is somewhat encumbrous:—

JOHANNES SKINNER

Hujus loci (Camerton Camerlaerton Camulodunum) quondam serviens necnon Rector dictus.

Obiit die   mensis   183

nec Ostorius armis Rector nomine Skinner rexerunt post annos dehinc perditus sit titulus Rectoris nam Plebi omnia parent.

Boodle called to offer his services. Mrs. Boodle had kindly offered to come to Anna but the day was so unpromising we could not think of her doing so.

Boodle drove over his Wife to be with Anna: after dinner we continued in conversation till tea, which change to my ideas proved of great service to me, as it composed my nerves and I slept better than I have done for a long time.

After breakfast I endeavoured to fill up the time by reading aloud to Mrs. Boodle and Anna. About three o'clock Boodle drove over with Georgiana, Boodle promising to perform the Service on Sunday morning.

I went early to bed as Owen was expected in the evening and I did not like to enter into any conversation which might harass my mind.

As I had fully determined not to permit either word or look to draw anything from my now only remaining son, I met him at breakfast as usual. He had appointed 10 for the funeral and the men who were to attend had their meal as breakfast in the kitchen.

We went to the Church and Boodle performed the Ceremony —happy had it been for me if I myself were the object instead of Joseph, but my hour is not yet ripe. After Boodle had left us, Owen produced his brother's Will folded up as a letter and dated 2nd January, in which he bequeathed whatever he died possessed of to his brother and sister, leaving his brother his Executor.

Owen said if I wished to have the Livy returned to me, which I had given Joseph, as it was an Elzevir edition it was at my service.

I wrote thus far before I went to bed, having first read the Prayers to the servants, which custom has been broken in upon during Joseph's illness.

The servant brought me the following letter from my son Owen who is I am happy to find, come to a sense of his misconduct and solicits my forgiveness. The hand of Providence is surely in this. I was nearly driven beyond myself by the ingratitude of my children, but now I may look for a little respite.

"MY DEAREST FATHER,

"I have been wrong, very wrong in my conduct to you, and on my ride home I have thought on it with shame and although my pride forbad me to acknowledge it, yet I have at length determined to overcome all such feelings which are prompted by an evil agency.

"I had made a resolution on the night of poor Joseph's death and again on the morning I went over his concerns never again to give you any needless provocation, but alas, it has been like too many others, broken; but shall not be persisted in any longer. I have only again to express my sorrow at this behaviour and only hope we may in future renew our old feelings of affection and keep up that bond of union which I am convinced whatever I may endeavour to think, cannot be effaced or eradicated between Father and Son.

"I am my dear Father your very affectionate Son

"FITZ OWEN SKINNER.

"*Monday night.*"

I replied immediately—for Posthac meminisse juvabit.

Wednesday, February 6

I am not so early a riser as I wish to be, neither can I ask my daughter just now to be in the breakfast parlour at eight o'clock, but we have generally finished our meal by nine.

Sunday, February 10

It was a continued rain the whole of the day. In the morning very few attended, but in the evening the Church was crowded to excess owing to the funeral of young Hill, a quondam Preacher of the Ranters, who was killed by a stone falling on him in the Coal Pits. I preached the Sermon I had before written on the uncertainty of human life and the necessity of due preparation: the people were very attentive the whole of the time and I only wish what I said may be impressed on their minds.

I was so much exhausted by my exertions during the day I went to bed at nine o'clock, requesting Anna to read Prayers to the Servants in my stead.

A woman brought the child of Zebedee Moon's daughter to be named—it is now dead—I much fear foul play. I spoke to the Father of the child on Monday about marrying the girl and he said decidedly he would not. I hear the sister of this Ranting family is with child—at least they attend to the concern of peopling the Earth if they fail in instructing the people!

I got a letter from Mr. Phelps saying Sir Richard Hoare had invited him to meet me at Stourhead next week, but I have not heard from the worthy Baronet himself.

I had to bury that poor little child of Zebedee Moon's daughter and I had an opportunity of requesting he would endeavour to keep his daughter at home and prevent a recurrence of similar *new births*. Mr. Zebedee is one of the very pious, I am informed, but the getting of bastards with them, I am induced to believe, is accounted as manifesting the fruits of the Spirit: at any rate, I can prove by my own observations the Spiritual are more addicted to this than those they look down upon as Carnal.

Stourhead

I proceeded to Stourton, where I got in good time to dress for dinner.

Sir Richard is looking better than I have seen him for some time, only his son and Mr. Phelps are with him at present.

We had a rubber in the evening or rather two, in which I was not a loser, having Sir Richard as my partner. I got to bed before eleven. It blew a hurricane the whole evening and night which kept me awake for hours.

I was in the Library a little after seven. The present Rector of Stourton joined our company at dinner, and we had cards and music in the evening—that is, Mr. Phelps played some sacred pieces on the Organ which stands in the Drawing Room.

Southfield House

We got to Southfield a little before five but did not dine till six.
Mr. Shuttleworth, a clergyman residing in Town was, I found,
arrived and made one at our Whist Table after tea. I did not get to
bed till after eleven.

I accompanied Mr. Peter Hoare in his walk to Nunney and Frome
and returned a little after five. I had in the evening some interesting
conversation with my kind host.

On returning to Camerton I learnt that old Cottle was found
drowned in the Canal Wednesday night last and was to be buried
in the evening of this day. The appearances were so singular as to
induce some to suppose it was not accidental, but God knows. The
Coroner gave his verdict simply "found drowned."

I got [a letter] from Mr. Doveton saying the Clerical Meeting will
be held at Mells on Monday, March 4th, which I shall attend if
nothing very particular intervenes to prevent me.

This being my Tithe Day I dined with the farmers at Coombs'
public house. My Receipts were £105 and £31 due.
I forgave my son £86 and Mr. Purnell had paid his £15 before.
In the course of the evening a girl from Red Hill brought a child
to be named, pretending it was ill, but it had not that appearance.
After prayers I was very glad to get to my bed, being very tired.

I felt too much fatigued and unwell after tea I did not get up to
read prayers—my daughter officiating for me, but I got no sleep
till past one o'clock, as independently of my bodily sufferings, the
rats made so much noise behind the wainscotting of my dormitory,
I could not close my eyes.
In vain I struck hard against the pannels with the poker, but they
again returned to the Charge and seemed as though they would eat

through the wood and I was obliged to let them have their own way; as I am obliged to let the two-legged vermin have their way in my Parish, since they return to the Charges when drawn away and mind neither check or control; but I have to do my duty without fear or favour and must leave the account to Providence.

I walked into the Park after breakfast and called on some of the people.

Monday, November 25

I walked into the village to call on Rose's wife whom I did not see yesterday, and spoke to Heal the Book-keeper—a canting Methodist and one of the *Clan* meeting about his good-for-nothing cousin, Mores, who once lived with me and cheated me under the mask of the greatest civility, till I found him out, and then he was as malevolent as any of them.

George[1] Coombs, whom I also spoke to in my way to Durcot, where Rose lives, said the farmers were very fearful there would be a loss through Rossiter, since he kept the accounts just as he chose. That he had taken the goods of the person sent to Jail from Tunley and means to sell them by auction.

Coombs moreover said Rossiter had cheated him out of two casks which he had of him and had never paid anything.

I said I knew Rossiter of old and the public, one of these days would know as much as I did of him when his time was come. That I had endeavoured to do everything I could for the benefit of the Parish, but had met with nothing but insult, and it was high time to leave them to themselves, which I was determined to do unless called upon to speak for myself.

Coombs said he could not blame me and I mentioned to this man my determination to take no more interest about Parish matters—I mean, as to their money, and that he might mention it to the farmers, as not a word I speak but what is carried from Dan even into Beer Sheba.

[1] George Coombs died in 1810. This must be his son, Joseph.

1834

I RODE with Anna to Combe Hay to see my God-daughter, who is so altered that I should scarcely have known her.

On our return we dressed and now dined with Trelawney Collins at Timsbury: there was a large Party—Mr. and Mrs. Hammond and two pupils, Mr. and Mrs. Paul, Mr. Hill and his sister Anne, and Boodle. We had some political skirmishing as Hammond is a strong Whig. The party dispersed early and after Prayers I retired to my dormitory.

I rose early and walked in Collins's garden which is kept in beautiful order, abounding in rare plants—but as I do not admire the desecration of the Ancient Church Font as a receptacle for flowers I scratched on it with a sharp stone—"O Fons Timsburiae videre nunc velior alga olim praesidium et dulce decus *clerum*—'; perhaps the hint may be of service.

Boodle has done the same with the old font of his Church, and both he and Collins have substituted a foolish carved toy of wood to hold the basin containing the Consecrated Water—and Thomas Boodle, the curate of Compton Dando has his Font in the stable yard! As all these my brethren are far more stiff laced in their Clerical habits than the Rector of Camerton, I wonder at their doing so: perhaps they do not attach so much value to Fonts on another account as I do, besides that of their Consecration, namely that of their antiquity which frequently decides the period of the building of the Church.

I rose tolerably early (at Radstock Rectory) and read for an hour before breakfast. The Radstock Font is put to the same use as that at Timsbury, namely that of a flower pot—O Tempora, O Mores—I do not approve of such desecration, for it may put a stumbling block in the way of the ignorant who already are not inclined to hold anything belonging to the Church in any great veneration.

After breakfast whilst the horses were getting ready for our return to Camerton, Boodle taught me some of the moves of the Chess men with which I was unacquainted, but I fear I shall prove a dull scholar.

1839

EDITOR'S NOTE. Since 1834 Skinner had written little of interest in his Journal concerning Parish matters, and the very considerable deterioration in his mental health is clearly shown by the page entitled "Liber Niger", a hymn of triumph over his enemies based on the seventy-third psalm . . .

LIBER NIGER

Oh how suddenly do they consume, perish and come
to a fearful end! Yea even as a dream when one
awaketh—so shalt thou make their image to vanish
out of the City——

N.B. It is a singular completion of the foregoing quotation that
of all the actors in the scenes here described only two farmers are
remaining at Camerton, viz. William Collings, of Durcot, and old
Stephen Rossiter and neither of these have prospered—

Burfit is on the Parish at Maiden Bradley
William Goold died in great distress in Wales
Aaron Heal was reduced to break stones on the road
Emery is still alive, turned out of his farm and in great
poverty—died 1825
Lancaster of Cridlingcot is a bankrupt reduced to great
poverty.
Charles Dando after having spent everything was killed by a
fall from his horse.
Cook of Cridlingcot after having cheated me of upwards of
£60 is on the Parish & Lippeat the Overseer is a bankrupt in
Poverty. The Reynolds are both dead in poverty.—George
Coombs of the public house died by his own debaucheries.
Lowe the gardener I believe is dead.
Stephens the lord of the manour died in France & had
scarcely a decent burial.
Old Goold and his wife died in great poverty. She had
assistance from the Parish when she died—
Kelson Junior reduced to poverty, as well as his father—

James Widcombe the Clerk and Overseer was imprisoned for embezzling parish money and is now a labourer.

Joseph Goold died in poverty and worn out by his debaucheries.

One by one, his enemies pass before us; they come to a fearful end! but his own end was near.

On September 30 Squire Purnell lay dying in his house at Woodborough across the Fosse. Richard Boodle came from Radstock to read prayers, then, as he tells us in his Diary, he walked to Camerton, and at Skinner's gate met a servant with a letter from Mr. Skinner requesting his immediate attendance. He found him agitated, but had a long conversation with him and hoped he had left him more calm.

On October 1, and again two days later he saw Skinner, but gave no indication of the state of his mind.

Then, on October 11 he records, "Mr. Hammond called in on me to announce the death of Mr. Skinner. I rode with Mr. Hammond and called at Camerton Rectory".

Extract from the "Bath Chronicle" of Thursday, October 17 (also in the "Bath and Cheltenham Gazette"—Tuesday, October 15)

An Inquest was held on Saturday morning by Mr. Uphill on the body of the Rev. John Skinner, Rector of Camerton.

The Rev. gentleman's health had been declining for some time and his mind had latterly been very much affected.

On Friday morning, in a state of derangement, he shot himself through the head with a pistol, and was dead in an instant.

Verdict accordingly.

Appendix I

Memorandum

As I have mentioned in my Will it is my desire that my executors the Rev. Richard Boodle of Radstock, and the Rev. John Hammond of Priston, as soon after my death as convenient apply to Sir Henry Ellis of the British Museum, and tell him that event has taken place, and that I have commissioned them to deliver up the MSS vols. specified in my Will, in number one hundred and fifty, containing journals and productions of various kinds, but chiefly on the subject of antiquities, with the chests in which they are deposited and with the keys thereof, for the sole use and benefit of *The British Museum* and the public in general.

My wish and request that no extracts might be taken from these books till fifty years after my death alone proceeded from the fear of giving offence by the free remarks made when writing on passing events.

As the Rev. Messrs. Boodle and Hammond may not so conveniently spare time to see the books delivered themselves into the custody of Sir H. Ellis, I should wish my son F. Owen Skinner, would take the charge, who being settled in London may better fulfil it.

JOHN SKINNER.

CAMERTON PARSONAGE,
NEAR BATH, SOMERSET.
August 13, 1839.

Appendix II

*Description of a Day spent in College during the
Winter of 1792*

To W. P——, Esq.

WHY with such jangling notes and shrill
The hateful harbinger of ill
   Resounds that ceaseless bell;
Say, Scout, who thus uncall'd dost creep
Like some foul fiend to frighten sleep
   Be quick, the reason tell?

Rouse, Master, rouse, and dress in haste
The quarter's chime is nearly past
   Two minutes wants at most.
I've put your breeches by your head
And thick greatcoat have also laid
   For bitter is the frost.

He vanishes: at once I rise
Rubbing my dim and misty eyes
   And leap upon the floor,
But not the coldest marble hearth
Not plunge into Carshalton's bath
   Could chill my limbs much more.

Bell stops: unjustly blaming scout
For stockings turning inside out
   I hurry on my clothes.
Stiff fingers, bungling much thro' haste
But more so from the eastern blast
   Which thro' my casement blows.

With little time to wash or comb
Slipshod I quit my dressing-room
   And clatter down the stairs.
One instant finds my cap on pate,
My gown o'er coat y'cleped great,
   My band beneath my ears!

APPENDIX II

Now shuffling to the Chapel door
Behind two sloven students more
   I follow up the aisle.
Displeas'd, good natur'd Chapman stares,
For nearly half done are the prayers
   And Lessons read meanwhile.

At length the benediction said
The President he takes the lead
   And Fellows follow fast,
Scholars and commoners behind,
Precedence, form, nor order mind.
   The devil catch the last.

This sketch, dear Will, with flowing pen
I draw, to shew how College men
   Commence the morning here.
Doubtless their more restricted lot,
Yourself at ease, you envy not
   This season of the year.

Rolls smoking hot, at half-past eight
And George and butter on a plate
   The scarecrow Thomas brings,
Laying a napkin passing white,
Tea equipage he puts in sight
   Whilst loud the kettle sings.

At half-past nine tea-drinking o'er
And cups returned thro' pantry door
   Our books we take instead.
By turns Virgilian murmurs please
Or thunders from Demosthenes
   Hurl'd 'gainst the tyrant's head.

This author chiefest of the set
We lecture in to Tutor Kett
   Must therefore come prepar'd.
At one, exactly on the stroke
The time expir'd for sporting oak,
   My outer door's unbarr'd.

If day prove only passing fair
I walk for exercise and air
   Or for an hour skate,
For a large space of flooded ground
Which Christchurch gravel walks surround
   Has solid froze of late.

A quarter wanting now of three
On ent'ring gates of Trinity
   For dressing will suffice.
As Highland barber, far fam'd Duff
Within that time will plenty puff
   Of lime in both my eyes.

Now shrilly pealing kitchen bell
We find a diff'rent errand tell
   To that for Morning Prayers;
It dinner, dinner, seems to call
Enticing students to the hall
   By dozens down the stairs.

Fellows then march in garments sable
To upper seat y'clept High Table
   And range them on each side
Where Commoners of first degree
In silk gowns clad, seem equally
   With them in state allied.

The Batchelors upon the right
And Scholars' Table standing by't
   Are lower in the Hall,
Because some space it does require
For the large grate and flaming fire
   Which blazes 'gainst the wall.

Extending from the high raised floor
In length: we count two tables more
   For me and my compeers,
That is, for Youths with leading strings
And sleeveless gowns, poor awkward things
   Entitled Commoners.

Our Hall arrangement being said
We must add too the Griffin's head
  In centre, made of brass.
For what? You ask—why not to eat
But for a kind of after treat
  Whilst grosser viands pass.

'Tis then before concluding grace
Some gownsman, rising from his place
  Whilst servants bustle out,
Towards the Griffin walking slow
To Fellows makes initial bow
  And then begins to spout.

Μηνιν ἀειδε Θεα then
Or verses from the Mantuan pen
  Sound in melodious strains.
Or lines from Milton's Paradise
With emphasis delivered nice
  A just applause obtains.

And here *en passant* I will state
A dialogue we heard of late
  Betwixt Vice Pres. and chap,
Why not a friend to spouting stood
At Griffin's head in sulky mood
  The verses in his cap.

But not being able to see well
To read them there, much less to spell,
  He silent kept his place.
Silent meanwhile were gownsmen all
At least five minutes in the Hall
  Full staring in his face.

He, blest with impudence enough
Now smil'd and now look'd grim and gruff,
  At verses now would peep,
Now with cap tassel would he play
Now turn his body quite away
  From where the Fellows keep.

Moulding, Vice Pres., with visage round
As is a cheese of twenty pound
   Or moon in Harvest week,
Than these not boasting more pretence
To features emanating sense,
   At length began to squeak.

Why, why, you stupid fellow, why
Are you thus silent, and not try
   Your tongue for to unloose?
Better behaviour, sir, I beg.
You stand as foolish on one leg.
   As any silly goose.

This sharp reproof when Freshman heard
A moment at fat Moulding stared
   Not knowing what to do:
But slow returning to his seat
He splutter'd out in rage and heat
   "I ain't more goose than you."

Narrare finish'd and grace said
Vice Pres. and Fellows take the lead
   And march away to wine.
We in our turn their steps pursue,
Gen. Coms., A.B's, and scholars too,
   Where'er our steps incline.

For now some ten or dozen get
By 'fore appointment in a set
   To taste inviter's port.
He glasses, plates and spoons prepares,
Decanters, knives and forks and chairs,
   But each his own dessert.

For with large baskets enters soon
A wily fruitr'er styled Balloon
   Who hands around his store:
Apples and pears and chestnuts too
And oranges deck'd out to view
   With many a *bonne bouche* more.

Should guest from other college come
Of course the master of the Room
 Provides for his supply.
Our inmates carry to account
In Fruit'rer's book each day's amount
 Of what they taste or buy.

Meanwhile the jovial toasts go round
The bottles guggle, glasses sound
 As each one drinks his fair.
The Chairman watches, bawls and raps
Should any fill upon heel taps
 Or his good liquor spare.

At five, the Chapel bell again
Rings a loud peal: but rings in vain
 To move a single guest,
For whiles delightful they behold
Within all warm, without all cold,
 Each loves fireside the best.

At six, dame Prudence well may see—
It is high time to order tea
 If Prudence has her eyes,
But Bacchus, sly enchanter, draws
His hoodwink'd captive to his laws.
 In short—now none are wise.

For lo! they tea and coffee spurn
Whilst unsnuff'd the candles burn,
 Some hiccough and some snore.
The Chairman vainly strives to speak
And mouths his English worse than Greek.
 In short, the game is o'er.

At nine, the blinking Scout appears
Whilst most are nodding in their chairs,
 And bottles moves away,
For from the Kitchen he has brought
What each one sober might or ought
 Have order'd—on his tray.

Boil'd fowl, salt herrings, sausages,
Cold beef and brawn and bread and cheese
   With tankards full of ale.
The sated guests he with delight
Counts o'er—for this his perquisite
   Is—when their functions fail.

Altho' in some respects he earns
The solace of these good returns
   For putting them to bed,
As many a curse and many a kick
And many a pinch and many a lick
   They give whilst being led.

Hush! Hush! cries Tom across Quadrangle
In lantern stuck his two-inch candle—
   "The President will hear,
Be quiet Sir, and come along;
I wish you would not pull so strong,
   Nor yet so loudly swear."

Yet my friend Will, you don't suppose
That thus alike all evenings close
   And gownsmen are all such.
No, no! believe me, now and then
They will exceed like other men,
   So did the grave phiz'd Dutch.

Warren and self in gloomy weather
Oft times a number get together
   Immediately we dine,
Who sit and chat till half-past five
With jest and song are all alive
   With quite sufficient wine.

Then Crotch[1] and two Musicians more
And amateurs near half a score
   To play in concert meet.
Our chairs to Warren's rooms we move
And those who strains melodious love
   Enjoy a real treat.

[1] William Crotch, *b*. 1775, *d*. 1847, composer.

Crotch as Director of the Band
On Harpsichord with rapid hand
   Sweeps the full chord; this youth,
Of late through Britain's realms was styl'd
The wondrous boy: Apollo's child,
   And such he was in truth.

Whilst pause the Flutes' and Viols' sound,
The tea and toast are handed round
   Till each has had enough
And then brisk Punch and Lemonade
May suit when a full piece is played
   Better than weaker stuff.

At half-past nine the supper things
In order Master Thomas brings
   And puts them on with care,
For now the cunning rascal sees
He has a different set to please
   Than those who tipsy are.

The cloth remov'd, some Negus sip
And some regale on hot egg flip
   And some sing Catch and Glee.
For each in turn must something do,
Attempt old songs or bawl out new
   By way of harmony.

Eleven strikes: and strangers strait
Pass to their homes thro' College gate
   The Porter lets them out.
Meanwhile the rest to bed retire
Thus ends the day: and your desire
   To hear what we're about.

Appendix III

Paper given to the Bath Field Club in 1872 by H. J. Hunter Esq. M.D.

Mr. Skinner, the subject of this paper was a man whose character presented itself under very different aspects to the various persons or classes of persons who had access to him. Not alone was he to excite the sympathies of the gentle and celebrated, mixed with something not always acceptable to our ruder neighbours, but there was from time to time frequent change in him as seen from any fixed point. The barometer of his spirits showed a wide range of exultant rise and moping fall, and to know him well required that he should be approached from different sides and also at different times. It was observed that with sympathetic friends Mr. Skinner was notably lively and enthusiastic, but the presence of a companion whose tone of mind was tinged with a little bustle of vulgarity would wither him into silence almost morose. It is now thirty-three years since his death, and no-one (so far as I know) has glanced at his character, reviewed his works, or noted the chief incidents of his life. It is under these circumstances, and in the presence of this omission only that I have ventured to undertake to say what I know about this gentleman, poet, artist, scholar and dutiful country priest, and to show of how much more I am ignorant. It is not my purpose to support his opinions, nor to condemn them, but to make the Club acquainted with them so far as I can. To persons whose natural genius leads them to dislike all but the plainest positive reasonings, much of what Mr. Skinner wrote and said will appear too fanciful, and his exploded errors hardly worth recalling . . .

When your attention is asked to Mr. Skinner's opinions, I do not mean to ask more than that a man of singularly tasteful scholarship who in the days when Antiquaries Field Clubs were not, occupied his leisure in the pursuits which occupy our leisure, should be remembered by us, who may in some sense be considered as his successors and heirs to a delightful field of observation. In 1830 Mr. Hunter read at this Institution a paper of Mr. Skinner's "On the Early History of Bath" which proved to be an attempt to show that the name of Bath is not given to the place in respect of its being a place for bathing, but that the name BADUN existed as the name of this fortified hill on Hampton Down, and the *Dunum of the Water Passage*, as he analyses it, and that this became in the mouths of the Saxons, BATHUN.

I have been led to take the more interest in Mr. Skinner's character, because he was, from the time of their first introduction by Mr. Warner in 1817, to nearly the time of Mr. Skinner's death, a sympathetic friend and fellow antiquary of Mr. Joseph Hunter. Of a visit made to Camerton in 1820, I find an account in Mr. Hunter's diary. "I spent a very pleasant day with Mr. Skinner yesterday. I found him living with his son and daughter at the rectory house which he has embellished with the hand of true taste, and not less so the five acres of ground which adjoins it. We walked to see a beautiful piece of the Fosseway about two miles from his house. His theories are too bold for any more cautious temper. In the embellishment of his house and grounds he seems to have been eminently successful. There is not the fritter and glitter of the Leasowes, there is more of a just economy combined with the elegance, and the inscriptions which abound are in purer taste. In the porch he has the Votum Horatii, and I could not but observe one thing which none but a very tasteful antiquary would have thought of. Barker of Bath had painted a portrait of a great trout which he had taken. This he gave to Skinner, who suspended it in his porch having added the word IXOYE: serva nos in characters but just perceptible. In the hall there are the more curious of the remains which have been discovered at his supposed Camalodunum, and in the windows in stained glass, and in other parts of the house he has figured British and Romano-British emblems, and especially such as relate to Cunobelin and Boadicia.

The study of antiquity was but the amusement of his leisure; his duty was that of a parish priest, and it was in that character that he was to suffer in the cause of enlightenment and religion. After another visit to Camerton during which Mr. Skinner seems to have opened his heart to him about his troubles, Mr. Hunter writes as follows:— "Looking upon this beautiful residence seeing the owner, a gentleman of refined taste, of extensive acquirements, with various objects of interesting pursuit, withall of a very amiable disposition, with a good fortune, promising children, and many friends and acquaintances, one would be apt to say, surely this man if any, is happy! The last inscription, even when an allowance is made for the melancholy which should attend the sepulchre, shows a sorrow of another kind, which indeed is sometimes apparent in his conversation. He has all the wilder species of Methodism around him, and ignorant preachers among the colliers of his parish, so that his church is almost deserted. Hinc illae lachrymae!"

Mr. Skinner's tender conscience and fine taste could not bear rough usage; . . . he found a dispute with his parishioners a very different thing from a controversy among polite and friendly antiquarians. The year 1831–2 was in many respects not a happy time for country parsons; there were sorry people who found delight in tormenting with their threats and forebodings sensitive men who had made the clergy their profession. I then remember Mr. William Lisle Bowles coming into our house on Belvedere with the air of a man who had a mob at his heels, and anticipating with tears the destruction of his beautiful parsonage at Bremhill by incendiaries. In that year Mr. Skinner's son died at his house of a decline, and the family was seriously agitated by the visit of the cholera. In that year a friend writes of him "Skinner is very lively and ingenious, said to be sometimes hasty, but he has much to try his patience among the farmers of Camerton".

As in mind, so was Mr. Skinner irritable in bodily system, and in the pangs of neuralgia he sought the fleeting friend of irritable men—opium. His mind fell from her seat, and then he fell, and in such a way that, although when the Pastor calls His sheep together he will not be forgotten, still to the visitor to Camerton his tomb is not, and can never be exactly that which he in hopeful and poetic, though even then in pensive thought designed it.

Appendix IV

EXTRACTS FROM THE WILL OF REV. J. S. SKINNER
(Public Record Office Ref: PROB/11/1919)

Proved at London, with two Codicils, on 14/NOV/1839.

Will dated 1/FEB/1839.

Executors: Rev. Richard Boodle of Radstock.
Rev. John Hammond of Priston.

Witnesses: Samuel Batchellor of Corston, Esquire.
Elizabeth Wherret of Camerton, Spinster.

" . . . *my household furniture, plate, books (except such books as I*
"*may, by any Codicil, give to the President of Trinity College, Oxford),*
"*china, Linen Prints, Drawings and implements to my daughter Anna;*
"*and also the sum of £1,050 under the powers given to me by the*
"*Marriage Settlement, being the sum equal to that already given to my*
"*son, Fitz Owen Skinner under the said Settlement.*

"*I give to my son Fitz Owen Skinner all the Plate & China having the*
"*Crest & Coat of Arms of my family thereon, all my Oil Paintings and*
"*my Greek & Latin Classical Books*".

£1,000 was left in Trust to the Executors, £800 of which was for the
publication of his Manuscript entitled "An Analysis of Language and
Symbols of worship of the Sun". The profits and sale of Copyright to
be used for the benefit of his two children.

£100 to Rev. J. Hammond "for the trouble he may have in arranging publication" and the remaining £100 to a competent scholar to
peruse and correct the work.

Then follow the instructions regarding his Journals, 146 volumes
in all, contained in five Iron Chests, which were to be deposited in the
British Museum and not to be opened until the expiration of fifty
years.

His coins, about 1,600 in number, were left to the Trustees of the

Bristol Institution, together with various other items of Roman remains, fossils etc., and an ancient chair.

To the Bath Institution his copper plates of the Wellow Roman Pavement, also a Manuscript collection of correspondence between Sir Richard Colt Hoare Bart and Rev. James Douglas on the subject of the Roman Colony of Camelodunum.

He left £50 each to his Executors, £50 to the son of Rev. John Hammond; £50 each to Georgiana & Alfred Boodle, with the Residue to be divided equally between his children Anna & Fitz Owen.

In a First Codicil dated 13/Aug/1839 and witnessed by Arabella Hoare and Elizabeth Wherret he revoked his instructions regarding the publication of his Manuscript (An Analysis of Language . . .) and instead, left it in trust of his son Fitz Owen and his son-in-law R. Boyle to provide a fund for the sending of his grandson Fitz Owen John Skinner to Trinity College, Oxford.

He left a further sum of £1,000 which was deposited at Hoare's Bank, Fleet Street, for sending any son of his daughter Anna and Robert Boyle to Trinity College, Oxford.

He left a large picture of Noah's Sacrifice to Peter Hoare, of Southfield House; a copy of the Bayeux Tapestry to Dr. Holland of Chichester; an antique seal of Romulus and Remus to his old friend Rev. C. Burrard of Yarmouth, Isle of Wight, and to Rev. W. L. Bowles of Bremhill "a little useful poney which his friend Mr. Wiltshire gave me and for the same reason, because I know that he will have it taken care of as long as he lives". To his son Owen, a choice of clocks, and the gold ring with the family crest that was his grandfather's.

In a Second Codicil dated 17/Aug/1839 and witnessed by John Baber and Elizabeth Wherret he directed that all the money which had previously been willed to his daughter Anna Skinner, should now be left to the Trustees of the Settlement made at her marriage with Robert Boyle.

There were numerous alterations, deletions and ambiguities in the Will, and before Probate could be granted the Witnesses had to attend the Prerogative Court at Canterbury to give evidence regarding these irregularities.

Appendix V

*MSS. of the Journal in the British Museum. Journals of
Travels and Parochial Matters*

APPENDIX V

APPENDIX V

Index

INDEX

Bowles, Charles, 258
    Rev. W. L. (Rector of Bremhill, Wilts), 121, 360, 362
Boydell (artist), 82, 181, 232, 424
Boyle, W. R. A. (married Anna Skinner), 3
Braysdown, 278, 426
Bremhill, 121, 360
Brent Knoll (South Brent), 2, 361, 422
Briant, Mr. (Clerk-Gen. Meetings, Ilminster), 10
Bridle, Mr. (gaoler, Ilchester), 164
Bristol
    Fair, 415
    Riots, 472
    Port, 89
British Museum, iii, iv, 82
Britten, James, 58–9
Brougham, Lord, 332
Buckland Down, 257
Bumstead, Rev. 320
Burfitt (farmer), 32–3, 35, 55–6, 62, 387, 492
Burrard-Neale, Sir Harry, 17, 20, 359
Burrard, Rev. George (Rector of Yarmouth, I. of W.), 88, 97, 159, 250, 359, 374, 380, 405
Bush, Wm. (see Skinner, J., Domestic Staff)
Bush (prominent Methodist of his day), 79–81, 182
Butleigh, 362
Butler, Col., 418

Cambridge University, 8, 351, 362, 380–2, 397
Cameley, 110
Camerton
    Club, 42, 128, 164, 230, 302, 388
    Coal Works (see also Strikes), v, 11–12, 105, 117, 128, 137, 150, 164, 177, 198, 226, 244, 246, 264, 332, 394, 405, 424–5, 472
    Glebe Farm, 225, 448–9, 471
    Manor House, 2, 4, 101, 409, 422
    National School, 176, 242, 244, 246, 485
    Overseers, vi, 12, 27, 63, 71, 75, 76, 87, 130, 137, 218, 236, 250, 253, 263, 279, 293, 302, 323, 359, 367, 394, 426
    Parsonage, v, 24, 264, 271, 325–6, 330–1, 377–8, 448
    Poor House, 236, 250–1, 299

Schools, 25, 36, 114–5, 173, 176, 183, 242–3, 246, 254, 315, 323, 332–4, 369, 420
    Sunday School, 36, 92, 115, 173, 176–8, 213, 241, 264, 266, 269–70, 284, 304, 324, 332–4
Camerton Inn (now The Jolly Collier)— see Inns
Campbell, Capt., 254
Canal (see Somerset Coal Canal)
Carew family (Lords of Camerton Manor, 1584–1750) 102–3, 173, 290
Cassan, Rev. S. H. (Rector of Mere), 287, 291, 360
Catherine, Empress of Russia, 45, 183, 241
Catholicism, 4, 26, 155, 158, 162, 167, 177, 187, 237–9, 248, 258–9, 262–3, 275, 279–82. 295, 299–300, 347, 353–4, 370, 384
Champneys, Mr. T. S. (Orchardleigh House, Frome), 162, 257
Charles I, 111
    II, 430
Cheam School, 1, 140, 433
Cheddar, 139, 245, 360, 421, 443
Chelwood, 359, 459
Chewton Mendip, 52, 245
Chilcompton, 21, 74, 239, 245, 253, 310
Chipping Sodbury, 27
Church wardens (see also Goold, Hicks, Rossiter and Weeks), 36, 55, 57, 87, 113, 159, 171, 176, 195–6, 203, 223, 297–8, 383–4, 398, 404
Cirencester, 146, 154
Clandown, 143, 179, 244, 330, 400, 421
Clarence, Duke of, 359
Clarke (Mayor of Bath), 87, 178
Clarke, Mr. and Mrs. (Church-school), 169–70, 175–8, 181–2, 197, 213, 264
Claude (Painter), 168
Claverton, 1, 14, 82, 149, 232, 243
Clifton, Bristol, 71, 127, 131–3, 254, 300
Cloford, 214
Clutterbuck of Bradford (Steward to Mr. Gore-Langton), 139, 141
Clutton, 62, 189
Colchester, 259
Coleford, 336
Collins (miller at Radford), 205, 261, 429, 476
    Mrs. 245–6
    Rev. Trelawney, 368, 373, 422, 442, 491
Colville, Mr., 358, 364
Combe Down, 336, 443

512

INDEX

INDEX

INDEX

Maiden Bradley, 110, 257
Maiden Castle, 18
Manningham, Mrs. (*née* Laura Skinner), 224, 228, 340
Mark, 119
Marksbury, 282
Marlborough, 82, 120, 155
Marriage Act, 224
Marston Bigot, 184
Maule (attorney), 262, 282, 301
Meade, Rev. (Rector of Marston), 184, 351, 395
Meadyates, 181, 262, 281–2, 358, 367, 400, 429, 455
Medical
  Alcoholism, 36
  Blooding, 131, 243, 255, 378, 384, 402, 438, 445, 450
  Burns, 216
  Bladder, 229, 251
  Calomel treatment, 143
  Childbirth, 413
  Cholera, 446–7, 449–55, 457, 464, 468, 470, 472–4
  Consumption, 3, 4, 8, 11, 38, 45, 71–2, 79, 86, 127 seq., 186, 201, 311, 375, 389, 437, 444, 458
  Digitalis, 45, 50
  Dropsy, 76, 247, 376
  Fever, 142, 288–9, 318
  Gallstones, 215
  James's Powders, 255
  King's Evil, 328–9
  Laudanum, 73, 327, 434, 450, 467
  Leeches, 313–4
  Leprosy, 398, 416
  Measles, 139, 141, 334
  Opium, 479
  Rheumatism, 58, 108, 250
  Rupture of blood vessel, 311
  Scotts Pills, 317–8
  Smallpox, 281
  Stroke, 69
  Syphilis, 61
  Typhus, 74, 156, 478
  Vaccination, 281
Mells, 110, 139, 160, 169, 183, 193–4, 224, 257, 269, 293, 304–5, 320, 352, 436, 489
Mendips, 1, 136
Merick, Mr., 258
Methodists, 24, 26, 30, 40, 42, 47, 66, 68, 79, 81, 91 seq., 108, 111, 141, 167, 182, 185, 191, 203–4, 213, 222, 224–5, 229, 233, 240, 248, 259, 281, 283, 299, 303, 324, 328, 340, 443, 490

Meylers Library, 347–8
Midsomer Norton, 129, 161, 206, 246, 262, 364–6
Mogg, Rev., H. H., M.A., 1814–36 (Chewton Mendip), 469
Monmouthshire, 366
Montgomery, Mr., 395
Morals, 14, 299
  Begging, 63
  Dishonesty, 27, 31, 33, 52, 53, 64, 76, 97, 105, 112, 119, 130, 137, 172, 195–6, 263, 270, 303, 320–1, 415, 490
  Illegitimacy, 26, 33, 60, 67, 236, 279, 488
  Marriage, 27, 32, 35, 42, 63, 128, 183, 255–6, 279, 296, 327, 401–3, 409, 416, 427, 488
  Murder, 53, 90
  Obscenity, 40–1, 55, 63, 321
  Prostitution, 27, 60–1, 69, 73, 75, 89, 131, 279 seq., 306, 315 seq., 395, 420, 428, 458
  Rape, 22, 61–2, 73
  Suicide, 26, 39, 244
Moysey, Dr. (Archdeacon), 177, 205, 207–8
Mulgrave, Lord (1st Lord of Admiralty, 1807), 46, 50

Napier, Mr. (Sherriff of Somerset and great nephew of Prowse), 126
Newnham family, 245, 267, 307 seq., 471
Newton St. Loe, 288
Newbury, 287
Norman, Dr., 313 seq., 318, 438, 443, 455
Norton St. Philip, 109, 166
Nostell Priory, 393
Nunney, 160, 193, 257, 287, 352

Oakhill, 253
O'Connell, Daniel, 347
Offley, Mr., 258
Orchardleigh, 162, 257
Oxford University, 146 seq., 289, 291, 311, 320, 473, Appendix II
  Balliol, 149
  Barnes, Dr. (Christchurch), 147
  Barrington, Hon. Mr. (Oriel), 147
  Barter (Sub-warden, New Coll.), 150–1
  Bodleian Library, 82, 148, 150
  Buckland (Prof. Mineralogy, Corpus Christi), 150, 152–4
  Christchurch College, 147, 152–3

516

INDEX

INDEX

MORE OXFORD PAPERBACKS

The Diary of a Country Parson, 1788–1802

James Woodforde

Edited by John Beresford

James Woodforde was parson at Weston Longeville, Norfolk, from 1774 until his death in 1803. His life was obscure and tranquil, his character uncomplicated; he loved his country, sport, good food, and established institutions, and was warm-hearted and generous. His diary covers nearly every single day in his life from 1758 to 1802. What makes it a classic as well as a remarkable document of social history is Parson Woodforde's rare ability to bring vividly to life the rural England of two centuries ago.

OXFORD PAPERBACKS

The Diary of a Georgian Shopkeeper

Thomas Turner

Introduction by G. H. Jennings

'I cannot say I came home sober.' Recurrent drunkenness (and attendant guilt) might be called the leading theme of the diary of Thomas Turner of East Hoathly in Sussex – a most candid, perceptive, entertaining personal document with unique social and historical overtones. The subjects Turner touches on are many and varied: his activities as shopkeeper, church-warden, and Overseer to the Parish Vestry; the principal historical events of the period (1754–65), with Turner's (often unexpected) reactions to them; reflections on marriage; accounts of his first wife's illness and death, and of his courting of a new wife; the races, cockfighting, cricket; poverty, boredom, illness, and death; and of course continual drinking.

OXFORD PAPERBACKS

The Dillen

Memories of a Man of Stratford-upon-Avon

Edited by Angela Hewins

Foreword by Ronald Blythe

George Hewins was born in a Stratford doss-house at the zenith of the Victorian age. He grew up in desperate poverty, barely literate, underfed, and under-sized (hence his nickname of 'the dillen' or runt). But George did possess one extraordinary gift: he was a storyteller of genius in the old oral tradition. *The Dillen* is his story, told to his grandson's wife as he approached his hundredth year. 'It is funny and heartbreaking by turn, packed with incidents and curiosities.' *Sunday Times*

'It takes the reader by the scruff of the neck and forces him to taste the food, smell the smells, agree to the tricks and breathe the air of a cheerful, dreadful England which would do for you if it could.' Ronald Blythe

The Wynne Diaries

The Adventures of Two Young Sisters in Napoleonic Europe

Edited by Anne Fremantle
New introduction by Christopher Hibbert

The diaries of Betsey and Eugenia Wynne provide one of the most detailed and vivid accounts we have of the Napoleonic era, as well as a delightfully amusing picture of the lives of two young women. The rich, rather unconventional Wynne family spent its time travelling in Europe with a large retinue of servants. The girls' diaries record the family's progress, their own romantic secrets, and later, when Betsey marries a captain in Nelson's navy, impressions of some of the Admiral's great sea-battles.

The Wynne family, and especially the sister diarists, Betsey and Eugenia, are very good acquaintances to make.' Marghanita Laski, *Country Life*

OXFORD PAPERBACKS

A Victorian Poacher

James Hawker's Journal

Edited by Garth Christian

Illustrated by Lynton Lamb

James Hawker was born in 1836, a tailor's son, in the village of Oadby, Leicestershire. Times were hard and Hawker lived according to his own moral code, poaching with great dexterity in order to feed his family. Rather than face unemployment he worked at many labouring trades, but never gave up the habit of poaching. His memoirs, first published in 1961, portray the life of a remarkable man: shrewd, vigorous, humorous, learned in country lore, a first-rate field naturalist, and eloquent in his exposition of the poacher's craft.

Selected Letters of Sydney Smith

Edited by Nowell C. Smith

With an introduction by Auberon Waugh

The wit and charm of Sydney Smith runs throughout his letters as he comments on the people and events of his day with an eye for both the tiny detail at home and more general affairs. A clergyman himself, he was ever ready to poke fun at the Church, in the nicest possible way. Those who took themselves too seriously were also subjects for his scorn. But he was not merely amusing – his outspokeness on literary, political and religious affairs betrayed a rare moral courage, which went alongside the warmth and generosity he showed in his daily life.

'No man writing in English combined wit and common sense in more nicely balanced proportions than Sydney Smith . . . Auberon Waugh brings affection as well as insight to his introduction, and the whole book is one by no means to be missed.' David Williams, *Punch*

The Private Memoirs and Confessions of a Justified Sinner

James Hogg

Edited by John Carey

Written in 1824, James Hogg's masterpiece, *The Private Memoirs and Confessions of a Justified Sinner*, is a brilliant portrayal of the power of evil. Set in early eighteenth-century Scotland, the novel recounts the corruption of a boy of strict Calvinist parentage by a mysterious stranger under whose influence he commits a series of murders. The stranger assures the boy that no sin can affect the salvation of an elect person. The reader, while recognizing the stranger as Satan, is prevented by the subtlety of the novel's structure from finally deciding whether, for all his vividness and wit, he is more than a figment of the boy's imagination.